The City in the Seventies

the city
IN THE SEVENTIES

EDITED BY **ROBERT K. YIN** New York City– Rand Institute

ITASCA, ILLINOIS 60143 **F. E. PEACOCK PUBLISHERS, INC.**

Table of Contents

Preface

A short book justifies only a short prefatory note. I would like to take this opportunity to thank several people who contributed to the manuscript.

My greatest immediate debt is to the authors and publishers of the articles appearing in the book, both for allowing me to include their work and for allowing me to make numerous editorial changes in the interest of keeping the total volume down to manageable size. I am also grateful to Hans-Lukas Teuber, Nathan Glazer, and David Riesman for their stimulating comments on early versions of the introductory passages. To Edgar Borgatta I owe particular thanks for providing the intellectual inspiration for the book and for his continuing interest and suggestions throughout its preparation. Finally, I owe a special debt to Barbara Fern Yin, who remains a special resource in all my endeavors.

NEW YORK, N.Y.   ROBERT K. YIN
October, 1971

Introduction

The events of the 1970's may come as a surprise to those who witnessed closely the urban scene of the 1960's. In that scene, the federal government committed itself to aiding the cities via the antipoverty, model cities, and crime prevention programs. The urban riots called public attention to the deplorable conditions in the central city, with the Kerner Commission Report[1] raising hopes for basic improvements in the ghettos. Moreover, the election of many liberal and reform-minded mayors sparked even further optimism about the ultimate fate of the American city. As a result, one might have predicted clear signs of improvement in the large cities by the 1970's. One might have thought that the cities would be providing better opportunities for living and working, particularly for the poor; if not better opportunities, at least safer streets; if not safer streets, at least cleaner ones.

Not only is progress dubious on these fronts, but recent woes suggest that things may even get worse before they get better. First, the migration to the suburbs has continued at a rapid rate, as fewer people find the city an attractive and desirable place to live. Second, the marshaling of municipal employees into public labor unions has made round-the-year negotiations and employee strikes into not uncommon events. Third, a severe lack of money now threatens to reduce other municipal services previously taken for granted, such as the operation of public libraries and museums and the maintenance of public parks. Thus, as we enter the mid-1970's, the dilemmas facing the cities seem as critical and as awesome as ever.

The urban debate

Several arguments have been used to explain the continuing crisis in the cities. The arguments differ drastically, posing a formidable challenge for anybody trying to develop his own view of the urban dilemma. The first

---

[1] *Report of the National Advisory Commission on Civil Disorders* (New York: Bantam Books, Inc., 1968).

argument claims that the nation as a whole has simply not provided enough money for the cities. Were the federal government to give as clear a priority to the solution of urban problems as it has to the support of underdeveloped countries, to the waging of military conflicts, to the landing of a man on the moon, or even to the building of new highways, many of the urban ills would disappear. In other words, a greater financial commitment alone could provide dramatic relief for the cities.

A second argument is based on the traditional hue and cry that there has not been enough urban research. According to this argument, our understanding of urban problems is still too rudimentary. Even if more money were available, few workable solutions could be proposed. Thus, although the social sciences are now concentrating heavily on urban problems and policy research, this development is quite recent, and much more research lies ahead.[2] The same argument supports the drive to recruit engineers and scientists into urban research from other fields. The presumption is that urban problems can be more effectively attacked if they are studied by men who have already demonstrated their talents in other ways.

These first two arguments have in common the notion that an immediate and massive commitment of more resources, money in the first instance and research talent in the second, is the key to dealing with the urban crisis. Two other arguments, however, are based on a contrasting premise, that the rapid outpouring of such resources may not do any good and may indeed have detrimental effects. The first is made by Edward Banfield in his recent book, *The Unheavenly City*.[3] Banfield maintains that (a) the cities are not quite as badly off as they seem to be, (b) many of the current urban problems have obvious and simple solutions, and (c) political barriers, and not the lack of money or of knowledge, generally prevent the implementation of such solutions. To take one example, Banfield argues that unemployment is aggravated by minimum-wage laws. The laws may ensure higher wages for some jobs, but the laws also make employers eliminate the marginal jobs that are unprofitable at the minimum wage, thereby reducing the number of jobs available (p. 95 ff.). One solution proposed by Banfield would be to *lower* the minimum wage, allowing the price of labor to fall to a level where it would be purchased. Such a move would clearly be unacceptable, though, both to organized labor and to public opinion. If anything, they would want to follow the opposite policy by raising the minimum wage. Banfield suggests that other urban problems also have feasible but politically unaccept-

---

[2]For a recent and broad assessment of policy research and sociology, see "Sociological research and public policy," *The American Sociologist,* Vol. 6 (June, 1971), whole "Supplementary Issue."

[3]Edward C. Banfield, *The Unheavenly City: The Nation and the Future of Our Urban Crisis* (Boston: Little, Brown & Co., 1970).

able solutions and that in fact the political reality usually dictates the pursuit of self-defeating public policies and programs.

The second of these arguments is made, although in a very different manner and on quite different grounds, by Jay Forrester in his book *Urban Dynamics*.[4] Forrester claims that a city is best depicted as a complex system, in which all elements, like the availability of housing or the amount of underemployment, interact in a dynamic manner. Using a computer simulation of such a system, Forrester demonstrates that policy changes often have unexpected and counterintuitive long-term effects that more than negate any short-term gains. In fact, a vicious cycle may even develop, in which ". . . the action erroneously assumed to be corrective makes the problem worse and the worsening calls forth still more of the presumed remedial action, which only further aggravates the situation" (p. 70). For example, this cycle is hypothesized to occur with the construction of low-income housing, presumably for the purpose of reducing the number of ill-housed people in the city (p. 65 ff.). The desired reduction may indeed occur at the outset, but the longer term effect is just the opposite. More low-income people subsequently move into the city because they perceive that better housing opportunities exist. According to Forrester's analysis, the construction program, rather than satiating the demand for low-income housing, has produced an even greater demand and has also incurred other undesirable side effects.

These two arguments by Banfield and Forrester have been used to support a more conservative view of the urban crisis. From this view, part of the current crisis may be attributed not to the lack of resources, but to an overindulgence in the use of similar resources in the past. Furthermore, if it is true that most of the appropriate solutions are still politically unacceptable and that most of government's actions can only further aggravate any given situation, then a do-nothing policy, construed for example under the slogan of "benign neglect,"[5] may turn out to be not only less costly but also more beneficial.

This debate over what should be done to help the cities will not be settled easily. On the level of national affairs, the fact that no national urban policy has emerged may be partial testimony to the existence of a deadlock. Nevertheless, the debate unavoidably forms part of the milieu within which research on the city is to be carried out. As such, it forms the background for the main question raised by *The City in the Seventies:* How should the social sciences structure the study of the contemporary city?

---

[4]Jay W. Forrester, *Urban Dynamics* (Cambridge, Mass.: The M.I.T. Press, 1969).

[5]This slogan was applied by Daniel P. Moynihan to part of a proposed national policy on matters dealing with race (see *The New York Times,* March 1, 1970, p. 1). For a recent examination of the substance of the proposal, see Thomas J. Cook, "Benign neglect: Minimum feasible understanding," *Social Problems,* 18:145–152 (Fall, 1970).

The social sciences and urban research

Before suggesting an answer, it may be useful to reconstruct a conversation overheard at a recent conference on technology and urban problems. In the conversation, the president of an aerospace firm asked a municipal official how the firm could help the city. The president was interested in obtaining guidelines for his firm's research program, and the municipal official had a succinct and specific recommendation: The firm should change its present location and move from its suburban base to some neighborhood in the central city. In other words, the act of relocating would provide more benefits to the city than would any work that the firm could perform. The reply caught the president by surprise, and, as one might expect, he discarded it as being somewhat facetious.

The conversation highlights a duality of roles, however, that has become confused in recent years, especially in light of the continued crisis in the cities and the debate over what shall be done. The confusion has arisen over the roles of social scientists as part of a scientific research profession and as private citizens. As a private citizen, anyone who has felt concern for the welfare of the city should not hesitate to devote his own personal resources to the solution of urban problems. This can be done by participating in local affairs, exercising power as consumers in the marketplace, and dealing directly with grievances, political issues, and political campaigns (even more revolutionary ones). In other words, those who are motivated simply by a desire to "solve urban problems" may best do so by relocating their "firms" and by living and working in the central city. At the same time, this action orientation is not necessarily the route to be followed by social scientists as members of their profession. This role should be guided more by intellectual instincts and the lessons of formal training, the general goal being to develop the best strategy for understanding the nature of the city..It seems that only in this manner can knowledge about the city be advanced.

The confusion between these two roles seems to be epitomized by the "problems" approach to urban research, an approach that has come increasingly in vogue. Dazzled by the apparent success of the natural sciences in solving complex engineering problems and prodded by the gap between what was being studied in the universities and what was occurring outside of them, the social sciences in the 1960's firmly embraced a problem-solving approach to the study of society. The problems of concern were not limited, of course, to those of the cities. Nevertheless, certain major social problems such as racial discrimination, poverty, and drug addiction were inevitably dominated by the urban setting, while other problems, such as street crime, neighborhood and housing deterioration, and civil disorders, were virtually restricted to the cities. In responding to the crisis of the cities, the social sciences attempted to develop a more relevant curriculum for studying the city. Since a major criticism had been that the curriculum was too divorced from the problems of the day, the simple solution was to allow the problems of the day to become the curriculum. Whether one was a student of political science, sociology, economics, or psychology, the study of the city therefore became a loosely arranged series of inquiries into housing, race, poverty, community control, and the like.

All this happened while most social scientists themselves continued to live and work under cloistered conditions, with personal lives often far removed from the central city. Few of them developed an inner-city style of life. The suggestion here is that, rather than changing the curriculum to make it more relevant, maybe what was really needed was to change the social scientists as individuals and make *them* more relevant.[6] Moreover, the suggestion seems appropriate today, like the recommendation to relocate the aerospace firm. Essentially, those social scientists who are mainly concerned with the solution of contemporary urban problems will have more impact in their role as private citizens than any study of urban problems will have. And, it may very well be that the conditions of the central city would be substantially improved if professional people in all fields would bring the weight of their income, education, and resourcefulness to bear on the urban scene.

From action to research

As for the study of the city, the problem-solving orientation surely leaves much to be desired. Studying the city on a problem-by-problem basis is an overwhelmingly expensive proposition, in both time and money. Cities have always had serious problems, and there is no end to the amount of study that can be devoted to them. (One may contrast the writings of Jacob Riis, Lincoln Steffens, and Upton Sinclair with some of the current literature on urban poverty, politics, and public health.) Especially costly is the situation where a research project also involves direct assistance to specific community or client groups. There again, the number of such groups is endless, and social science verges on the brink of becoming social work. Other objections to the problem orientation include the difficulties of forming generalizations and the tendency toward oversimplifying human

---

[6]This is not meant to be a criticism of social scientists alone. A not unusual situation along the same lines occurred during the 1968 teachers' strike in New York City, where none of the main figures "responsible" for the strike—not the mayor, the president of the board of education, the president of the teachers' union, or even the administrator of the local demonstration project around which the strike focused—had their own children in the New York City public school system (see Martin Mayer, *The Teachers Strike, New York, 1968,* [New York: Harper & Row, Publishers, 1969] p. 89). The main point is that in the area of social problems, there is often a vast discrepancy between the actors and those acted upon.

phenomena by ignoring second, third, and higher order consequences.[7] But most important of all, the problem orientation leaves the initiative for deciding what questions and issues ought to be studied in the hands of society, or worse, in the hands of government bureaucracies and other research-sponsoring agencies.[8] This abdication takes place because the problems approach typically defines social problems by their societal context, and rarely in a theoretical context.[9] In contrast, one has to believe that if social science has anything to offer to the world, it is the ability to determine the issues likely to lead to new and fundamental insights about society and, therefore, the ability to initiate inquiry.

As an alternative to the problems approach, it may be advantageous to renew attempts aimed simply at developing a better understanding of the nature of the city. One potential organizing theme can be derived from Don Martindale's prefatory note to Max Weber's *The City.*[10] In his note, Martindale describes how European urban theory had, by the turn of the 20th century, developed into a basically institutional theory of the city (p. 46 ff.). Fustel de Coulanges, for instance, took religion to be the critical institution of the city; Marx and Pirenne attempted to explain the city in terms of economic institutions; others emphasized kinship and family, or jurisprudence, or even the city garrison as the key institutions. Martindale then goes on to show how, for Weber, the urban community was distinguished not by any single institution, but by *an order or system of institutions.* Weber's complete urban community included a fortification, a market, a court and partially autonomous law, other civic associations, and some degree of self-government and administration. Finally, Martindale notes that, as thus defined, the Weberian city appeared only under certain conditions and during certain periods of time. The American city, for instance, does not qualify because it lacks its own fortification and army. The military and other functions performed by cities in other ages have been granted by our society to another polity, the nation.

---

[7]Even technologists and businessmen, those often given the most credit for successfully dealing with problems, are just beginning to realize the complex nature of the repercussions following their actions. See, for example, Raymond A. Bauer, *Second-Order Consequences: A Methodological Essay on the Impact of Technology* (Cambridge, Mass.: The M.I.T. Press, 1969).

[8]For instance, the National Science Foundation has recently embarked upon a new program of applied research titled "Research Applied to National Needs" (RANN). This program will involve the expenditure of almost $100 million annually, and the agency has identified several target areas for research. What one would like to know is how these areas were defined, and the decision-making process by which the agency officials arrived at their conclusions. See "NSF: Is applied research at the take off point?" *Science,* 172:1315–1317 (June, 1971).

[9]Herbert Blumer, "Social problems as collective behavior," *Social Problems,* 18:298–306 (Winter, 1971).

[10]Max Weber, *The City,* trans. and ed. by Don Martindale and Gertrud Neuwirth (Glencoe, Ill.: The Free Press, 1958).

One need not accept Weber's peculiar definition of the urban community, however, to see the value of interpreting the city as an order of institutions. First, this approach places emphasis on institutions, and hence on the fact that social interactions and roles are the basic phenomena to be studied and explained. Second, it presents the city as a confluence of different institutions that complement, conflict, and overlap to create distinctive by-products. Third, it calls attention to the facts that the institutions are related and do not operate in isolation and that a satisfactory analysis of the city must include the explicit examination of relationships, not just institutions. Fourth, it suggests that relationships and institutions change over time, and that the concepts used in dealing with the city similarly need to accommodate a state of continuing change.

It is the task of the study of the city, then, to identify and explain the nature of specific urban institutions and interactions. Among other things, the study should explain the ways in which such phenomena are uniquely urban and not mere aspects of the society at large; the goal might be much like showing how the family is a very special kind of small group. In addition, because of the many changes that have occurred on the urban scene, the study should be placed within the milieu of contemporary events.

No comprehensive piece of research currently covers such a view of the study of the city. However, there have been individual studies, appearing in isolation and in different academic disciplines, from which this type of study can be shaped. Thus while no new urban theory has emerged that can identify the relevant urban institutions and their relationships, the individual studies do permit one to speculate about the likely components of such institutions and the research methods that will be used to study them. *The City in the Seventies* attempts to pull together some of the fragments and to present the research themes that may be of increasing importance in the next few years. Given such a rationale, it is hoped that the answer to the inevitable question, "Why another urban reader?" has by now also become obvious.

Part One of the reader focuses attention on some of the components of the city. These include people, neighborhood change, local government, and the physical environment. Some emphasis has been placed on suggesting how the components interrelate. For instance, the ethnic identification of people is accentuated in some cities; the ethnicity in turn exerts a strong influence on the residential patterns of the city and the organization of local government. Because the length of the reader has been deliberately kept within manageable proportions, the topics covered should not be construed as an exhaustive list. Notable among missing topics is discussion of the economic factors in the city—e.g., jobs, transportation networks, and industrial production. A second omission is the relationship between the city and its region. As people move into and out of the city with increasing ease, and as national, state, and local governments become more interlocking, the interaction between city and region has gained great importance. Nevertheless, to cover either of these two topics would perhaps have required separate volumes.[11]

Part Two of the reader emphasizes some of the methods for studying the contemporary city. Again, for reasons of space, the topics are necessarily a sampling, with coverage given to some newer developments, such as systems analysis and social indicators, as well as to more traditional methods, such as participant-observation and survey research. The articles in Part Two also raise one important general issue: the relationship between a research investigator and the human subject whom he wishes to study. More than with any other kind of research, recent urban studies have had to contend with the problems of this researcher-subject interface. Although there have been many laboratory studies dealing with experimenter effects and biases, and there is a considerable literature on research design and methodology, few persons have discussed in a serious way the simple questions that often confront the urban researcher—Should the research be done in the first place? Who should decide how the study is to be designed and carried out? Who has access to the research findings? One hopes that the selected articles will be a sufficient reminder that the research probe is in itself a social act and that it has genuine and permanent consequences of its own.

Several of the articles in Parts One and Two cover topics of potential importance to the future function and study of the city. However, nowhere is the urban future dealt with explicitly, and thus Part Three contains one article that dares to speculate about the likely future of the central city. The article is an interview with a prominent urbanologist and blends together many themes into a comprehensive view of the city.

As a group, the selected articles have two characteristics that deserve mention. First, the articles have been written by authors from a wide variety of professions and academic disciplines. Among those represented are business, journalism, political science, sociology, psychology, anthropology, economics, engineering, operations research, city planning, environmental science, and history. Such a multidisciplinary selection was not consciously sought. However, it suggests that a student must be conversant over a much wider range of research than ever before, even though the wide span of knowledge should by no means be attained at the expense of mastering one discipline to a fair degree of specialization and sophistication. The main point is that different disciplines bring different orientations, methods, and

---

[11]For a recent volume on economic aspects, see, for example, Harvey S. Perloff and Lowdon Wingo, Jr. (eds.), *Issues in Urban Economics* (Baltimore: The Johns Hopkins Press, 1968).

theories to the study of the city. The contemporary social scientist should have a breadth and depth of knowledge that his intellectual ancestors may never have imagined.

Second, the articles do give more coverage to issues in large American cities, particularly New York City. The assumption is that large cities like New York have many experiences with greater intensity than in other cities, but the basic issues like the use of the environment or the developments in local government remain similar to those of other cities. Some have even claimed that the large cities like New York undergo new crises and situations slightly earlier than do other cities and in this sense provide a small glimpse into the future.[12] Whatever the merits of that claim, there seem to be several advantages in studying urban issues from the perspective of the larger cities. Because of the greater numbers of people involved, research observations can be made more frequently and in finer detail. In addition, many issues are simply more readily visible in the larger cities, though one always has to beware of overgeneralizing the experiences of one city to those of another.

In summary, *The City in the Seventies* is an attempt to present the American city in a contemporary research perspective. The detective working on such a case cannot afford to be thrown off by current crises, but neither can he ignore them. By the same token, he does not have the time to examine ancient historical parallels and cross-cultural evidence in detail, but he must be careful not to overlook the obvious clues. Lastly, he must use his imagination and not fear to speculate about the future course of events, but he cannot become overly utopian. At this stage of his thinking, the detective should have as his goal not the development of solutions, nor even the statement of problems. He should be satisfied if he can only pose the appropriate questions regarding the nature of the city and its expected development.

---

[12]See "Focus on New York," special issue of *The Public Interest,* No. 16 (Summer, 1969), especially the article by Nathan Glazer, "Beyond income maintenance—A note on welfare in New York City," pp. 102–20.

PART ONE

Components of the City

A. PEOPLE AND ETHNIC SUBCULTURES

Of all the factors that make cities distinctive, perhaps the most important ones stem from the characteristics of the urban populace. First and foremost, cities are centers of population and human activity. The great numbers of people and the density of their settlement in the city produce a huge diversity of occupations, marketplaces, and life styles.[1] Furthermore, they enable a city to develop and support establishments that in the past have been uniquely urban, e.g., subways, professional team sports, museums, cultural centers, specialized shopping districts, and skyscrapers.

The first section of *The City in the Seventies* focuses on two important characteristics of a city's people: their ethnicity and their residential mobility. In certain respects, these two characteristics go together, for mass migrations from other countries to the United States have been an important part of American history.[2] Contrary to what one may think, the total number of people currently migrating to the United States has again become quite large, following passage of the Immigration Act of 1965, which abolished the national origins quota system.[3] In fact, the size of the influx is surpassed only by the massive migrations that occurred at the beginning of the century, although the ratio of immigrants to base population is of course much lower now (see Table 1). The new immigration act has also resulted in shifts in the countries of origin of immigrant populations. In the shifts, the number of immigrants from southern Europe, Asia, and the Caribbean region has increased, with many more people now coming from Greece, Portugal, the Philippines, and Jamaica.

---

[1]This is the major theme of the now classic article by Louis Wirth, "Urbanism as a way of life," *American Journal of Sociology*, 44:1–24 (July, 1938).

[2]Oscar Handlin, *The Uprooted: The Epic Story of the Great Migrations That Made the American People* (Boston: Little, Brown & Co., 1951), p. 3.

[3]For a full discussion of the policy changes involved in the Immigration Act of 1965 and some of the recent trends in migration patterns attributable to the act, see Charles B. Keely, "Effects of the Immigration Act of 1965 on selected population characteristics of immigrants to the United States," *Demography*, 8:157–169 (May, 1971).

Traditionally, the new immigrants have settled in the cities, thereby helping to develop distinct urban villages and ethnic subcultures. Thus ethnic identifications have played an important role in American urban development, although in some cities more than in others.[4] Ethnic identifications, for instance, can greatly influence people's residential choices, with the tendency being to select places of residence that are near other people of the same ethnicity.[5] Similar influences can be found in the jobs people choose, voting preferences, and the organization of local government.

Most importantly, however, ethnic identifications have not disappeared as quickly as previously thought. Milton Gordon has described the shortcomings of the traditional "melting pot" analogy, whereby immigrant groups are seen as intermarrying and assimilating rapidly into the American culture.[6] In the excerpt of his book reproduced here (Selection 1 of this reader), Gordon discusses the origins of the melting pot view and its basic inadequacies. Nathan Glazer (Selection 2) presents a contemporary picture of assimilation, or the lack of it, in New York City. Glazer's article is a 1969 critique of the views that he and Daniel P. Moynihan expressed several years earlier in the widely read book *Beyond the Melting Pot.*[7] Finally, Elena Padilla (Selection 3) and Stan Steiner (Selection 4) provide brief descriptions of urban life from the perspective of two of the larger contemporary immigrant groups, the Puerto Ricans and the Mexicans. These last two selections should be taken as illustrative of the general problems faced by new ethnic groups in cities, rather than as mere accounts of two particular ethnic groups. As for the future, the assimilation challenges to be faced by Filipinos, Jamaicans, and other new immigrant groups may be worth anticipating.

Residential mobility within the United States has also been marked by a significant migratory trend: the movement of black people into the cities and the concomitant movement of nonblacks out of the cities and into the suburbs. To a lesser degree, there has also been a movement of rural whites from Appalachian areas into major cities in the eastern half of the United States. These migratory patterns are difficult to study, with census data being the only comprehensive (though still quite incomplete) information base. It is difficult, for instance, to distinguish accurately between a popula-

---

[4]Stanley Lieberson, *Ethnic Patterns in American Cities* (New York: The Free Press, 1963); and Daniel N. Gordon, "Immigrants and urban governmental form in American cities, 1933–1960," *American Journal of Sociology,* 74:158–171 (Sept., 1968).

[5]For example, see Nathan Kantrowitz, "Ethnic and racial segregation in the New York metropolis, 1960," *American Journal of Sociology,* 74:685–695 (May, 1969).

[6]Milton M. Gordon, *Assimilation in American Life: The Role of Race, Religion, and National Origins* (New York: Oxford University Press, 1964).

[7]Nathan Glazer and Daniel P. Moynihan, *Beyond the Melting Pot: The Negroes, Puerto Ricans, Jews, Italians, and Irish of New York City* (Cambridge: The M.I.T. Press, 1963, rev. 1970).

Table 1
Immigration into the United States

Years	Average annual immigration	Total U.S. population at end of decade
1891–1900	369,000	76,000,000
1901–1910	880,000	92,000,000
1911–1920	574,000	106,000,000
1921–1930	411,000	123,000,000
1931–1940	53,000	132,000,000
1941–1950	104,000	152,000,000
1951–1960	252,000	180,000,000

Year	Annual immigration	
1962	284,000	–
1964	292,000	–
1966	323,000	–
1968	363,000*	–
1969	359,000	204,000,000

SOURCE: *Statistical Abstract of the United States, 1970,* Table Nos. 2 and 128.

*Does not include Cuban refugees already in the United States who were allowed to adjust their status through special legislation (Act of November 2, 1966). See footnote 3 of text above.

Table 2
Percentage of Negro population in large central cities

City	1950	1960	1970
New York	10%	14%	21%
Los Angeles	9	14	18
Chicago	14	23	33
Philadelphia	18	26	34
Detroit	16	29	44
Baltimore	24	35	46
Houston	21	23	26
Cleveland	16	29	38
Washington, D.C.	35	54	71
St. Louis	18	29	41
Milwaukee	3	8	15
San Francisco	6	10	13
Total, United States	10	11	11

SOURCE: *The World Almanac,* 1969, p. 604 and *The New York Times,* April 4, 1971, p. 1, and May 19, 1971, p. 39; based on the 1950, 1960, and 1970 censuses.

tion growth due to in-migration and one due to natural increase. But what is clear is that large central cities now contain significant and growing proportions of black people (see Table 2). Charles Tilly (Selection 5) describes some of the issues connected with the black migration to the cities, looking mainly at two issues: first, whether the migration per se is responsible for the social problems often associated with it, and second, the extent to which the traditional view of ethnic assimilation is applicable to the black people. The last article of this section is a report of research done in Chicago by Gerald Suttles (Selection 6). Suttles covers some of the aspects of the black subculture as it has formed in another establishment that up until now has been distinctively urban, the public housing project.

1. Theories of assimilation: The melting pot

MILTON M. GORDON

. . . . .

In 1908, Israel Zangwill's drama, *The Melting Pot,* was produced in this country and became a popular success. It is a play dominated by the vision of its protagonist, a young Russian Jewish immigrant to America, a composer whose goal is the completion of a vast "American" symphony which will express his deeply felt conception of his adopted country as a divinely inspired crucible in which all the ethnic divisions of mankind will divest themselves of their ancient animosities and differences and become fused into one group signifying the brotherhood of man. In the process he falls in love with a beautiful and cultured Gentile girl. The play ends with the completion and performance of the symphony and, after numerous vicissitudes and traditional family opposition from both sides, the approaching marriage of David Quixano and his beloved. During the course of these developments, David, in the rhetoric of the time, delivers himself of such sentiments as these:

> America is God's crucible, the great Melting Pot where all the races of Europe are melting and re-forming!. Here you stand, good folk, think I, when I see them at Ellis Island, here you stand in your fifty groups, with your fifty languages and histories, and your fifty blood hatreds and rivalries. But you won't be long like that, brothers, for these are the fires of God you've come to —these are the fires of God. A fig for your feuds and vendettas! Germans and Frenchmen, Irishmen and Englishmen, Jews and Russians—into the Crucible with you all! God is making the American.

Abridged and edited from Milton M. Gordon, *Assimilation in American Life: The Role of Race, Religion, and National Origins,* pp. 120–131. Copyright © 1964 by Oxford University Press, Inc. Reprinted by permission.

The author is Professor of Sociology, University of Massachusetts, Amherst, Mass.

And later,

> Yes, East and West, and North and South, the palm and the pine, the pole and the equator, the crescent and the cross—how the great Alchemist melts and fuses them with his purging flame! Here shall they all unite to build the Republic of Man and the Kingdom of God. Ah, Vera, what is the glory of Rome and Jerusalem where all nations and races come to worship and look back, compared with the glory of America, where all races and nations come to labour and look forward.[1]

Here, then, we have a conception of a melting pot which admits of no exceptions or qualification with regard to ethnic stocks which will fuse in the great crucible. Englishmen, Germans, Frenchmen, Slavs, Greeks, Syrians, Jews, Gentiles, even the black and yellow races, were specifically mentioned in Zangwill's rhapsodic enumeration. And this pot must patently boil in the great cities of America.

Thus, around the turn of the century, the melting pot idea was embedded in the rhetoric of the time as one response to the immigrant-receiving experience of the nation. It may be found, for instance, in the writing and speeches of two presidents: Theodore Roosevelt and Woodrow Wilson,[2] and, significantly enough, the published volume of Zangwill's play on the theme was dedicated to the first Roosevelt to lead the nation. However, as must now be apparent, a certain ambiguity surrounds the melting pot concept, allowing its adherents to interpret it in various ways. Neither Roosevelt nor the mature Wilson favored theories of racial superiority (although it is possible to detect a preference for the earlier immigration sources in their writings),[3] and both believed that the new immigrants from Southern and Eastern Europe were essentially capable of being absorbed into the American scene. However, Roosevelt, while viewing America as a nation in which "the representatives of many old-world races are being fused together into a new type," maintained at the same time that "the crucible in which all the new types are melted into one was shaped from 1776 to 1789, and our nationality was definitely fixed in all its essentials by the men of Washington's day."[4] And a similar view, according to a careful study of the matter, was shared by Wilson. In the minds of both Roosevelt and Wilson, writes Edward Saveth, "unlike the frontier melting pot, which occurred earlier and was accepted as part of the process of nation making, the later mingling of peoples was looked upon more as an assimilative process whereby the peoples from southern and eastern Europe were indoctrinated in canons of Americanism established by earlier arrivals."[5]

The melting pot idea ... continued to draw ... attention and discussion ... [well into] the twentieth century. In the middle 1940's a sociologist, Ruby Jo Reeves Kennedy, who had carried out an investigation of intermarriage trends in New

---

[1]Israel Zangwill, *The Melting Pot* (New York: The Macmillan Co., 1909), pp. 37–199.

[2]Edward N. Saveth, *American Historians and European Immigrants* (New York: Columbia University Press, 1948), pp. 112–121 and 137–149.

[3]*Ibid.*

[4]Quoted in Saveth, *op. cit.,* p. 121; original source given as "Speech at the unveiling of the Sheridan statue in Washington, cited in introduction to *The Jews in Nazi Germany* (New York, 1935), p. viii."

[5]Saveth, *op. cit.,* p. 148.

Haven, Connecticut, described a revised conception of the melting process as it had taken place in that city and suggested a basic modification of the theory. In New Haven, Mrs. Kennedy reported, after a study of intermarriage from 1870 to 1940, the rate of in-marriage, or endogamy, among the various national origins groups was high over the whole period, although it had dropped from 91.20 per cent in 1870 to 65.80 per cent in 1930 to 63.64 per cent in 1940. But while there was a decreasing emphasis on national origins lines in choosing a mate, there was still a considerable tendency to marry within one's own religious group. In 1940, 79.72 per cent of the British-Americans, Germans, and Scandinavians intermarried among themselves— that is, within a Protestant "pool"; 83.71 per cent of the Irish, Italians, and Poles intermarried among themselves—a Catholic "pool"; and 94.32 per cent of the Jews married other Jews. (The question of intermarriage between Jews of Central European origins and Jews of Eastern European origins was not studied.) Where Catholic-Protestant marriages took place—and it should be noted that in 1940 both the Irish and the Italians, when they did marry outside their own national group, preferred British-Americans to any other single national origins group—the majority of such marriages were sanctioned by Catholic nuptials, thus prescribing that the children would be brought up as Catholics. In other words, intermarriage was taking place across nationality background lines, but there was a strong tendency for it to stay confined within the basic influential field of one or the other of the three major religious groups: Protestants, Catholics, and Jews. Thus, declared Mrs. Kennedy, the picture in New Haven resembled a "triple melting pot" based on religious divisions, rather than a "single melting pot."[6] Her study indicated, she stated, that "while strict endogamy is loosening, religious endogamy is persisting and the future cleavages will be along religious lines rather than along nationality lines as in the past. If this is the case, then the traditional 'single-melting-pot' idea must be abandoned, and a new conception, which we term the 'triple-melting-pot' theory of American assimilation, will take its place as the true expression of what is happening to the various nationality groups in the United States."[7] The triple melting pot thesis was later taken up by the theologian, Will Herberg, and formed an important sociological frame of reference for his analysis of religious trends in American society, published as *Protestant—Catholic—Jew.*[8]

Having now examined the rise and development of the melting pot idea, let us examine it with the aid of our analytical scheme, and against the background of the realities of American group life. We shall deal first with the "single melting pot" version, since this version is not only historically and logically prior but is the form in which this idea has captured the imagination of a number of articulate interpreters of American society for over a century and a half.

Partisans of the idea of America as one huge melting pot, like adherents of Anglo-conformity, have provided no systematic delineation of their views. Indeed,

---

[6]Ruby Jo Reeves Kennedy, "Single or triple melting-pot? Intermarriage trends in New Haven, 1870–1940," *American Journal of Sociology,* 49:331–339 (January 1944); see also her "Single or triple melting pot? Intermarriage in New Haven, 1870–1950," *American Journal of Sociology,* 58:56–59 (July 1952).

[7]Kennedy, 1944, *op. cit.,* p. 332 (author's italics omitted).

[8]Will Herberg, *Protestant—Catholic—Jew* (New York: Doubleday & Co., Inc., 1955).

the concept is one which singularly lends itself to expression in vague rhetoric which, however noble its aims, gives minimal clues as to the exact implications of the term for the manifold spheres of societal organization and behavior. Nevertheless, certain logical inferences can be made, and one feature appears to be envisaged in all the statements of the idea: a complete mixture of the various stocks through intermarriage—in other words, marital assimilation, or amalgamation.

With regard to cultural behavior, the most characteristic implication is that the cultures of the various groups will mix and form a blend somewhat different from the cultures of any one of the groups separately. However, a neglected aspect of this model of cultural intermixture is whether all groups will make an equally influential contribution to the boiling pot, or whether there is to be a *proportionate* influence depending upon the size, power, and strategic location of the various groups. If, to illustrate hypothetically and simply, there are 100,000 Sylvanians occupying their own country, and 2000 Mundovians enter as immigrants, under the melting pot model of cultural interpenetration will the resulting blend—assuming some rough measurement were possible—consist of equal parts of Sylvanian and Mundovian culture, or will the Sylvania cultural contribution be fifty times as important and pervasive as the Mundovian contribution? The answer to this question obviously has significant consequences for the contributing societies, in relation to the questions of both objective cultural survival and group psychology.

Indeed, at one extreme of interpretation—a loose and illogical one, to be sure —the melting pot concept may envisage the culture of the immigrants as "melting" completely into the culture of the host society without leaving any cultural trace at all. It would appear that some exponents of the idea came close to feeling that this was the proper role for Southern and Eastern European immigrants to play in the American melting process. In this form, of course, the melting pot concept embraces a view of acculturation which is hardly distinguishable in nature from that of Anglo-conformity, except that the conformity is to be exacted toward a cultural blend to which the cultures of immigrant groups from Northern and Western Europe have been conceded an earlier contribution.

With regard to the remaining assimilation variables, the analysis may proceed as follows: If large-scale intermarriage is to have taken place, then obviously the immigrants must have entered the cliques, clubs, other primary groups, and institutions of the host society and, in addition, placed their own impress upon these social structures to some extent. Thus the process of structural assimilation must somehow reflect a blending effect, also. Identificational assimilation takes place in the form of all groups merging their previous sense of peoplehood into a new and larger ethnic identity which, in some fashion, honors its multiple origins at the same time that it constitutes an entity distinct from them all. Prejudice and discrimination must be absent since there are not even any identifiably separate groups to be their target, and "civic assimilation" will have taken place since disparate cultural values are assumed to have merged and power conflict between groups would be neither necessary nor possible. This, then, is the "ideal-typical" model of the melting pot process. With this analysis and the previous discussion in mind, let us take a quick look at the American experience to see how well the model applies. A fuller discussion of some of the issues is reserved for later chapters.

While no exact figures on the subject are attainable, it is safe to say that a substantial proportion of the descendants of the non-English immigrants of colonial times and the first three-quarters of the nineteenth century (with the exception of the Irish Catholics and the German Jews) have by now been absorbed into the general white "sociological Protestant" sector of American life. That is to say, they do not live in communal subsocieties which are lineal descendants of those which their immigrant ancestors created, and so far as they understand it, are simply "Americans" who may be vaguely conscious of an immigrant forebear here and there from a non-English source but for whom this has little current meaning. This would include many descendants of the Scotch-Irish, German Protestants, Swedes, and Norwegians, among other groups from Northern and Western Europe, as well as, in all probability, a few with colonial Jewish ancestry whose early American progenitors converted to Christianity (not to mention occasional individuals who have a mulatto ancestor who, at some time, "passed" into the white group).[9] This does not mean that communal societies with appropriate institutions representing most of these ancestral groups do not still exist, but that, in relation to the total number of ethnic descendants, they become increasingly thinly manned as the third and fourth generation leave their rural or small town (occasionally urban) enclaves and venture forth into the broader social world.

The burden of our point should now be clear. Entrance by the descendants of these immigrants into the social structures of the existing white Protestant society, and the culmination of this process in intermarriage, has not led to the creation of new structures, new institutional forms, and a new sense of identity which draws impartially from all sources, but rather to immersion in a subsocietal network of groups and institutions which was already fixed in essential outline with an Anglo-Saxon, general Protestant stamp. The prior existence of Anglo-Saxon institutional forms as the norm, the pervasiveness of the English language, and the numerical dominance of the Anglo-Saxon population made this outcome inevitable.

Culturally, this process of absorbing Anglo-Saxon patterns has moved massively and inexorably, with greater or lesser speed, among all ethnic groups. Structurally, however, the outcome has, so far, been somewhat different, depending on whether we are considering white Protestant descendants of the "Old" immigration, white Catholics and Jews of both periods of immigration, or the racial and quasi-racial minorities. Here, then, is where the "triple melting pot" hypothesis of Kennedy and others becomes applicable. While Protestant descendants of Germans and Scandinavians can, if they wish, merge structurally into the general white Protestant subsociety with relative ease, Jews, Irish Catholics, Italian Catholics, and Polish Catholics cannot do so without either formal religious conversion or a kind of sociological "passing"—neither process being likely to attract overwhelmingly large numbers. Negroes, Orientals, Mexican-Americans, and some Puerto Ricans are prevented by racial discrimination from participating meaningfully in either the white Protestant or the white Catholic communities. Nationality background differences within the white population, however, appear to be more amenable to dissolv-

---

[9]Estimates of the number of very light Negroes who "pass" permanently into the white group range from 2,000 to 30,000 annually, although the practice is obviously so shrouded in secrecy that even these limits may not include the true figure. See Maurice R. Davie, *Negroes in American Society* (New York: McGraw-Hill Book Co., 1949), pp. 401–407; also Gunnar Myrdal, with the assistance of Richard Sterner and Arnold Rose, *An American Dilemma* (New York: Harper & Bros., 1944), pp. 129–130, 683–688.

ing influences, for reasons which we shall consider later. The passing of the "nationality" communities may be slower than Kennedy and Herberg intimate and the rate of Catholic-Protestant intermarriage has been shown to be substantially higher in the country as a whole than in New Haven.[10] However, a vastly important and largely neglected sociological point about mixed marriages, racial, religious, or national, apart from the rate, is *in what social structures the intermarried couples and their children incorporate themselves.* If Catholic-Protestant intermarried couples live more or less completely within either the Catholic social community or the Protestant social community, the sociological fact of the existence of the particular religious community and its separation from other religious communities remains.

The result of these processes, structurally speaking, is that American society has come to be composed of a number of "pots," or subsocieties, three of which are the religious containers marked Protestant, Catholic, and Jew, which are in the process of melting down the white nationality background communities contained within them; others are racial groups which are not allowed to melt structurally; and still others are substantial remnants of the nationality background communities manned by those members who are either of the first generation, or who, while native born, choose to remain within the ethnic enclosure. All of these constitute the ethnic subsocieties which we have described earlier, with their network of primary groups, organizations, and institutions within which a member's life may be comfortably enclosed except for secondary contacts with "outsiders" in the process of making a living and carrying out the minimal duties of political citizenship, if he so desires. Another pot besides the religious containers which is actually doing some structural melting is labeled "intellectuals." All these containers, as they bubble along in the fires of American life and experience are tending to produce, with somewhat differing speeds, products which are culturally very similar, while at the same time they remain structurally separate. The entire picture is one which, with the cultural qualifications already noted, may be called a "multiple melting pot." And so we arrive at the "pluralism" which characterizes the contemporary American scene.

---

[10]August B. Hollingshead's data on intermarriage in New Haven in 1948 support the Kennedy thesis. However, John L. Thomas's broader study of Catholic-Protestant intermarriage found that between 1940 and 1950, "mixed marriages sanctioned by Catholic nuptials approximated 30% of all Catholic marriages in the United States." To these must be added an unknown rate of mixed marriages involving one Catholic partner which are not sanctioned by Catholic nuptials. See August B. Hollingshead, "Cultural factors in the selection of marriage mates," *American Sociological Review,* 15:619–627 (October, 1950), and John L. Thomas, "The factor of religion in the selection of marriage mates," *American Sociological Review,* 16:487–491 (August, 1951). The Thomas quotation above will be found on p. 488.

2.   A new look at the melting pot

NATHAN GLAZER

The major part of *Beyond the Melting Pot* by myself and Daniel P. Moynihan dates from 1960–61. It was in those years, at the end of Mayor Wagner's second term, that the chapters on the five major ethnic groups (Negroes, Puerto Ricans, Jews, Italians, and Irish) were written. I had formulated the major themes sometime earlier—they were that ethnicity in New York remains important; that it would continue important for politics and culture; that, from the perspective of New York City, Negroes and Puerto Ricans could be seen as the latest of the series of major ethnic groups that had—oddly enough, two by two, beginning with Germans and Irish, going on to Jews and Italians—come as immigrants to make up the population of the city; that helping to make each group different, in its own development and its relation to the rest of the city, were its basic cultural characteristics, and particularly important among these was family structure.

The conclusion of the book was fashioned and attached in late 1962, and was based, in large measure, on Moynihan's experience in running the campaign of Henry Morgenthau for Governor of New York State in that year, an experience which seemed to be consistent with and to confirm the basic assumptions of the book. The book was published in 1963. An appropriately obscure final paragraph reads: "Religion and race define the next stage in the evolution of the American peoples. But the American nationality is still forming. Its processes are mysterious, and its final form, if there is ever to be one, is as yet unknown."

It is a combination of obtuseness and perception that more or less sums up how the book reads today. Obviously, at this point in time, during New York's primaries and election campaign of 1969, it hardly seems as though religion defines the present, or the future, major fissures in New York life. Race has exploded to swallow up all other distinctions, or so it would appear at the moment. Yet, ten years ago, and to some extent even today, one of the major splits in New York City was between Catholics and Jews. The rise of the reform Democratic clubs was a means whereby the liberal upper-middle-class Jewish population of the city tried to seize the Democratic Party, dominated until then by Irish, and latterly some Italian, Catholic politicians. True, the issues on which they divided often seemed less important than the images of the leaders they felt comfortable with. And even in those distant years there was already some fudging evident between the liberal values of Jews and the conservative values of Irish and Italian Catholics when it came to matters of race, and in particular to school integration. But there *were* issues, such as support to parochial schools, and these issues were live enough to help account for the defeat of a new constitution for New York State not long ago.

Abridged and edited from Nathan Glazer, "A new look at the melting pot," *The Public Interest*, No. 16 (Summer, 1969), pp. 180–187. Copyright © 1969 by National Affairs, Inc. Reprinted by permission.

The author is Professor of Education and Social Structure, Harvard University, Cambridge, Mass.

By now, it hardly seems that the religious split matters. Catholics have become more liberal—in particular, on such matters as the role of traditional authority, censorship, sex, and morals, on which they used to diverge sharply from Jews—and Jews have become far more aware of the virtue of conservative working-class and middle-class values, which they always practiced but refused to celebrate. Even the American Jewish Congress, the most liberal of the major Jewish organizations, seems to spend as much of its energy these days, perhaps more, on the threats from black militants as on older concerns such as keeping inviolate the line between church and state. In any case, the administration of President Kennedy seems to have reduced the salience of that latter issue.

.   .   .   .   .

Thus, religion as a major line of division in the city is for the moment in eclipse. Race dominates the city more than could ever have seemed possible in 1963. That was, after all, before the first summer riots. The civil rights revolution had not yet broken out of the south. Nor had it yet raised the economic issues, and even less, the issue of potential separatism, that were to prove so much more explosive than the issues of political equality, which were, after all, part of the American creed all along. It seemed hardly possible then that the violence one had always associated with southern race relations could be transferred bodily to New York—its racial violence seemed far in the past (it had not had a race riot in either World War I or World War II, as had other northern cities). One looked at the demands of the civil rights movement in 1963—equality in the vote, equality in the courts, equality in representation in public life, equality in public accommodations—saw that they existed more or less in New York City, and concluded that the political course of the northern Negro would be quite different from that of the southern Negro. He would become part of the game of accommodation politics—he already was—in which posts and benefits were distributed to groups on the basis of struggle, of course, but also on the basis of votes, money, and political talent, and one concluded that in this game the Negroes would not do badly.

A number of considerations led to this outlook, which seemed reasonable enough at the time.

First, other New York groups had started at the bottom economically and politically, and had risen. What was to keep the Negro from doing the same, particularly since the crude evidence available suggested there had already been substantial shifts in occupation—from domestics and laborers to clerical workers and semiskilled workers, for example? On the basis of the experience of other ethnic groups, it was hard to see that this economic rise would need any additional direct commitment by local government. It would come through growth in the national economy, change in the structure of job market, higher levels of education (which were already evident), and movement into specific but rewarding parts of the economy and labor market—certainly the civil service, possibly the great private bureaucracies of New York businesses, hardly through entrepreneurial activity though there were opportunities there too.

Second, there seemed to be no major obstacle to this development in the form of a massive, institutionalized racism. There was prejudice, of course, but other groups had met that. And compared to the greater scale of prejudice Negroes had met, there were now in existence well-funded city and state agencies devoted to fighting prejudice and discrimination in jobs, education, housing (though that was admitted to be an enormous problem), and indeed in the actions of both public and significant private bodies.

Third, *Beyond the Melting Pot* did suggest that a significant check to the economic rise of the Negroes might be found in the values of American Negroes themselves; these played some large but not fully explicated role in economic development. But the suggestion was tentative—no warning sign was flashed—because the economic and sociological fundamentals seemed so secure.

What was wrong with this optimistic outlook? First, it was based on poor data. As David Gordon points out,[1] . . . the analysis of the distribution of population by income is a late development, and even so we are in bad shape between censuses. When the work on *Beyond the Melting Pot* began, the figures for the decade 1940–50, were available, and showed remarkable change, owing to the war. The stagnation of opportunities for the Negro after the Korean war was to be discovered in the statistics available for 1950–60, but I didn't discover them. There was a serious undercount of Negro males in New York (as in the whole country) which probably led to an overstatement of the economic position of the Negro. The undercount was first pointed out in 1955 in an article by Ansley J. Coale, but it was not until after our book was published, amazingly enough, that this became general knowledge among social scientists, aside from some specialists in demography. Since the analyses of income data were then so scanty, one depended on occupational data, and these, interestingly enough, showed more change for Negroes than the income data. After the book was published, Herman P. Miller demonstrated that the Negro had moved not at all in relation to whites since the mid-1950's; Michael Harrington helped rediscover poverty; the civil rights movement for the first time took up economic aims (only in late 1963, it will be recalled); and the relatively optimistic view of the Negro's economic future in our book collapsed.

And yet, one must still remember how different things looked in the first two years of the Kennedy administration. Then the problem of poverty and inequality, it seemed, could be handled by a tax cut, an Area Redevelopment Administration program for the by-passed areas, a manpower training program for workers displaced by automation. The poverty program was still, in those days, a juvenile-delinquency-fighting program. Life was simpler then!

Still, one wonders how far off the prognosis of *Beyond the Melting Pot* was, after all. If one were so inclined, though hardly anyone is, I am afraid, one could still find remarkable progress since the early 1960's, using the criteria of numbers of Negroes in colleges, the number in high positions in government, the numbers in high-paying jobs. David Gordon's analysis is sobering and in some ways hard to understand, perhaps a metropolitan-wide analysis of the position of Negroes and Puerto Ricans would show a less despairing picture. Certainly the situation of New York seems unique when compared with the changes the census records for the Negro in metropolitan areas for the country as a whole, and one is at a loss to understand *why* Negroes do comparatively so much worse here, when the city has (still) one of the more enlightened governments and bodies of public opinion.

---

[1] David M. Gordon, "Income and welfare in New York City," *The Public Interest,* No. 16 (Summer, 1969), pp. 64–88.

If one looks at the Puerto Ricans, who are economically no better off than Negroes, one does find a substantial move in the second generation that seems to correspond to what one expected for new groups in the city. Thus, Nathan Kantrowitz, comparing second generation Puerto Ricans in 1950 and 1960 (small groups in both years, but their numbers are rapidly growing) showed they improved their position, both in terms of numbers of graduating high school and college, more rapidly than other white males in the city. And while the story on occupational mobility is mixed, even there one sees some grounds for optimism in a substantial shift into white collar work.

I have not seen such an analysis for Negroes (that is, one based on movement of Negroes born in the city), but the basic question remains: if one had it, would it really matter? And one must conclude sadly, it would not. There is one basic reason for this. Perhaps it made sociological sense at the time to treat Negroes as an ethnic group in New York, parallel to other ethnic groups, to evaluate their place in the city in contrast to that of immigrant groups, and record how rapidly this position was changing, but it did not make *political* sense. It is even a question, of course, how much sociological sense it made. It made some, I still think. After all, Negroes themselves often saw their place in the city in these terms, viewed themselves as fighting not an undifferentiated white society but an ethnically diverse one, and in such a society some groups, for some purposes, were allies. That Negroes were, or were becoming, one group in a group society was the basic assumption of the book, and in that sense, perhaps, it was closer to social reality than some analyses of American society which saw assimilation and integration as already more advanced for most groups in the society than was actually the case.

Where the book failed was in determining what *kind* of group Negroes would form. As an ethnic group, they would be one of many. As a *racial* group, as "blacks," as the new nomenclature has it, they form a unique group in American society. In a sense, of course, they always have been; they are old settlers whose presence shaped our Constitution, they were the only group held as slaves, they dominate a good part of American culture and literature—no one could forget that or deny that. But New York City, *Beyond the Melting Pot* argued, while it was America, was also different from America. It accentuated and heightened one distinctive goal of American society—its openness to new groups and its even-handed distribution of opportunity. Here, the larger American experience of the Negro, based on slavery and repression in the south, would be overcome, as the rest of the Negroes joined society, in conflict and accommodation, as an ethnic group.

It didn't happen. Groups may preexist in sociological reality, but they shape themselves by choice—they define their own categories (and this, curiously enough, was also a major theme of the book). In 1963, it looked as if the categories could still be defined as ethnic, and that seemed to us most human. In 1969, we seem to be moving to a new set of categories, black and white—and that is ominous. On the horizon stand the fantastic categories of the "Third World," in which all the colors, Black, Brown, Yellow and Red (these are the favored terms for Negro, Mexican-American and Puerto Rican, Chinese and Japanese, and American Indian—a biologically and humanly monstrous ordering it seems to me—among the militants of southern California), are equated as "the oppressed" in opposition to the oppressing whites.

.　　　.　　　.　　　.

Another reality that was less clear in 1960–61 was how massively Negroes (and Puerto Ricans) abstained from politics, in some of the key ways that counted, for example, voting. They abstained *more* in the 1960's than in the mid-1940's in New York City and the reasons are unclear. Arthur Klebanoff has studied this for the city, particularly for Brooklyn. Between 1950 and 1965, the proportion of Negroes and Puerto Ricans in Brooklyn rose from 9 percent to 29 percent of the population. This should have meant a massive change in political representation, and presumably in rewards. It didn't.

.　　　.　　　.　　　.　　　.

Klebanoff's analysis demonstrated that while Negroes and Puerto Ricans formed approximately 30 percent of Brooklyn's total population and 25 percent of its eligible voting population, they were no more than 15 percent of Brooklyn's registered voters. It is understandable, then, that the Ocean Hill–Brownsville Local Governing Board should have declared, "Men are capable of putting an end to what they find intolerable without recourse to politics." Unfortunately, when they do, only uncertainty, insecurity, and disorder can result.

Beyond the Melting Pot explored some of the reasons why Negroes and Puerto Ricans would not organize as rapidly and effectively as other groups. For the Negroes, it suggested that the mere fact that they did not form a self-consciously foreign group, with special cultural demands that had to be met (food, language, religion) meant that the bases for organization were restricted. For Puerto Ricans, it suggested that the attitudes developed toward the paternalistic government of Puerto Rico were easily transferred to the government of the City of New York. Thus, in both groups, the push to organization and self-help were somewhat muted. But in the very nature of the ethnic analysis, this could not be expected to last— the groups would become more self-conscious, better organized. What could not be foreseen, of course, was what form this organization would take.

In the Negro communities, we have seen a wholly admirable and impressive rise of self-assertion and pride. The distinctive aspects of the Negro experience in America and Africa are being explored, reported, recorded, analyzed, and increasingly taught, both in private and in public schools. Aspects of Negro experience that were previously considered by Negroes themselves, unimportant, or matter-of-fact, or even shameful, are becoming part of the curriculum for this new movement of self-assertion. All this deserves encouragement and support. When it is combined, as it so often is, with an effort to teach an unreal past and an unreal present, one can still understand it—every group has its own similar tendencies. But when it is combined with an effort to separate Negroes from the mechanisms by which varied groups, in this most mixed of nations, participate in a common society and a common state, then we can only be saddened and frightened.

All the work of incorporating Negroes into a common society—economically, culturally, socially, politically—must be pushed as hard as possible. All those—and they still, from all evidence, form the large majority, if a quiet one—who want to be part of a common society must be given every aid and encouragement, and must be associated in every common enterprise. It is hard to believe that the genius for compromise and accommodation which has kept this a single city, despite the fact that it was made of minorities, will now fail. But the possibility, in 1969, is a haunting one.

3.   Race relations: A Puerto Rican view

ELENA PADILLA

There is no question that the character of race or ethnic relations has changed in tone and quality in New York City. Racism as a fact of social life, of economic dimensions, of culture, politics, and survival has surfaced. Old and powerful mechanisms for discriminating against members of minority groups continue to operate, although now through more complex and subtle channels. They permeate the social and political fabric of the city.

This surfacing is largely a product of the impact and spillover effects of the black movement on the political process of the city. The myth of the melting pot has finally fallen into discredit, and New York City minorities openly struggle to maintain their social and cultural plurality, their distinct identities, but this time, also openly struggle for access to political power. Puerto Ricans have joined in this struggle and the Puerto Rican society in New York City has been profoundly affected and has begun to affect the political scene.

The payoffs have yet to come. Overall, the conditions of life of Puerto Ricans in New York lag behind those of blacks and, by far, behind those of poor whites. Puerto Rican communities have been decaying physically and economically, with minimal services and programs addressed to protect the Puerto Rican population. The deterioration of East Harlem, South Bronx, Bedford-Stuyvesant, or Brownsville —the major Puerto Rican ghettoes in the city—has proceeded swiftly while intermittent wars over funding and distribution of resources are presided over by agents of the city bureaucracy. The conditions of life of the large masses of Puerto Ricans in New York are, to say the least, distressing. In 1964, Puerto Ricans had the lowest median family income when compared to whites and to blacks. In 1966, the unemployment of Puerto Ricans was 9.8 percent.

There is a rising sense of discontent and anger among Puerto Ricans about these conditions. What many used to consider to be a fault of the Puerto Ricans, now is regarded more as a fault of the social and the political systems.

In the past decade, Puerto Ricans have made a massive entry into the political arena, moving from marginal positions in ghetto clubhouses into the new politics of the communities and the urban world. More aggressive and proliferated efforts have been organized for self-help, self-development and self-enhancement. Politics has become a major vehicle for action. Yet, Puerto Rican politics in New York follows rules that are more expressive than instrumental, and more responsive to charisma of leadership and promise of immediate solution than to organized and

"Race Relations: A Puerto Rican View" by Elena Padilla is reprinted from Lyle C. Fitch and Annmarie H. Walsh (eds.), *Agenda for a City: Issues Confronting New York* (1970), pp. 557–562, by permission of the Publisher, Sage Publications, Inc., Beverly Hills, California.

The author is Professor, Department of Psychiatry, College of Human Medicine, Michigan State University, East Lansing, Mich.

sustained pressures. It is a nationalistic brand of politics that can also be characterized as reactive and defensive. In short, it is minority group politics, addressed to
self-protection and self-preservation.

A Puerto Rican, Herman Badillo, dared to defy the political organization of
the Democratic Party and to run in a primary for mayor of the city in 1969.
Although he lost the contest, his primary constituency well surpassed that of the
incumbent mayor who later sought and obtained his support. The contest established Badillo as a spokesman on urban problems in the city and the country. An
urbane, New York-educated lawyer, Badillo, who has a profound understanding of
New York City politics and American government, is not confined to the politics
of a Puerto Rican leader in the city. Affirming his Puerto Rican identity, he has
transcended the constrictions of ethnic politics, yet his defeat in the Democratic
Party primaries was indicated by a leading radio station as proof that city voters
were not yet ready for "a mayor with a Puerto Rican image." In this sense, the
political career of Herman Badillo epitomizes the "mobility ceiling" which still
restricts and obstructs the life chances of Puerto Ricans in New York as the 1970s
begin.

At the level of interpersonal relations, discrimination is part of the daily life
experience of any Puerto Rican in New York who comes into direct, face-to-face
contact with white America. As racial and ethnic factors have become more intense
in setting the climate of interpersonal relations in the city, more subtle, yet effective,
modes of expressing discrimination have become commonplace. Prejudice is clothed
today in sophisticated-sounding theories of group identity and of persistent or
glorified cultural patterns. These theories tend to lock persons of Puerto Rican
origins into an identity they may not feel and a caricature they may resent. Individual achievements by Puerto Ricans are seldom recognized as such. Many of
their relationships with white society seem humiliatingly tainted with patronizing
behavior. Stereotypes mar friendships, professional relationships, and opportunities.
Even sophisticated, educated New Yorkers feel that they must confess to us how
much they are doing for "your people." In turn, all educated persons of Puerto
Rican origins are expected to know the best and cheapest tourist hotels or abortion
mills in San Juan, and to be able to provide social services for other Puerto Ricans,
from scholarships for medical school to child placement. These kinds of stereotypes
—degrading as they are—stimulate defensive group identity, resentment, and discontent.

In the 1960s, several trends developed in the Puerto Rican society of New York.
First, there was an exodus away from New York to other states; also there was a
pattern of returning to Puerto Rico. The movement represents a "brain drainage"
since it contains a relatively large proportion of males in the professional, technical,
and managerial occupations. This movement, however, has been paralleled by a rise
of Puerto Rican leadership, with a strong component of individuals reared and
educated in the United States. Puerto Rican organizations and pressure groups have
proliferated and provided a multiplicity of fulcrums for social and political activities.
Puerto Ricans have been elected to city and state offices. There is an increased
Puerto Rican population of middle-class professionals in New York drawn from
Puerto Rico itself, and a growing second generation of college-educated adults of
Puerto Rican parents, whose roots and orientation are in New York.

Active participation in the labor movement and the organization of Puerto Rican communities have become vital ingredients of Puerto Rican society in New York. Puerto Rican migrants, who settled the New York slums as a "lumpen-proletariat" from a colonial existence, have increasingly become a potent political force in the city, involved in struggles for self-determination through community control. Their support is coveted both by politicians from San Juan and from New York. The slums have become the centers for community politics, for demands for resources for self-solution, with city-wide, middle-class Puerto Rican leadership lending its support and occasionally taking over roles of spokesmen and power brokers. The leadership of student uprisings in the Spring of 1969 at the City College included both black and Puerto Rican young people committed to transforming the City College into an instrument for educating large numbers of blacks and Puerto Ricans. Puerto Ricans also have played a crucial part in the school decentralization movement. In other words, the Puerto Ricans have become activated and have started to articulate aspirations and goals to the bureaucracy and to the political hierarchy, both within the traditional channels and through confrontation.

These efforts have not been altogether successful when compared to the achievements of the black communities, although in many ways blacks and Puerto Ricans are facing similar predicaments and defeats. The Puerto Rican "experience" is not unlike the black "experience." In many respects, Puerto Ricans are worse off than blacks in New York City. The proportion of Puerto Rican adults with no schooling or some grade school education by far exceeds that among blacks (37.9% to 16.5%). Among blacks, higher proportions than Puerto Ricans are high school graduates (23.7% to 16.3%), and higher proportion of blacks than Puerto Ricans are college graduates (5.9% to 3.4%). The proportion of blacks in professional, managerial, and technical occupations (9.5%) is four times that of Puerto Ricans (2.5%) in the same occupations. Puerto Ricans are young, with a median age of 21.7 years; families tend to be larger than among whites or blacks. Almost two-thirds of all Puerto Rican workers in 1960 were engaged in low-paid work. Greater proportions of Puerto Ricans than blacks are in blue-collar work, lesser proportions in service occupations and in white-collar occupations.

One might have expected that the commonality of experience between Puerto Ricans and blacks with white America would have encouraged a joint effort in the struggle for political power, to make this a more humane society. Puerto Rican and black coalitions, however, are generally short-lived and based on a specific issue or set of interrelated issues. Yet it is not infrequent now to find Puerto Ricans who have joined in a common cause with black organizations, particularly within neighborhoods of the city fighting some part of the Establishment that keeps them down. Politically, black and Puerto Rican identities, however, are different social categories: the first is based on race, the other on nationality. Alliances between blacks and Puerto Ricans recognize and respect this difference, but more importantly recognize a common social bond between blacks and Puerto Ricans as oppressed minorities sharing in the total experience resulting from such oppression.

In the Puerto Rican tradition concepts of race are blended with socio-economic class. First and foremost, being Puerto Rican is an affirmation of the Spanish heritage, a condition which overrides racial considerations. Yet, racial connotations are intrinsically webbed into social and interpersonal relations among Puerto Ricans and between Puerto Ricans and other ethnic groups. Puerto Rico has been a colonial outpost of Spain for four centuries, and of the United States in the twentieth century. Slavery and its associated institutions which formed the nucleus of colonial plantation society are part of the biological and social Puerto Rican heritage and have left their strong mark on the contemporary social institutions, the culture, and the social psychology of Puerto Ricans.

American influence and political control no doubt have intensified the racial dimension in Puerto Rican standards of behavior, which not only affect the relations between Puerto Ricans and and black Americans but also the relations between white and black Puerto Ricans, and between Puerto Ricans and white Americans. Neither the quantum nor quality of Puerto Rican attitudes toward race, however, can be measured or understood in American terms. More distinct manifestations are an expressed preference for looking "white" and denial and suppression of "color." Being considered white means bypassing oppression and achieving social mobility, and conversely not being considered white is a sign of subjection to an unbearable oppression. For militant Puerto Ricans, however, an association with being black is now becoming a more acceptable part of the politics of protest. But being Puerto Rican remains a distinct social identity in New York. Thus, the statistical categories of "Puerto Ricans," "other whites," and "Negroes" in which New York City residents were classified by the Puerto Rican Development Project assured Puerto Ricans access to the antipoverty pie in an acceptable framework.

Under the impact of the poverty program, the politics of blacks and Puerto Ricans have come both closer and into clearer opposition. Knowingly or innocently, bureaucrats have promoted antagonistic competition between black and Puerto Rican antipoverty organizations. Governmental decisions regarding the distribution of funds—projects, recognition, leadership, and jobs—have also generated rivalries and violence within Puerto Rican communities which could have been prevented if the bureaucrats in city government had been more perceptive about the problems, issues, and styles of Puerto Rican and black communities around the city.

First, there has been a tendency for patronizing administrators to equate blacks and Puerto Ricans. Since blacks have much greater political leverage, Puerto Rican leaders retaliate with specific demands for Puerto Ricans. The result has been intensification of the struggle for resources between blacks and Puerto Ricans. Second, Puerto Rican leaders, like black leaders, have been challenged by the Establishment as "not representative." Since in fact there is not a unified Puerto Rican leadership "representing" the Puerto Rican community, it has been possible for some time to use this mechanism to keep Puerto Ricans "out of the action," although, in the context of American politics, to expect such "representative" community leadership for whites, blacks or any group is simply absurd. Feeling mounting pressure from Puerto Rican organizations, and from the effects of the riots in Brownsville, East Harlem, and South Bronx, the bureaucracy and partisan leadership started to handpick their own designated Puerto Rican "representatives," and to make token appointments of Puerto Ricans to bureaucratic positions. It has even become fashionable to go to Puerto Rico to recruit individuals for the New York City bureaucracy. It has not been particularly difficult for Puerto Ricans to enter city service in positions at manual, clerical or starting levels (although still the proportion of Puerto Ricans in government service is extremely low), although higher positions are seldom, if ever, occupied by Puerto Ricans except in services specifically for Puerto Rican users. Thus, Puerto Ricans have had important positions only in the Human Resources Administration and narcotic addiction services.

In response, Puerto Rican particularist demands have increased—for example, demands for a Puerto Rican district superintendent in a Manhattan school district, Puerto Rican candidates for the presidency of a city college, Puerto Rican members of health, hospitals, and mental health boards. None of these demands has been granted, although a few other high level appointments went to Puerto Ricans, just as the 1969 electoral campaign started. In some of these struggles for political access, there has been active support from black communities and such reciprocity is likely to increase.

In short, as racial tensions have become more sharply defined, a sense of social identity and internal defense among Puerto Ricans has taken on political expression in the city. Political expediencies and developments originating outside the Puerto Rican community itself have brought the Puerto Ricans into the political arena to make their claims. In the 1960s, New York Puerto Ricans began making claims on city and state politics, with special thrusts in the protests of community politics; in the 1970s, the outreach will move into the Congress and the national bureaucracy.

4.   La Raza

STAN STEINER

URBAN VILLAGES

. . . . .

The barrios of Los Angeles are the third largest Mexican City in the world. Guadalajara and Mexico city alone have greater populations. No one knows for certain, but barrio leaders say that from 800,000 to 1,000,000 Mexicans live in Los Angeles. Either population is larger than the population of Washington, D.C., or Cleveland, Ohio. The people of La Raza in the city, by themselves, constitute one of the ten largest cities in the United States.

Los Angeles is the capital of La Raza. It is to the Mexicans what Boston has been to the Irish and New York City has been to the Jews.

Many people are extremely poor. And yet there is a beauty in the barrios. Roses entwine the junked cars in the backyards, much as the tropical flowers cover the poorest Indian hut in Mexico. In one of the cities in the San Joaquin Valley, there is a Community Poverty Council that has a eucalyptus tree on its front lawn, a lemon tree at its back door, and roses blooming on the windowsill of the "welfare

Abridged and edited from Chapters 11 and 12 in *La Raza: The Mexican Americans,* by Stan Steiner. Copyright © 1969, 1970 by Stan Steiner. Reprinted by permission of Harper & Row, Publishers, Inc.

lady's" office, where the poor come for their alms. The poverty of a rural home is not visible from outside, especially when the home is in a city.

Ever since the Aztecs built the City of Mexico the people of La Raza have been people of the cities. The conquistadors thought their city as magnificent as any in Europe. Bernal Díaz del Castillo, the chronicler of Cortés, wrote: "Some of the soldiers among us who have been in many parts of the world, in Constantinople and in Rome, said that so large a market place and so full of people and so well regulated and arranged, they had never beheld before." And Spaniards, too, were of the city: "The civilization of Spain is an urban thing," one historian says. "In America it is the one city that symbolizes the rule of Spain," another writes. It is not surprising, then, that 85.4 percent of the Chicanos of California live in urban areas.

In the Southwest the number of city dwellers is but slightly less; only in New Mexico are the urban Chicanos a minority—little more than one-third of the state. The population of La Raza in urban areas from Arizona to Texas ranges from 69.3 to 78.6 percent. The Chicano population of Los Angeles, Denver, and Phoenix is 10 to 20 percent of the city; in Albuquerque it is 25 percent; in San Antonio and El Paso 40 to 50 percent; in Laredo 85 percent.

Even so, the barrios of the Chicanos are not like the gray tenement tombs of the ghetto. The barrios sprawl over the hills and into the arroyos and valleys, amid the weeds and flowers, like wandering Indian villages. They are a paradox that defies easy comparisons.

Ghettos are the refuse dumps of the industrial city.

"Who creates the ghetto?" asks Eliezer Risco, the editor of *La Raza*, the newspaper of the barrios of East Los Angeles. "The ghetto is where you are forced to live by housing discrimination. But La Raza has been living in the barrios for hundreds of years. No one has forced us. The barrios are not ghettos, although we do have ghettos in the barrios. There are suburbs and there are skidrows; there are ghettos of the poor and there are neighborhoods of the rich. We have everything here that you have in the larger city, but one thing—you, in the larger city, govern us. We do not run our own lives because you do not let us. You run the barrios and you don't know how."

"Barrio" is a Spanish word that simply means "neighborhood." In the colonial era of Mexico the Spanish rulers subtly changed the meaning by using barrio to designate the "native quarter," where the Indians lived. It was a word of contempt. The word barrio, as it is used in the United States to designate the Mexican or "Spanish" neighborhood, is a modern version of that colonial term; except that today the Chicanos have once more changed the demeaning meaning of the old colonial word to one of pride.

It is a city within a city within a city. Wherever the outsider sees one barrio, there are not one but many barrios within the boundaries of family ties, origins in Mexico, or simply street-map geography. Each barrio has its own loyalties, churches, local shrines, shopkeepers, gangs of boys, customs, history, and old village patriarchs.

"Urban villages" may be a better definition of "barrios." In these communities the Chicanos try to live in the best of both worlds: those of the village and those of the city.

"Why do you still live in East Los Angeles?" a man on the street is asked by *La Voz,* the newspaper of the Community Service Organization. "Just a matter of being in a place something like the old country," one man replies. Incongruous? Where in Los Angeles is Mexico? He feels it is in the barrios.

Men and women who come from the rugged mountain towns of northern Mexico and the rural valleys of the Southwest to seek jobs in the city do so warily. In self-protection they bring their village ways with them. The rural feeling of independence, the little gardens, the religious ecstasies, the large and comforting family loves, the communal ways of life—all of these give the urban villages and villagers a resilience that resists the numbing conformity of the concrete streets. None of these human exuberances fit within the confines of gray ghetto walls.

In the old days a goat and a vegetable garden were more of a necessity for the survival of a barrio family than a car port. Some of the barrios are still derisively referred to by outsiders as "Goat Hill."

"Years ago Los Angeles was rural. It was all farms," says Eduardo Pérez, a barrio leader. He remembers that it was just one generation ago. "Where I was born, in East Los Angeles, there were Japanese farmers. Hundreds of vegetable farms. In World War II the Japanese farmers were put in concentration camps. And their land was confiscated. Up to then the Mexican people used to come to Los Angeles to work on the farms."

It was not simply out of migrant camps that the barrios grew. The people of the Sonoran deserts and mountains on both sides of the border could have moved into the ghetto tenements, but they would have been suffocated. "We need open sky," Pérez says, "or we would die."

"Our people in northern Mexico are rural people," Pérez says. "We're in the mess we're in partly because of that. Mexicans coming to this country head for the countryside. We're always going to the rural towns first to work in the fields, to do stoop labor. We're being displaced by automation on the farms. So we go to the cities. In the barrios we know our countrymen will help us. We're desperate. Where else can we go?"

.   .   .   .   .

THE CONQUERED COUNTRY

"Gabachos!" a community leader curses. "It is the white cop. The *gabacho* with the gun. He is conditioned, he is programed to treat us Mejicanos that way. He sees a lot of brown faces and he doesn't see human beings. He feels he can treat us any way he likes and get away with anything. Years and years he has been doing this.

"They are not preventing violence. They are creating it. They are not building community relations. They are building up animosity."

"But why? Why do they do this to us?" asks the suburban community leader.

.   .   .   .   .

"We are a conquered people," says Bert Corona, the past president of the Mexican-American Political Association. "The behavior of the police toward our people will not let them forget that."

Few if any, of the white officers live in the barrio they patrol, and few know the language of the people. The barrio is not home to them, but a strange place of strangers who have unfamiliar ways and an unknown culture. "We are foreigners to them," says Eliezer Risco, the *La Raza* editor, "and they are foreigners to us." In the routine of barrio life there is mutual fear of these "foreigners." "The police [have] fear of the Mexican American and would kill him out of fear rather than out of justice," D. C. de Herrera writes in Denver's *El Gallo.*

The officers of the law are familiar strangers: abstract, respected, cursed, and feared. In the barrio they are not called *policía* in proper Spanish, but by the name of their stigma, *"placas,* pigs, *gabachos, chortas,* dog pack, *pendejos,* Mister, motherfuckers, *los muertes,* the Man."

One young man in the Boyle Heights barrio of Los Angeles tells me: "The cops are just nothing but Anglo Pachucos. Man, we learn everything we know about street fights from them. They teach us from when we were little kids. It's like basic training, except they use live ammo."

In the streets there is unseen warfare, not between gangs of boys, the Pachucos of legends—that is a daily headline—but between ordinary citizens and police. One family fight, of many, was that of the Santoyo family. The police were duly summoned, and *La Raza* reported the consequences: "The Santoyos, father, mother, and daughter, were beaten; the father into unconsciousness—he was kicked, slapped, pushed, pulled by the hair and insulted verbally with terms like 'Mexican animals!' " Five of the Santoyo brothers, mother, daughter and father, were tried and convicted, not of fighting each other, but of fighting the police.

These are minor skirmishes that do not become headlines. But from time to time there is deadly violence.

Here are a few who were shot by police in one barrio in one city in one year:

A young boy, Louis Pinedo, is killed in a dark street in Denver by an officer's bullet. Patrolman John Cain argues self-defense and is acquitted of wrongful death. "Gunshot wound, back," says the medical autopsy on the teen-ager. He was seventeen and small. The barrio leaders march on the City Fathers.

On a downtown street, Andrew García—he is twenty-three—shot to death by an officer moonlighting as a bouncer in a bar. Two women who are walking by say they have to pull Patrolman Harold MacMillen from the body of the dying boy: he was clubbing the youth with his revolver.

In the bedroom of his home, in his girl's arms, Richard Medina, age twenty, was shot three times. He was thought to be armed, but his girl says, "While I was holding him the policeman came in and started shooting. After he stopped, Richard dropped from my arms to the floor." He did not die.

Joey Archuleta died on the street on a summer day. Patrolman Theodore Zavashlak says he tripped and his gun went off. Joey was 15. The officer is cleared, the shooting "accidental." Once more the barrio marches through downtown Denver to City Hall and the Police Headquarters.

Robert Gene Castro, age fifteen, is shot to death in his home.

The shootings were reported in *El Gallo* within a single year. Yet there are those to whom "police brutality, harassment and inhumanity is only a figment of the poor peoples' imagination," the barrio newspaper caustically wrote. "Denver has had no riot to date [the summer of 1968], but the toll of injured and killed in the Mexican American community [at the hands of the police] continues to mount. . . ."

Hardly a year after this editorial there was a riot in the Denver barrios. The police had shot still another Chicano youth, and high school students rampaged through the streets in protest, overturning cars, smashing windows, until dozens of school children were injured, or arrested.

"More Chicanos are killed by cops on the streets of the Southwest than any other minority group in the population," writes a young man in a barrio newspaper. He calls it "Chicano birth control."

Yearly "the wild-West shooting of minorities by the police" grows worse, charges investigator D. C. de Herrera, the chairman of the Denver barrio's own Police Review Board. "To the Mexican American in Denver, the Police Department presents one of the biggest problems. They have absolutely no respect for our rights. They search our homes, our automobiles, and our own persons without any search warrants and due process of law."

.   .   .   .   .

In Los Angeles the newspaper *La Raza* describes the nature of the "degrading" behavior by the police. The "frisking, harassment, name calling and brutality" is a "daily occurrence" in the streets. *La Raza* cites what it says is a typical incident on an ordinary day: One summer afternoon five young and unemployed Chicanos who enrolled in a job-training program at a "Skill Center" are having lunch. They are horsing around. Local police arrest the restless youths on "suspicion" of being high, possessing narcotics. In the trunk of one boy's car they find a tool box; so they charge him with theft of that, too. But the tool box turns out to belong to the boy's father, none of the youths has any narcotics, and they are released for "lack of evidence" after a night in jail.

The youths voice hatred of the police. "Racism!" they charge, and the barrio newspaper editorializes: "The suspicion was based solely on the fact that they were Mexican." All the natives look suspicious to an "occupying army" of colonialists, and so "the Chicano is always the criminal," a young man writes to the newspaper.

"Americans of Mexican descent are subject to discriminatory treatment by law-enforcement officers," Dr. Hector P. Garcia, a United States Civil Rights Commissioner, says flatly. Investigation in the barrios across the Southwest, by staff lawyers of the federal body, revealed a state-by-state pattern of legal and police harassment, the Commissioner asserts. These investigators report: "The most serious issue encountered in the course of the Commission's study is harassment and abuse of Americans of Mexican descent by law-enforcement officers. Such conduct ranges from unjustified arrests to insults, threats and, not infrequently, physical assaults," Dr. Garcia told the Senate Subcommittee on Migratory Labor.

In the courts the complaints of injustices suffered by La Raza defendants were equally prevalent. The "unfair legal practices" reported in the barrios, Dr. Garcia testified, involve widespread charges that Chicanos are "excluded from jury service, denied equal access to bail and adequate counsel, and [are] employed in disproportionately low numbers in law-enforcement agencies."

The legal system is often designed "to keep Mexicans in their place," the Civil Rights Commissioner concluded. He termed such practices "rather sordid."

Laws are written, laws are enforced, and laws are judged by those outside the barrio. The Chicano who obeys the law of his traditions, the moral codes of his family, and the social customs of the barrio may find himself opposed by the laws of the outside society. Even the way dispute is settled by a barrio family may violate half a dozen laws of the Anglo society. What the Chicano does may not seem unlawful to him, but he is a criminal simply by being a Chicano.

"Law and order doesn't seem to be the practice of the Los Angeles Police Department," says *La Raza*. "The Eastside [of Los Angeles] is becoming a no man's land in which the people have no protection whatsoever from the services rendered by the Police Department."

5.   Race and migration to the American city

CHARLES TILLY

.   .   .   .   .

WHO MIGRATES? WHY?

We often encounter the argument that if a town improves its living conditions and public services too energetically, it will simply see its resources consumed by a rush of new, poor, dependent migrants—drifters, welfare chiselers, and problem families. There are two things wrong with this idea. First, living conditions and public services play only a small part in determining the number of migrants to any particular city. Second, migrants to cities are drawn especially from favored and vigorous elements of the general population.

When interviewers ask American migrants why they have moved, the migrants give answers relating to jobs far more than any other answers; the largest number usually report a specific job brought them to the city, but another sizable number say they came looking for work.[1] This is about as true for Negroes as it is for whites. However, since workers in relatively unskilled occupations more often migrate without having a job already nailed down, and since Negroes include a higher

---

Excerpted by permission of the publishers from pp. 135–157 of James Q. Wilson (ed.), *The Metropolitan Enigma* (Cambridge, Mass.: Harvard University Press, 1968). Copyright © 1968 by the President and Fellows of Harvard College; 1967 by the Chamber of Commerce of the U.S.A.

The author is Professor of Sociology and History, University of Michigan, Ann Arbor, Mich.

[1]Ralph H. Turner, "Migration to a medium-sized American city," *Journal of Social Psychology,* 30:229–249 (November 1949), and Henry S. Shryock, Jr., *Population Mobility within the United States* (Chicago: Community and Family Study Center, University of Chicago, 1964), Chapter 12.

proportion of workers in relatively unskilled occupations, Negroes who migrate are more often looking for work than migrating whites.

Our information on why migrants choose one destination rather than another is less abundant.[2] For people who have received specific offers of jobs, the climate, amenities, and services of a given city normally enter in a secondary way into their evaluation of the offer. For people retiring or in bad health they often determine the choice. But for people moving without a guarantee of a job the presence of friends and relatives matters a great deal more than such things as the housing supply or the availability of public assistance. If these conditions do make some marginal difference in the volume of a city's migration, most likely it is through the encouragement or discouragement friends and relatives already there give to potential migrants, rather than through a general spreading of the word among the would-be freeloaders.

If we move away from what people *say* about their own motives for moving and toward the *objective conditions* differentiating cities receiving many migrants from cities receiving few, we find jobs looming even more important than before. In the United States, the net migration to an area corresponds very closely to its income level and its production of new jobs as compared with other potential destinations for migrants. An exhaustive analysis of net migration from 1870 to 1950 conducted by the demographers and economists of the University of Pennsylvania shows that during this period Negroes as a group, even though they had less to hope for, responded more sharply to changes and regional variations in economic opportunity than did whites.[3] We have no good reason to think the situation has changed. Though booming cities often have both good public services and numerous migrants, there is no sign that public services themselves affect the volume of migration, and there is every sign that new employment does.

Anyway, who comes?[4] The "Grapes of Wrath" picture of migrants as the dispossessed has such a grip on American imaginations that one of the most popular

---

[2]See Leonard Blumberg and Robert Bell, "Urban migration and kinship ties," *Social Problems,* 6:328–333 (Spring 1959); John S. MacDonald and Leatrice MacDonald, "Chain migration, ethnic neighborhood formation, and social networks," *Milbank Memorial Fund Quarterly,* 42:82–97 (1964); Morton Rubin, "Migration patterns of Negroes from a rural northeastern Mississippi community," *Social Forces,* 39:59–66 (1960); and Harry Schwarzweller, *Family Ties, Migration, and Transitional Adjustment of Young Men from Eastern Kentucky* (Lexington: University of Kentucky Agricultural Experiment Station, 1964).

[3]Hope T. Eldridge and Dorothy Swaine Thomas, *Demographic Analyses and Interrelations* (Philadelphia: American Philosophical Society, 1964). Vol. III of *Population Redistribution and Economic Growth, United States, 1870–1950.* Memoirs of the American Philosophical Society, No. 61.

[4]In addition to Shryock, Rubin, Schwarzweller, and Eldridge and Thomas, cited above, *see* Karl E. Taeuber and Alma F. Taeuber, *Negroes in Cities* (Chicago: Aldine Publishing Co., 1965); C. Harold Brown and Roy C. Buck, *Factors Associated with the Migrant Status of Young Adult Males from Rural Pennsylvania* (University Park: Pennsylvania State University Agricultural Experiment Station, 1961); Ronald Freedman, "Cityward migration, urban ecology, and social theory," in Ernest W. Burgess and Donald J. Bogue (eds.), *Contributions to Urban Sociology* (Chicago: University of Chicago Press, 1964); C. Horace Hamilton, "Educational selection of the net migration from the South," *Social Forces,* 38:33–42 (1959); and Arnold M. Rose, "Distance of migration and socio-economic status of migrants," *American Sociological Review,* 23:420–423 (1958).

explanations of the big-city riots of 1964, 1965, and 1966 has been the arrival of unhappy wanderers from the South. In reality, cityward migrants tend to be *above* the average in education and occupational skills at their points of origin. They come heavily concentrated in the most energetic age groups—the late teens and early twenties. *And they even tend to rank higher in education and occupation than the population already in the city.* (Of course, those who leave any particular city also average high in occupation and education, so the net effect of migration in and out is often to depress the level of skill in a city's population.)

People moving off farms are a little different. They are not consistently better off than the people they leave behind: both the least and the most educated predominating in the younger ages, the least educated in the older ones. They tend to be even younger than other migrants, and they are on the whole below the standard levels of education and occupational skill for the city's population. But migrants from farms are only a small part of all people coming to any particular city, and so their arrival does not significantly depress the population's level of qualifications.

We already know that nonwhite migrants to cities have more often come from farms and from regions with generally low educational standards than have white migrants. We also know that nonwhite persons, whether migrants or not, generally get less education and hold poorer jobs than white persons. No one should be surprised to learn that the average nonwhite migrant comes to the city with less education and occupational skill than either the white migrant or the bulk of the urban population. *But compared to the nonwhite population already in the city,* the average nonwhite migrant has a distinct *advantage* in age, occupation, and education.

These complicated comparisons hold an ironic implication for those city fathers who wish they could speed the departure of Negroes from their towns and keep new Negro migrants from coming in. Such a strategy would be a very good way to depress the average level of qualification of the city's Negro population. It would probably increase the proportion, if not the absolute number, of the Negro population heavily dependent on public services. The way to insure a young and skilled Negro population would be to attract new migrants and make sure that the mobile people already in the city were too satisfied to depart. Of course, stimulating job opportunities and providing a decent education for Negroes already in the city would complement such a policy.

One part of this prescription is already in effect without much help from the city fathers. More and more of the recent Negro migrants to big cities are people with relatively good job skills and educational backgrounds moving in from other metropolitan areas. If these new migrants have not attracted as much attention as the displaced croppers from depressed farming areas of the South, maybe it is because they do not fit everyday prejudices so well.

DOES MIGRATION DISORGANIZE?

If we come to realize that most Negro migrants are neither drifters nor dregs, we may have to abandon other commonplace prejudices concerning the disorganizing effects of migration. No doubt it is true—as a long line of acute observers from W. E. B. DuBois to Gilbert Osofsky have noted—that migration from the South to an urban North in which Negro women had a niche (if not a very pleasant one), while Negro men often had no place at all, wrenched and reshaped the family lives of Negroes.[5] No doubt this wrenching even affected the later generations born in the city. Although the difference in family stability between whites and Negroes of the same income or occupations is less than many people think, Negro households do break up and regroup more often than do white ones. Rates of divorce and separation are generally higher for Negroes.[6] The greater frequency of divorce and separation in turn helps make families headed by women more common among Negroes. . . . Though the majority of Negro families are unbroken, a substantially higher proportion of Negro children than of white children grow up without a father continuously at hand, and suffer both economically and psychologically from the absence of that father.

All this amounts to saying that the situation in the city, rather than the fact of moving, shook Negro family life in the time of the great northward migration. The distinction may seem academic: the impact of any move on the individual always includes the differences in living conditions between the origin and the destination. Yet it matters a great deal. For in the one case we might conclude that as migration slowed down and the immediate shock of moving faded, the troubles of Negro families would disappear. In the other case, we could hardly expect much improvement until the opportunities open to Negro men and women in the big city changed.

$$\cdot \qquad \cdot \qquad \cdot \qquad \cdot \qquad \cdot$$

THE ASSIMILATION OF THE NEWCOMER

Sociologists and politicians alike have often tried to analyze what has been happening to racial minorities as a process of assimilation "into the mainstream of American life." They have relied on analogies with the fairly regular ways in which Italians or Poles went from isolation, deprivation, and cultural distinctness toward the normal rewards and involvements of American life.

The basic argument stands out in both the title and the text of Irving Kristol's stimulating *New York Times Magazine* article: "The Negro Today Is Like the Immigrant Yesterday."[7] The article rightly reminds us how much of the ugly language and uglier fact of current accounts of Negro urban life applied to the Irish of our cities only a few generations ago and holds out assurances that this crisis, too, will pass away. A number of historians of American immigration and assimilation, like Oscar Handlin, have urged the same thesis.[8]

---

[5] W. E. B. DuBois, *The Philadelphia Negro* (Philadelphia: University of Pennsylvania, 1899), and Gilbert Osofsky, *Harlem: The Making of a Ghetto* (New York: Harper & Row, Publishers, 1966).

[6] See, for example, U.S. Department of Health, Education, and Welfare *Divorce Statistics Analysis,* National Center for Health Statistics, Series 21, No. 7 (Washington, D.C., 1965).

[7] *The New York Times Magazine,* September 11, 1966.

[8] Oscar Handlin, *The Newcomers* (Cambridge, Mass.: Harvard University Press, 1959). See also Marc Fried, "The transitional functions of working-class communities," in Mildred Kantor (ed.), *Mobility and Mental Health* (Springfield, Ill.: Charles C Thomas, Publisher, 1965).

The idea is attractive because of its simplicity and its optimism. Even if they didn't come from overseas, many Negroes have recently made the big move from region to region and from country to city. Over the last century Negroes and Orientals have won access to significantly better jobs, incomes, and education. These changes make the assimilationist idea plausible. The argument also makes it easier for the descendants of nineteenth- or twentieth-century immigrants to reply to Negro demands with: "We made it on our own . . . Why can't you?"

The idea of an inevitable movement toward assimilation faces some difficult facts, however. The ancestors of most of America's Negro population were here well before most of the Europeans on whose assimilation the scheme is based. Some forms of racial discrimination and segregation (the World War II roundup of Japanese, the rising residential segregation of big cities in the 1940's, the earlier elaboration of Jim Crow legislation are examples) have worsened several times in the memory of living men. And Negroes (if not Orientals or American Indians) have publicly expressed a greater sense of alienation from the rewards and involvements of American life in recent years than before.

In some broad ways, to be sure, assimilation has been moving on. Over the last few decades Negroes have been gaining better jobs, more education, higher incomes, sounder housing, fuller medical care, even greater life expectancy. But so have whites. In all these respects, the gap between whites and Negroes has closed little (if at all) over the last twenty years. Negro unemployment rates remain consistently higher, especially in bad times. Broken families remain common, illegitimacy rates rise, the need of Negro households for public assistance persists. The essence of assimilation is not just material improvement in absolute terms, but a closing of the gap between a group of newcomers and the rest of the nation. For a process often billed as steady and irreversible, the assimilation of Negroes does not seem to be working right.

At the beginning of their discussion of the position of Negroes in New York City, Nathan Glazer and Daniel Patrick Moynihan seem to accept the standard argument: "The Negro population is still in large part new to the city. In 1960 half of the entire nonwhite population of the city above the age of 20 had come from the South. These Americans of two centuries are as much immigrant as any European immigrant group, for the shift from the South to New York is as radical a change for the Negro as that faced by earlier immigrants."[9] Then the qualifications begin. As their analysis unfolds, Glazer and Moynihan slowly come to the conclusion that the conditions for getting ahead have changed too much, that the Negro family has suffered too much damage, that the internal cohesion of the Negro population is too low, for anyone to expect an updated repetition of the classic American success story. Now, this is not exactly the argument of civil rights leaders or of radical critics of American society, but it differs greatly from the more optimistic assimilationist account of what is going on.

At first glance, these disagreements may look like tedious professorial wrangling over definitions and historical analogies. In fact, they set the terms of one of

[9]Nathan Glazer and Daniel Patrick Moynihan, *Beyond the Melting Pot* (Cambridge, Mass.: The M.I.T. Press, 1963), p. 26.

the great questions for research and action in urban life over the next decade. Has there been a standard process of assimilation into an American mainstream via the big city, one that is still working today for Negroes and other racial minorities? Or have the mechanisms broken down, has the economic situation changed too much, has the system of exclusion become too efficient, are the groups now seeking inclusion too different in character? Or is the notion of assimilation into the mainstream itself based on a misunderstanding of how American life works?

If the standard process of assimilation is still working, then designers of American public policy could reasonably seek ways to speed up an established pattern of change. If the process is not working, then they would have to envisage changes in the very structure of American society. For once, a problem with extensive theoretical implications and a question of great significance for public policy come together. Although I cannot guarantee that the social scientists, the policy makers, or the critics will come up with satisfactory answers, I am sure that they will all soon be pouring an extraordinary effort into the analysis of assimilation.

That prediction is all the safer because when forced to account for racial protests or ghetto riots, Americans so readily turn to migration and its aftermath as the explanations. The Governor's Commission on the Los Angeles Riots (the McCone Commission), after pointing out the hardships suffered by Negroes everywhere in the United States, had to ask, "Why Los Angeles?" Here is what they said:

> Yet the riot did happen here, and there are special circumstances here which explain in part why it did. Perhaps the people of Los Angeles should have seen trouble gathering under the surface calm. In the last quarter century, the Negro population here has exploded. While the County's population has trebled, the Negro population has increased almost tenfold, from 75,000 in 1940 to 650,000 in 1965. Much of the increase came through migration from Southern States and many arrived with the anticipation that this dynamic city would somehow spell the end of life's endless problems. To those who have come with high hopes and great expectations and see the success of others so close at hand, failure brings a special measure of frustration and disillusionment. Moreover, the fundamental problems, which are the same here as in the cities which were racked by the 1964 riots, are intensified by what may well be the least adequate network of public transportation in any major city in America.[10]

Migration bears the blame.

That migration is to blame seems at first glance to be confirmed by the special census of South Los Angeles conducted after the Watts riots. From 1960 to 1965, unemployment stayed almost constant (in the face of dramatic increases in employment elsewhere), incomes had dropped, housing had deteriorated, and broken families had become more common.[11] When unveiling the census report, Andrew Brimmer, Assistant Secretary of Commerce for Economic Affairs, interpreted it to mean that "the most successful families had moved to more desirable neighborhoods and had been replaced by lower income groups moving in from other parts of the

---

[10] *Violence in the City—An End or a Beginning?* (Los Angeles: Governor's Commission on the Los Angeles Riots, 1965), pp. 3–4.

[11] U.S. Bureau of the Census, *Special Census Survey of the South and East Los Angeles Area, November 1965,* Series P–23, No. 17, 1966.

state and nation."[12] The new findings seemed to corroborate the Commission's explanation of the riots.

But the facts are more complicated. If migration is such a powerful factor, we should find that cities receiving many underprivileged migrants are more violent than the rest, we should expect violence in those sections of cities where populations are swelling with new migrants, and we should discover that recent migrants are peculiarly prone to violence. What is the evidence?

The efforts of sociologists to get at the origins of collective violence have not revealed any reliable tendency for high-migration cities to produce more interracial mayhem or more frequent ghetto explosions than the rest. An analysis of 76 urban riots during the years 1913–1963 done by Stanley Lieberson and Arnold Silverman of the University of Wisconsin identified some revealing tendencies for riots to break out in cities where Negroes were underrepresented in the police force or in the city council, but detected no difference attributable to migration.[13] In any case, the Watts of just before the 1965 riots was actually a *declining* community in population as well as in standard of living, not a staging area for new arrivals. And the Los Angeles County Probation Department found:

1. Over half the juveniles picked up for participation in the riots were California born.
2. More than three quarters had lived in the country at least five years.
3. Only one in twenty had been there less than a year.
4. The proportions of natives and long-term residents were even higher among those juveniles whose cases the courts considered worth prosecuting.[14]

... It apparently takes time to learn to riot. Again we discover that the way assimilation to the city works is more important than how much stress and strain moving around creates.

MIGRATION AS A PROBLEM FOR PUBLIC POLICY

The most acute problems we have encountered in this survey of race and migration are not really problems created by migration at all. Some are difficulties faced by members of racial minorities wherever they are in America, difficulties that migration simply transplants and concentrates in cities. Job discrimination is one important example. In these cases, a change in the conditions of migration might affect which communities had to take the largest direct responsibility for meeting the problem, but it would not make much difference in the gravity of the problem as a whole.

---

[12]According to a report in *The New York Times*, March 9, 1966.

[13]Stanley Lieberson and Arnold R. Silverman, "The precipitants and underlying conditions of race riots," *American Sociological Review*, 30:887–898 (December, 1965).

[14]*Riot Participant Study, Juvenile Offenders* (Los Angeles County Probation Department, 1965). According to a *New York Times* article of September 4, 1966, a similar study of adult offenders done by the state's Bureau of Criminal Identification and Investigation yielded the same conclusions. After I wrote this paper, in 1966, much more evidence pointing in the same direction came in. See especially Louis H. Masotti (ed.), "Urban violence and disorder," *American Behavioral Scientist*, Vol. 2 (March-April, 1968), entire issue.

Other problems are forms of discrimination more prominent in cities than elsewhere and therefore aggravated by the movement to the cities of more of the people they hurt. Big city residential segregation is like that. In these cases, a slowdown of migration might ease the problem, but it certainly would not eliminate it.

As for problems directly produced by migration, my main message has been that they have been seriously misunderstood and exaggerated. Migrants as a group do not notably disturb public order, their arrival does not lower the quality of the city's population, they place no extraordinary demands on public services, and they do not arrive exceptionally burdened with personal problems. These things happen to them later. The difficulties faced by inhabitants of ghettos and by cities containing them are not to any large degree products merely of migration.

Yet in two ways the migrant *does* present a challenge to public policy. First, moving over long distances often imposes hardships and confusion on families at the same time as it cuts them off from the agencies that might be able to help them; instead of recognizing the special problems of people on the move, American public services tend to discriminate against them. Second, the newcomer—already by definition an innovator, having an advantage in age, education, and skill, bound to the old ways of his new city by fewer commitments and routines—is in an extraordinarily good position to take advantage of programs breaking down racial barriers, if only they are open to him. The challenge is to make maximum use of the migrant's talents, give him the greatest possible access to the rewards the city has to offer, make sure he can get past the personal crises almost all big moves involve without breaking down, and assure that he has attractive alternatives to the social and geographic isolation of the ghetto.

.   .   .   .   .

6.   The projects and the Negroes

GERALD D. SUTTLES

THE HERITAGE OF POLITICAL ARRANGEMENTS

In relative numbers, the Negroes make up only about 14–17% of the total population in the Addams area. They achieve their importance, however, more by what they portend than what they are. On the West Side the proportion of Negroes

Abridged and edited from Gerald D. Suttles, *The Social Order of the Slum: Ethnicity and Territory in the Inner City* (Chicago: University of Chicago Press, 1968), pp. 119–131. Copyright © 1968 by The University of Chicago. Reprinted by permission.

The author is Associate Professor, Department of Sociology, University of Chicago, Chicago, Ill.

has been steadily increasing for a long time. All the other ethnic groups have retreated from them, and the general assumption is that they will eventually "take over." Oddly enough, it is the lowly status of the Negroes that makes them such a portentous enemy. Because of the universal fear of stigma in being associated with them, it is assumed that no group in the area can halt their invasion. Thus even this small group of Negroes is considered a far more serious contender than any combination of other ethnic groups.

To understand how the Negroes fit into the Addams area, it is necessary to locate them in the context of both past and present political arrangements. For several years the Italians have held a near monopoly on all political power and patronage. The other ethnic groups have been propitiated by a variety of "favors" on condition they support the Italians. Until recently, however, there has been no serious contender to the Italians' right to represent the area and to dispense whatever favors they could command. The Italians have been content with the privilege of distributing patronage even if they did not receive the lion's share. In the present case, the benefits of this position have been considerable. Since the Addams area is in the First Ward, its influence penetrates the "Loop," the main business section of the city. In turn, a variety of legitimate businesses and vice interests have found it convenient to accommodate the Italians by giving them somewhat more than their share of the exemptions, goods, and privileges that can be distributed through political means.

.   .   .   .   .

These precedents have left a heritage of institutional and moral arrangements. Their most important outcome is the pervasive belief that political power is not something that another ethnic group would willingly share. The Italians simply assume that any opponent will never be satisfied with less than total usurpation. Thus, like their Irish predecessors, they hesitate to yield an inch lest their opponents take a mile. Consequently, they believe that every gain by the Negroes is necessarily a loss to the Italians. The ultimate outcome, then, is a political struggle carried out with the understanding that "winner takes all."

Recently the Italians' suspicions and fears have been corroborated by still other events. Ever since the Negroes took over the Jane Addams Projects, many of the Italians have recognized the importance of federal funds as an omen of Negro invasion. Thus, portions of the urban renewal program and even the University of Illinois are often referred to as "something for the niggers."

It would be quite misleading to suggest that very many of the adults and even a few of the adolescents are aware of the area's political history or the likely consequence of the University and urban renewal program. Of course, a few do have this knowledge and pass it on to others. Most generally, however, it is expressed in the abbreviated form, "The niggers want everything," without further explanation. In fact, a verbal transmission of the historical particulars is really unnecessary. Throughout the area the visible effects of history are encoded in the current arrangements that obtain for almost every facility in the area. The streets, the businesses, the parks, and the schools are all marked off as the exclusive domain of one or another ethnic group. Most often, the symbolic paraphernalia that decorate an establishment are also ethnic-linked. Thus the "collective memory" of the local people need not always be transmitted in verbal form. Instead it is codified in the objective effects and practices that function as continuing reminders of long-forgotten historical origins. All that seems to differentiate the various groups is the points on which they focus attention. The Italian boys are concerned over who shall take control of the streets, the schools, and a wide variety of local hangouts. Their parents may share some of the same apprehensions, but they are also worried over the future state of their homes, jobs, and business places. The Negroes are equally convinced that the Italians will never voluntarily yield any of the benefits vested in the Addams area. Thus, by their suspicions and distrust of each other, both groups are caught in a struggle from which they can rest only after total victory or total defeat.

PROJECT LIVING

In their struggle with the Italians, the Negroes are burdened by a number of other circumstances. First, the Negroes are almost wholly confined in public housing. In Chicago public housing, ADC recipients are especially favored, and the general view is that all the residents of the projects are "public wards." Moreover, the standardization and restrictive rulings that govern the projects almost totally eliminate all those overt signs that families customarily depend on to present themselves to the outer world. The Jane Addams Projects are a drab and uniform continuity. Undoubtedly the apartments are fairly clean and roomy. However, they entirely lack most of the ordinary external embellishments, adornments, and decorations that families use to notify others of their tastes, beliefs, income, practices, and background. Thus, the first line of family impression management is lost, and an outsider can only surmise that all the residents are alike.

Second, project living is one of the most permanent and inflexible forms of absentee landlordship. In the history of most ethnic groups, there has been a constant alteration and accommodation of existing facilities to their own uses. Today the same progression goes on among the Italians, Mexicans, and Puerto Ricans in the Addams area. The lower floor of a residence is turned into a business place. Family members, relatives, and friends are drawn in as "sweat labor." Sometimes, by great frugality, a building is purchased and cut up into additional "flats" which can be squeezed for every cent they will produce. At every turn, personal labor supplants that which requires hard cash. In the eyes of the wider community these ventures are "abuses" or, at best, result in an eyesore on the face of the city.[1] For the local residents, however, such ventures are the first rungs on the social ladder that reaches up to where such judgments can be passed.

Among those who live in the projects, however, all these minor entrepreneurial ventures are totally out of reach. This has the obvious effect of eliminating several of the more devious pathways of upward mobility and social differentiation that have been so important in the career of various ethnic groups.[2] As a result, the Negroes are reduced to the most abject and menial "hustles" that are left: pimping,

---

[1]The general pattern is outlined by Daniel Bell, "The breakup of family capitalism," in *The End of Ideology* (New York: Collier Books, 1961), pp. 39–45, and George Orwell, *The Road to Wigan Pier* (New York: Harcourt, Brace & World, 1963).

[2]Daniel Bell, "Crime as an American way of life: A queer ladder of social mobility," in *The End of Ideology*, pp. 127–150.

casual prostitution, shoplifting, "policy," and occasional traffic in "reefers." All of this, however, must be managed under the oppressive suspicion that the CHA (Chicago Housing Authority) has planted "finks" on every floor to spy on them. The residents are thereby further estranged from one another, and whatever level of trust might already exist is undermined.

In the long term, however, the most important consequence of project living may be the way it restricts most opportunities to achieve a stake in the prospects of the local community and to develop the kind of leadership and social differentiation that is so critical in forming a stable moral community. In the Jane Addams Projects the Negroes can never alter the buildings to their own use, and all that keeps them there are a few friends and an income too small to rent better housing. If they become more affluent, they leave. Even this decision is outside the realm of personal choice. According to the rules of the CHA, anyone who earns beyond a certain income level is obliged to leave. The result is an overwhelming homogeneity in which differences of income, education, political influence, and occupation are so lacking as to fail to designate potential leaders and spokesmen. The Negroes often resort to several formalized community organizations, small groups that are usually engendered by some of the local welfare agencies. These groups are usually short-lived and transient in their membership. Leadership within them tends to be rather artificial, since the elected officers seldom have any social credentials aside from rare instances of personal acclaim. Otherwise there is a dearth of leadership and a tendency to take lightly the pretensions of those who get pressed into leadership positions by some of the welfare agencies.

In addition to the oppressive homogeneity, there are a plethora of other problems involved in project living: the inability of friends and relatives to settle near one another and create a little moral world exempt from the insinuations of the wider community; a fear of accumulating "immovable" property lest it be taken as a sign of excessive income; the inability to "put up" a relative or friend for an extended period of hardship; a special police force created to watch over them; the myth that any effective political organization among project dwellers will be subverted by transfers and evictions; a series of rather strict rules that constrain high decibel parties and other forms of socializing; some rather restrictive measures on the ownership of telephones and television sets.

The project residents do not always hold each other responsible for their lowly position. Quite often, they will explain that the other people in the projects are there because of circumstances they could not avoid. However, this explanation provides them no comfort at all. Whether a person has been reduced to an abject position by his own efforts or by those of someone else, he is still outside the realm of easy trust and companionship. A desperate man is still a desperate man no matter who is responsible for his predicament.

STYLE OF LIFE

In large part the conditions of project living seem only to extenuate patterns that already have their historical precursors. A certain level of transiency is implicit in the housing regulations that remove people after they have gone beyond a given income range. The inability to settle around kinsmen and long-term friends is perhaps greater in the projects than in private housing. In any case the projects do not increase the conditions for stable relations, and the ultimate result seems to be a highly fluid population in which acquaintances are temporary or; at least, expected to be temporary.

In the Jane Addams Projects these conditions of impermanence seem to elicit a variety of novel social signs that function to introduce people to one another. Greetings, conversations, and clothing are highly subject to fads and fashions. Considered in the context in which they occur, all of these novelties and "exoticisms" seem to serve a very necessary communicative function.

Negroes living on the West Side and in public housing face every sort of misgiving, suspicion, and fear. To become eligible for an orderly social relationship they must either try to assuage these fears and doubts or take up such an awesome appearance of power that they are guaranteed "free passage." In either case, they must exaggerate the available signs that let others know what they "really are." The most direct means of doing this is simply to extend, emphasize, and elaborate existing styles of clothing, manners of speech, walk, stance, and demeanor. Colors become extremely loud or entirely lacking, styles advance to the very forefront of the period, and mannerisms become "way out."

In the Jane Addams Projects there is a constant round of fads, novelties, and extemporaneous feats. Dances, speech, clothing, gestures, and even sex practices undergo a continual change, elaboration, and attrition. There seems to be an unending search for the signs that will surely identify those worthy of merit, trust, or power. These signs, however, seem to be always imperfect, since the search goes on and on.

Concurrently, there is also a strong undercurrent of uneasiness and skepticism about what people "really are." Sometimes this is evident in the extremely effusive greetings that seem to be necessary to assure one of friendship although both parties may have seen each other only the day before. Upon meeting, a handshake is an essential start especially with whites. Throughout the remainder of the encounter other bits of physical contact regularly punctuate the general flow of interaction. An extraordinary repertoire of "insults" and instances of license provide intermittent guarantees that they can afford such liberties. "Signifying," "mommy-rapping," or "jiving" seem only the more stylized of these.

At the same time, there is steady appeal to force where familiarity and exceptional signs of trustworthiness or power do not furnish a clear indication of one's future safety. Acts of violence without material gain, for example, reach their apex among the Negroes in the area. The extent of "gun-packing" may be exaggerated, but still it is an omnipresent threat. Less drastic but more common are bluffing contests in which both parties search for an end to the indeterminancy that overshadows their relationship. Boys cow one another by "stare-downs," denigrate each other by the term "boy," and sometimes become so vociferous and threatening that they are said to be "woofing." Often, of course, these efforts end in a draw and can be settled only if verbal threats and promises are recast in the heat of physical combat. Afterwards the combatants do not necessarily become permanent enemies. Somehow, the ambiguities of their past have been settled by gaining sure knowledge of where they stand.

The same problem is evident in the project residents' perpetual apprehension of deception, "con-artists," or "phonies." Apparently no one is willing to accept another at face value, and extreme proofs of one's identity and sincerity are required. Effusive greetings, name-dropping, "woofing," "rapping," and other verbal trials are only some of the more direct ways of doing this. Dress, grooming, decorum, stance, and even one's way of walking can be enlisted to eliminate doubts and suspicion. Among the Negroes in the Addams area, the major identities that have to be avoided are those denoted by the labels "country," "savage," "nigger," and "Uncle Tom." Thus, to show their sophistication, some girls go to school in high heels, "fix" their hair into fantastic shapes, and in recent months have shortened their skirts to a perilous level.

In contrast to the girls, the Negro boys in the Jane Addams Projects face a somewhat more ambiguous dilemma. If the boys completely repudiate the image of an "Uncle Tom," they risk being mistaken for a "savage." In this Scylla and Charybdis, two alternatives are open. On the one hand he can become a "gauster," by wearing the "rag," "shaping" his hair, belonging to a gang, adopting the "pimp's walk," and wearing a belted coat and baggy trousers. On the other hand, he can become "Ivy" by wearing a button-down collar, tight pants, and always keeping himself in immaculate order. The "gauster," however, runs the risk of being considered a "savage," while the "Ivy" may be suspected of being "sissy."[3] In either case, "keeping cool" may preserve a questionable identity when others would be discountenanced.

From a distance, these seem to be what often strike outsiders as so "crude" and "vulgar" about the dress of Negroes as well as many other minority groups. In the perspective of polite society all this is far too "obvious" and, for that reason, "vulgar." However, in the eyes of the Negroes in the Addams area, the obviousness of these signs is their central virtue. Only in this way can they be sure of alerting other people that they are a safe associate or too acute and powerful to be treated as "fair game." Thus, much of this "vulgarity" seems only an *amplification of the signs* that presage most social relations.

· · · · · ·

MIXED BLESSINGS

While the Jane Addams Projects are not an unmixed blessing, the Negroes there are quick to point up some of the advantages. Compared to most other housing projects, these projects make up a relatively small unit. Thus, many of the residents know each other rather well, and an even higher proportion can recognize one another by face. In a situation where anonymity may foretell unknown dangers or provide an opportunity for predation exempt from retaliation, it is very comforting to be surrounded by familiar faces. At the same time, however, people are often so well "cast" in the minds of local residents that any attempt at personal change meets a stone wall of doubt. In this context it is nearly impossible for someone to "turn over a new leaf," even when everyone agrees it would be for the better.

---

[3]Here "sissy" means a homosexual, not a preadolescent boy who acts like a preadolescent girl.

Secondly, the Jane Addams Projects are a "low rise" development that never reaches beyond four stories. In local circumstances this conveys several assurances missing in a "high rise." For instance, there is the recognition that the police might actually be able to provide some measure of surveillance and protection. Correspondingly, the necessity of taking similar coercive measures into their own hands is somewhat less pressing than in the "high rise." Moreover, each entrance into the Jane Addams Projects is used by only four to eight families. Among such a small number of people, facial recognition is easy, and a stranger is especially obvious. By contrast, those who live in the "high rise" must face from five to seven hundred people without knowing for certain why they are there. Similarly, many of the trouble spots and minor "no-man's-lands" of the "high rises" do not occur when a project is no more than four stories high. There are no elevators, the roofs are not altogether outside ground level observation, and the stairwells do not extend into regions where one can achieve almost total anonymity.

A third advantage to the Jane Addams Projects is that they were built in 1936 when the amount of space considered necessary to a family was less than it is today. Thus, most of the apartments have only a few rooms, and with adjustments to present standards, there is a tendency for them to be occupied by small families. The ratio of dependents to adults is rather low compared to most projects, and while most of the adults are unaware of their favored position, in relation to the rest of the city, they can still appreciate each particular situation in which they outnumber the adolescents. Like most persons, the adults in the projects assume that young people have not reached the age where they "know what's good for them." Sometimes they will cross the street rather than confront a group of young boys lounging on the sidewalk. Occasionally, these same adults may resort to such blatant defensive maneuvers that the adolescents are left without any honorable line of retreat. In either case, little is accomplished except to estrange further the young and the old. To the advantage of the adults in the Jane Addams Projects, situations of this kind are less frequent than they are for those who live in projects with apartments for families with many more children.

A fourth condition that affects the Negroes in the Addams area, but which is somewhat difficult to appreciate, is the fact that along with all the other groups in the area they are in the minority. Within the entire neighborhood, there is fairly sure knowledge that no group could muster a clear quorum and that each must hesitate before it goes too far. As a rule, then, they equivocate by engaging in numerous minor skirmishes but back off from a full-scale confrontation. Actually this may multiply the incidence of minor displays of force, but it also keeps in abeyance anything that might reach the dimensions of a riot.[4]

---

[4]Allen D. Grimshaw suggests, with some doubt, that this may have been one reason certain ecological areas were free of racial riots during their heyday. See his "Urban racial violence in the United States: Changing ecological considerations," *American Journal of Sociology,* 66:109–119 (September, 1960).

B. NEIGHBORHOOD CHANGE

The neighborhood has been generally accepted as a geographically based social group with certain shared concerns, including housing, facilities for raising children, shopping, employment, and government. The neighborhood differs from other more regional or national groups in that these daily functions are normally carried out within walking distance of each other, and neighborly relations therefore often consist of personal, face-to-face interactions. Charles Horton Cooley considered these interactions important enough to regard neighborhoods as primary groups, which are defined as groups whose activities bear directly on the socialization and development of the individual.[1] Regardless of the precise impact of the neighborhood on the individual, however, neighborhoods are important because they tend to exist wherever people live, whether in rural or urban areas, and whether on one continent or another.

The contemporary urban neighborhood has attracted attention for at least three reasons.[2] First, the extent to which the urban neighborhood differs from the more traditional rural community has been a topic of continued debate over the past thirty years. On the one hand, Louis Wirth and others have emphasized that urban neighborhoods exercise far less influence on the individual than do rural neighborhoods.[3] This point of view is part of the more general interpretation of the effects of urbanization, in which secondary contacts, via industrialization and bureaucratization, for instance, gain great prominence. The urban neighborhood becomes merely

---

[1]Charles H. Cooley, *Social Organization* (New York: Schocken Books, Inc., 1962, orig. pub. in 1909), pp. 23–31.

[2]For a general but brief survey on the urban neighborhood, see Suzanne Keller, *The Urban Neighborhood: A Sociological Perspective* (New York: Random House, Inc., 1968); see also Phillip Fellin and Eugene Litwak, "The neighborhood in urban American society," *Social Work,* 13:72–80 (July, 1968).

[3]Louis Wirth, "Urbanism as a way of life," *American Journal of Sociology,* 44:1–24 (July, 1938). The general issue is reviewed in Herbert J. Gans, *People and Plans: Essays on Urban Problems and Solutions* (New York: Basic Books, Inc., 1968), pp. 34–52.

a place to live and no longer serves the numerous social functions that the traditional neighborhood does. On the other hand, there is considerable evidence that urban neighborhoods do continue to play a significant role in people's lives. Such evidence comes both from analyses of the amount of human interaction in urban neighborhoods and from general studies of life in various types of urban villages, i.e., neighborhoods dominated by a single ethnic group.[4] The debate suggests that no simple answer is possible. Certainly many people, including those who are occupationally mobile or who have routine access to a car, may be less dependent on their immediate geographic environment, whether for shopping or for social activities. Other people in the city, however, still make great use of their neighborhoods and establish strong identifications with them. Furthermore, the recent trend toward citizen participation and community control over municipal services has probably reinforced these neighborhood identifications.

Second, the urban neighborhood can exist in great variety, even in one city, and much research has been devoted to the examination of different types of neighborhoods, like ethnic villages, hobohemias, the downtown area, high-rise residential neighborhoods, and ghettos.[5] The variety of neighborhoods may be a reflection of many basic factors, like the ethnicity and income levels of the residents, the types of housing, the physical terrain, and the degree of mixture among residential, commercial, and industrial functions. One aim of studying the diversity of neighborhoods is to develop neighborhood typologies, or schemes within which the different neighborhoods can be classified. Shevky and Bell's social area analysis, for instance, was an attempt to account for small-area variations in terms of three basic population factors: socioeconomic status, family status, and ethnicity.[6] A viable typology would seem to be part of any basic understanding of the structure of urban neighborhoods, and of why neighborhoods differ in the first place.

---

[4]For example, see Scott Greer and Ella Kube, "Urbanism and social structure: A Los Angeles study," in Marvin B. Sussman (ed.), *Community Structure and Analysis* (New York: Thomas Y. Crowell Co., 1959), pp. 93–112, and Herbert J. Gans, *The Urban Villagers: Group and Class in the Life of Italian-Americans* (New York: The Free Press, 1962). An example of one of the many firsthand accounts of life in individual neighborhoods is Piri Thomas, *Down These Mean Streets* (New York: Alfred A. Knopf, Inc., 1967).

[5]The original Chicago school of sociology produced many studies of this sort. For example, see Louis Wirth, *The Ghetto* (Chicago: University of Chicago Press, 1928), and Harvey Warren Zorbaugh, *The Gold Coast and the Slum* (Chicago: University of Chicago Press, 1929).

[6]For a comprehensive discussion of social area analysis, see Wendell Bell, "Urban neighborhoods and individual behavior," in Muzafer Sherif and Carolyn W. Sherif (eds.), *Problems of Youth* (Chicago: Aldine Publishing Co., 1965), pp. 235–264.

Third, urban neighborhoods can and do change very rapidly. The rapid rate often poses a real dilemma, for in many cases the change results in the eventual abandonment of a whole area and the undesired displacement of people. Understanding the change process seems vital to understanding the nature of the city, for the aggregate effects of neighborhood changes across the city are an important element in the changing structure of the whole city. Burgess's concentric ring theory, for instance, was an attempt to explain the growth of the city according to zonal and neighborhood changes.[7] Furthermore, neighborhood change may be a barometer of the quality of life in different neighborhoods, for it may reflect the desire people have for living in a given neighborhood.

The articles in this section of the reader all deal with this last aspect of urban neighborhoods, neighborhood change. The emphasis is on change because it is a major aspect of urban life and because it is closely related to the questions of ethnic identifications and residential mobility that were treated in Section One. For the contemporary city, another challenge may be to forecast what new aspects of neighborhood condition are attributable to changes like population turnover. Increases in fires and fire alarms, for instance, have only recently become dramatic enough to be studied as possible concomitants of neighborhood change.[8]

Our current understanding of neighborhood change is still quite rudimentary, and perhaps the articles presented here will stimulate further empirical research on the topic. In the first two articles, R. D. McKenzie (Selection 7) and Harrison White (Selection 8) each describe an important factor in the change process: the movement of people into and out of the neighborhood (McKenzie), and the mechanisms by which changes occur in the housing market (White). These two discussions are followed by three scenarios of neighborhood change. Gilbert Osofsky (Selection 9) reviews the dramatic changes that occurred during the early decades of this century in Harlem, as Harlem changed from a predominantly white to a predominantly black neighborhood. Murray Schumach, a reporter for *The New York Times* who specializes in local neighborhoods, gives a brief account of changes currently taking place in Chinatown, primarily as a result of increased immigration (Selection 10). Schumach's article highlights the direct and immediate impact that immigration can have on a neighborhood and suggests that one way of anticipating future changes is to monitor immigration patterns. George Carey (Selection 11) speculates about one possible way (besides urban renewal) whereby a higher income population can displace a lower income population in a neighborhood.

---

[7]Ernest W. Burgess, "The growth of the city," in Robert E. Park *et al., The City* (Chicago: University of Chicago Press, 1925), pp. 47–62.

[8]Robert K. Yin, "The development of social indicators: The case of fire alarms," New York City-Rand Institute, mimeographed paper, November 1971.

The last two articles of this section present more theoretical aspects of neighborhood change. First, Otis and Beverly Duncan (Selection 12) discuss neighborhood change that is dominated by racial succession, or the displacement of one racial group by another. Racial succession has been widely studied,[9] and the Duncans present their own characterization of the invasion-consolidation process, based on their analysis of census tracts in Chicago. Then, David Birch (Selection 13) tests a stage theory of neighborhood change. The main goal of such a theory is to determine whether all urban neighborhoods experience similar sequences of social and housing change, even though the neighborhoods may change at different rates and in different eras. Birch's article suggests that at least in one city, New Haven, they do.

7. The neighborhood

RODERICK DUNCAN McKENZIE

.   .   .   .   .

Mobility of population may be considered under three heads: change of residence from one community to another, change of residence from one neighborhood to another within the community, and mobility without change of residence. The official sources of information on these subjects are very inadequate. The census reports furnish data concerning nationality and interstate migrations, but aside from that we know nothing about the movements of people from one community to another much less the movements that take place within the community itself.

That the mobility of modern life is intimately connected with many of our social problems there is general consensus of opinion. Assuming that a reasonable amount of mobility is both inevitable and desirable, nevertheless it is unquestionably true that the excessive population movements of modern times are fraught with many serious consequences.

Perhaps the most obvious effect of the mobility of the population within a city is the striking instability of local life. Neighborhoods are in a constant process of

---

[9]For example, see Chester Rapkin and William G. Grigsby, *The Demand for Housing in Racially Mixed Areas: A Study of the Nature of Neighborhood Change* (Berkeley: University of California Press, 1960), and Karl E. Taeuber and Alma F. Taeuber, *Negroes in Cities: Residential Segregation and Neighborhood Change* (Chicago: Aldine Publishing Co., 1965).

Abridged and edited from McKenzie, Roderick Duncan, *The Neighborhood,* Arno Press edition 1970, pp. 145–68, originally published in 1921. Footnotes enlarging on the author's text have been omitted.

R. D. McKenzie (1885–1940) was an eminent sociologist trained at The University of Chicago.

change; some improving, others deteriorating. Changes in incomes and rents are almost immediately registered in change of family domicile. Strengthened economic status usually implies the movement of a family from a poorer to a better neighborhood, while weakened economic status means that the family must retire to a cheaper and less desirable district. So in every city we have two general types of neighborhood; the one whose inhabitants have located there on the basis of personal choice, and the other whose inhabitants have located there as the result of economic compulsion. The former, as we shall see later, contains the possibilities for the development of neighborhood sentiment and organization, while the latter lacks the necessary elements for reconstruction.

Rapid community turnover also plays havoc with local standards and neighborhood mores. It is impossible to have an efficient local opinion in a neighborhood where the people are in constant move. It has repeatedly been affirmed by students of society that the decay of local standards is a pertinent cause of moral laxness and disorderliness.

The flux of modern life also intensifies all problems connected with government, national, state, or local. The fact that we have a residence qualification for voting leaves an increasingly large number every year of disfranchised citizens. This too applies especially to a class, the migrant laborer, which has no other means of participation in social control.

Students of municipal government are constantly calling attention to the difficulty of creating interest in municipal affairs among a people who are in constant move. Stability of residence, as a rule, implies home ownership, which in turn gives rise to local sentiment and interest in neighborhood surroundings. In a region where the population is continually shifting there is little opportunity for the development of neighborhood sentiment, and as a result, local concerns are usually left to take care of themselves. It is hard to develop interest in neighborhood affairs among families who are the while conscious of the temporary nature of their domicile within the district.

The problems which the mobility of population presents to political reformers are likewise common to social workers in other fields. Organizations dealing with delinquency and dependency are hampered in their efforts by the frequent movements of their "cases." Similarly the church, trade union, and other voluntary forms of association lose in their efficiency through the rapid turnover of their local membership lists.

In considering the general causes of the present mobility of population it is important to view the subject from both its psychological and its social aspects. Thomas and Znaniecki have grouped the dominant individual wishes or desires into four general classes: "the desire for recognition or status; the desire for safety or security; the desire for power; the desire for new experiences." . . . Of the four types of desires just mentioned the desires for security and recognition find their chief satisfactions in the solidarity and intimacy of the small local group; while the desires for power and new experience attain their fullest fruition in a wider social milieu. The rigoristic codes of the small stable community have never afforded adequate satisfaction to the human impulses of the more energetic members of the group. The solidarity of the primitive neighborhood group was undoubtedly, to a greater extent, the product of a hostile external environment rather than the result of spontaneous human impulses.

. . . . .

On the social side it is scarcely necessary to draw attention to the leading causes of intercommunity migration. The sudden change from a predominantly agricultural to a predominantly industrial society has occasioned a mobility of life unknown before. As long as the soil furnished the chief basis of economic income man was obliged to live a comparatively stable life in a fixed and definite locality. With the development of the modern capitalistic régime, the presence of the individual is no longer necessary to insure the productivity and security of his property. He may now, if he chooses, invest his savings in interest-bearing securities which require neither his personal presence nor his attention to insure an income. He is thus left free to live, if he so desires, a nomad life. Of course all classes in society are not equally free to move about. The middle-class tradesman and many of the professional groups are more or less tied to definite localities by the very nature of their work. On the other hand, the well-to-do and the day-laborer are free to move almost at will.

. . . . .

8.   Multipliers, vacancy chains, and filtering in housing

HARRISON C. WHITE

Houses and families can be likened to husbands and wives only if divorce is endemic and praiseworthy. As an American family evolves through stages of a normal life cycle its housing aims change.[1] With young children comes the goal of

Abridged and edited from Harrison C. White, "Multipliers, vacancy chains, and filtering in housing," *Journal of the American Institute of Planners,* 37:88–94 (March, 1971). Copyright © 1971 by American Institute of Planners. Reprinted by permission.

The author is Professor of Sociology, Harvard University, Cambridge, Mass.

[1]A good general analysis and a survey of pre-1960 data can be found in Chapters 5 and 7, "Consumer Strategies" (Abu-Lughod and Foley, 1960). Life-cycle data are treated in detail in the recent survey by Lansing, Clifton, and Morgan (1969). In their cross-tabulation of moves by life-cycle stage of predecessor and successor families in a given house, a substantial fraction of successors is earlier in the cycle. But different families have different absolute standards about space, tenure status, and the like. The relevant tabulations are of changes in housing over the careers of given families.

a house.[2] As children and families grow, pressure is felt for more room (White, 1969a). From time to time, the family may pull up stakes and move to a new job in a new city, and thus a new home.[3] As income grows so does the desire for a more gracious house and so does the ability to respond to the desire for space: space for children, for leisure, for flexibility. In later years, the house may yield to an apartment on retirement, or a widow may be forced to leave a house for a room (White, 1969a). There is little residue of sentiments, never very effective, for a permanent house defining the family locus.

HOUSING POLICY AND A MOVING MODEL

One reads much about the "housing market," or net of interrelated markets, localized in a given city's region (Grigsby, 1963). Yet families and houses do not constitute a market in the sense of classical economics. Houses, like families, are largely indivisible units and are dispersed among fixed locations, characteristics that violate the classical axioms (Koopmans, 1957). One could think of a stream of new houses being built in subdivisions for a stream of families coming to jobs in a new industrial park. A price structure would emerge to clear the markets in houses of various costs and families of various incomes; perhaps indivisibility and dispersed locations could be neglected. But wait awhile. Houses are not "consumed." Their life span is indefinite (Smith, 1966). As families move out, the same houses reappear vacant. They attract other families from a whole region just as the former inhabitants may have been pulled to larger or more desirable houses elsewhere. Net yearly increments to houses and to families in a metropolitan area cannot be seen as real flows to be matched to each other in a market. A different view is required, a model of continuing realignment between huge existing stocks of houses and families. In this model, price levels are no longer the dynamic element in the housing "market." Moves fit together in chains of cause and effect identified by the careers of *vacancies*.

Housing policy should be seen in a new light. Each family has recurring needs to move in order to adjust its housing to changing circumstances, as evaluated by themselves, not by some planner or according to statistical norms for a category of people devised by an outside observer. Intelligent social policy will focus on aiding this continuing process of voluntary moves scattered throughout the population. Priority may be given to certain underprivileged sectors (or often, in fact, to privileged groups), but effects on one group cannot be separated empirically from the overall process of adjustment. Each family's move changes the context in which others move.

.   .   .   .   .

---

[2]See Graph 6 in Lansing, Clifton, and Morgan (1969), which is a plot of percent of movers who buy houses by income level and life-cycle stage.

[3]Only a minority of all housing moves are associated with job changes (Lansing *et al.,* 1969, and Paxton, 1956).

INDEPENDENT FLOWS AND VACANCY CHAINS
IN HOUSING SYSTEMS

New houses are built by investors, not by their first occupants, in all save a tiny fraction of cases.[4] These investors try, in part, to anticipate consumer desires, but their predictions cannot be made with accuracy. Most new houses must attract families already ensconced in the huge existing stock of houses rather than some easily identifiable stream of newly founded families.[5] Investors also are responding to pressures quite independent of consumer desires: interest rates, tax advantages, alternative opportunities in commercial building (Smith, 1966). The *stream of new houses* can be treated as a flow relatively independent of the exact state of any current "housing market" in one area.[6] The combination of inaccurate and slow data reports with erratic variations in actual rates suggests that the new housing stream is not causally determined by the state of the housing system even over long time periods. Treat this stream as an exogenous variable that can change arbitrarily regardless of the state of the housing system. The system is the population of houses and their occupants in given metropolitan areas.

For families, flows *out* of the local housing system tend to be independent of the state of the system. Death of the head of a household obviously is not affected by the demand for housing, nor is sudden loss of income attendant upon retirement. A widow or widower will not always vacate a house, nor will a retired couple, but the tendency is strong, and more important the move is little affected by nuances in the current housing system. Moves of families from one city to another must be included as the equivalent of death in a local system. They are almost invariably tied to changes in job and thus are nearly independent of the housing situation in the city left behind. All these *flows of families* out of a local system can be treated as one aggregate flow.

These two flows of houses and families, though opposite in physical direction, add together to measure the volume of opportunity to move introduced into the local housing system. It is the size of this total flow of vacancies (and its distribution among types of houses) which determines the amount of movement as well as the net changes in stocks of houses and families. This is the assertion to be contrasted with the classical economic idea that price levels evolve within the system—in terms of the relation between supply schedules of houses and demand schedules of consumers, and that prices thereby determine numbers of houses sold and new families housed. With few exceptions, a family controls the disposition of the house it occupies, even if ownership is not complete. It can leave voluntarily but cannot be forced out.[7] By the same token the family cannot force its way into occupancy of another house. Each move into a house is contingent on the prior occupants volun-

---

[4]For data, see the 1965 survey of new home builders in *Better Homes and Gardens.* The decision power of investors is a main theme in Smith (1966).

[5]Confirmed in all the surveys cited here.

[6]For a discussion of the difference between exogenous and dependent flows to a system, see Simon (1957).

[7]Obviously, there are exceptions: leases end; men default on mortgages; Public Housing Authorities force tenants out for misbehavior or financial reasons.

tarily moving to another house, whose occupants in turn must have moved. Thus, moves follow one another in chains. The beginning of a chain is either the "death" of a family in an existing house or the creation of a new house.[8] The number of chains formed annually equals the total flow of new opportunity into the system. The average length of a chain is the *multiplier*, the total number of moves caused by the initial arrival of a vacancy.

Five or ten different families and houses may be involved in a given chain. It is highly unlikely that those at one end are even aware of the existence of those at the other. What gives a chain identity is not a particular family or house but a particular interaction. It is logical to name the interaction a *vacancy*. Though there may be no appreciable lag between the actual departure of the predecessor family and arrival of the successor's,[9] there is still a delay between the formation of the former's and the latter's intentions.

.   .   .   .   .

The main alternative to vacancy chains is a "market" for matchmaking: families leave houses before they have located a new place so that at any given time a pool of vacant houses and a pool of unsettled families confront each other. As families spontaneously left houses, an addition would flow into each pool. No longer would new houses and deaths be the cause of mobility by opening up the possibility for chains of moves. Such matchmaking situations could arise only when there is a large surplus of available houses of all kinds. A family's need for housing is pressing and continuous enough to make them reluctant to leave a house voluntarily without assurance of another being available. Even given surplus housing, matchmaking is unlikely. If other houses are surplus, it will be clear that one's own will be hard to sell. In any case, most owners have mortgages, and until they have sold their existing houses they are unlikely to have the means to enter matchmaking pools.

.   .   .   .   .

Flows which terminate vacancy chains in the housing system are dependent in volume on the state of the system, unlike the flows of new houses and deaths which initiate chains of moves. These dependencies are viable, in part, because of the existence of the more flexible apartment system. Consider the flow of new living groups—most often married couples but also other groups of kin or friends—into the system of houses. The argument is that the volume of this flow depends on number of houses available, that is the number of vacancies active in chains at that time. Yet obviously the number of new couples formed per year is in large part a demographic and cultural fact,[10] rather independent of the availability of housing space. Any gap between the flow of available vacancies in houses and the flow of

---

[8]Again there are exceptions. For example, large older houses may be converted into a number of apartments (Lansing *et al.,* 1969, and Smith, 1966).

[9]The best data on this point are in Appendix C of Lansing *et al.* (1969). Families often take temporary quarters between houses and are available to move in immediately, when they do buy a house.

[10]The evidence is that the post-1940 trend toward higher frequencies of independent household formation, especially by the elderly and by young adults, will continue through 1985 (U.S. Bureau of the Census, 1968). It seems clear that increasing income levels are the prime force behind this trend (Campbell, 1966).

new households can be seen as accommodated by apartments or doubling up in homes of kin.

The other dependent flow is of houses leaving the system by demolition, abandonment, and the like. There is no definite lifespan or even distribution of lifespans for a given group of houses or type of house. It is plausible that the proportion of houses abandoned depends on the number of houses vacant in the current state of the system. Furthermore, abandonment of an individual house is unlikely to be considered until after the current occupants have moved out.

A simple picture of housing dynamics emerges. Families adjust to evolving needs by moving to vacancies; each vacancy is originally created either by a death or by construction of a new house. Vacancies jump from house to house until extinguished either by recruitment of a family from outside the system or by abandonment of a house removed from the system. Once the vacancy jumps and extinctions can be predicted, then mobility and change in the housing system can be predicted from the rates of creation of vacancies.

HOUSES AND JOBS

Models for systems of jobs and men, developed and tested with data from three large bureaucracies over fifty years, suggested the housing system described here (White, 1970a). Many of the details and much of the argument must be recast, but the essential dynamics of the systems seem the same. Men correspond to families, jobs to houses, and vacancies in jobs to vacancies in houses. A Markov chain model can be used for each type of system, and its limitations are similar in the two cases.

Through recent research, it has become clear that houses like jobs are largely obtained through networks of personal contacts.[11] Economists and other social scientists emphasize the role of rational institutions in disseminating information and opportunity among whole categories of people, as in the classical "market." But, in reality, even when people frequently use impersonal agents and media, as they do in housing, they find their effectiveness is low. Thus, a given person anxious to move may learn of but a few realistic opportunities, scattered in what seems a whimsical pattern from a market point of view, unified only because each is known to someone in his various circles of acquaintances. Conversely, banning some miraculous transformation in our social institutions, each opportunity will tend to become known to only a scattering of potential customers. It is very difficult as yet to supply useable models of such complex processes of interaction along networks of informal and formal ties.

. . . . .

DATA ON HOUSING CHAINS

The pioneer work by Lansing, Clifton, and Morgan (1969) provides the first systematic discussion of and data on vacancy chains in housing. They trace over 1,000 vacancy chains initiated by a national sample of new housing units (40 percent

---

[11]On house searches, see Rossi (1955); on job searches, see Reynolds (1951). Reynolds' assessment is confirmed in recent work on professional occupations by Mark Granovetter.

apartments, 60 percent houses). Each chain had to be established by interviews with the new occupants of a mover's previous home, at successive steps.[12]

The average length of chains begun by new houses was over 4.0, which shows the magnitude of the multiplier effect (apartments are included in the system to which this figure refers). The average price of houses declined steadily with position in the chain from $26,000 at the first step (the new houses) to $18,000 at the sixth and higher steps. Chains begun by new apartments were about one move shorter, as one would expect, and also decreased in length with the rent for the new apartment.

It is clear that price is a good criterion for defining categories among which vacancies move, but Lansing *et al.* do not attempt to define strata. They do not give the cross-tabulations of moves by origin and destination strata from which transition probabilities among categories could be estimated. They do show that the average length of chain doubles as the price of the new house increases from under $15,000 to over $30,000. . . . Vacancies in the more expensive new houses make more moves to other units in the system before reaching units with price levels low enough to make termination likely (from recruitment of newly married couples, demolition, and the like).

The observed fraction of vacancy chains terminated at their first step is less than a quarter and rises to over 30 percent beyond the fourth step. Overall, about 20 percent of all the chains end by demolition of the housing unit or the like. Half the chains end by recruiting newly married couples from their parents' houses. The remainder end by recruitment of people, mostly young, who also do not leave behind vacant housing units in the U.S. This distribution among types may be much the same in all price categories of houses, just the total frequency of terminations varying with the price category in which the vacancy lies.

Lansing *et al.* do not estimate the distribution of new houses and thus vacancy creation by price range, but existing surveys can yield such estimates. These authors do report, after comparison of national housing statistics with their own data, that about half of all moves in U.S. housing lie in chains set off by new housing. The other half are moves set off by deaths of families.

HOUSING POLICY IMPLICATIONS OF FILTERING

The picture of housing systems developed here . . . can be regarded as a specification of the much-debated—because it is quite vague—concept of *filtering* in housing (Grigsby, 1963). Lansing *et al.* so regard their empirical analysis. Filtering has been described variously, but it generally refers to the tendency of houses over time to depreciate in value, eventually falling into the hands of families with lower incomes.

The basic fact is that every new unit built, given the distribution of prices, thus types, now found in the new housing market in the U.S., enables four families to move. They move voluntarily and thus must be meeting their needs in a way they see as better. More extensive data [are] needed, and [they] must be analyzed in terms

---

[12]Lansing *et al.* (1969) correct observed chain lengths for the bias introduced by the greater likelihood of non-response from families in a long chain.

of price strata, before specific recommendations about desirable housing programs can be made. . . . Subsidized new housing will not, in general, be the most effective path to the national policy goal of improving the overall match of families' needs with available houses. Subsidized housing will not have as large a multiplier effect as new housing units built for middle and higher income groups.

Nor does it follow that the existing streams of new housing are optimal. As Wallace Smith (1966) has argued, they are created by investors who do not aim to maximize overall benefits nor do they have reliable information even on desires of persons able to afford new houses. The stream of new housing is not really determined by the state of the market in the classical sense. It is not an endogenous variable responding to needs expressed through a market, but rather it is a somewhat arbitrary exogenous variable. Policy should be directed to improving the match between needs and supply without losing the multiplier effect.

REFERENCES

Abu-Lughod, J., and Foley, M. M. "Consumer strategies." In N. Foote *et al.* (eds.), *Housing Choices and Housing Constraints.* New York: McGraw-Hill Book Co., 1960.

Campbell, B. O. *Population Change and Building Cycles.* Urbana: Bureau of Economic Research, University of Illinois, 1966.

Grigsby, W. G. *Housing Markets and Public Policy.* Philadelphia: University of Pennsylvania, 1963.

Koopmans, T. C. *Three Essays on the State of Economic Science.* New York: McGraw-Hill Book Co., 1957.

Lansing, J. B.; Clifton, C. W.; and Morgan, J. *New Homes and Poor People.* Ann Arbor: Survey Research Center, University of Michigan, 1969.

Paxton, E. T. *What People Want When They Buy a House.* Housing and Home Finance Agency, 1956. p. 8.

Reynolds, L. *The Structure of Labor Markets.* New York: Harper & Row, Publishers, 1951.

Rossi, P. H. *Why Families Move.* Glencoe, Ill.: The Free Press, 1955.

Simon, H. A. *Models of Man.* New York: John Wiley & Sons, Inc., 1957.

Smith, W. F. *Aspects of Housing Demand—Abrogation, Demolition, and Differentiation.* Research Report No. 29. Berkeley: Center for Real Estate and Urban Economics, University of California, 1966.

U.S. Bureau of the Census. "Population estimates." In *Current Population Survey.* Series P-25 (1968).

White, H. C. "Consumer needs in housing." Unpublished memo, 1969a.

White, H. C. "Control and evolution of aggregate personnel." *Administrative Science Quarterly* 14:4–11 (1969b).

White, H. C. *Chains of Opportunity.* Cambridge, Mass.: Harvard University Press, 1970a.

White, H. C. "Matching, vacancies, and mobility." *Journal of Political Economy* 78:97–105 (1970b).

9. Harlem

GILBERT OSOFSKY

A GENTEEL COMMUNITY

In the last three decades of the nineteenth century Harlem was a community of great expectations. During the previous quarter century it had been an isolated, poor, rural village. After the 1870's, however, it was transformed into an upper- and upper-middle-class residential suburb—Manhattan's first suburb.

Prosperity had come to Harlem before. Throughout the colonial period its lands brought wealth to farmers. The estates of some of America's most illustrious colonial families were located there—Delanceys, Beekmans, Bleeckers, Rikers, Coldens, Hamiltons and others. The stamp of respectability and distinction colored Harlem's name and later settlers recalled its past glories proudly: "Who among [you] then," a lecturer on the history of the community said in 1882, "with Harlem's . . . history before you, and the goodly prospects in store, are not proud of being called Harlemites. . . . The spirit which animated their [the founders'] breasts," he concluded romantically, "is rooted in the soft rich soil of Harlem. . . ."

The phenomenal growth of Harlem in the late nineteenth century was a by-product of the general development of New York City. From the 1870's on, the foundations of the modern metropolis were laid. This urban revolution was characterized by improvements in methods of sanitation, water supply, transportation, communication, lighting and building. As the city expanded, so did its population. In 1880, for the first time in its history, and in the history of any American city, the population of Manhattan alone passed the one million mark (1,164,673), and "New Immigrants" had just begun to arrive. This increase in population coincided with an expansion of commercial and industrial activity and both made serious inundations on living quarters in formerly staid residential sections. The only way for the island city to grow was northward. Many older residents and older immigrants, attempting to avoid the bustle of the new metropolis and escape contact with its newest settlers, looked to Harlem as the community of the future: "In our family, we were always careful to explain that we lived in Harlem, not in New York City," a man whose family moved uptown in these years recalled. "It was our way of avoiding contact with such uncouth citizens as might be found downtown. . . ." The neighborhood would become "the choicest residential section of the city," predicted another resident. "Upper Seventh Avenue in Harlem has become one of the finest streets in New York. . . . Rows of trees and pretty gardens . . . lend to it a semi-suburban aspect."

Harlem expanded gradually in the 1860's and was annexed to New York City in 1873. The city filled some 1,350 acres of marshland in 1870, sold them to the

Abridged and edited from Chapters 5, 6, and 8 in *Harlem: The Making of a Ghetto*, by Gilbert Osofsky. Copyright © 1966 by Gilbert Osofsky. Reprinted by permission of Harper & Row, Publishers, Inc. Footnotes enlarging on the author's text have been omitted.

The author is Professor of History, University of Illinois at Chicago Circle, Chicago, Ill.

public, and constructed houses over them. A few city fathers in the heyday of the Tweed Ring appropriated promising lands for themselves and built fashionable homes there. The turning point in Harlem's history came in 1878–1881. During these years three lines of the elevated railroad came as far north as One Hundred and Twenty-ninth Street and, by 1886, the elevated line came even further north. Rows of brownstones and exclusive apartment houses appeared overnight: "Business grows, blocks and flats go up with apparently so little effort, that the average Harlemite is in a continuous swim of development and prosperity," the local newspaper commented in 1890. Practically all the houses that stand in Harlem today were built in a long spurt of energy that lasted from the 1870's through the first decade of the twentieth century. Electric lights were first installed in 1887 and the telephone followed the next year. Shanties, doomed by "the wilderness of brownstone, brick and mortar . . .," took with them Harlem's celebrated goat, the subject of much newspaper lampooning. An irate "Harlem Goat" begged the *New York Herald* to leave it in peace: "I feel as if my browsing days in Harlem are over, and I can hardly find a . . . blade of fresh grass. . . ." "No more goats in Harlem/There's prosperity in Harlem," sang the Harlem Board of Commerce at a neighborhood fete. "When Harlem was a Prairie," echoed the motto of the Harlem Old-Timers Association. An Irish resident of the community since the 1840's saw a "one horse town . . . turned into a teeming metropolis. . . ."

Speculators made fortunes buying Harlem land, holding it for a short while, and reselling at great profit. Builders purchased land, constructed houses and sold them as soon as they were completed. They used the profits for reinvestment. Oscar Hammerstein I, Henry Morgenthau, and August Belmont were among them. "Hammerstein bought and sold properties in that area with great speed and generally at a profit," his biographer wrote. Edward H. W. Just, another speculator, born in Eisleben, Germany in the 1830's, came to New York City as a young man when the ready-made clothing industry was becoming a major source of city wealth. He became a successful shirt manufacturer and invested heavily in Harlem property. When he died in 1893 he left an estate worth more than $2,000,000. One plot of land purchased in 1852 for $3,000 was worth $200,000 in 1890. "When I see the prices that real estate is now bringing in Harlem," one old-timer bemoaned in 1889, "it makes me feel that I was a fool for not making . . . investments years ago when property was so cheap. Twenty years [ago] the meadow lands of Harlem were not considered worth paying taxes for."

. . . . .

People generally took it for granted that Harlem would develop into an exclusive, stable, upper- and upper-middle-class community: "a neighborhood very genteel." The newly built elevator apartment houses, many equipped with servants' quarters, rented for prices that could be paid only by the wealthy. The most magnificent was a group of spacious, luxurious brownstones built on One Hundred and Thirty-eighth and One Hundred and Thirty-ninth Streets in 1891. Stanford White, the well-known architect so closely associated with the architectural history of the city (he designed Madison Square Garden, Washington Arch, Grand Central Station), had been commissioned to build one hundred and six distinguished homes, each with ten to sixteen rooms and flower-bedecked driveways. They were advertised to be as "distinctive as a suburban colony but with all the advantages of city life": "These driveways are ornamented at their intersections by circular beds of flowers, making a decorative feature even of their utility. Great care is taken of the property to preserve its exclusive appearance, and a general air of being well-looked-after pervades the surroundings." Houses set back twelve feet from the street added privacy and rear entrances "permitted the business of housekeeping to be kept out of sight." In a society whose working-class families paid an average of $10-18 a month rent, the rents for these homes *started* at just under $80, and ranged between $900 and $1700 a year.

Another group of twenty-eight three-story exclusive homes, Astor Row, constructed in the 1890's on West One Hundred and Thirtieth Street, provided large porches and shade trees. They were known "as one of the most attractive and exclusive home centres" in Harlem, and "presented a picture of domestic tranquility and comfort which few other . . . blocks in the city possess," a *New York Times* reporter noted. In spite of high rentals Astor Row had a long waiting list of prospective tenants.

Prosperity and optimism seemed the order of the day. One merchant built a large department store on One Hundred and Twenty-fifth Street in 1890 and had such confidence in Harlem's future that he offered to pay half the rent for five years of any businessman who followed him. Local citizens could attend the Harlem Opera House, built by Oscar Hammerstein I in 1889, or go to one of Harlem's many theaters. In 1900 they might dine at the luxurious German Pabst Harlem: "Where Gentlemen and Ladies can enjoy good music and a perfect cuisine amid surroundings which have been rendered as attractive to the eye and senses [as] good taste, combined with expenditure, could make them."

The people attracted to this "residential heaven" were obviously older and wealthier New Yorkers—"people of taste and wealth." Few neighborhoods in the entire city at the turn of the century had so disproportionate a number of native Americans or immigrants from Great Britain, Ireland and Germany, including German Jews, living in it. In 1902, of the 103,570 families in the Twelfth Ward, only 10,786 could be classified as "New Immigrants." Many late-nineteenth-century Harlemites were born in downtown Manhattan or immigrated to America in the years 1830–1850, and subsequently moved to the community after 1870. One man came to visit a friend in Harlem in 1889 and was surprised "to see so many downtowners who have come here to live. It looks as if everybody will be rushing up here from downtown before long," he said. A future director of the Harlem Board of Commerce moved to the neighborhood in the 1880's and was surprised to meet so many Greenwich Village friends there. The homes of municipal and federal judges, mayors, local politicos (including Tammany boss Richard Croker), prominent businessmen and state politicians (Chauncey M. Depew, for example), were scattered throughout Harlem. Their children attended Grammar School 68, "referred to as the 'Silk Stocking School' of the City" because its "pupils were practically all from American families, and . . . more or less prosperous people." Their daughters could go to "Mme. De Valencia's Protestant French and English Institute for Young Ladies," one of the many private schools for the wealthy that flourished in the nineteenth-century city. A young Jewish boy moved to Harlem from the Lower East Side in the first decade of the twentieth century and recalled seeing rich German Jews, "Uptown Jews," strutting down Seventh Avenue in top hats, black coats and canes.

·   ·   ·   ·

Those who lived through the transition of Harlem to a Negro ghetto tended to forget that substantial numbers of Negroes were also scattered throughout the neighborhood in the late nineteenth century. It seemed to many that Negroes came to Harlem suddenly in the twentieth century; older white residents never really understood the nature of the change that reshaped their entire community. In reality, the Negro sections of Harlem predated those of its late-nineteenth-century residents. The first Negroes to live and work in Harlem were slaves and references to them are found in seventeenth-century documents. The original wagon road constructed between New Amsterdam and Harlem was built by the "Dutch West India Company's Negroes." Slaves worked on farms and estates in Harlem in the seventeenth and eighteenth centuries and colonial Harlem even had its own "Negro Burying Ground." One local farmer bequeathed his slaves to his children in 1752. The New York Census of 1790 listed 115 slaves for the "Harlem Division," just under one-third of its total population.

·   ·   ·   ·

ROOTS OF INSTABILITY

Harlem life altered radically in the first decade of the twentieth century. The construction of new subway routes into the neighborhood in the late 1890's set off a second wave of speculation in Harlem land and property. Speculators who intended to make astronomic profits when the subway was completed bought the marshes, garbage dumps and lots left unimproved or undeveloped in the 1870's and 1880's. Between 1898 and 1904, the year that the Lenox Avenue line opened at One Hundred and Forty-fifth Street, "practically all the vacant land in Harlem" was "built over," the *Real Estate Record and Builders' Guide* noted in 1904. "The growth of . . . Harlem . . . has been truly astonishing during the last half dozen years."

The real estate boom created a wave of new building activity in Harlem dominated primarily by speculators, although some individuals made long-term investments. It was taken as business gospel that investments would be doubled and trebled after the completion of the "tunnel road." "Even a 5-story single flat in Harlem would net . . . at the end of . . . three to five years . . . at the utmost . . . a very handsome unearned increment," a realtor concluded. "It would be impossible to err." Another supposed expert in urban real estate maintained that no "other class of public improvements had such a great, immediate and permanent effect upon land values as rapid transit lines. . . ."

·   ·   ·   ·

This real estate fever "seized upon [the Jewish] Ghettos of Greater New York" too. Offices were set up in people's homes, investments were discussed in Lower East Side restaurants, as workers with modest savings conceived themselves as budding realtors. Abraham Cahan, the well-known Jewish newspaper editor and novelist, graphically described the "boom atmosphere" which even pervaded the immigrant ghettos of the city: "Small tradesmen of the slums, and even working-men, were investing their savings in houses and lots. Jewish carpenters, house-painters, bricklayers, or installment peddlers became builders of tenements or frame dwellings, real-estate speculators. Deals were being closed and poor men were making thousands of dollars in less time than it took to drink a glass of tea or the plate of sorrel soup over which the transaction took place. Women, too, were ardently dabbling in real estate. . . ."

In the section of Harlem north of Central Park to One Hundred and Twenty-fifth Street, and west of Lexington Avenue to Seventh Avenue, new tenements and apartment houses went up in the late 1890's. These properties seemed to offer "good profit on investments," as East European Jews spilled out of the Lower East Side in search of better homes—part of the migration to lower Harlem and other boroughs that reflected their economic mobility. The disintegration of the Jewish sections on the Lower East Side that began in the first decade of the twentieth century continued for thirty years. As Russian and Polish Jews replaced German Jews in the garment industry in these years, they now began to encroach on the residential center of "Uptown Jewry." To live in lower Harlem became a symbol of good times to many East European Jews. Some families who moved into the neighborhood, one contemporary recorded, "speak apologetically and at times are actually embarrassed when their former residence in the lower parts of the city is mentioned." The newspapers called this section of Harlem "Little Russia."

The University Settlement, founded on the Lower East Side, followed its people to Harlem. An "Experimental School in Harlem" established in 1902 became the "Harlem Guild of the University Settlement" in 1903. Maurice H. Harris, a social worker, started another settlement on East One Hundred and Fifth Street in 1906. "It is from the inspiration . . . I obtained from your Settlement that I have been enabled to start a humble venture of my own," he wrote his mentor Lillian D. Wald. Jewish synagogues bought property in the neighborhood: "Calvary Presbyterian Church is now one of the prettiest little Jewish synagogues in . . . New York." A variety of social institutions arose: the Harlem Home of the Daughters of Israel, Harlem Hebrew School, Harlem Hebrew Educational Institute, Harlem Hebrew Retail Grocers' Association, and so on. Local libraries began to acquire books of Jewish history and Yiddish literature for their newest readers.

Older residents objected to the "migration of the better class of East Side Jews into the district north and east of the Park, then the new quarter of the most prosperous Russian Jews," in terms similar to those previously reserved for Italian immigrants and Negroes. "Foreigners are crowding up the whole length of the island," the *Harlem Local Reporter* said in an editorial. Elmer Rice and his family, like many of their Harlem neighbors, moved away from One Hundred and Sixth Street in 1903 because the "neighborhood had been growing less 'refined'. . . ." The sometimes bitter response of German Harlemites to the settlement of East European Jews in their community was symbolized by a to-let sign which hung on one building: *Keine Juden, und keine Hunde.* [No Jews, No Dogs.]

.   .   .

Speculation in West Harlem property led to phenomenal increases in the price of land and the cost of houses there—increases inflated out of all proportion to their real value. John M. Royall, Negro realtor, recalled that "from 1902 to 1905 real

estate speculative fever seized all New York City. The great subway proposition
... permeated the air. Real estate operators and speculators [imagined] becoming
millionaires, and bought freely in the West Harlem district in and about the
proposed subway stations. Men bought property on thirty and sixty day contracts,
and sold their contracts ... and made substantial profits. I have known buyers to
pay $38,000 and $75,000 for tenements which showed a gross income of only $2600
and $5000 a year. On they went buying, buying. ..." Houses continually changed
hands. Each time a house was sold, Royall said, it brought a higher price. In the
urge to get rich quick on Harlem property, few persons realized how artificial
market values had become.

The inevitable bust came in 1904–1905. Speculators sadly realized afterward
that too many houses were constructed at one time. West Harlem was glutted with
apartments and "excessive building ... led to many vacancies." No one knew
exactly how long it would take to construct the subway and many houses built four
and five years in advance of its completion remained partly unoccupied. The first
of them to be inhabited by Negroes, for example, was never rented previously. Rents
were too high for the general population ($35–$45 per month) and precluded any
great rush to West Harlem even after the subway was completed. There was a
widespread "overestimation of ... rental value," a contemporary remarked. When
the market broke, landlords competed with each other for tenants by reducing rents,
or offering a few months' rent-free occupancy to them. Local realtors unsuccessfully
attempted to eliminate these cutthroat practices.

By 1905 financial institutions no longer made loans to Harlem speculators and
building-loan companies, and many foreclosed on their original mortgages. The
inflated prices asked for land and property in West Harlem "solemnly settled
beneath a sea of depreciated values." In the aftermath of the speculative collapse,
and as a consequence of the initiative of Negro realtors, large numbers of colored
people began to settle in West Harlem.

.   .   .   .   .

A NEIGHBORHOOD TRANSFORMED

But not all property owners were ready to open their houses to colored people.
It seemed unbelievable to some that theirs, one of the most exclusive sections in the
entire city, should become the center of New York's most depressed and traditionally worst-housed people. Some owners banded together in associations to repulse
what they referred to as the Negro "invasion" or the Negro "influx." The language
used to describe the movement of Negroes into Harlem—the words "invasion,"
"captured," "black hordes," "invaders," "enemy," for example, appear repeatedly
in denunciations of Negroes—was the language of war.

In the 1880's and 1890's Harlemites annually celebrated the historic Revolutionary Battle of Harlem Heights. These patriotic fetes were symbols of community
pride and pamphlets were widely distributed informing the neighborhood of the
dignitaries participating in them. In the early twentieth century, however, Harlem's
residents gathered not to preserve the memory of a Revolutionary conflict, but to
fight their own battle—to keep their neighborhood white.

Most of the formal opposition to Negro settlement in Harlem centered in local associations of landlords. Some were committees representing individual blocks, others were community-wide in structure. Property owners on West One Hundred and Fortieth, One Hundred and Thirty-seventh, One Hundred and Thirty-sixth, One Hundred and Thirty-fifth, One Hundred and Thirty-first, One Hundred and Thirtieth, One Hundred and Twenty-ninth Streets, and so on, in descending order as the Negro community spread southward, and along the avenues, signed restrictive agreements. Each swore not to rent his apartments to Negroes for ten or fifteen years—till when, it was thought, "this situation . . . referred to . . . will have run its course": "The premises, land, and buildings of which we . . . are the owners . . . shall not be used as a . . . Negro tenement, leased to colored . . . tenants, sold to colored . . . tenants . . . or all [other] persons of African descent," one agreement reads. "Each of the parties," another maintains, "does hereby covenant and agree [not] to . . . hereafter . . . cause to be suffered, either directly or indirectly, the said premises to be used or occupied in whole or in part by any negro, quadroon, or octoroon of either sex whatsoever. . . ." Some covenants even put a limitation on the number of Negro janitors, bellboys, laundresses and servants to be employed in a home. Following a pseudo-legal procedure which was supposed to make these agreements binding, each signer paid all the others a fee of one dollar. The finished products were notarized and filed at the County Clerk's Office in the New York City Hall of Records where they may be read today. The streets covered by such restrictive codes were known in the Negro community as "Covenant Blocks," and Negroes took pride in being the first colored landlords or tenants to live in them: "to knock [the covenants] into a cocked hat," one said. "Although organizations to prevent the settling of colored citizens in certain . . . sections of Harlem mushroom overnight," the *Age* quipped, "the colored invasion goes merrily along."

These movements permitted whites the opportunity to vent their anxieties and the chimerical hope that restrictive agreements "safeguarded the neighborhood . . . for all time," but they did not end Negro settlement in Harlem. All the organizations failed. That it was necessary to found so many in a relatively short period of time was a reflection of the general failure of each. Private housing covenants had not, during the life of the HPOIC, been ruled constitutional (from 1917 to 1948 the United States Supreme Court barred segregation by public ordinance but not separation in private agreements). Although at least two people were sued in New York City for violating their original commitments, local courts never convicted them. Negro realtors, like John M. Royall, ridiculed the proposal for a voluntary line of segregation as an agreement to "capitalize on prejudice," and "a joke." . . .

The basic cause of the collapse of all organized efforts to exclude Negroes from Harlem was the inability of any group to gain total and unified support of all white property owners in the neighborhood. Without such support it was impossible to organize a successful neighborhood-wide restrictive movement. Landlords forming associations by blocks had a difficult time keeping people on individual streets united. There also continued to be speculators, Negro and white, who, as in 1904 and 1905, sought to exploit the situation for their own profit. They bought tenements and opened them to Negroes to try to force neighbors to repurchase them at higher prices. Nor was it possible, and this is the major point, to create a well-organized and well-financed movement of Negro restriction (the HPOIC plan called for the contribution of one-half of one percent of the assessed valuation of all property to a community fund) in the disrupted and emotional atmosphere that pervaded Harlem in the first two decades of the twentieth century. The very setting in which whites were confronted with Negro neighbors for the first time led to less than level-headed reasoning. The first impulse of many "in a rather panicky state of mind" was to sell at whatever price their property would bring and move elsewhere. Realtors called this "panic selling" and, in spite of efforts to prevent it, it continued. Between 1907 and 1914, two-thirds of the houses in or near the Negro section were sold—practically all at substantial losses to the original owners. Since the already weak real estate market was flooded with property in a short time, and only a relatively few Negroes were wealthy enough to buy—"there was no market for real estate among the newcomers"—prices continued to depreciate rapidly: "realty values have tumbled by leaps and bounds." "The coming of Negroes to this locality without any financial backing brought about a decided change, as the colored people . . . were unable to adhere to the standard formerly observed by the whites," a Harlem banker wrote. "Hence there was a deterioration in values. . . ." In the 1870's and 1880's fortunes were made in soaring Harlem land prices; by 1917 white realtors tried to encourage interest in the neighborhood by advertising how cheap property had become: "Changes in the character of Harlem population," a member of the Harlem Board of Commerce wrote, have led "to remarkable bargains, both for rental and purchase. . . . Such properties in good condition can now be purchased at less than the assessed value of the land alone."

    ·   ·   ·   ·

The creation of Negro Harlem was only one example of the general development of large, segregated Negro communities within many American cities in the years *preceding* and following World War I. Harlem was New York's equivalent of the urban ghettos of the nation. "The Negroes are being relegated to the land of Goshen in all our great cities," Kelly Miller commented. "Niggertowns," "Buzzard's Alleys," "Nigger Rows," "Black Bottoms," "Smoketowns," "Bronzevilles," and "Chinch Rows" developed elsewhere, North and South, by 1913—and they would continue to emerge in the future. The District of Columbia was noted for its supposedly decadent Negro alleys: "Tin Can Alley," "Coon Alley," "Hog Alley," "Moonshine Alley," and "Goat Alley." (Life in "Goat Alley," was the subject of a play by that name in the 1920's.) "So closely have the terms Alleys and Negroes been associated," a historian of Washington's Negro section wrote, "that in the minds of the older citizens they are inseparable." "There is growing up in the cities of America a distinct Negro world," George Edmund Haynes said in 1913. These were neighborhoods "isolated from many of the impulses of the common life and little understood by the white world," he concluded.

    ·   ·   ·   ·

In 1914 Negroes lived in some 1,100 different houses within a twenty-three-block area of Harlem. After a house-to-house survey in that year, the Urban League estimated Harlem's population at 49,555—the entire Negro population of Manhattan in 1910 was 60,534. *Prior to World War I,* the neighborhood was already the "largest colony of colored people, in similar limits, in the world"—and it continued to expand. By 1920 the section of Harlem bordered approximately by One Hundred and Thirtieth Street on the south, One Hundred and Forty-fifth Street on the north and west of Fifth to Eighth Avenue was predominantly Negro—and inhabited by some 73,000 people. Two-thirds of Manhattan's Negro population lived there in 1920. "If my race can make Harlem," one man said, "good lord, what can't it do?" Harlem had become "the Mecca of the colored people of New York City."

10. Neighborhoods: Chinatown is troubled by new influx

MURRAY SCHUMACH

At Bayard and Mulberry Streets, among congested tenements, is Public School 23, one of the few schools left with the outdoor fire escapes of the last century. Inside it is immaculate. The school's monthly attendance frequently exceeds 99 percent, about 10 percent above the city average. Nearly all the students are of Chinese origin.

"They enjoy school," says Mrs. Grace Mok, a teacher there who grew up in Chinatown and was graduated from this school, and whose children, who are now married, did the same. "That's the trouble sometimes. They enjoy school so much they'll come to school with fever, with whooping cough, with measles."

Yet at Seward Park High School, where 600 of the 4,000 students are Chinese, the dropout rate for them often reaches a surprising 15 percent.

SURGE IN IMMIGRATION

This contrast is one result of the immigration wave that has been drastically altering Chinatown since the repeal of the immigration quota system in 1965. About 25 percent of the 45,000 residents of the community arrived in the last two years. The boundaries, once generally regarded as Canal Street on the north, Park Row on the south, Mulberry Street on the west and the Bowery on the east, extend uptown to Grand Street—with some clusters near 14th Street—and to Essex Street on the east.

Gangs of loitering dropouts have become as commonplace in Chinatown's narrow streets as the smiling children, the aromatic restaurants, the stores of exotic merchandise and the camera-clicking tourists.

Abridged and edited from Murray Schumach, "Neighborhoods: Chinatown is troubled by new influx," *The New York Times,* June 16, 1970, p. 49. Copyright © 1970 by The New York Times Company. Reprinted by permission.

"The Chinese are a people New Yorkers tend to neglect," says the Rev. Denis Hanly, pastor of the Roman Catholic Church of the Transfiguration, which took root at Mott and Park Streets in 1848, a couple of decades before the section began changing from Irish to Chinese.

The problems of this community, which have been obscured by those of black and Puerto Rican areas, are serious. They include the following:

1. Housing shortages have resulted in payments of "key money" ranging from $500 to $2,000 for tenement flats.

2. Language problems have made it difficult for Chinese immigrants to get jobs and obtain education.

3. Debts incurred in getting to the United States have obliged wives as well as husbands to work. Sometimes children, after school, stand beside a sewing machine at which their mothers are working.

4. Crime, mainly robbery, but with some purse-snatching and mugging, has grown in this area, once known for its low crime rate.

SUTTON CITES NEED

"There's a great need for help in Chinatown," says Percy E. Sutton, Manhattan Borough President, "and no special attention is being paid. But I'm determined that within a year we're going to get a language laboratory there. I think it's terribly important."

The lack of what has come to be known in the area as "survival English" has been the main cause of the difficulties of students in high school, according to many community workers in Chinatown. The language problem is much more serious among adolescents than among children in the grade school. These bilingual workers point out that very few of the community's school dropouts were born in this country.

Part of the trouble has been the reluctance of the Chinese-American community here to press for government assistance. A recent study of Chinatown by Chinese-speaking college students, under the auspices of Columbia University and the Ford Foundation, found that: "The Chinese have always relied upon their family or relatives for aid in times of need, and children are expected to take care of their parents in their old age. Thus few are willing to accept welfare."

In addition, the Chinese Consolidated Benevolent Association, with some 60 member groups, the Establishment of Chinatown, has been challenged by the Chinatown Planning Council and the Chinese Youth Council, both largely publicly financed, which direct their appeal to the young, arranging English classes and seeking jobs.

There are indications, however, that, except for a tiny Maoist-directed group, efforts are being made to reduce frictions. Representatives of the different groups join in meetings with public officials and a number of men in the dissident groups, in private conversation, seem in basic agreement.

Though residents of Chinatown are learning how to use the government—they have even staged a few demonstrations—the dominant qualities of the community are still self-reliance, industry and ingenuity.

Residents are buying many of the area's tenements and factories. Volunteers teach English and the benevolent association operates the New York Chinese School, after regular school hours, which teaches Chinese and Chinese culture to more than 2,600 children. At the Chatham Square branch library, the children burrow tirelessly among the English and Chinese books.

An example of the Chinese businessmen's resourcefulness is the line of men at the curb every weekday, at Elizabeth and Bayard Streets, at 10 A.M. and 3 P.M. They are restaurant workers who are picked up by car and driven to and from restaurant jobs in Queens, Long Island, New Jersey and Westchester County at the expense of the restaurant owners.

HAVE MOBILITY

One of the major assets of Chinese Americans is their mobility. Unlike some minorities, if they have the money they can live almost anywhere in the city or suburbs.

But there is some concern—most people agree it is very little—about the possibility that if hostilities break out between the United States and Communist China, they might be put in concentration camps as security risks.

That Chinese Americans do not take this possibility very seriously is a tribute to them. For many years they were persecuted in this country. Early immigrants were brought to the United States as cheap labor in the goldfields of the West and as railroad laborers.

They began settling in New York City, driven from the West by the humiliation of being limited to the most menial work. Sometimes they were even lynched.

Despite this unhappy history and present problems, the adaptability of Chinese immigrants here is reflected by the cheerfulness of the children. Says Mary Gee, a young woman who has never moved from the Chinatown tenement in which she was born:

"The little kids are happy."

11. Hippie neighborhoods and urban spatial systems

GEORGE W. CAREY

The phenomenon of neighborhood change as a concomitant of urban growth has repeatedly drawn the attention of scholars. Earlier in this century when the dominant demographic question in America seemed to be the absorption of vast numbers of foreign immigrants into city life, the University of Chicago School of sociologists put forward the celebrated ecological theme of invasion and succession as an interpretive mechanism by means of which the social evolution of urban areas might be understood.[1] This process required a continuous stream of young, low-status newcomers (such as the immigrants from Europe and Asia) to pour into the metropolis, like successive applications of syrup to a stack of pancakes, spreading out—other things being equal—in circumferential waves whose advance was matched by the progressive retreat of the other, older, and wealthier residents before them. Thus any part of the landscape which the metropolitan fringe approached would tend to be developed first as an area of single-family residences housing high-status commuters who were backing away from the teeming immigrants, then subsequently as middle-class apartment buildings, later becoming a zone of deteriorating tenements inhabited by a poorer population, and finally, an area of mixed uses into which commercial uses, transient residents, and the very poor could be expected to intrude. Eventually we might behold a central urbanized area, devoted largely to commerce, in which relict structures of previous modes of occupancy were to be found scattered here and there like fossil remnants in a stream delta.

Since the heyday of this school of thought, much criticism and modification have been directed toward it. One of the most powerful is based upon the fact that invasion and succession do not constitute a unidirectional process. Neighborhoods sometimes change from low status to higher status—the "invasion," in other words, occasionally represents the privileged displacing the underprivileged.[2] One social mechanism by which this is notoriously accomplished is urban renewal, which operates through direct political intervention. Another class of instances operates informally through what Jane Jacobs has strikingly called "unslumming."[3] In the process of unslumming, a revolution in perception seems often to be effectuated

"Hippie neighborhoods and urban spatial systems," by George W. Carey, was presented as a paper at the December, 1969 meeting of the American Association for the Advancement of Science, Boston, Mass. This article appears by permission of the author.

The author is Chairman, Division of Urban Studies, Livingston College, Rutgers University, New Brunswick, N.J.

[1] Robert E. Park, Ernest W. Burgess, and R. D. McKenzie, *The City* (Chicago: University of Chicago Press, 1925), pp. 47–62.

[2] Karl E. Taeuber and Alma F. Taeuber, *Negroes in Cities* (Chicago: Aldine Publishing Co., 1965), pp. 99–125.

[3] Jane Jacobs, *The Death and Life of Great American Cities* (New York: Random House, Inc., 1961).

which opens the eyes of individuals to the desirable attributes of neighborhoods previously considered slums—a perceptual revolution which results in the bidding up of land values and the instituting of restoration and development activities in the area affected. The Georgetowns, Greenwich Villages, Brooklyn Heights and Park Slopes are examples.

This paper suggests that the mechanism by which some neighborhoods are unslummed may involve the action of the "hippie" subculture as a deviation-amplifying subsystem acting as a regulator for a deviation-minimizing system.

Many examples abound which apply the concept of deviation-minimizing systems to population data. Such systems operate through negative feedback to produce a tendency toward steady state, after the manner of a thermostat. If the temperature of a room oscillates below a certain set norm, the regulator—or thermostat—detects this deviation and turns on the furnace. Subsequently, if the temperature exceeds the norm, the regulator detects this and shuts off the furnace. Thus the room temperature oscillates about the norm to a greater or lesser degree, depending, in part, on the "stickiness" of the regulator.[4]

Suppose the thermostat is wired differently, however, so as to respond in the same direction as the oscillation, instead of the opposite. The direction of feedback is now positive instead of negative, with unfortunate results to the norm. If the initial disturbance were a drop below the norm, the thermostat would allow the furnace to remain shut off, letting the room temperature continue to drop. If the initial disturbance were to rise above the norm, on the other hand, the furnace would be turned on, heating the room indefinitely. This process is a deviation-amplifying system.[5]

While a deviation-minimizing system of the first sort tends toward a steady state which is independent of the initial condition of the system, the deviation-amplifying system has no built-in tendency toward steady state and is dependent on the initial kick given to it.

As a neighborhood declines in status from a "residential apartment" to a "tenement" district, the decline sometimes proceeds only to the point where rents begin to fall into a range that is attractive to the kind of culturally deviant group that—at various times in our national experience—we have called "hippies," "beatniks" or "bohemians." This kind of group has often turned away from the traditional American profit-oriented work ethic, frequently aspiring to a new ethical, esthetic, or religious orientation. Its deviance from the cultural norm sometimes includes a rejection of conventional family structure. It is possible to view the formation of such a group as a positive-feedback, deviation-amplifying process. Wilkins has remarked that persons who deviate from generally accepted social norms may

> be "defined out" of the system. . . . Definition by the society of an individual as unacceptable may lead to a self-identification as unacceptable to the culture,

[4]Edward S. Deevey, Jr., "General and urban ecology," in Leonard J. Duhl (ed.), *The Urban Condition* (New York: Basic Books, Inc., 1963), pp. 20–32.

[5]Magoroh Maruyama, "The second cybernetics: Deviation-amplifying mutual causal processes," in Walter Buckley (ed.), *Modern Systems Research for the Behavioral Scientist* (Chicago: Aldine Publishing Co., 1968).

and hence the culture as unacceptable to him. When sanctions are applied to the deviants within any society which are perceived by them as extreme, the persons so defined become alienated from the values of the parent system. Sanctions may become devalued. . . . This type of positive feedback process . . . (is) a deviation-amplifying system.[6]

The hippie subculture is one such group. There are others. Wilkins, in his paper, was specifically concerned with the drug subculture, for example.

The culturally deviating group's choice of neighborhood is often related to its special esthetic perspective and life style. Perhaps there are intrinsic properties of the area that constitute amenities to them: unstructured loft space for the creation of new living styles, declining but inherently well-designed old brownstone dwellings, park space, or—especially in the case of Chelsea and the East Village in New York City—proximity to an older bohemia, such as Greenwich Village, where a tradition of cultural permissiveness still remains.

Here they gather, forming a dense social space where the norms of behavior can be partly defined in their terms, and in which most of their daily needs may be met. This effectively minimizes the social sanctions imposed upon them elsewhere. As Wilson has said, their behavior becomes the proper behavior in the public places of the neighborhoods. "Bohemian or 'hippie' sections (despite their loud disclaimers of any interest in either restraint or constraint) establish and sustain a characteristic ethos."[7]

The mass communication media act like extended organs of perception to society as a whole, as they constantly "hunt" over the physical and social landscape. Very rapidly they detect the now-flourishing hippie neighborhood, which—precisely because of its cultural deviance—has produced interesting, exotic, and visible manifestations. Persons of means are now drawn there out of curiosity and nostalgia for some of the values and life ways which—in their view—the hippie may have discovered or rediscovered. This gathering density of middle-class observers implies a gathering density of purchasing power which is equivalent to turning on the economic furnace. Heat, in the form of investment, enters the neighborhood. Shops are established and elements of the housing stock which are rehabilitated are purchased by persons of means—often, at first, from professional worlds which lay emphasis on artistic creativity, later from the more cosmopolitan wing of the upper middle class. As land values and rents are bid up, developers may acquire parcels of tenements suitable for razing and rebuilding in town house or luxury apartment blocks. In the process, previous neighborhood residents are squeezed out. The hippies along with the "old timers" must either move, or exploit the new trend. In this way some hippies will be co-opted into playing a middle-class-shopkeeper role in the ensuing commercialized bohemia of which Greenwich Village in New York is archetypical. Aspects of this process are implicit in the study by Ware.[8]

When the "development temperature" of the area rises to the point where development costs approximate development returns, the economic furnace turns

---

[6]Leslie T. Wilkins, "A behavioral theory of drug taking," in Buckley, *op. cit.*, p. 424.

[7]*Ibid.*, p. 463.

[8]Caroline Ware, *Greenwich Village, 1920-1930* (Boston: Houghton Mifflin Co., 1935).

off after one or two sputterings represented by late investors who fail. In the long-range view, the neighborhood has first fallen below the status norm of the city and then oscillated above it. Presumably the relative status may once again start to dip—only to rise again, if all goes well. Overall, in other words, deviations are corrected, and tendencies towards an oscillating steady state are observed. But the mechanism which achieves this involves a cultural subsystem created by a deviation-amplifying process acting as regulator.

Perhaps the analogy of the thermostat is less apt than one from natural ecology. In a balanced environment, moribund elements are detected by specialized organisms that play a scavenger role, recycling them. In this fashion, the way is paved for a continuation of the steady state. But as the dead matter in one locus is dealt with, the scavengers must also remove. In turn, the scavenging organisms may have assumed that role through evolutionary development. But biological evolution has been cited as being a deviation-amplifying process in many ways.[9]

This suggests to us that the tendency toward steady state in some social systems is maintained through regulatory subsystems which are partially evolved through deviation-amplifying processes. Or, in other words, in terms of our example, the hippie may be the vanguard of the middle class as well as its offshoot.

12. Stages of succession

OTIS DUDLEY DUNCAN AND BEVERLY DUNCAN

CONCEPT OF SUCCESSION

An area undergoes "succession" when one type of land use replaces another. The term "residential succession" means, more specifically, the replacement of one population group in an area by another. The initial population and its successor may differ with respect to economic function, social status, ethnic or national background, race, or other socially significant characteristics or a combination of characteristics.[1] In [our] study, . . . attention [was] focused on racial succession, and the question [was] raised of whether racial succession is associated with changes in other

---

[9]Maruyama, *op. cit.*, p. 308.

Abridged and edited from Otis Dudley Duncan and Beverly Duncan, *The Negro Population of Chicago: A Study of Residential Succession* (Chicago: University of Chicago Press, 1957), pp. 108–132. Copyright © 1957 by the University of Chicago. Reprinted by permission.

The senior author is Professor of Sociology, University of Michigan, Ann Arbor, Mich.

[1]For a discussion of the concept of succession, see Harold A. Gibbard, "The status factor in residential successions," *American Journal of Sociology,* 46:835–842 (May, 1941).

aspects of population composition. Accompanying residential succession may be changes in the density of population, the composition of households, the way in which residential structures are used, the character of local institutions, and the like. Such changes, however, are not assumed to be invariable concomitants of succession; their occurrence and intensity must be established by research.

Succession is a normal aspect of city growth.[2] Growth requires areal expansion, hence a shift of some areas from non-residential to residential use. Growth of commercial and industrial functions leads them, in turn, to encroach upon previously residential areas, particularly in the belt surrounding the center of the city, which is referred to as the "zone in transition," but in other parts of the city as well. A population group with high socioeconomic status often vacates a residential area, as the area ages and its housing becomes less desirable, in favor of newer residential developments; the area may then be taken over by a group of somewhat lower status. Cressey has shown that each of the major groups of immigrants to Chicago originally took up residence near the city's center and then moved toward the periphery over a period of years. Many areas near the center have therefore undergone residential succession, in terms of ethnic characteristics, several times.[3]

To make the notion of residential succession quite explicit, consider the following simplified situation: During year t_0 a given area is exclusively inhabited by members of population group A. In year t_1, some members of group B move into the area, and, by the end of year t_n all the residents of the area are members of group B. We would then say that over an n-year period the area underwent a succession from an area of A residents to an area of B residents. In practice, the initial and terminal dates of a succession cycle can seldom be dated precisely, both for lack of data and because the displacement of group A by group B may never be 100 percent complete. Other complications may arise, too. The area under study may, throughout its history, be inhabited by several groups. Yet a unidirectional change in the relative importance of these groups may signify that succession is occurring, even though an entire, simple cycle of succession may never be completed. For example, group C may begin to take over the area from group B before the latter has completely superseded group A. There is also the theoretical possibility that population turnover may cease at some point short of complete replacement of one group by another. The area may then have a mixed population in relatively stable proportions for a period of years. Little is known about the conditions necessary to produce a stable mixed area, and one must be careful not to assume that a given area is, in fact, one of this type, without making certain that the mixture is homogeneous, i.e., that there are no subdivisions of the area in which practically complete succession has occurred.

The concept of succession, as defined here, does not intrinsically involve considerations of conflict between the initial population and its successor or of resistance

---

[2]See E. W. Burgess, "The growth of the city," in R. E. Park *et al., The City* (Chicago: University of Chicago Press, 1925); E. W. Burgess, "Residential segregation in American cities," *Annals of the American Academy of Political and Social Science,* 140:105–115 (November, 1928).

[3]Paul F. Cressey, "Population succession in Chicago, 1898–1930," *American Journal of Sociology,* 44:59–69 (July, 1938); Richard G. Ford, "Population succession in Chicago," *American Journal of Sociology,* 56:156–160 (September, 1950).

by the former. In some instances succession does indeed involve overt conflict and organized resistance, but these phenomena may be so unimportant as to go unnoticed in other cases. Rather than beg the question by definition, it seems best to regard succession as involving population turnover, pure and simple, and to leave it an open question for research to determine whether and under what conditions succession is accompanied by intergroup friction.[4]

It should be clear that the rate of succession may be quite variable, i.e., the complete cycle may take only a short while or may occur over a long period of years. Moreover, the population turnover may be rapid at first and then slow down, or vice versa. Hence the time relationships involved in succession become a subject for study. Another possibility is that any period group B may move into an area more rapidly than group A moves out, and the gross population density may consequently increase. Unless there is simultaneously a succession from non-residential to residential uses of land, net density must likewise increase. In fact, in some types of succession it may well be that an increase in residential density is a necessary concomitant, if it is true that only by using the land more intensively can the incoming group afford to occupy the area.

Ideally, to study residential succession in an area, one would like to have a large number of observations on the characteristics of the area in the form of a time series covering the period during which succession occurs. In practice, data are likely to be available only for a few, widely separated points in time. When succession occurs rapidly, this may mean that an entire cycle takes place within a period between two observations, and one has, so to speak, only "before and after snapshots" of the situation rather than the ideal "moving picture" of the succession process.

Specifically, with the decennial census data used in [our] study, one can identify areas which turned over from virtually complete white occupancy in 1940 to virtually complete non-white occupancy in 1950. In other areas succession may have been well advanced by 1940 and completed by 1950; or the turnover of population may not have begun by 1940 but [been] well on its way by 1950; and so on.

STAGES OF SUCCESSION

Succession is considered to have four main stages: penetration, invasion, consolidation, and piling up—recognizing, of course, that succession logically need not continue through all stages and may be interrupted at any point and that there is no sharp dividing line between any two consecutive stages.

"Penetration" is the stage of initial entry of Negroes into an area occupied by whites. "Invasion" occurs when penetration is followed by the movement into the area of substantial numbers of Negroes; in this study no tract is considered "in-

---

[4]Both Burgess, "Residential segregation in American cities," and Gibbard, "The status factor in residential successions," describe stages of succession that involve resistance of the old residents of the area to the influx of new residents. In this study it has seemed preferable to delineate stages solely on the basis of the extent of population turnover. For a methodological study of racial tension in relation to succession, see Shirley A. Star, "Interracial tension in two areas of Chicago: An exploratory approach to the measurement of interracial tension" (unpublished Ph.D. dissertation, University of Chicago, 1950).

vaded" until it has at least 250 non-white residents. "Consolidation" refers to the continued increase in number and proportion of Negroes in an area, after invasion has been accomplished. Consolidation may proceed to virtually complete occupancy of the area by Negroes, after which, if Negroes continue to increase in numbers, the stage of "piling up" is reached.

The first stage—penetration—is disregarded in the analysis. Data on non-white population characteristics are not available for a tract until it has sufficient numbers of non-whites to place it beyond the penetration stage.

.   .   .   .   .

With regard to the remaining stages, the spatial arrangement of the tracts . . . is about what one would expect from a knowledge of the pattern of expansion of Negro settlement in Chicago. The piling-up tracts, with the exception of one in the northwest corner of the Near West Side community, are located in the center of the South Side "Black Belt." Most of the late-consolidation tracts are adjacent to or near the piling-up tracts in the "Black Belt" and on the Near West Side; the remainder are found in the southern part of the Near West Side, in the "Lilydale" Negro community, and in the Negro settlement in Morgan Park. The consolidation tracts are more widely scattered, appearing not only on the periphery of the piling-up and consolidation tracts in the "Black Belt" and in the Near West Side community, but also in the Near North Side, Englewood, West Englewood, South Chicago, and Morgan Park communities and adjacent to the older portion of the Lilydale settlement. The early-consolidation and invasion tracts are also somewhat scattered, although the bulk of them appear to be extensions of the "Black Belt" and Near West Side areas of Negro settlement.

In interpreting the results of our succession study, several things need to be kept in mind. First, the concept of stages of succession is an abstract and somewhat idealized scheme which, at best, can describe the actual process only approximately. Second, census tracts are arbitrary units, not at all homogeneous in size of area or population. Their classification according to stage of succession is to a considerable extent a matter of judgment, tempered by the necessity of working within the limits of the available data. Above all, the fact that the time period covered is fixed at ten years means that some tracts may proceed through a whole cycle of succession or several stages thereof, while others go through but a single stage. For example, tract 624 changed from 0.2 to 98.4 percent non-white between 1940 and 1950, while tract 450 changed from 0.3 to 12.4 percent non-white over the decade. Yet both are classified as "invasion" tracts because both were invaded only after 1940. To some extent, the study design overcomes the limitations of the data, for both cross-sectional comparisons among the several categories of tracts and measures of change over a ten-year period are possible. Even this combination, however, affords only an approximation to the theoretically preferable plan of following each tract through an entire succession cycle.

A further limitation on the study is occasioned by the lack of certain data. [Table 1] summarizes the situation in this regard for the five classes of tracts. The symbol "a" means that census data on population and housing characteristics are available separately for whites and non-whites. The symbol "b" means that data on characteristics of the total population essentially represent non-whites only (piling-up tracts) or whites only (invasion tracts, 1940). The symbol "x" refers to the

Table 1

	1940	1950
Piling up	a,b	a,b
Late consolidation	a	a
Consolidation	a	a
Early consolidation	x	a
Invasion	b	a

absence of data adequate to describe either the white or the non-white population separately (except for one or two characteristics). The most complete data are those for the total tract population in 1950, the second most complete those for total population in 1940. The data available by color are materially less detailed, especially those for 1940. This means that the best information (in terms of coverage of the data) is available for the piling-up tracts, and the poorest information for the early-consolidation tracts, with the other three groups falling in an intermediate position.

Despite these limitations, our results indicate that in the early stages of succession the movement of Negroes into formerly white areas is led by those who have lived in the city for some time rather than by recent migrants. This is not in contradiction to the observation that tracts in the later stages of succession have a higher proportion of migrants in their total population than those in the early stages. The proportion of migrants in the former group is low because their Negro population is large to begin with and they may be unable to absorb as many migrants relative to their initial population as can areas where Negroes are displacing whites.

In summary, the fragmentary data on migration that are available permit the following inferences: The bulk of the Negro migrants to Chicago enter areas of established Negro settlement—by and large, tracts in the late stages of succession. The migrants contribute disproportionately to the Negro population growth of these areas, as contrasted to areas of invasion and early consolidation. Conversely, older residents, rather than recently arrived migrants, constitute a disproportionate number of the Negroes moving into areas of former white occupancy.

13. Toward a stage theory of urban growth

DAVID L. BIRCH

. . . . .

STAGE THEORY

A *stage theory,* in its simplest form, is based on the premise that each element in a system evolves through a sequence of stages over time. The elements might be plants in a field, individuals in a society, stars in a galaxy, or nations in a world economy. Following Kuznets' (1965) guidelines, in a proper stage theory: (1) the characteristics of each stage should be distinct and empirically testable; and (2) the analytical relationship of any stage to its predecessor or successor should be well-defined—that is, it must be possible to identify what processes cause an element to move from one stage to the next.

In the stage theory of urban growth proposed here, an *element* is a neighborhood in a metropolitan region. It is hypothesized that each neighborhood changes character over time, following a well-defined sequence. When neighborhoods are aggregated, regional patterns become apparent. When neighborhoods are looked at in detail, the history of human flows through them can be documented and related to the aging process. Thus, it is possible to match physical development against social change and trace the effect of one upon the other.

The promise of a stage theory has not gone unrecognized. Burgess put forth a concentric ring theory in 1929. Homer Hoyt (1939) found it useful to superimpose radial sectors over Burgess' rings. Neither Burgess nor Hoyt paid much attention, however, to the evolutionary process experienced by particular neighborhoods.

In 1959, Hoover and Vernon took a major step forward in *Anatomy of a Metropolis.* After describing in empirical detail the trends and forces which they observed in the New York metropolitan area, they suggested, in a section titled "How Neighborhoods Evolve," five stages of development:

Stage 1. Residential development in single-family houses.

Stage 2. Transition in which there is substantial new construction and population growth in the area but in which a high and increasing proportion of the new housing is apartments so that average density is increasing.

Stage 3. A down-grading stage, in which old housing (both multifamily and single) is being adapted to greater density use than it was originally designed for.

Stage 4. The thinning-out stage . . . most of the shrinkage comes about through a decline in household size.

Stage 5. The renewal stage, in which obsolete areas of housing, after arriving at Stage 4, are being replaced by new multifamily housing.

Abridged and edited from David L. Birch, "Toward a stage theory of urban growth," *Journal of the American Institute of Planners,* 37:78–87 (March, 1971). Copyright © 1971 by American Institute of Planners. Reprinted by permission.

The author is Associate Professor of Business Administration, Harvard University, Boston, Mass.

Hoover and Vernon also began to relate, in general terms, the migration of different ethnic and social groups to the changing of neighborhoods. They noted the shift from white to black paralleling a shift from Stage 2 to Stage 3, the predominance of older couples in Stage 4, and the movement of younger and wealthier couples from older to younger neighborhoods in search of open space.

These proposed stage definitions were based on observations of different neighborhoods at more or less the same point in time and were buttressed by whatever time series and small area statistics were to be had. Nevertheless, they remained conjectures for lack of more refined, time-series data.

This article describes the development and testing of a stage theory based on New Haven data. It has been possible quantitatively to define stages quite similar to those of Hoover and Vernon and to show that: (1) the tendency for any given neighborhood to move from one stage to the next is quite strong; and (2) the location and movement of various ethnic and social groups between and among neighborhoods in different stages of development can be identified.

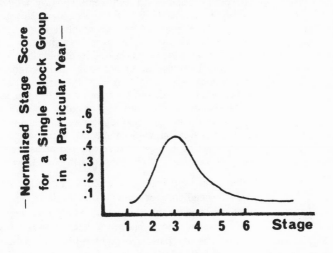

Figure 1
Example of a stage intensity score

APPROACH

In defining stages, the choice of parameters is critical. After some preliminary factor analysis and mapping, it was decided to follow Hoover and Vernon's lead and define stages in terms of residential types and population densities. The hope, supported by the initial analysis, was that other properties, such as ethnic concentrations and location of jobs, could be expressed in terms of the stages so defined.

Initial experiments uncovered six stages of residential development in New Haven. A description of the actual parameters and equations used to define the stages for analysis purposes is found in the Appendix. The stages may be described as follows:

Stage 1: *Rural.* This stage is characterized by low population densities and a predominance of single family units.

Stage 2: *First wave of development.* Subdivision begins with high rates of new construction, predominantly single-family units.

Stage 3: *Fully developed, high-quality residential.* The initial development has run its full course. In some cases, single-family units still prevail, but densities are considerably higher than in Stage 2. In other cases, an increasing number of multi-unit structures have been built. In either case, property values and rents are close to their maximum relative to other neighborhoods in the area.

Stage 4: *Packing.* As the age of the structures built during Stage 3 increases and rents fall, lower income groups begin to inhabit the dwellings, and, in order to bridge the gap between their old and their new rents, more people pack into the units than they were originally designed to hold. Densities are at their maximum. In many cities these areas might be called "new slums."

Stage 5: *Thinning.* By now, the buildings in Stage 4 have deteriorated still further, and the children of low-income parents who originally moved into them are leaving, probably for a Stage 4 or Stage 2 area somewhere else in the city. Population declines absolutely, leaving older couples behind. These areas might be called "old slums."

Stage 6: *Recapture.* At some point the land occupied by an old slum becomes too valuable to justify its use as an old slum, and its inhabitants become too weak politically to hold on to it. Property is then reacquired, leveled or rehabilitated, and put to more efficient use, such as high-income apartments or office buildings or public housing. When recapture is completed, the area may appear to have many of the properties of a Stage 3 area, but with significantly higher densities. At some point there must be a Stage 7, as recaptured areas themselves begin to decay, but this has not yet happened in New Haven.

Obviously there is great oversimplification involved, and it is not surprising, when we consider the size of the neighborhoods and the time it takes a neighborhood to evolve, that at any point in time a neighborhood would have the characteristics of more than one stage. If the stage concept has any validity, however, we would expect that, for any particular area at a particular point in time, the characteristics of one stage would dominate, that the characteristics of the preceding and succeeding stages would be the next most prevalent, and that evidence of other stages would exist only in small traces. Or, if, for each area, we computed the extent to which the characteristics of each stage were present at a point in time—a *stage intensity score*—and if these scores were made comparable (through normalization) and plotted, we would expect the resulting curve to have the shape shown in Figure 1. In other words, the block group in Figure 1 is predominantly a high-quality, moderately dense area (Stage 3) with some new single-family development still in process (Stage 2) and the first signs of packing (Stage 4). Characteristics of all other stages are present only to a nominal degree.

RESULTS

The actual curves for five randomly selected block groups are shown in Figure 2. As can be seen in the figure, the curves do have the unimodal properties described,

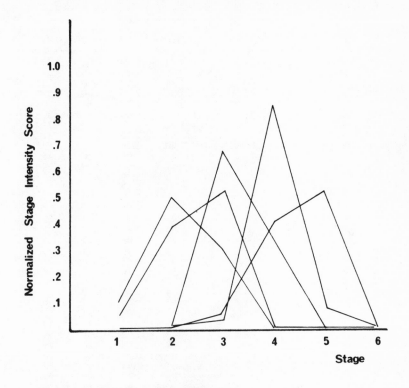

Figure 2
Five sample neighborhood (block group) stage intensity curves

and they are relatively "tight," that is they tend to peak at one particular stage and fall off quickly on either side.

Since the stage intensity scores have been normalized, it is possible to view the stage intensity curves as probability density functions, and to view the Stage 3 "score" as the probability that a neighborhood is in Stage 3 at a particular point in time. It is interesting to interpret the mean of this density function. The mean is simply the weighted-average "age" of the neighborhood on the stage scale. In Figure 1, the block group has an age of, say, 3.1.

If the stage theory is valid, we would expect each small area to increase in average age between successive time periods. Since some areas are changing faster than others, there is no reason to expect equal "stage aging" between two fixed calendar dates, but there should be no neighborhood that moves backward. . . .

Unfortunately, block group data are not uniformly available prior to 1967. Tract data are, however, and the aging test was performed on tracts, using the 1960–1967 interval. The results are shown in Table 1. With two exceptions, all tracts aged. The major exception—Tract 2—is in the process of being redeveloped. Thus, in 1967, it took on many of the properties of a rural area, reflecting large amounts of vacant and/or unpopulated land.

Table 1

Stage aging from 1960 to 1967 by tract for the New Haven SMSA

Tract	Age in 1960	Age in 1967	Age difference	Tract	Age in 1960	Age in 1967	Age difference
1	4.24	4.53	.29	32	2.43	2.52	.09
2	4.83	4.73	−.10	33	2.24	2.29	.05
3	4.03	4.63	.60	34	2.17	2.20	.03
4	3.93	4.03	.90	35	2.79	3.05	.26
5	4.13	4.14	.01	36	2.62	2.62	.00
6	4.11	4.12	.01	37	1.84	2.16	.32
7	4.21	5.18	.97	38	2.01	2.23	.22
8	3.90	4.00	.10	39	2.12	2.43	.31
9	3.90	3.98	.08	40	2.08	2.27	.19
10	3.13	3.26	.13	41	1.91	2.36	.45
11	2.52	2.75	.23	42	2.68	2.98	.29
12	3.36	3.47	.11	43	3.39	3.49	.10
13	2.93	3.56	.63	44	3.17	3.33	.16
14	3.67	3.92	.25	45	2.89	2.93	.04
15	3.95	4.11˙	.16	46	2.95	2.96	.01
16	4.18	5.04	.86	47	2.54	2.83	.29
17	4.29	4.29	.00	48	2.72	2.74	.02
18	3.20	3.80	.60	49	1.69	1.93	.24
19	3.46	3.74	.28	50	1.88	2.11	.23
20	4.12	4.33	.21	51	2.38	3.02	.64
21	4.31	4.65	.34	52	2.26	3.22	−.04
22	4.51	4.64	.13	53[a]			
23	4.11	4.16	.05	54	3.09	3.32	.23
24	4.17	4.38	.21	55	3.47	3.57	.10
25	3.96	4.12	.16	56	2.98	3.21	.23
26	2.84	3.27	.43	57	2.46	2.79	.33
27	3.33	3.40	.07	58	2.73	3.04	.31
28	2.81	2.89	.08	59	3.10	3.30	.20
29	2.55	3.22	.67	60	3.26	3.50	.24
30	2.12	2.36	.24	61	3.44	3.57	.13
31	2.64	2.83	.19	62	1.51	1.58	.07

[a] Tract 53 is a large hospital and has been excluded from the analysis.

The geographical pattern of aging has long been of interest. According to Burgess and, to a certain extent, Hoover and Vernon, at any point in time we would expect to find older neighborhoods concentrated in the central city, middle-aged neighborhoods ringing the central city, and younger neighborhoods in the further reaches of the region. . . . In the New Haven SMSA, . . . [We found] that the relative position of the younger and older areas is more or less as predicted, but that the pattern is hardly one of concentric circles. Rather, we see a series of protrusions and subdevelopments. If this pattern is typical of other cities, it suggests that the standard central city/suburb division used in much urban analysis misses most of the interesting developments with the region and that the case for disaggregated data should be made more strongly than ever.

So far, we have gained considerable support for the notion that tract-sized neighborhoods evolve through a predictable sequence over time. We have not, however, verified the stage theory, at least in terms of Kuznets' guidelines. In the first place, if neighborhoods truly move through stages, then they should remain stable for relatively long periods and shift quickly to another stage. While we note great variations in the rate of aging in Table 1, we have no idea what the pattern looks like for individual neighborhoods over a long period of time. We can conjecture that the shifts from rural to the first wave of development and from thinning to recapture are probably quite abrupt, and that the shifts from Stage 2 to higher densities and the subsequent thinning process are likely to be more gradual. Further research will be required, however, to establish that these hunches are, in fact, correct.

Second, we have not yet been able to identify and quantify what specific factors cause a neighborhood to move from one stage to the next. Again, further research will be required to relate the flows of migrants into and out of the SMSA and the changing structure of the economy to the evolution of individual neighborhoods.

Finally, while the data show neighborhoods progressing with great regularity along the stage scale, this certainly does not ensure that all buildings or blocks within a tract-sized area will follow exactly the same pattern. In fact, there are numerous instances where a family or a group of families have "recaptured" small sections of a neighborhood before it reached Stage 6. Thus, small-scale movements from Stage 5 to Stage 4 or Stage 3 are common. Although such movements were not sufficiently numerous in New Haven between 1960 and 1967 to reverse an entire tract, in some instances they may well have slowed the rate of evolution.

In summary, while we are still a long way from verifying a full stage theory, the New Haven data strongly suggest that tract-sized neighborhoods seem to progress positively along a scale based on the stage concept. The question remains: can we meaningfully match this physical evolution to social changes?

While it has not yet been possible to examine all forms of social change, a number of checks were made on the Hoover-Vernon postulates. As mentioned earlier, Hoover and Vernon suggested a model of the movement of individual family units through stages. According to their model, wealthy families have more choices, and by and large they choose to use their wealth to purchase low-density living. The motives behind this choice are complicated and have to do with a desire for more space, better schools for children, and a basic American instinct for privacy. As one generation of housing becomes rundown or too closely packed, the wealthy will continuously open up new land and build new housing.

The poor, in Hoover and Vernon's analysis, have far fewer choices. They cannot afford the high costs of new construction. They must, therefore, inherit the rundown, lower cost housing abandoned by the wealthy. To the extent that they have large families, though, they too will push outward for lower density and better schools.

At any point in time, then, we would expect to find the better educated, wealthier families living in younger neighborhoods; poorer, less well-educated families living in older neighborhoods; and families with more children, regardless of wealth, living in younger neighborhoods. It is clear from Table 2 that, for New Haven, all of these phenomena occur as predicted. In each case, there is a smooth gradient in the anticipated direction from the younger to the older neighborhoods.

If there were no mobility within the region, this would be a discouraging finding. As neighborhoods aged, as we have seen that they do, families at all levels would experience a frustrating decline in their environment relative to their aspira-

Table 2
Income, educational achievement, and family size by stage age

Stage age	Average family income ($000)	Average years school completed	Average family size
0–2.5	12.2	11.8	3.8
2.5–3	11.3	11.4	3.6
3–3.5	10.0	10.7	3.4
3.5–4	9.2	10.1	3.4
Over 4	7.8	9.8	3.3

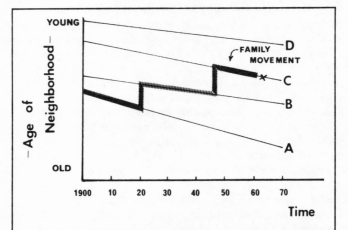

A family enters the area in Neighborhood A in 1900. The family's resources grow while Neighborhoods A and B decline. (The straight line rates of decline in the fringe are simplified for illustration.) Finally, the jump from A to B is possible, and it is made. In the same fashion, the family moves to Neighborhood C, where it remains until the death of the family head. To an outside observer, or to a family rooted in Neighborhood A, or frequently to the mayor, Neighborhood A, and the city as a whole, are declining. Our family, however, is experiencing, on the average, continuous upward mobility. The region is serving its needs very well. The fact that certain parts of the region—most notably the older sections of the central city—are suffering in the process is of little consequence to the family.

Figure 3
An illustrative example of family movement

tions. Implicit in Hoover and Vernon's model, however, is a constant shifting of individual families from older to younger stages, which might be diagramed in simplified form as shown in Figure 3.

While it is not possible to trace, with existing census data, movement of individual families, it is possible to identify specific groups that entered the system at well-known times and places, to predict their pattern of location at a later date, and to check the prediction against actual data. Two quite different groups in New Haven afford a good opportunity for this kind of check—the Italians and the blacks. The Italians constitute a large immigrant group which has been in New Haven for some time. We would expect, therefore, that by 1967 they would be found in neighborhoods of all ages, but that, due to their lower starting point on the economic ladder, their incomes would still be lower. Table 3 shows that our expectation has some validity. An Italian neighborhood has been defined as any block group which contains greater than 40 percent Italian foreign stock—the median for New Haven as a whole. We see that there are Italian concentrations in all neighborhood age groups, and that, as with the population as a whole, wealthier Italians use their wealth to live in younger areas. Furthermore, the average family income in Italian neighborhoods is consistently lower than the corresponding SMSA average.

Table 3

Average family income versus stage age for Italian neighborhoods in the New Haven SMSA

Stage age	Number of neighborhoods	Average family income for Italian neighborhoods ($000)	Average family income for all neighborhoods ($000)
0–2.5	41	11.1	12.2
2.5–3	49	10.4	11.3
3–3.5	66	9.5	10.0
3.5–4	41	8.7	9.2
Over 4	72	7.3	7.8

The Italian experience thus offers considerable support for the Hoover-Vernon model. A much better test, however, would be the experience of blacks. They are a relatively new immigrant group and thus should be less well along in the process of upward mobility. According to Hoover and Vernon, however, as economic gains are made by the black community, its more prosperous members should be motivated to move to younger neighborhoods for many of the same reasons that the Italians did so before them. In contrast is the view held by many analysts and observers that blacks must forever remain trapped in the less desirable sections of the region, due to racial prejudice and lack of economic opportunity.

We can see from Table 4 that blacks are, in fact, concentrated in the older stages within the central city and that they form a good test group. The next question, then, is whether or not they are moving upward and outward through the system.

A first sign of movement appears in Table 4, where we note that the suburban concentrations, small as they are, are in the middle-aged neighborhoods, not the older ones. This suggests that blacks who do move out do not simply move into neighborhoods similar to the ones they left behind.

The next question is: how fast is the movement of blacks into suburbs taking place? Recent data at the national level (Table 5) indicate that, within recent years, black growth rates in suburban areas are rising sharply. This is reflected in the jump in the growth rate from 0.7 percent per year to 8.0 percent per year. While these data are based on a fairly thin sample, the 100 percent sample in New Haven revealed an average growth rate among suburban blacks of 19.3 percent per year between 1960 and 1967.

This very rapid suburban growth would be of little consequence to the blacks, of course, if it were not accompanied by an improved way of life. Outward movement, in short, is of little value without upward movement. The movement into middle-aged rather than older areas suggests that improvement is indeed taking place. Table 6 gives a much stronger indication of improved life style. For each racial mix, suburban neighborhoods have higher average family incomes than corresponding central city neighborhoods. Of greatest interest is the high family income in the 10 to 30 percent black suburban neighborhoods, and the relatively low income in the neighborhoods more than 30 percent black. The over-30 percent-black suburban neighborhoods are almost universally dominated by public housing projects, accounting for the relatively low income. The 10 to 30 percent black suburban neighborhoods are almost all privately settled areas, a natural product of the mobility process. Further data on years of school completed and value of owner-occupied dwelling units reveal a similar pattern.

Table 4
Percent black in central city and suburbs by stage age

	Percent black	
Stage age	Central city	Suburbs
0–2.5	..	.8
2.5–3	1.2	2.7
3–3.5	2.9	2.5
3.5–4	14.5	1.7
Over 4	26.9	.2
Average	19.5	2.0

Table 5
Average annual change in U.S. metropolitan population,
1960-1966 and 1966-1968

	Average annual change	
	1960—1966	1966—1968
White		
Central city	−.03	−1.0
Suburbs	3.0	2.0
Black		
Central city	3.4	1.0
Suburbs	.7	8.0

Table 6
Average family income for central city and suburb on block groups
in the New Haven SMSA, by percent black

	Average family income ($000)	
Percent black	Central city	Suburbs
0—.01	10.2	10.9
.01—2	9.7	10.9
2—5	10.1	10.5
5—10	8.4	9.2
10—30	7.4	11.2
Over 30	7.6	8.0

Of great interest is the pattern of southern immigration. The experience of the central city is as expected. A significant proportion (50 percent) of blacks coming to the area come from the South, and it is reasonable to expect them to settle in existing black neighborhoods. The substantial southern migration into the suburban black areas was not expected. Evidently better educated, wealthier blacks are bypassing the old, central city way stations and are migrating directly into more attractive suburban neighborhoods. Should this pattern continue, it would, of course, further accelerate the rate of black suburban growth. If the phenomenon is a national one, as the data in Table 5 suggest, the results of the 1970 census could considerably alter our perception of this nation's racial problems.

Finally, the spatial pattern of suburban black growth is of great interest. Recent surveys have suggested that blacks tend to live in clusters in the suburbs, as do many other ethnic groups. Figure 4 is a three-dimensional view of the New Haven SMSA in which higher black concentrations are represented as higher altitudes. A pattern of clusters or enclaves is clear. A closer look at the data shows that, in many cases, suburban black enclaves are located in neighborhoods which were formerly oc- cupied by poorer Italians living in relatively inexpensive housing. In short, at least in New Haven, a rising economic position has given blacks the same kind of opportunities for mobility available to other immigrant groups before them and they appear to be capitalizing on them in the same way.

Figure 4
Percent black in the New Haven SMSA, 1967

CONCLUSION

Neighborhoods in New Haven appear to evolve through a predictable sequence of stages over time. Furthermore, an understanding of this aging process appears to be very useful in anticipating the movements of different social and economic groups and thus in predicting the aggregate pattern of metropolitan development.

To some the stage theory may seem pessimistic, foretelling the inevitable decay of urban regions. For someone who is rooted to a particular neighborhood, it is indeed pessimistic. Neighborhoods do seem to evolve, and eventually decay. To those on the move, however, evolution is hardly a drawback. It is the process which brings higher quality neighborhoods within their reach. What may appear as decay to an older Italian couple earning $5,000 a year, or to a city planner, may be viewed as opportunity by a black whose income is just beginning to rise.

Whatever viewpoint is taken, the research in New Haven strongly suggests that the evolution takes place with remarkable regularity and that upwardly mobile classes of all sorts take advantage of it in meeting their needs for open space and a more satisfying environment.

APPENDIX

Toward a Stage Theory of Urban Growth

The stage intensity scores used in the New Haven analysis are derived using a three-step process.

First, raw intensity scores are computed for each block group or tract (depending upon the availability of data) for each stage. The key to developing the stage score formulas is to select variables and analytical relationships that identify, unambiguously and consistently, the dominant characteristics of each stage. The formulas presented below were used in computing the data for the figures and tables in this article.

Stage 1: Rural Low density and the absence of multiunit structures are the dominant characteristics of Stage 1. The formula is:

Stage 1 Score $= 1000/Density \times Exp$ (–1 $\times$ % *MUS*/10),

where density is measured in population per square mile and *"Exp"* stands for the exponential operator—that is, Exp(–1 $\times$ % MUS/10) is shorthand for:

$$e^{\frac{-1 \times \text{Percent Multiunit Structures}}{10}}$$

The exponential function serves to give low scores to areas with high proportions of multiunit structures. The "10" is a scaling factor which governs the rate at which the exponential function "falls off." Similar functions are used in the other stage score formulas.

Stage 2: First Wave of Development The key indicators of initial development are the presence of new, single-family housing and the absence of multiunit structures. We are thus led to the formula:

Stage 2 Score $= \% NH \times \%$ *SFU* $\times Exp$ (–1 $\times$ % *MUS*/15),

where % *NH* is the percent of new housing in the area, % *SFU* is the percent of single family units in the area, and once again, an exponential "filter" is used on multiunit structures.

Stage 3: Fully Developed, High Quality, Residential The well developed, high-quality area is characterized by high rents and moderate densities. To define moderate density, an exponential filter is used, this time falling off with the absolute value *(Abs)* of the difference from 6,500 people per square mile,

Stage 3 Score $= \% HR \times Exp$ [–1 $\times$ *Abs* (Density–6,500/6,000)], where % HR stands for the percent of rental units in the top category (which is adjusted over time for inflation), and the fall-off of the exponential function is governed by the constant 6,000.

Stage 4: Packing The newly developing slum is characterized as having high density and a low percentage of high-rent units thus:

Stage 4 Score = ($Density$/1,000) $\times$ (100 – % HR).

Stage 5: Thinning After considerable experimentation, it was discovered that the only consistent indicator of thinning in a neighborhood was an actual population decline and that the extent of the decline was a good measure of the extent of thinning. We are thus led to the formula:

Stage 5 Score = Max (0, % PD),

where % PD is the percent population decline and Max is an operator which assigns a score of zero if the population is level or growing and the value of the percentage decline (with a positive sign) if, in fact, the population declined.

Stage 6: Recapture This was perhaps the most difficult stage to express analytically because recaptured areas generally look like younger areas. It turned out, however, that the recaptured areas tended to have much higher densities, reflecting perhaps the high cost of recapture, and that they were predominated by rental units. The following formula was thus used:

Stage 6 Score = % NH $\times$ Exp [–1 $\times$ Abs ($Density$ – 20,000)/5,000] $\times$ Exp [–1 $\times$ Abs (% ROU –80)/30],

where % NH is, as before, the percent of new housing, the first exponential filter singles out areas with high density (centering around 20,000 in New Haven), and the second exponential filter picks up areas with high percents of renter-occupied units (%ROU).

Once the raw scores have been calculated for all areas, they are scaled so that, for each stage, the highest score is 100 and the lowest score is zero. To take an example, one block group had a density of 4,905, a percent multiunit structures of 84, a percent new housing of 5, a percent of single family units of 16, a percent of high rent units of 18, a population decline of 26 percent, and a percent renter occupied units of 98. Its raw stage scores were thus:

Stage	Score
1	.0
2	.3
3	12.6
4	401.6
5	26.0
6	.1

After each score was scaled using comparable scores of other areas, the scaled scores were:

Stage	Scaled score
1	.0
2	.0
3	15.8
4	19.1
5	32.5
6	.0

In order to convert these scaled scores into probability density functions for further use, the scaled scores are normalized so that they add to 1.0, yielding:

Stage	Normalized stage score
1	.00
2	.00
3	.24
4	.28
5	.48
6	.00

This completes the scoring procedure, unless a weighted average "age" of the neighborhood is desired. If it is, the number of the stage is weighted by its normalized score to yield the weighted average. In this case it is 4.2.

REFERENCES

Burgess, E. W. "Urban areas." In T. V. Smith and L. D. White (eds.), *Chicago: An Experiment in Social Science Research.* Chicago: University of Chicago Press, 1929. Pp. 114–118.

Hoover, E. M., and Vernon, R. *Anatomy of a Metropolis.* Cambridge, Mass.: Harvard University Press, 1959. Pp. 190–207.

Hoyt, H. *The Structure and Growth of Residential Neighborhoods in American Cities.* Washington, D.C.: Federal Housing Administration, 1939.

Kuznets, S. *Economic Growth and Structure: Selected Essays.* New York: W. W. Norton & Co., Inc., 1965. Pp. 213–216.

C. GOVERNMENT

The role of government in providing services and allocating public resources is seldom more directly felt than at the local level. City politics and municipal services, whether involving the election of school board members or the schedule for garbage collections, often have an immediate and visible impact on everyday affairs. Unlike politicians at the national level, a city's political leaders constantly live close to their constituents and cannot avoid the attentive and sometimes harsh eye of the local press and media. The mayor of the city may even choose to associate himself directly with the welfare of individual people, such as by mourning the death of a policeman or fireman or personally intervening to reduce community conflicts. Finally, the time lag between a city government's actions and the policy impact on the city's population can be short, further reinforcing the closeness of the city government to the lives of citizens.

City government thus forms another major component of the city. The first question that arises is the adequacy of political leadership, primarily as represented by the mayor, and James Cunningham (Selection 14) compares the performance of four mayors as effective leaders. In addition, the general role of the mayor may also be changing. Historically, the mayor's office has been a political dead end.[1] However, much public attention has recently been given to mayors across the country, particularly as young and reform-minded men have been elected mayors and as the management of the city has become more complex.[2] It is too early yet to make any predictions about whether the combination of young, vigorous talent and the increasing importance of cities in national affairs will radically transform the traditional role, but the possibility remains that in the future mayors will

---

[1]Marilyn Gittell, "Metropolitan mayor: Dead end," *Public Administration Review,* 23: 20–24 (March, 1963).

[2]See, for example, Jeffrey Hadden, Louis H. Masotti, and Victor Thiessen, "The making of the Negro mayors, 1967," *Transaction,* 5:21–30 (January–February, 1968), and Leonard Ruchelman (ed.), *Big City Mayors: The Crisis in Urban Politics* (Bloomington: Indiana University Press, 1969).

collectively become a stronger political force and will individually use the mayor's office as a step toward more important ventures.

As in the previous sections of this reader, the selections on city government attempt to capture some of the intricate relationships among urban institutions and processes. The continued presence of ethnic identifications, for instance, has had much to do with the style and structure of the party system and the urban bureaucracy. Elmer Cornwell, Jr., (Selection 15) describes the relationship between the old-style political machine and immigration. For Cornwell, the machine would not have been nearly as prominent without the succeeding waves of immigrants, and he attributes the decline of the machine to the decline in immigration during the 1930's and 1940's. The ethnic influence on politics can also be strongly felt well beyond the first generation of immigrants if one closely examines urban voting patterns. Political scientists have only recently become aware of the strong persistence of ethnic voting patterns, and the revelation is part of the evidence that has been used to dispel the general myth of the melting pot.[3] One researcher suggests that the peak influence of ethnicity should not even be expected until the second or third generation, since time is required to mobilize the ethnic group into a viable political force.[4]

A second political force on the governmental scene, and a rather new one, is the development of public employee unions. Everett Kassalow (Selection 16) attempts to place this new trend within a broader context. He suggests that the serious and often militant strikes by public employees are characteristic of the early stages of union development and that as the unions mature, the strikes and harsh demands will diminish. To some urban dwellers, even the acceptance of Kassalow's optimistic outlook does not allow for the fact that the cities may simply not survive the demonstrations of power associated with the formative period of union development. A. H. Raskin (Selection 17) describes some of the strikes, for instance, that confronted New York's Mayor Lindsay during his first term of office.

If one views the union development in a broader context, however, another interesting fact emerges: the rise to power of public unions has been paralleled in part by the growth of community action groups and an incipient movement toward neighborhood government. The causal relationship, if any, between the organizing of the unions and the organizing of the communities is not a simple one. The communities initially became much

---

[3]See, for example, James Q. Wilson and Edward C. Banfield, "Public regardingness as a value premise in voting behavior," *American Political Science Review,* 58:876–887 (December, 1964); Michael Parenti, "Ethnic politics and the persistence of ethnic identification," *American Political Science Review,* 61:717–726 (September, 1967); and Daniel N. Gordon, "Immigrants and municipal voting turnout," *American Sociological Review,* 35:665–681 (August, 1970).

[4]Raymond E. Wolfinger, "The development and persistence of ethnic voting," *American Political Science Review* 59:896–908 (December, 1965).

more politicized as a result of the federal antipoverty program,[5] but this occurred about the same time that the issuance of new regulations by the Kennedy administration and some local governments served to encourage the formation of public unions. Since then, some of the most controversial political issues, as in the New York City school decentralization plan, have involved the unions and the communities as adversaries. According to one political analyst, as the unions have increased in power, it has been to the interest of both the mayor and the community to foster a strong alliance with each other in order to offset the union power; hence the recent surge of interest in decentralization and neighborhood government.[6] Not to be overlooked in all of this are the differences in ethnic and racial composition of the unions and the communities. In the main, the unions have been dominated by whites belonging to the older ethnic groups—the Jews, the Italians, and the Irish. The communities, on the other hand, have most often been dominated by blacks and other new ethnic groups like the Puerto Ricans.

The continued unfolding of the union-community relationship is likely to be a dominant feature of urban government in the near-term future. Consequently, the remaining articles of this section all deal with some aspect of the relationship. Albert Reiss, Jr., (Selection 18) describes the basic interaction between municipal civil servants as suppliers of service and community clients as consumers of service. Among other points, Reiss discusses the frequent failure of the public bureaucracy to be client-centered, and he suggests some remedies that are currently available. Sherry Arnstein (Selection 19) next discusses some of the early experiences of the Model Cities program and various kinds of citizen participation. Her discussion indicates that the achievement of effective community control requires an extreme form of citizen participation that has rarely occurred. Finally, Douglas Yates (Selection 20) analyzes some of the major issues surrounding decentralization and the formation of neighborhood government. The spectre of neighborhood government has been raised in many cities,[7] yet, as Yates points out, there has been little historic precedent for neighborhood government in the urban context, and most neighborhood government schemes are likely to involve complex and controversial steps that most city governments may not be prepared to take.

---

[5] For a general but controversial account of community action and poverty programs, see Daniel P. Moynihan, *Maximum Feasible Misunderstanding: Community Action in the War on Poverty* (New York: The Free Press, 1970; paperback edition with special introduction).

[6] Herbert F. Kaufman, "Bureaucrats and organized civil servants," in Robert H. Connery and Demetrios Caraley (eds.), *Governing the City: Challenges and Options for New York* (New York: Praeger Publishers, 1969), pp. 41–54.

[7] George J. Washnis, *Neighborhood Facilities and Municipal Decentralization* (Washington, D.C.: Center for Governmental Studies, 1971).

14. Urban leadership in the sixties

JAMES V. CUNNINGHAM

The four cities explored in these pages are important. In a sense, they represent all cities. They have been and will be for a long time large centers of human life. It is imperative that resources be garnered and utilized so that life can flourish there. This requires organization, and organization requires hierarchy. So there are inevitably men on top in the cities. By their position, by the strength of the organization, by the way they develop resources, by their personality, these men possess power.

With power, leaders can make plans and carry them out. They can influence men and other organizations. There is self-satisfaction in this—status gives pleasure to the holder. Through power men can seek to hold their position. Therefore they covet power, seek to expand it, give many of their waking hours (perhaps almost all their waking hours) to coveting and nourishing it. What use they make of their power, not how much they have, is of first importance to the cities.

The four cities are complex organizations. In each we saw a group of leaders and a mayor concerned with power. Each mayor, however, acted in a different way, used his power differently, as we have seen.

Mayor Daley held more power than the other three mayors together, and he used it to impose control over Chicago toward a stated goal of keeping "the people of Chicago the healthiest, best protected, and most prosperous city in the nation."[1] He rejected suggestions of sharing power with the poor as likely to cause new conflict and power struggles, declaring flatly that "elected officials have responsibilities they should not delegate."[2] This led him to inflexibility and increased reliance on police and National Guard. His hard-line method blew up in a gory melee seen on the nation's television screens August 28, 1968.[3]

His political ramparts began to crack as the sixties ended. His aldermanic candidates were defeated in the once safe First and Forty-fourth Wards during 1969, when black voters and middle-class voters revolted.

Mayor Daley's administration during the sixties was traditional, with few creative undertakings. He avoided risk, particularly when an opportunity required some sharing of power as in the case of resident participation in the anti-poverty program. Initiative for new projects and programs came largely from outside city

---

Abridged and edited from James V. Cunningham, *Urban Leadership in the Sixties* (Waltham, Mass.: Lemberg Center, 1970), pp. 77–88. Copyright © 1970 by Lemberg Center, Brandeis University. Reprinted by permission.

The author is Associate Professor, University of Pittsburgh, Pittsburgh, Pa.

[1]Inaugural address of Mayor Richard J. Daley, April 20, 1955 (mimeographed).

[2]Interview with Mayor Daley, June 29, 1966.

[3]Daniel Walker, *Rights in Conflict* (New York: Bantam Books, Inc., 1968), makes clear there were a number of options open to Mayor Daley and his police which might have avoided violence at the Democratic National Convention—e.g., unfettered use of Lincoln Park, parade permits.

hall, although he was ready to support a new program if it appeared safe and profitable.

He was an energetic man, constantly in touch with the city and personally maintaining control. While he was willing to consider ideas from the outside, entry into any power position in his administration for individuals or groups was severely limited. His organizational abilities involving both city hall and his party were high, but he aimed always for tight control.

His office had massive power, and when he chose to promote an idea or project, he obtained results. It was a productive promotional skill he had, but little ingenuity was needed or used. Political scientists and others have pointed out that innovation requires "slack," a certain amount of looseness, freedom, and spare resources in an organization.[4] There was little slack to be seen in the Chicago city government during the sixties.

In Pittsburgh, Mayor Barr held the inherited leadership of city hall and the local Democratic Party. His potential power was great, but he personally did not exercise much of it unless pushed to do so by someone else. He retained in his administration some aggressive and innovative officials and appointed others with similar qualities. And he let those under him have fairly free rein to be innovators or non-innovators, as they chose.

The result in Pittsburgh was sporadic, uneven progress in a city which had long been shaped by powerful financial interests, interests whose concern was largely limited to one part of the city, the non-residential part. Mayor Barr never mobilized his potential power to challenge the renewal strategy which had been imposed on the city by financial interests.

Creative ideas for Pittsburgh did not come out of Joseph Barr. His risk-taking was limited to what others in his administration might do that he would tolerate, a kind of indirect risk-taking. He seldom took initiative on any of the city's problems or proposed new directions, though sometimes he backed up staff members who did. Not surprisingly, few of his staff members thought in terms of new strategies for the city, beyond the so-called "Renaissance" strategy, except when it was a matter of adopting a federally funded program offered the city. He allowed citizens some control over staff, budget, and program in the anti-poverty program.

The Pittsburgh mayor's energy level was limited, and he suffered from poor health part of the time he was in office. He was open to individuals and groups with ideas, though he seldom would push even an idea he liked; he was more likely to allow others to do it. The full force of the mayor's personal power and figure seldom was visibly behind an idea.

Mayor Barr seemed to have some organizational ability, although more of it appeared to go toward building the party than building the city. In his last years in office he did not appear to be applying organizational talent to city or party (or to be able to hold some of his creative staff members). His party organization suffered a stunning defeat in Pittsburgh during his last year in office, with his chosen successor for mayor defeated by City Councilman Peter Flaherty. The mayor's skill at promotion was low. He generally left this up to others. This turned out to be one

---

[4]See, for instance, Victor A. Thompson, "How scientific management thwarts innovation," *Transaction,* June, 1968.

of his candidate's weakest points in the 1969 primary campaign. Pittsburgh had great opportunities during the sixties and lagged on many of them. Permissiveness was not enough. Pittsburgh's experience showed that there is no substitute for the mayor himself being the entrepreneur.

Mayor Locher of Cleveland was a tragic figure, a captive of the white ethnic tradition in politics, much as Daley was. But while Daley expanded his power, Locher hoarded his. Locher exhibited no sense of innovation and daring. He surrounded himself with inflexible leaders of the past. He turned his back on opportunity for a new opening to the poor and to black constituents. Under his tutelage, participation of the poor was a mere ritual. Even the business community became estranged from him.

While Cleveland's problems called for bold moves against racism and poverty, Locher was concerned with putting utility wires underground and getting children to pick up candy wrappers. No large creative projects came out of his administration. His tenure was a holding action and risk was avoided whenever possible.

His enthusiasm for meetings, ceremony, and bowling indicated a rather high energy level, but it was frittered away. Any openness he had in the beginning of his time in office gradually disappeared, and in the last years of his regime he was an inaccessible mayor huddling with a few advisors who seemed as unimaginative and tradition-bound as he was. He showed no great organizational ability or promotional skill. Cleveland under Locher was a living demonstration that a city which tries to stand still goes swiftly downhill.

In New Haven, Mayor Lee was expansive with his power, sought endlessly to build new things with it and to affect many with its use. He was always ready to risk it as long as the stakes were high and he thought he could keep control of the game. He held back undertaking a full utilization of community talent for fear of losing some control. But he was the one mayor who saw that citizen participation might be a plus for a mayor, even if it was merely to see neighborhood organizations as sources of information through which he could receive an early warning on problems before voters complained.

Mayor Lee himself was a man with a creative urge. He was constantly searching, sensing, finding, adopting ideas. How many original ones he created himself is hard to say, but they certainly poured out of his office. And he was never fearful of hiring creative people to work for him.

Probably his strongest quality was that of risk-taker. He resisted temptations to play it safe, to move only incrementally. His physical disruptions of the city were ventures of high risk.

His drive and initiative were strong at all times, even when his energy level dipped during times of ulcer attacks. His openness for listening to others was considerable. As a former newsman and university publicist he was a professional at promotion, a master of every technique from the news release and the big dinner to the handwritten note and the wave from an automobile window.

Of course it would be foolish to portray Lee as a saint or even as a totally successful mayor. He wanted the people let into his administration to be under his control, not citizens involved on their own terms. He did not seem to see that his goal of a better life for citizens was not to be achieved only by new housing and services but also required the more direct means of letting citizens help work out the programs that affect them. He created a large citizens' board to give sanctions to urban renewal, but he kept the board relatively powerless.

In short, with all his strong qualities and federal money, Richard C. Lee was a long way from solving New Haven's problems when he stepped out at the end of the sixties. Nevertheless, when this has been pointed out, it must be acknowledged that he extended his neck as none of the other mayors extended theirs.

.   .   .   .   .

This study of four cities in the sixties reveals that even with tremendous innovative efforts as in New Haven the city is a long way from solving its problems. In New Haven, less than a third of the poor were reached. Large numbers of families still lived in substandard housing, and in a sense the whole citizenry was stunted by the paternalistic rule of an executive-centered coalition. Even when energetically and imaginatively utilized, the physical resources of a city are not enough.

The results point to the importance of attempting to utilize community talent more fully and creatively. Quality of life is determined by more than government expenditures. But the results also indicate that the mayors at the 1969 U.S. Conference of Mayors meeting in Pittsburgh were right in asking for more federal resources. The more innovative a mayor becomes, the more he will need federal resources. It appears that, indeed, cities cannot solve many of their present physical problems under current circumstances.

No mayor can be a complete hero in the contemporary city. The disruptive forces, physical and social, are too great. The mayor's authority over many forces is small or non-existent. And he is too limited by talent and resources. But some mayors can do better with what they have than others. Perhaps it is no accident that the mayor who rated as most innovative was the only one who had no trouble with the voters anytime during the sixties.

City hall takes a great toll of the man who tries to run it. None of our four mayors has gone on to higher office (although Lee is reported to have had the chance to run for the U.S. Senate in 1959). Sayre and Kaufman found the same situation among the mayors of New York City. They concluded, "The office uses up the man."[5]

It can be expected that the innovative mayors of the seventies will be those who create and risk opening their administrations to wider participation by the citizenry so that this added source of talent and energy can not only have more say in government but can help the mayor understand the problems of the poor and can help share the burden of solving problems. Talented leaders from previously neglected sectors of the city can help persuade the federal government that it must insure jobs, income, education, and housing for all citizens. The cities will never have enough money to do all these things themselves. The programs of the sixties, even when fully exploited by innovative urban leaders, provided training and jobs for a few, inadequate incomes for a limited number, houses for only those on a small part of a city's waiting list, and token experiments in education. Goals for the seventies should be programs that provide the full needs of all those in need. Toward

---

[5]Wallace Sayre and Herbert Kaufman, *Governing New York City* (New York: Russell Sage Foundation, 1960), p. 697.

the end of 1969 President Nixon opened up debate on these issues with sweeping new proposals for government welfare programs.

The urban areas have two needs: more resources and innovative leadership to use those resources fully and well. The cities need leaders who are willing to be used up. How are they to be developed? Lee came out of a city council. And perhaps we should look more to the city legislatures as preparatory grounds, just as the nation now seems to look more and more to the Senate as the training ground for Presidents. This means that local political parties, political clubs, newspapers, and other organizations concerned with the quality of elected officials must give more attention to the caliber of men being supported both for mayor and city council. The universities and business corporations probably have a role to play here, also, for they are often the source from which candidates can come. Any potential candidate might well be scrutinized in accordance with the seven marks of the public entrepreneur.

Innovation and entrepreneurship in the leadership of public organizations appears to be a vast and profitable area for study and search. This essay has concentrated on mayors, and only in passing has it looked at the myriad of key posts below the mayor. Many of these, too, need innovative leadership if they are to contribute to building a human city. There are rich fields here for studies from which we could probably learn much about the leadership needed by cities.

More ought to be known about the activities carried on by contemporary public executives, about how to measure innovativeness in the executive, about how to measure the output of his organization, and the relation between executive innovativeness and output. How do we recruit and train young executives who are most likely to be innovators? How important is background? How important is personality? How important organizational context? The tasks for researchers are large and significant.

No longer can we afford to let ethnicity, inheritance, party loyalty, and chance be the dominant factors in choosing our urban leaders. There are now other qualities of greater importance. Contemporary cities cannot be run successfully by ordinary men.

15. Bosses, machines, and ethnic groups

ELMER E. CORNWELL, JR.

Though the direction of the causal relationship may be difficult to establish, the classic urban machine and the century of immigration which ended in the 1920's were intimately intertwined phenomena. This fact is not always recognized as fully as it should be. Much of the literature on bosses and machines, beginning with the muck-rakers, but not excluding more recent studies with less overt moralistic flavor, carries the implication that such factors as the dispersal of power in urban government—under weak mayor charters and through rivalries among state, county, city and special district authorities, all plowing the same field but none with full responsibility for its cultivation—invited the machine's extra-legal reconcentration of power. It is also true that attitudes engendered by a business society whose prime movers characteristically had their eye on the "main chance"—and specifically on traction franchises and the like—also fostered the growth of the essentially entrepreneurial role and amoral attitude of the boss.

RELATION OF MACHINE TO IMMIGRATION

When all this has been said, however, the fact still remains that the classic machine would probably not have been possible, and certainly would not have been so prominent a feature of the American political landscape, without the immigrant. Essentially, any disciplined grass roots political organization rests upon a docile mass base which has in some manner been rendered dependable, predictable, and manipulable. The rank and file of the Soviet Communist party is disciplined by a combination of ideological allegiance, fear, and hope of reward. The average party supporter in a liberal-democratic society cannot be so disciplined under ordinary circumstances, at least not for long. The newly arrived immigrant was a special case, however. He was characteristically insecure, culturally and often linguistically alien, confused, and often in actual want. Thus, even if he had valued the franchise thrust upon him by his new political mentors, its careful exercise would have taken a low priority in his daily struggle for existence. In most cases, he did not value or even understand the political role into which he was being pushed.

Thus, it was the succeeding waves of immigrants that gave the urban political organizations the manipulable mass bases without which they could not have functioned as they did. And, until immigration dried up to a trickle in the 1920's, as one generation of newcomers began to espouse traditional American values of political independence, there was always a new group, often from a different country of origin, to which the machine could turn. As long as this continued to be possible, machines persisted, and once the immigrant base finally began to disappear, so did

Abridged and edited from Elmer E. Cornwell, Jr., "Bosses, machines, and ethnic groups," *The Annals,* 353:27–39 (May, 1964). Copyright © 1964 by The American Academy of Political and Social Science. Reprinted by permission.

The author is Professor of Political Science, Brown University, Providence, R.I.

most of the bosses of the classic model. In a very real sense, then, the one phenomenon was dependent on the other.

The argument can be made that there were other machines that clearly were not immigrant based in this sense. All generalizations, especially those in the social sciences, are but proximate truths. At the same time, machines based on white, Protestant, "old-stock" clienteles were not wholly unrelated in their motivation and operation to the factor of immigration. Platt's smooth-functioning organization in New York State[1] and Blind Boss Brayton's contemporary operation in Rhode Island[2] were both based, in the immediate sense, on what Lincoln Steffens called "the good old American stock out in the country."[3] And yet recall that both of these states were highly urbanized even in the 1890's and early 1900's when these two worthies flourished and had ingested disproportionate numbers of immigrants. As of 1920, when 38 percent of the total United States population was foreign born or of foreign parentage, the corresponding percentages for New York and Rhode Island were 64 and 71.[4] These facts alone suggest what the political history of both makes clear: these rural "old-stock" machines existed largely as means of political defense against the newcomers and doubtless would not have existed had there been no immigrants.

The point, then, is that, whereas in the cities the immigrants sold their political independence for the familiar currency of favors and aid, their rural native cousins were sometimes prompted to do the same, in part out of desire for cultural-religious as well as political, and perhaps at times economic, self-protection. Recollection of the Know-Nothing era of militant nativist activity a half-century earlier suggests that this kind of cultural-religious antagonism can be a very potent political force indeed. An analogous explanation could even be offered for the existence of machines in the South like that of Harry Byrd in Virginia, by simply substituting the perceived Negro threat for the danger of engulfment by foreigners in the North. And, curiously enough, the two examples of reasonably thoroughgoing machine-like organizations that flourished in the otherwise inhospitable English soil—Joseph Chamberlain's Birmingham caucus[5] and Archibald Salvidge's "machine" in Liverpool[6]—also were at least indirectly related to the problem of Irish home rule, and, in Liverpool, to actual rivalry with Irish immigrants over religion and jobs.

In short, whatever else may be said about the conditions and forces that spawned the classic machine, this kind of disciplined political entity must rest at bottom on a clientele which has felt it necessary to exchange political independence —its votes, in a word—for something seen as more essential to its well-being and

---

[1]See Harold F. Gosnell, *Boss Platt and His New York Machine* (Chicago: University of Chicago Press, 1924).

[2]See Lincoln Steffens, "Rhode Island: A state for sale," *McClure's Magazine,* 24:337–353 (February 1905).

[3]Lincoln Steffens, *Autobiography* (New York: Literary Guild, 1931), p. 367.

[4]E. P. Hutchinson, *Immigrants and Their Children* (New York: John Wiley, & Sons, Inc., 1956), p. 27.

[5]See J. L. Garvin, *The Life of Joseph Chamberlain,* 3 vols. (London: Macmillan & Co., Ltd., 1932–1934).

[6]Stanley Salvidge, *Salvidge of Liverpool* (London: Hodder and Stoughton, 1934).

security. In general, such a group will be the product of some kind of socioeconomic disequilibrium or cultural tension which finds its members in an insecure or seriously disadvantaged situation. Thus, the immigrant was willing to submit to the boss in exchange for aid—real or imagined—in gaining his foothold in the new environment, and the old-stock machine supporters, North or South, submitted in part for protection against swarming aliens or a potential Negro threat to white dominance.

.   .   .   .   .

THE DECLINE OF THE MACHINE

The decline and fall of the boss as a political phenomenon has often been chronicled and explained. It is argued, *inter alia,* that reforms like the direct primary, nonpartisan systems of election, voting machines and tightened registration requirements, and city manager schemes often dealt crippling blows. In the aggregate, they doubtless did, though many exceptions can be found to prove the rule. One particular contribution of the reformers which has had unquestioned importance—though circumvention has not proven impossible—was the elimination of patronage with the installation of civil service based on the merit principle. And, generally, educational levels have risen, and occupational levels and incomes have risen as well. Even where patronage remains available, the latter development has rendered it less attractive, and to fewer people. Finally, and most often cited, there was the impact of the New Deal. Its installation of publicly sponsored welfare programs eliminated many of the rough-and-ready welfare functions of the precinct captain, though the more imaginative recouped part of their loss by helping to steer constituents through the bureaucratic maze, claiming credit for the benefits thus obtained.

Granting the importance of all of these developments, in the long run the decline of immigration doubtless proved the most important blow to the traditional machine operation. New arrivals had been entering the country at a rate in excess of four million each half-decade up to the First World War. The rate averaged barely more than one-third of that between 1915 and 1930 and dropped to a mere trickle for most of the period down to the present. Sharply restrictive legislation passed in 1921 and 1924 was responsible. Obviously, the impact on the machines came in the form of a delayed reaction, but most of them gradually withered. The few that survived did so through shrewd adaptation to changed conditions, specifically through judicious self-administered doses of reformism, as, for example, with the Daley organization in Chicago.

Thus ended an era. Immigration may not have called the boss into being, but the two in most cases were closely linked. Two questions remain to be dealt with. What contemporary counterparts are there, if any, of the immigrant influx of yesteryear and how are the parties dealing with them? And what can be said of the current political behavior of the children and grandchildren of the former immigrants?

THE PARTIES AND THE NEW IMMIGRATION

There are, of course, two major groups that do represent close parallels with the earlier influx and at the same time carry important differences. These are the

Negroes who have been migrating in increasing numbers from the South to northern urban centers since the First World War and the Puerto Ricans who began coming to New York City, for the most part, after the Second World War.[7] Both resemble their alien predecessors in the magnitude of their numbers, their basic and important cultural differences from the population into whose midst they are moving, an almost invariable need of assistance in adjusting to a new environment, and their potential impact on the political balance of forces.

The major points of difference are also worth noting. Both come bearing the credentials of American citizenship, which was not the case with the earlier groups. Though this factor should make for easier adjustment, other group characteristics operate to make acceptance more difficult. For the Negro, there is the fundamental problem of color, coupled with cultural characteristics which, though acquired ostensibly in the American environment, operate to make assimilation more difficult. These include all the long deposit of servitude and enforced inferior status: loose marital ties and correspondingly weak family ties generally, a poverty of leadership potential, low literacy and skill levels, and the like. For the Puerto Ricans, there is language, plus differences of culture, and a partial color barrier which operates to cause at least some Spanish-Americans to be classified—against their will—as Negroes. On balance, it is probably true that, so far as these two groups are concerned as groups, they face higher barriers to integration into American life than almost any earlier group save, possibly, the Orientals.

But the society itself has changed enormously from the society to which the Irish, Italians, and Jews sought entrance. Urban areas are now equipped with facilities to which the newcomer can turn for aid that counterbalance to some degree the particular hostilities which members of these two groups arouse. There are now elaborate public welfare programs, there is Aid to Dependent Children for the many fatherless families, there are numerous private agencies and charities which stand ready to help, and, in the case of the Puerto Ricans, their land of origin has taken a unique interest in the welfare of its emigrants. There have even been legislative efforts to ban the discrimination in housing or employment which they encounter.

Though these facilities stand ready to ease aspects of the economic and social integration of these latest immigrants, there still remains the question of political absorption. Here, too, the situation today sharply differs from the past. The political parties now have neither the incentive nor the means with which to perform the functions they performed for the earlier immigrants. The machine in most affected areas is gone beyond recall, and there remain in its place party organizations that are hollow shells of their former strength and vigor. Party in general, given the proliferation of both public bureaucracies and the mass entertainment industry, has been pushed to the fringes of the average citizen's attention span and often to the fringes of the governing process itself. The debilitating impact of reform legislation contributed to the same end, needless to say. Thus, in general, the new immigrants

---

[7]Two recent books are especially useful discussions of these groups: Nathan Glazer and Daniel Patrick Moynihan, *Beyond the Melting Pot* (Cambridge, Mass.: The M.I.T. Press, 1963), and Oscar Handlin, *The Newcomers: Negroes and Puerto Ricans in a Changing Metropolis* (Cambridge, Mass.: Harvard University Press, 1959).

can look to the parties for little of the former assistance they once provided in gaining entrance and leverage in the political processes of their new homes.

Returning for a moment to the current status of descendants of earlier immigrants, the assumption that significant cultural distinctions and tendencies toward common political attitude and behavior would disappear in two or three generations has proven erroneous. Ticket-balancing, for example, in ethnic or religious terms is as prevalent, perhaps, as it ever was and shows few signs of disappearing in the immediate future. The election of an Irish Catholic President in 1960, if anything, enhanced the importance of such balancing tactics, as the discussion in early 1964 of Democratic vice-presidential candidates indicated. In psychoanalysis, it is well recognized that problems have to be clearly recognized and frankly made explicit before they can be eliminated. The same may in a sense be true of ethnic factors in American politics. Only the frank recognition of the once-potent barrier to a Catholic in the White House paved the way for the Kennedy election. At the state and local level, it is probably also true that only after various groups have achieved and enjoyed the recognition they feel they are entitled to and have done so for a long enough period to transform a privilege into a quasi-right will it become possible, gradually, to choose candidates without these criteria in mind. The unfortunate thing is that American parties have decayed as organizations to the point that they can make far less contribution to this process of adjustment than they could and did in the past.

16. Trade unionism goes public

EVERETT M. KASSALOW

Strikes of public employees, once a novelty, are no longer unusual. During one three-month period, not so long ago, a casual check showed social workers' strikes in Chicago, Sacramento, and White Plains; slowdowns of firefighters in Buffalo and of policemen in Detroit; strikes among university maintenance employees at Ohio State, Indiana, and the University of Kansas Medical Center; a three-day "heal-in" by the interns and residents of the Boston City Hospital; "informational" picketing, with a strike threat, by the Philadelphia School Nurses' Association; teachers' strikes in a dozen communities, ranging from West Mifflin, Pennsylvania, and

Abridged and edited from Everett M. Kassalow, "Trade unionism goes public," *The Public Interest*, No. 14 (Winter, 1969), pp. 118–130. Copyright © 1969 by National Affairs, Inc. Reprinted by permission.

The author is Professor of Economics, University of Wisconsin, Madison, Wis.

Gibraltor, Ohio, to South Bend, Indiana, and Baltimore, Maryland. Such strikes and slowdowns among teachers, policemen, firemen, etc. have become daily occurrences. Because there had been a growing feeling that industrial relations were becoming more "mature," strikes of this sort in sectors hitherto unidentified with unionism have led to confusion. Large-scale unionization of government workers is a relatively new phenomenon in this country, although it has been common in almost all other democratic industrial countries of the world. That large-scale public-employee unionism was also inevitable in the United States at some time is clear. But why now? What new forces account for the current upsurge of public unionism?

THE RESPECTABILITY OF UNIONS

The first of these forces has been the institutionalization of trade unionism in American life. Unions date back more than 150 years in the United States. But large-scale unionism dates only from the late 1930's, and it has only been in the past decade or so that collective bargaining has become widely accepted as the appropriate way to settle wages and working issues. During this decade unionists have become respectable. Union leaders have been named to innumerable presidential commissions dealing with every conceivable problem area of the country's foreign and domestic business.

It is not surprising thus that, despite the revelations in the senate investigations of the malfeasance of Jimmy Hoffa and a few other union leaders, public opinion surveys show that union officers have registered a significant gain in occupational prestige between 1947 and 1963. This gain is clearly attributable to the widespread acceptance of the basic value of unionism in society, and this legitimacy is being transferred to public employees as well. For this reason, unionism among government workers has begun to advance rapidly, and there is every prospect it will continue to grow.

There is a second, more specific reason for the recent growth of government unionism, and this is Executive Order 10988 issued by President John F. Kennedy in January 1962, which encouraged unionism in the federal service. In its support of public unionism, this order was as clear and unequivocal as the Wagner Act of 1936 had been in its support for unions and collective bargaining in the private sector. It declared that "the efficient administration of the government and the well-being of employees require that orderly and constructive relationships be maintained between employee organizations and management."

In New York City, earlier orders issued by Mayor Robert Wagner resulted in the "breakthrough" of unionism in 1961 among 44,000 teachers. Kennedy's order has a spillover effect in legitimating unionism in state and local public service. Further, the reapportionment of state legislatures seems to have had a generally liberalizing effect, and a flow of new legislation in a dozen states has expedited public employee bargaining.

The enormous growth in public employment has also acted to transform the state of the government worker. Between 1947 and 1967, the number of public employees increased over 110 percent. (During the same period, private nonagricultural employment increased only 42 percent.) Clearly, the day has passed when being a civil servant is a prestigious matter. At a time when unions and bargaining have become increasingly accepted elsewhere in the society, this expansion of public employment, with its consequent bureaucratization and depersonalization of relationships, has undoubtedly encouraged unionization in the public sector.

.   .   .   .   .

PUBLIC MANAGEMENT AND COLLECTIVE BARGAINING

The growth of unionism in the public sector has been so rapid that public management has found it difficult to assimilate it in recent years. Even with the best intentions, the process would pose problems to public managers who until recently have had complete authority in personnel matters, within civil service laws and regulations. In many cases the older practices of benevolent paternalism persist, and new ideas about bargaining come slowly. Even though unionism has become accepted in every major industry, the personnel officers in government often have little notion of how to deal with a union, and episodes quaintly reminiscent of labor history thirty years ago frequently occur. One federal union organizer describes his experience in dealing for the first time with an old line air-base personnel director. The union had only recently won its exclusive bargaining rights, and the organizer led his committee into a small personnel office. The director sat behind a small table and told the union committee to remain standing in the crowded office as it prepared to present its demands. The organizer refused to negotiate under these circumstances and eventually a larger office and a large table and sufficient chairs were found. Eventually, too, the old personnel director was eased out of his position. At various levels, this experience has been and will be repeated countless times before the new bargaining process takes hold.

The civil service commissions present the most fundamental problem. In the federal government, as well as in many states, these bodies have been the unilateral source of rules and regulations for government employees. In the first stages of the new unionism, these commissions have become the principal management authority. But these commissions often serve both as employer and arbiter, and determine what groups of employees can or should be grouped together for bargaining purposes, or what the proper scope or area of this bargaining should be. In private unionism, the NLRB has been the arbiter of such questions, and it is unlikely that the government unions will allow the "employer" both to make such crucial determinations and also to bargain.

It is sometimes difficult to remember that one of the original reasons for the creation of civil service commissions was to protect the employees from political attack and insecurity of tenure. To trade unions, seeking to assert their rights and to modify old rules and regulations, the commissions now appear primarily as retrograde authority. Thus, efforts by the federal government to continue the Civil Service Commission as executor of the various federal laws regulating employment, while trying to graft on to it new rights and duties of administration in the new collective bargaining process, have drawn much criticism. The "depression psychology" and its memories of insecurity has come to an end in the minds of most government workers today, and similarly the old "concept of Civil Service," as President Jerry Wurf of the American Federation of State, County and Municipal Employees has argued, "falls by the wayside." Wurf notes that his "own union's early history was concerned with the bettering of the Civil Service. But, if you look at Civil Service today, it is really a management tool, which is unilaterally established, and the workers have no say in how it functions."

Several states have already acted to empower a separate new agency to certify unions, help select mediators and arbitrators, define union rights and protections, etc., and the federal government is seriously considering similar action. Clearly, what most public employee unions want is their own version of the Wagner Act's National Labor Relations Board to do for collective bargaining in the public sector what the NLRB did for the private sector in the 1930's. Civil Service Commissions just don't fit that picture, and many are likely to be phased out of this new area of public administration.

STRIKES IN THE PUBLIC SERVICE

No subject in recent years has provoked as much heat as the matter of strikes among public employees. It is probably the most difficult problem in the public employee field. Even expert arbitrators and mediators, men of hard-headed, pragmatic experience, have taken surprisingly rigid, ideological positions on this matter.

Curiously, this issue is being debated as though the American experience was unique. But the fact is that many other countries have faced this same problem, and a wide range of solutions have been tried. Some countries have substituted compulsory arbitration for the right to strike, thereby presumably offering the unions a fair alternative to break "impasse" situations. Other countries have widely conceded public employees the right to strike, though a few groups such as policemen, firemen, or the military may be excepted by law or voluntary agreement.

Although the United States has its own history, it is difficult in the light of experience both here and in other nations to swallow the categorical judgment of a distinguished American labor arbitrator that: "Neither compulsory arbitration nor strikes are appropriate in public employment relations." His argument rests on the traditional citizen-taxpayer's absolute right "to establish priorities of competing executive agencies." But this does not take into account the countless ways in which this absolute fiscal right has been transferred to independent boards of education, transport authorities, public utility agencies and the like, over the years.

Before taking hard and arbitrary positions, it is well to put strikes in a proper perspective. Over the past two decades or so, strikes in the United States have generally been declining. Occasional upsurges occur, particularly during periods of war- or defense-induced inflation, but generally the number of strikes have declined as union-management relations have matured. There is good reason to believe that, once the organizing phase is over, public employee unions will prove even less strike prone than those in private industry. For one thing, working conditions are generally more secure and often more pleasant and less onerous than in private industry. For this reason it is important to note that as unionism and the bargaining process is extended for the first time to millions of new employees and new institutions (public agencies) considerable friction and tension will occur. The very inexperience of the new union leaders and the public managers guarantees this. But neither should the historic trajectory of unionism be ignored either.

Because there are inherent difficulties in the adjustment to new bargaining public officials need to approach these difficulties with caution, rather than be obsessed with strikes and punishment for strikes. Admittedly, in today's transition period, most cities or states are not likely to concede the right to strike to public employees. However, rather than setting forth elaborate punishment systems for strikes which may occur, officials should take positive steps wherever possible to improve relations.

.   .   .   .   .

17. Why New York is "Strike City"

A. H. RASKIN

In one of a thousand dark hours of labor crisis at Gracie Mansion, with the city's teachers on strike and the police and firemen and the garbage collectors all making menacing noises, a mediator came upon Mayor Lindsay with his head sunk in his hands. "What an idiot, what an idiot! I could have had that Senate nomination and been away from all this," the Mayor said.

A few minutes later, he had redonned the mask of good cheer that is part of the armor any mayor must wear in this most tortured of cities. But Lindsay's momentary dip into despair was the culmination of three years of almost continuous conflict on the municipal labor front—conflict of such intensity that it had forced aside most of his hopes for civic regeneration, put heavy new strains on an already bloated budget and, worst of all, unleashed racial hatreds that threaten to make our metropolis unlivable.

The regularity with which one crippling stoppage in a vital service is succeeded by an even worse one has caused many New Yorkers to wish for a return to the "palsmanship" that kept the city's labor relations relatively tranquil through the 12-year mayoralty of Lindsay's Democratic predecessor, Robert F. Wagner, Jr. Unions chiefs felt comfortable with the son of the author of labor's Magna Carta, the Wagner Act; and Mayor Wagner neglected no chance to build up their sense of security by proclaiming that New York was a "union town." Strike threats were a fixture in transit and other civil-service negotiations, but strikes were almost never the end of the line. Pleasanter still, the price of peace was a half or third the level that has prevailed in the Lindsay administration—which has often paid the price without getting the peace.

Abridged and edited from A. H. Raskin, "Why New York is 'Strike City' " *The New York Times Magazine,* December 22, 1968. Copyright © 1968 by The New York Times Company. Reprinted by permission.

In exploring the roots of this conflict, the first thing to recognize is that any mayor, including Wagner, would be having trouble on the labor front these days. High prices, high taxes, high wage settlements in private industry and the jingle of money in every sector of the overfat metropolitan economy have given the rank and file of all New York unions a far-out view of how much is enough in new wage contracts.

In the civil service, the inflationary itch is aggravated by the extra hazards and torments that go with being the visible symbol of the municipal establishment in dealings with the angry residents of the ghetto (or with those outside the ghetto who are angry about the ways the poor express their anger). On top of all that is the general breakdown in respect for institutions that permeates every corner of American life. The policeman, the fireman, the teacher and the rest of the city's 320,000 employes are the targets of that rebellion; they are also caught up in it, to the embarrassment of their union leaders, who find dream contracts being tossed back by their memberships as unworthy of serious attention.

"Wagner got out just in time," is the way Lindsay's labor-relations director, Herbert L. Haber, sums it up. Civil servants all over the country are beginning to feel their muscle, heedless of the restraints imposed by no-strike laws; even the most assertive union leaders today could not win their members over to a deal hatched in a back room at City Hall.

Substantial as these factors are in explaining the down spiral that carries New York ever closer to paralysis, it is nonsensical to pretend that friction between Lindsay and the satraps of labor does not add a big downward push of its own. Even before taking office, the Mayor stressed that one of the things he liked least about the Wagner administration was the wheeler-dealer atmosphere that enshrouded its handling of labor matters, especially in transit. Lindsay promised to banish the "power brokers" from City Hall and put contract negotiations on a tidy basis, with deadlocks to be resolved by impartial fact-finders.

That plan got off to a disastrous start. In the 12-day subway strike that began five hours after Lindsay was sworn in, Michael J. Quill, then president of the Transport Workers Union, attacked the whole concept of fact-finding so vituperatively that the chairman of the panel which the Mayor had counted on to put forward a peace formula threatened to pack his bag and go home to Wisconsin if Lindsay insisted on recommendations. The strike wound up with a $62-million settlement, double the largest sum Wagner ever had given.

Some of the roots of discord lie in the shadowland of personal chemistry—in the clash of life styles, of cultures and generations. The easy friendliness that Lindsay radiates as he walks bareheaded through the ghetto disappears when he is in the presence of old-line leaders of the Central Labor Council. Then there's just the way he looks: a handsome Yalie, always casually elegant and up on the grooviest of mod expressions, the epitome of everything that makes the unionists feel clumsy and out of it, for all their power.

[In February 1968, the strike by] the Uniformed Sanitationmen's Association ... nearly buried the city in uncollected garbage. Lindsay's appeal to Governor Rockefeller to call out the National Guard brought threats of a general strike by all New York labor. The Governor and the bipartisan leadership of the Legislature, not unhappy at the prospect of humiliating the Mayor, prepared to push through a union-appeasement package. The only thing that stopped them was an outraged howl from the voters, galvanized into action by Lindsay's statement that the package was the same as paying "a little bit of blackmail."

But if the Mayor came out on top with the public, he won no friends in labor. The call for the National Guard was like waving a bloody shirt, a reminder of Homestead and Pullman and the Haymarket Massacre. The unionists were still furious when the school year was ushered in with another citywide school strike. . . . When two early settlements collapsed because the local governing board would not put the disputed teachers back in their classrooms, the executive board of the Central Labor Council met with the Mayor and demanded assurances that the city would back up its commitment to have the teachers reinstated. The Mayor was as emphatic as he knew how to be—too emphatic, as it turned out. "We'll use every power, including bayonets if necessary," he promised. That carried the unionists right back to the sanitation strike, and the conference ended in anger.

.   .   .   .   .

[Later when] cracks were opening up inside labor, Lindsay mounted a frontal attack of his own on efforts by the [United Federation of Teachers] to take its case to Albany and thus push the Mayor out of command of the situation, in the same way that the sanitation union had tried [in] February. Lindsay accused [Albert] Shanker and his teachers of rejecting every peace plan short of unconditional surrender by the heads of the Ocean Hill experiment in community involvement.

The Mayor's TV assault on the U.F.T. violated all the kid-glove maxims of standard labor-management practice, which are built on the theory that the union can utter any insult it wants against the boss but he must never respond in kind. But Lindsay decided, as he had when he called for the National Guard to move the garbage, that revolutionary times demanded revolutionary methods. And once again his gamble seemed to pay off. Albany made it plain that it was not going to bail out the U.F.T.; more unions built a bonfire under [Harry] Van Arsdale [President of the Central Labor Council] and the teachers. The upshot was a creaky settlement that weekend at Gracie Mansion. "It was because of labor pressure that Shanker packed it in," a ranking Lindsay aide declares.

Where does this leave things? If you talk to Lindsay, you find him bravely insisting that the city is turning the corner toward greater harmony in labor relations. That hope got a bad setback when the rank and file of the Patrolmen's Benevolent Association overwhelmingly rejected the fat wage package the Goldberg panel had counted on to stabilize the pay balance in police, fire and sanitation—and thus stop the interunion leapfrogging that keeps pushing the city toward bankruptcy. Despite this upset, however, the Mayor remains convinced that the bulk of the civil-service union chiefs recognize the need for orderly procedure in their dealings with the city.

.   .   .   .   .

Lindsay's own touch is getting a bit surer; he is less dogmatic in his approach to union negotiators, more inclined to recognize that the exigencies of union politics can be as demanding as those of municipal politics. "In the teachers' strike," says one veteran mediator, "he startled me by vetoing one suggestion settlement on the ground that 'Shanker can never sell that; his members won't go for it.' " A police negotiator, no admirer of the Mayor, describes him as affable and conciliatory in this year's contract talks, with only rare lapses into the avenging deity role that marked his conduct last time around.

.   .   .   .

What emerges from the name-calling and the back-biting and the political posturing on every side of the municipal labor scene is the certainty of still more strife. The city's public-service system is a repository of money and power, the two things the ghetto wants most. Payroll costs take nearly $3.5 billion of New York's $6-billion expense budget. But the undereducated, underequipped people of the slums find their access to that pot of gold blocked by a wall of rules built up over the years to shield those already inside the civil service. The point of these rules, of course, is to ban the spoils system and enshrine merit as the sole test in appointments and promotions. To the job-hungry on the outside wanting in, however, the whole qualifications structure is part of a conspiracy by their white overlords to hold them in colonial subjugation and shut them out of either participation or control of the agencies that have most to do with their daily lives. The white civil servant becomes "the enemy," and the better union protectionism makes his job, the more intense the ghetto's resentment.

The Irish got there first in police, fire and transit, the Italians in sanitation, the Jews in teaching. Negroes and Puerto Ricans have moved into the vacuum in the fast-expanding field of health services, but even there their strongest hold is on the jobs at the bottom of the scale, those that are the messiest and that pay the least. So the fight over school decentralization may be duplicated in every other field in the months and years ahead. Jobs will be the prize, as much as community control, and the Mayor will be in the middle every time the line is drawn—as it has been in Ocean Hill and the Intermediate School 201 complex in East Harlem—on union rights vs. community rights.

Lindsay's whole effort since he got to City Hall has been to take the abrasive edges off this inescapable conflict by trying to persuade the militants on the Negro side that an orderly transfer of power can be effected without confrontations that trample on the rights of whites to build up rights for blacks. The Mayor's approach entails giving the people who are interested in change a voice in change. This explains his appointment of Negro-firsters like the Rev. Milton A. Galamison and William H. Booth to prestige posts in the Lindsay administration. Even Mau Mau leader Charles 37X Kenyatta has become a convert in the Mayor's attempt to cool it.

To many white workers, especially those whose municipal jobs expose them to daily danger and insult on the police beat or the fire engine or in the tumultous school system, this mayoral attitude seems a green light for black supremacists and vigilantes. The civil-service union leader, worried enough in his own right, finds a new dimension added to his merchandising problem as salesman for any agreement he negotiates with the city. "Dump Lindsay" was the sign the teachers carried at City Hall. "Dump Lindsay" was the slogan for the policemen, too.

Political vindictiveness, fear and race hate thus inflame the difficulties already created by the "gimme" spirit that is rampant in every union, public or private. The man with a good civil service job feels as pushed around as the man without one.

The policeman spurns a $10,350-a-year pay offer because he feels he ought to be top banana in the municipal wage system. The hospital or housing worker in the $4,000-to-$4,500 category insists he would be better off on relief. The mother on relief demands department store credit cards to supplement the public payments that give a welfare family of four an annual cash income of $4,000 and that will cost taxpayers in the neighborhood of $1.5 billion in this fiscal year. The taxpayers, including a growing number who work for the city, get away from it all, at least part of the time, by moving across the city line to Westchester, New Jersey, or Long Island. And the city's streets are full of Rolls-Royces, Cadillacs and Jaguars. Gleaming new office buildings mushroom in midtown. Cooperatives on the fashionable East Side sell for upward of $100,000. Tiffany's and Cartier's are as crowded as supermarkets.

Those who stand on either side of the municipal barricades wrap themselves in a mantle of self-righteousness and justify their excesses by pointing to the abuses of everyone else. Laws are something for other people to obey, an attitude that applies to alarmed white unionists and embattled black extremists alike. The ultimate idiocy was the way in which both sides in the Ocean Hill controversy hung out the banner of "due process" as a cover for their actions, while each used illegal tactics to make its position stick.

Injunctions issued under the no-strike provisions of the state's Taylor Law are treated like confetti by all the major municipal unions except police and fire, and no one is sure how long these two will defer to the law. Yet none of this seems relevant to any union chief as a possible explanation for the heedlessness of law exhibited by ghetto militants when they clash with the police on school steps or in the streets.

New mass walkouts by unions in housing and welfare and possibly other city agencies are threatened for New Year's Day. They revolve around money but also around demands that the city's bargaining rules be extended to give unions a much bigger voice in formulating basic municipal policy. And again the militant in the ghetto asks: "If you can strike to get more say about what you do and what the city does, why can't we? It's our lives, our homes, our safety, our children. We won't stand still any longer and let white society run them for us."

All in all, Santa Claus is bringing no gift of labor peace to John Lindsay—or community peace, either.

18.   Servers and served in service

ALBERT J. REISS, JR.

.   .   .   .   .

Beginning with the mid-sixties a new domestic issue has emerged that crosscuts programs: the form, control, and quality of the organization and administration of Great Society programs. There have been growing doubts about the responsiveness of federal programs to local needs and requirements, about local as well as federal bureaucratic administration of such programs, about citizen as opposed to bureaucratic control of programs. This new issue undoubtedly will emerge as a big issue of the seventies. Briefly, the issue is who shall serve whom, how, and for what in which ways. How, for example, shall those who serve meet demands to the satisfaction of those served?

Sociologists contributed to the rise of this new issue. They spawned the belief that the community had declined, even disappeared, as a viable organization in American society. For it, they substituted the mass society with its mass media, its mass middle class, and its mass opinion. At the same time, they undermined the very institutions and organizations of the Great Society by documenting the failures rather than successes of bureaucracy and by focusing on what they regarded as dysfunctional consequences of bureaucratic processing, such as labeling clients as deviant. In its vulgar form, sociologists held that both the organized political and administrative community and large-scale bureaucracy were bankrupt. The only remaining and saving grace was informal social organization where "people" solved problems together, a return to "community" with a small "c."

.   .   .   .   .

CITIZEN DEMANDS FOR SERVICE

Each day, a substantial number of citizens in any large community face a problem they regard as a crisis demanding immediate attention. Such problems include domestic crises, arguments between landlords and tenants or among neighbors, and crises of health or accident, to list a few. What shall they do? Generally, they call the police.

Calling the police in most cities is not surprising, since, apart from the limited emergency service provided by fire departments or ambulances, the police generally are the only service available twenty-four hours a day to serve citizens in need of help. Some years ago a police official in Chicago wryly commented:

"Servers and Served in Service" by Albert J. Reiss, Jr., is reprinted from John P. Crecine (ed.), *Financing the Metropolis: The Role of Public Policy in Urban Economics,* Vol. 4 of the *Urban Affairs Annual Reviews* (1970), pp. 561–576. Reprinted by permission of the Publisher, Sage Publications, Inc. Abridged and edited.

The author is in the Department of Sociology, Yale University, New Haven, Conn.

Where else in the City of Chicago can you put a dime in the telephone, call for help and it comes, and get your dime back? Any welfare agency is on a nine to five basis and even if you call them, they'll give you an appointment two weeks hence. But if you call the police, they go.

Setting aside the question of how and in what way the police should be involved in providing such emergency services, it is clear that communities face an enormous problem of linking citizens to emergency services. A major urban problem is to provide an appropriate range of services (undoubtedly in cooperation with the police) to deal with the range of problems citizens present twenty-four hours a day. This is no simple matter.

Let us consider an example. If a citizen gets into a family argument or a dispute with a landlord, and it escalates to the point where someone defines it as a law enforcement problem, the police will be called. On hearing the complaint, it helps neither the citizen nor the police very much for the officer to define it as a "civil" rather than a "criminal" matter and then to take leave. Though danger of altercation may have passed, the source of their dispute—the problem—remains. Suppose the officer is more helpful than that and suggests ways the citizens may proceed to deal with the problem—for example, by consulting a lawyer. If the citizen has no lawyer, cannot afford one, or doesn't understand how to go about handling the matter, such advice fails to meet the problem. Suppose we carry it a step further; suppose the police officer advises a citizen to go to a particular legal aid service if he is unable to afford legal help. How well is the legal service organized to meet the demand that would ensue were the police to do such a "good" job and the citizen to follow through? The answer, one suspects, is that legal organizations are unprepared to meet such demands through referral. Yet many of these demands appear to be legitimate ones and certainly ones that, in one way or another, the government is trying to meet through some new programs for the underclass.

Our consideration of this simple case suggests several requirements for any urban service model that would meet many citizen demands for service: (1) that there be provision for emergency response to crises as well as organized response to more routine matters, (2) that the citizen be linked to an agency that can deal with his problem, (3) that agencies be available to meet effectively the demand for service. It should not be assumed that either the police or an emergency service or crisis intervention unit is sufficient, for that is not the case. Such a unit is a necessary but not a sufficient condition for an urban service that meets client needs.

A CLIENT-CENTERED SYSTEM

Let us further examine current models for offering and providing services to clients. Most services to clients are offered on a model of the "walk-in," a client who presents himself at a place where diagnosis and treatment can take place—a hospital, a clinic, a welfare office, even a Community Action Center. Ideally, the client should be preprocessed before much is done. What this means is that, ideally, the professional person or decision maker wants information about the client before contact is made with him.

What is more, service agencies usually are structured on what used to be called "banker's hours"—a nine A.M. to five P.M. schedule of work. Over and beyond that, their high specialization of services often means that clients must move episodically to different specialists in different agencies. Such a system seems designed to cool clients out of their demands for service rather than to meet client demands. The client is required to adapt to the agency personnel's schedule rather than his own schedule.

There are other contingencies that arise in such a system. The client soon discovers that he loses contacts with previous agencies. The referral has been incorrect and he moves to another that refers to yet another. Often there is no agency to which one returns. Even where, as in some of the Community Action Centers, attempts are made to accommodate the clock and calendar of the client and to make some follow-up, all too often the referral for a client is to an agency that operates from nine to five. Employment offices, social welfare agencies, even parole agents generally are on a nine-to-five basis.

It must be recognized that life is more comfortable for the professionals that way and these agencies are and must be regarded as being professional rather than client-centered.

The capacity of professionals to subvert the goals of clients is enormous. Some years ago, in New York City, when the city attempted to speed up the processing of offenders in the system of criminal justice, courts were set up to operate "around the clock and calendar." However, someone had forgotten there were vacation schedules and the swing shift was eliminated when the judges wanted their vacation! Apart from the emergency services of police, fire, and hospital organizations, no provision generally is made for services where demand exists and where there are needs to be met around the clock and calendar.

One suspects that much of the success of voluntary organizations like Alcoholics Anonymous or Synanon depends not only upon the fact that they develop informal relationships among social deviants, but also because a call for service or help is readily met by those who are members. Indeed, movement to a client is a relatively rare event today apart from police, fire, and sanitation services—the latter being one of the few regularly programmed services. A visiting nurse association service is relatively uncommon in the system and, like most such services, is based on notions of client inability to become a walk-in.

Questions about professional criteria for client preparation for service abound. Do their distinctions about what constitutes emergency make sense? Is social work or correctional work outside the closed institution really a nine-to-five job? May not a parolee need attention more at one A.M. than at three P.M.? If the Traveler's Insurance Company can advertise that no matter where and when you are involved in an automobile accident, a simple call to a number brings the Traveler's agent to work on your problem, why can't many public urban services do so?

Should one think further about what clients mean when they say, "the system doesn't meet our needs"? They seem to say more than that it doesn't meet needs for equal rewards. Such needs are not to be slighted, but they point up the fact that "systems" do not treat clients as "persons," as people with integrity, dignity, and worth. Part of the clients' reaction to not being regarded as "people" arises from the way they are treated when professionals are in their presence; but much of it also arises from the way that we have organized the bureaucratic processing of people as *cases* (Scheff, 1966).

Recognizing this dilemma, some social work and clinical agencies have come to speak of developing "client-centered" agencies. What they emphasize is doing something *with* people rather than *to* people. Important as such a distinction may be, it also may miss the point people are making. What may be more important to many people is what it is like to be processed in any system. All too rarely do we look at systems from the standpoint of people who are processed within them. How many agencies apprise citizens of their rights? (The police may do a better job of this now than any welfare or correctional agency!) What attempt is made to communicate with citizens about what is happening *to* them, and why. Part of this failure to communicate lies in the fact that the system is built more for the professionals than for the clients. All too often a continuance in court, for example, is to suit the convenience of the lawyers or the judge—not to suit the convenience of the client. Recently I listened to a man describe the process of being arrested and processed in the criminal courts of Detroit. He saw it as a process of going up and down in elevators in the same building, and in his mind, there were no separate elements in the system of justice. The police, the prosecutor, the judge, and the agency were all one, not several. While one could argue whether a system of criminal justice should be designed so that people like it, one should hardly argue that ignorance of how clients view it is rational.

.   .   .   .   .

CIVIC ACCOUNTABILITY OF PUBLIC EMPLOYEES

Some of the fiercest debate about urban services today rages around the issue of how citizen complaints about service are to be handled. In many communities, there are sharp debates about citizen review boards for the police or grievance commissions to deal with citizen complaints of discrimination in housing or employment. There should be no doubt that, in a democratic society, citizens have both a right and an obligation to complain about treatment by public officials, whether or not their complaints prove warranted on proper and appropriate investigation. A central issue lost sight of is: how are we, on the one hand, to be regulated by any public service and yet make public servants accountable to us for that regulation?

Perhaps, we need to remind ourselves that the problem is a central one for all democratic societies. It only takes different forms at different times. The dilemma took a somewhat different form for citizens in our nineteenth century cities where service and accountability rested in a "spoils system." Good government rebelled against the spoils system and introduced the "merit system" of appointment to insure quality and responsibility for service by tenure rather than by political fealty. We also removed many offices from direct election and made them appointive on the theory that accountability to the electorate could be exercised more wisely if fewer persons are held responsible to the electorate. We are still engaged in this process of "streamlining" government. Finally, we developed vast bureaucratic, publicly sponsored welfare services that replaced the services of the precinct and ward committeemen in local parties.

In the cause of "good government," however, we have lost sight of some important consequences of "machine politics." When public servants were enmeshed in the local political system of cities, they had to be fairly responsive to the demands of citizens because their continuation depended upon a local electorate. This was particularly true for the underclass and for minority groups in our cities; an underclass or minority group vote was as good as any other. Indeed, the successive waves of immigrant domination of sectors of public service (for example, that of the German and Irish in police departments) rested less on merit than on the responsiveness of local government organization to the organized political pressures of each successive wave of immigrants. There is little doubt that local politics in the nineteenth century often made for the rapid movement of the underclass into positions in the urban polity, thereby representing their interests. Furthermore, the local political organization often served quite effectively as a channel for grievance. The decline of machine politics carried with it some measure of loss of accountability of public officials and servants to citizens (Cornwell, 1964).

.   .   .   .   .

EXTERNAL AND INTERNAL ACCOUNTABILITY OF PUBLIC AGENCIES

Any system must be considered from the standpoint of the people processed by it. . . . Consider first, the requirement that the citizen shall lodge and pursue his complaint through the very agency against which the complaint is lodged. If I have a complaint about a police officer, I should go to a police official; if I have a complaint about a school teacher, I should go to a school official; if I have a complaint about health service, I should go to the hospital or clinic staff.

No citizen should be required to make and pursue his complaint through the very agency against which the complaint is lodged. Such a system fosters reluctance on the part of citizens to make complaints because of fear the agency may be punitive. Furthermore, if one complains to the offending agency, one is open to organizational manipulation by personnel in the agency, often to "cool out" the complainant. In short, agency personnel are not "disinterested" parties; justice lies partly in disinterest in the outcome. A major requirement, then, for any complaint system that is accountable to the citizens it serves is that the registration of complaints lies outside the agency against which the complaint is lodged.

.   .   .   .   .

At the same time, proposals for making public agencies accountable to citizens all too often focus on how external agencies may audit the public agencies and make them accountable. There are demands for "civilian review," "citizen control," or an "ombudsman." In these days of quality control, it is surprising that agency administrators give so little attention to how they can monitor the quality of service their agency gives clients. A few examples of agency monitoring may make apparent how such means can be developed and foster accountability.

Many agencies could readily develop an internal audit unit that regularly and systematically samples the client population and assesses the adequacy of service from both the administrative and the client point of view. If that agency is the police department, for example, it is possible to make an immediate follow-up after the police have engaged in a transaction with a citizen. Since the computer can select such cases, it is difficult to "beat" the system by controlling selection. Where the agency does not wish to conduct the audit itself, it can secure the services of an independent agency that reports to it. Such audits have become an essential part of many private industrial establishments. They need to become part of management for any public agency as well.

[In summary,] it has been suggested that any system with a goal to make public organizations accountable to the citizenry must build in certain elements that now are generally absent. A number of these elements have been reviewed: (1) that the registration of any complaint and its final review must lie with an agency, other than the one against which the complaint is lodged; (2) that a single agency best meets the requirement of informing citizens where they may go to lodge a complaint; (3) that an organization, rather than persons, should be responsible for formulating the complaint and transmitting it for appropriate action; (4) that both a regular system of accounting and an auditing service for clients must be built into the agency; (5) that punishment systems of sanctions against offending agency personnel militate against changing the organization; (6) that the focus of action based on complaints should be on how the agency, rather than on how its staff, generates the complaints.

REFERENCES

Cornwell, E. E., Jr. "Bosses, machines, and ethnic groups." *Annals of the American Academy of Political and Social Science* 353:27–39 (May, 1964).

Scheff, T. "Typification of the diagnostic practices of rehabilitation agencies." In M. Sussman (ed.), *Sociology and Rehabilitation.* Washington, D.C.: American Sociological Association, 1966.

19.   A ladder of citizen participation

SHERRY R. ARNSTEIN

The idea of citizen participation is a little like eating spinach: no one is against it in principle because it is good for you. Participation of the governed in their government is, in theory, the cornerstone of democracy—a revered idea that is vigorously applauded by virtually everyone. The applause is reduced to polite hand-claps, however, when this principle is advocated by the have-not blacks, Mexican-

Abridged and edited from Sherry R. Arnstein, "A ladder of citizen participation," *Journal of the American Institute of Planners,* 35:216–224 (July, 1969). Copyright © 1969 by American Institute of Planners. Reprinted by permission.

The author is a consultant on urban affairs, Washington, D.C.

Americans, Puerto Ricans, Indians, Eskimos, and whites. And when the have-nots define participation as redistribution of power, the American consensus on the fundamental principle explodes into many shades of outright racial, ethnic, ideological, and political opposition.

There have been many recent speeches, articles, and books[1] which explore in detail *who* are the have-nots of our time. There has been much recent documentation of *why* the have-nots have become so offended and embittered by their powerlessness to deal with the profound inequities and injustices pervading their daily lives. But there has been very little analysis of the content of the current controversial slogan: "citizen participation" or "maximum feasible participation." In short: *What* is citizen participation and what is its relationship to the social imperatives of our time?

.   .   .   .

My answer to the critical *what* question is simply that citizen participation is a categorical term for citizen power. It is the redistribution of power that enables the have-not citizens, presently excluded from the political and economic processes, to be deliberately included in the future. It is the strategy by which the have-nots join in determining how information is shared, goals and policies are set, tax resources are allocated, programs are operated, and benefits like contracts and patronage are parceled out. In short, it is the means by which they can induce significant social reform which enables them to share in the benefits of the affluent society.

There is a critical difference between going through the empty ritual of participation and having the real power needed to affect the outcome of the process. . . . Participation without redistribution of power is an empty and frustrating process for the powerless. It allows the powerholders to claim that all sides were considered, but makes it possible for only some of those sides to benefit. It maintains the status quo. Essentially, it is what has been happening in most of the 1,000 Community Action Programs, and what promises to be repeated in the vast majority of the 150 Model Cities programs.

TYPES OF PARTICIPATION AND "NONPARTICIPATION"

A typology of eight *levels* of participation may help in analysis of this confused issue. For illustrative purposes the eight types are arranged in a ladder pattern with

---

[1]The literature on poverty and discrimination and their effects on people is extensive. As an introduction, the following will be helpful: B. H. Bagdikian, *In the Midst of Plenty: The Poor in America* (New York: Beacon Press, 1964); Paul Jacobs, "The brutalizing of America," *Dissent,* 11:423–428 (Autumn, 1964); Stokely Carmichael and Charles V. Hamilton, *Black Power: The Politics of Liberation in America* (New York: Random House, Inc., 1967); Eldridge Cleaver, *Soul on Ice* (New York: McGraw-Hill Book Co., 1968); L. J. Duhl (ed.), *The Urban Condition: People and Policy in the Metropolis* (New York: Basic Books, Inc., 1963); William H. Grier and P. M. Cobbs, *Black Rage* (New York: Basic Books, Inc., 1968); Michael Harrington, *The Other America: Poverty in the United States* (New York: The Macmillan Co., 1962); Peter Marris and Martin Rein, *Dilemmas of Social Reform: Poverty and Community Action in the United States* (New York: Atherton Press, Inc., 1967); Millie Orshansky, "Who's who among the poor: A demographic view of poverty," *Social Security Bulletin* 27:3–32 (July, 1965); and Richard T. Titmuss, *Essays on the Welfare State* (New Haven, Conn.: Yale University Press, 1968).

each rung corresponding to the extent of citizens' power in determining the end product. (See Figure 1.)

The bottom rungs of the ladder are (1) *Manipulation* and (2) *Therapy.* These two rungs describe levels of "non-participation" that have been contrived by some to substitute for genuine participation. Their real objective is not to enable people to participate in planning or conducting programs, but to enable powerholders to "educate" or "cure" the participants. Rungs 3 and 4 progress to levels of "tokenism" that allow the have-nots to hear and to have a voice: (3) *Informing* and (4) *Consultation.* When they are proffered by powerholders as the total extent of participation, citizens may indeed hear and be heard. But under these conditions they lack the power to insure that their views will be *heeded* by the powerful. When participation is restricted to these levels, there is no followthrough, no "muscle," hence no assurance of changing the status quo. Rung (5), *Placation,* is simply a higher level tokenism because the groundrules allow have-nots to advise, but retain for the powerholders the continued right to decide.

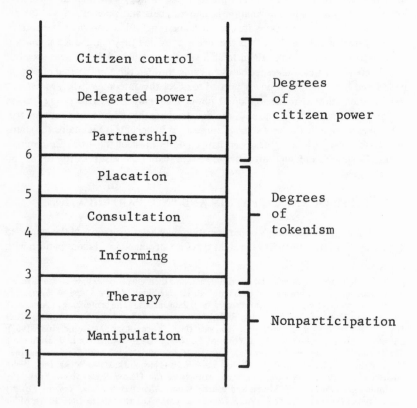

Figure 1
Eight rungs on a ladder of citizen participation

Further up the ladder are levels of citizen power with increasing degrees of decision-making clout. Citizens can enter into a (6) *Partnership* that enables them to negotiate and engage in trade-offs with traditional powerholders. At the topmost rungs, (7) *Delegated Power* and (8) *Citizen Control*, have-not citizens obtain the majority of decision-making seats, or full managerial power.

Obviously, the eight-rung ladder is a simplification, but it helps to illustrate the point that so many have missed—that there are significant gradations of citizen participation. Knowing these gradations makes it possible to cut through the hyperbole to understand the increasingly strident demands for participation from the have-nots as well as the gamut of confusing responses from the powerholders.

Though the typology uses examples from federal programs such as urban renewal, anti-poverty, and Model Cities, it could just as easily be illustrated in the church, currently facing demands for power from priests and laymen who seek to change its mission; colleges and universities which in some cases have become literal battlegrounds over the issue of student power; or public schools, city halls, and police departments (or big business which is likely to be next on the expanding list of targets). The underlying issues are essentially the same—"nobodies" in several arenas are trying to become "somebodies" with enough power to make the target institutions responsive to their views, aspirations, and needs.

.   .   .   .   .

CHARACTERISTICS AND ILLUSTRATIONS

It is in this context of power and powerlessness that the characteristics of the eight rungs are illustrated by examples from current federal social programs.

1. Manipulation

.   .   .   .   .

This illusory form of "participation" initially came into vogue with urban renewal when the socially elite were invited by city housing officials to serve on Citizen Advisory Committees (CACs). Another target of manipulation were the CAC subcommittees on minority groups, which in theory were to protect the rights of Negroes in the renewal program. In practice, these subcommittees, like their parent CACs, functioned mostly as letterheads, trotted forward at appropriate times to promote urban renewal plans (in recent years known as Negro removal plans).

At meetings of the Citizen *Advisory* Committees, it was the officials who educated, persuaded, and advised the citizens, not the reverse. Federal guidelines for the renewal programs legitimized the manipulative agenda by emphasizing the terms "information-gathering," "public relations," and "support" as the explicit functions of the committees.[2]

This style of nonparticipation has since been applied to other programs encompassing the poor. Examples of this are seen in Community Action Agencies (CAAs)

---

[2]U.S. Department of Housing and Urban Development, *Workable Program for Community Improvement, Answers on Citizen Participation*, Program Guide 7, February, 1966, pp. 1 and 6.

which have created structures called "neighborhood councils" or "neighborhood advisory groups." These bodies frequently have no legitimate function or power.[3] The CAAs use them to "prove" that "grassroots people" are involved in the program. But the program may not have been discussed with "the people." Or it may have been described at a meeting in the most general terms; "We need your signatures on this proposal for a multiservice center which will house, under one roof, doctors from the health department, workers from the welfare department, and specialists from the employment service."

The signators are not informed that the $2 million-per-year center will only refer residents to the same old waiting lines at the same old agencies across town. No one is asked if such a referral center is really needed in his neighborhood. No one realizes that the contractor for the building is the mayor's brother-in-law, or that the new director of the center will be the same old community organization specialist from the urban renewal agency.

After signing their names, the proud grassrooters dutifully spread the word that they have "participated" in bringing a new and wonderful center to the neighborhood to provide people with drastically needed jobs and health and welfare services. Only after the ribbon-cutting ceremony do the members of the neighborhood council realize that they didn't ask the important questions, and that they had no technical advisors of their own to help them grasp the fine legal print. The new center, which is open 9 to 5 on weekdays only, actually adds to their problems. Now the old agencies across town won't talk with them unless they have a pink paper slip to prove that they have been referred by "their" shiny new neighborhood center.

Unfortunately, this chicanery is not a unique example. Instead it is almost typical of what has been perpetrated in the name of high-sounding rhetoric like "grassroots participation." This sham lies at the heart of the deepseated exasperation and hostility of the have-nots toward the powerholders.

One hopeful note is that, having been so grossly affronted, some citizens have learned the Mickey Mouse game, and now they too know how to play. As a result of this knowledge, they are demanding genuine levels of participation to assure them that public programs are relevant to their needs and responsive to their priorities.

2. Therapy

In some respects group therapy, masked as citizen participation, should be on the lowest rung of the ladder because it is both dishonest and arrogant. Its administrators—mental health experts from social workers to psychiatrists—assume that powerlessness is synonymous with mental illness. On this assumption, under a masquerade of involving citizens in planning, the experts subject the citizens to clinical group therapy. What makes this form of "participation" so invidious is that citizens are engaged in extensive activity, but the focus of it is on curing them of their "pathology" rather than changing the racism and victimization that create their "pathologies."

---

[3]David Austin, "Study of resident participants in twenty community action agencies," U.S. Department of Housing and Urban Development, CAP Grant 9499.

... Common examples of therapy, masquerading as citizen participation, may be seen in public housing programs where tenant groups are used as vehicles for promoting control-your-child or cleanup campaigns. The tenants are brought together to help them "adjust their values and attitudes to those of the larger society." Under these groundrules, they are diverted from dealing with such important matters as: arbitrary evictions; segregation of the housing project; or why there is a three-month time lapse to get a broken window replaced in winter.

3. Informing

Informing citizens of their rights, responsibilities, and options can be the most important first step toward legitimate citizen participation. However, too frequently the emphasis is placed on a one-way flow of information—from officials to citizens —with no channel provided for feedback and no power for negotiation. Under these conditions, particularly when information is provided at a late stage in planning, people have little opportunity to influence the program designed "for their benefit." The most frequent tools used for such one-way communication are the news media, pamphlets, posters, and responses to inquiries.

4. Consultation

Inviting citizens' opinions, like informing them, can be a legitimate step toward their full participation. But if consulting them is not combined with other modes of participation, this rung of the ladder is still a sham since it offers no assurance that citizen concerns and ideas will be taken into account. The most frequent methods used for consulting people are attitude surveys, neighborhood meetings, and public hearings.

When powerholders restrict the input of citizens' ideas solely to this level, participation remains just a window-dressing ritual. People are primarily perceived as statistical abstractions, and participation is measured by how many come to meetings, take brochures home, or answer a questionnaire. What citizens achieve in all this activity is that they have "participated in participation." And what powerholders achieve is the evidence that they have gone through the required motions of involving "those people."

Attitude surveys have become a particular bone of contention in ghetto neighborhoods. Residents are increasingly unhappy about the number of times per week they are surveyed about their problems and hopes. As one woman put it: "Nothing ever happens with those damned questions, except the surveyer gets $3 an hour, and my washing doesn't get done that day." In some communities, residents are so annoyed that they are demanding a fee for research interviews.

Attitude surveys are not very valid indicators of community opinion when used without other input from citizens. Survey after survey (paid for out of anti-poverty funds) has "documented" that poor housewives most want tot-lots in their neighborhood where young children can play safely. But most of the women answered these questionnaires without knowing what their options were. They assumed that if they asked for something small, they might just get something useful in the neighborhood. Had the mothers known that a free prepaid health insurance plan was a possible option, they might not have put tot-lots so high on their wish lists.

·   ·   ·   ·   ·

5. Placation

It is at this level that citizens begin to have some degree of influence through tokenism is still apparent. An example of placation strategy is to place a few handpicked "worthy" poor on boards of Community Action Agencies or on public bodies like the board of education, police commission, or housing authority. If they are not accountable to a constituency in the community and if the traditional power elite hold the majority of seats, the have-nots can be easily outvoted and outfoxed. Another example is the Model Cities advisory and planning committees. They allow citizens to advise or plan ad infinitum but retain for powerholders the right to judge the legitimacy or feasibility of the advice. The degree to which citizens are actually placated, of course, depends largely on two factors: the quality of technical assistance they have in articulating their priorities; and the extent to which the community has been organized to press for those priorities.

It is not surprising that the level of citizen participation in the vast majority of Model Cities programs is at the placation rung of the ladder or below. Policymakers at the Department of Housing and Urban Development (HUD) were determined to return the genie of citizen power to the bottle from which it had escaped (in a few cities) as a result of the provision stipulating "maximum feasible participation" in poverty programs. Therefore, HUD channeled its physical-social-economic rejuvenation approach for blighted neighborhoods through city hall. It drafted legislation requiring that all Model Cities' money flow to a local City Demonstration Agency (CDA) through the elected city council. As enacted by Congress, this gave local city councils final veto power over planning and programming and ruled out any direct funding relationship between community groups and HUD.

HUD required the CDAs to create coalition, policy-making boards that would include necessary local power-holders to create a comprehensive physical-social plan during the first year. The plan was to be carried out in a subsequent five-year action phase. HUD, unlike OEO, did not require that have-not citizens be included on the CDA decision-making boards. HUD's Performance Standards for Citizen Participation only demanded that "citizens have clear and direct access to the decision-making process."

Accordingly, the CDAs structured their policy-making boards to include some combination of elected officials; school representatives; housing, health, and welfare officials; employment and police department representatives; and various civic, labor, and business leaders. Some CDAs included citizens from the neighborhood. Many mayors correctly interpreted the HUD provision for "access to the decision-making process" as the escape hatch they sought to relegate citizens to the traditional advisory role.

·   ·   ·   ·   ·

In most Model Cities programs, endless time has been spent fashioning complicated board, committee, and task force structures for the planning year. But the rights and responsibilities of the various elements of those structures are not defined and are ambiguous. Such ambiguity is likely to cause considerable conflict at the end of the one-year planning process. For at this point, citizens may realize that they have once again extensively "participated" but have not profited beyond the extent the powerholders decide to placate them.

· · · · ·

6. Partnership

At this rung of the ladder, power is in fact redistributed through negotiation between citizens and powerholders. They agree to share planning and decision-making responsibilities through such structures as joint policy boards, planning committees and mechanisms for resolving impasses. After the groundrules have been established through some form of give-and-take, they are not subject to unilateral change.

Partnership can work most effectively when there is an organized power-base in the community to which the citizen leaders are accountable; when the citizens group has the financial resources to pay its leaders reasonable honoraria for their time-consuming efforts; and when the group has the resources to hire (and fire) its own technicians, lawyers, and community organizers. With these ingredients, citizens have some genuine bargaining influence over the outcome of the plan (as long as both parties find it useful to maintain the partnership). One community leader described it "like coming to city hall with hat on head instead of in hand."

In the Model Cities program only about fifteen of the so-called first generation of seventy-five cities have reached some significant degree of power-sharing with residents. In all but one of those cities, it was angry citizen demands, rather than city initiative, that led to the negotiated sharing of power. The negotiations were triggered by citizens who had been enraged by previous forms of alleged participation. They were both angry and sophisticated enough to refuse to be "conned" again. They threatened to oppose the awarding of a planning grant to the city. They sent delegations to HUD in Washington. They used abrasive language. Negotiation took place under a cloud of suspicion and rancor.

In most cases where power has come to be shared it was *taken by the citizens,* not given by the city. There is nothing new about that process. Since those who have power normally want to hang onto it, historically it has had to be wrested by the powerless rather than proffered by the powerful.

· · · · ·

7. Delegated Power

Negotiations between citizens and public officials can also result in citizens achieving dominant decision-making authority over a particular plan or program. Model City policy boards or CAA delegate agencies on which citizens have a clear majority of seats and genuine specified powers are typical examples. At this level, the ladder has been scaled to the point where citizens hold the significant cards to assure accountability of the program to them. To resolve differences, powerholders need to start the bargaining process rather than respond to pressure from the other end.

Such a dominant decision-making role has been attained by residents in a handful of Model Cities including Cambridge, Massachusetts; Dayton, and Columbus, Ohio; Minneapolis, Minnesota; St. Louis, Missouri; Hartford and New Haven, Connecticut; and Oakland, California.

In New Haven, residents of the Hill neighborhood have created a corporation that has been delegated the power to prepare the entire Model Cities plan. The city, which received a $117,000 planning grant from HUD, has subcontracted $110,000 of it to the neighborhood corporation to hire its own planning staff and consultants. The Hill Neighborhood Corporation has eleven representatives on the twenty-one-member CDA board which assures it a majority voice when its proposed plan is reviewed by the CDA.

Another model of delegated power is separate and parallel groups of citizens and powerholders, with provision for citizen veto if differences of opinion cannot be resolved through negotiation. This is a particularly interesting coexistence model for hostile citizen groups too embittered toward city hall—as a result of past "collaborative efforts"—to engage in joint planning.

.   .   .   .   .

8. Citizen Control

Demands for community controlled schools, black control, and neighborhood control are on the increase. Though no one in the nation has absolute control, it is very important that the rhetoric not be confused with intent. People are simply demanding that degree of power (or control) which guarantees that participants or residents can govern a program or an institution, be in full charge of policy and managerial aspects, and be able to negotiate the conditions under which "outsiders" may change them.

A neighborhood corporation with no intermediaries between it and the source of funds is the model most frequently advocated. A small number of such experimental corporations are already producing goods and/or social services. Several others are reportedly in the development stage, and new models for control will undoubtedly emerge as the have-nots continue to press for greater degrees of power over their lives.

Though the bitter struggle for community control of the Ocean Hill-Brownsville schools in New York City has aroused great fears in the headline reading public, less publicized experiments are demonstrating that the have-nots can indeed improve their lot by handling the entire job of planning, policy-making, and managing a program. Some are even demonstrating that they can do all this with just one arm because they are forced to use their other one to deal with a continuing barrage of local opposition triggered by the announcement that a federal grant has been given to a community group or an all black group.

.   .   .   .   .

Among the arguments against community control are: it supports separatism; it creates balkanization of public services; it is more costly and less efficient; it enables minority group "hustlers" to be just as opportunistic and disdainful of the have-nots as their white predecessors; it is incompatible with merit systems and professionalism; and ironically enough, it can turn out to be a new Mickey Mouse game for the have-nots by allowing them to gain control but not allowing them sufficient dollar resources to succeed.[4] These arguments are not to be taken lightly. But neither can we take lightly the arguments of embittered advocates of community control—that every other means of trying to end their victimization has failed!

20. Neighborhood government

DOUGLAS YATES

In the 1969 New York mayoralty campaign, "power to the neighborhoods" was the battle cry of an unusual candidate, who was running, he said, to offer fresh answers to an old problem: the much lamented "urban crisis." The candidate was Norman Mailer, and since he claimed to be part visionary and part conservative, it was hard to tell whether the slogan "power to the neighborhoods" looked back to a fondly remembered past or pointed forward to an imagined future.[1] Coming at a time in American politics when a debate swirled around participatory democracy, it was not surprising that neighborhood government was a political issue. More puzzling, perhaps, is what is meant precisely by neighborhood government; what its origins are; what its benefits and deficiencies are thought to be; what the main obstacles are to its achievement; and what general problems it raises for local democracy and community development. I will explore these questions in light of the past and present experience of decentralized, neighborhood-based government.

---

[4]For thoughtful academic analyses of some of the potentials and pitfalls of emerging neighborhood control models, see Alan Altshuler, "The demand for participation in large American cities," an unpublished paper prepared for the Urban Institute, December, 1968, and Hans B. C. Spiegel and Stephen D. Mittenthal, "Neighborhood power and control, implications for urban planning," a report prepared for the Department of Housing and Urban Development, November, 1968.

This article appears for the first time in this volume, by permission of the author.

The author teaches political science at Yale University, New Haven, Conn.

[1]Mailer's position on neighborhood government is recorded in detail in Peter Manso (ed.), *Running against the Machine* (Garden City, N.Y.: Doubleday & Co., Inc., 1969).

HISTORICAL BACKGROUND

In terms of American urban history, the idea of neighborhood government is something rather new. Demands for neighborhood self-government have not been a familiar theme in political discourse, and there is little evidence, until very recently, of programs and policies designed to give power to urban neighborhoods. Thus while Thomas Jefferson certainly did argue for the creation of "republics-in-miniature," his little Republic was an agrarian one. Indeed, Jefferson was notoriously suspicious of and hostile to the city.[2] Nor have other previous analysts of local democracy paid much attention to the urban neighborhood as a locus for self-government. For example, the urban reformers at the turn of the century were obsessed with the fight against corruption and wanted to shift power away from grass-roots organizations to aloof, central administrators. The main debate in this century about local government has centered on whether the city as a corporate entity should enjoy more or less "home rule" in its relationship with state government.[3]

The practice of urban government under the great political machines also reveals little precedent for neighborhood government. While it is true that the ward bosses of legend carefully cultivated the grass roots by dispensing Christmas turkeys and patronage and by dealing with citizen complaints and problems, the point of these services was to oil a centralized political machine. Simply put, the political exchange rate in machine politics was patronage or favors for electoral support, and the currency was not used to purchase direct local democracy. Indeed, according to one historian, the essential purpose of Boss Tweed's machine, the first and most dramatic of the species, was to centralize power and therefore overcome the stalemate and inertia caused by existing governmental fragmentation.[4] The most that can be said of the old-time neighborhood bosses is that some special ones, like the Ahearns of New York's Lower East Side, did establish little baronies. But this is testimony to the existence of feudal power, not neighborhood democracy.

Other historical examples of "neighborhood government" that might be cited by present-day advocates tend to be slight or deceiving. New York and other cities may have had Borough governments (or the equivalent), but there is a considerable difference in scale between a borough and a neighborhood. Administrative field offices, district school boards, and community planning boards existed before the late 1960's, but their functions were usually strictly bureaucratic or merely advisory. Thus, it is only with the current urban crisis and with ensuing government programs that an explicit concern with participation, decentralization, and neighborhood

---

[2]Jefferson's view of the city as the locus of all "human depravity" is elaborated in Morton and Lucia White, *The Intellectual versus the City* (Cambridge, Mass.: Harvard University Press, 1962), p. 24 ff.

[3]See Anwar Syed, *The Political Theory of American Local Government* (New York: Random House, Inc., 1966).

[4]This interpretation is made by Seymour J. Mandelbaum in his *Boss Tweed's New York* (New York: John Wiley & Sons, Inc., 1965).

government has emerged. Specifically, the first traces of what might loosely be called neighborhood government were found in urban renewal, the war on poverty, and the Model Cities program. In the case of urban renewal, according to James Q. Wilson, citizen participation was limited to advisory planning and to bitter opposition of proposed renewal plans.[5] In the war on poverty's community action program, there was a constant struggle over the meaning of "maximum feasible participation," and as a result, the degree of local participation varied sharply from city to city. In most cities, however, poverty and political mobilization, not institutionalized neighborhood government *per se*, were the foci of community action. In contrast, Model Cities does focus directly on the urban neighborhood, but again, the legislation concerning participation is vague and ambiguous; and as in community action, the experience of Model Cities has varied widely, from total city hall control in cities like Chicago to substantial neighborhood control in cities like New Haven.

What is clear from the historical record is that, given these shallow roots, it is only certain contemporary and dramatic events like school decentralization in New York City that have focused political discussion on community control and neighborhood government.[6]

WHAT IS DECENTRALIZATION?

In discussing the historical background of neighborhood government, we have related a poorly defined notion to other equally vague concepts such as citizen participation and decentralization. Indeed, the central failing in the debate about neighborhood power and control is that it rests on analytical quicksand. Difficult as it may be to define "neighborhood," it is more difficult to pin down the concepts of "participation" and "decentralization," for they have been used indiscriminately to describe governmental arrangements as different as colonialism and community control. People can hardly be expected to decide whether neighborhood government is a good or bad thing, a promising policy or a totally impractical one, unless they know how the concepts are defined. The most important strand in this web of tangled concepts is decentralization. In order to give a firm meaning to this suggestive and ambiguous concept, it is necessary to ask three different questions: (1) What does the particular mode of decentralization entail in terms of power relations between the center and the locality? (2) What is being decentralized? (3) What are the reasons for decentralization?

The first question arises from the facts that there can be a whole range of power relations between the center and locality, and the relations may be obscured by

[5]James Q. Wilson, "Planning and politics: Citizen participation in urban renewal," in *Urban Renewal: The Record and the Controversy* (Cambridge, Mass.: The M.I.T. Press, 1966), pp. 407–421.

[6]The most controversial case of school decentralization occurred in the Ocean Hill–Brownsville experimental district. For accounts of this aspect of the New York experience see Maurice Berube and Marilyn Gittell (eds.), *Confrontation at Ocean Hill–Brownsville* (New York: Frederick A. Praeger, Inc., 1969); and Naomi Levine, *Ocean Hill–Brownsville* (New York: Popular Library, Inc., 1969).

superficial administrative arrangements. For instance, a strictly hierarchical administrative system, such as exists in France, decentralizes administrative offices, personnel, and the functions of intelligence gathering and consultation with citizens to departmental prefects and parish mayors. However, these local officials have virtually no autonomous decision-making power. They are, in law and practice, agents of the central administration whose authority derives from the center and who are responsible not to the locality but to Paris.

My contention would be that governmental forms increase in genuine local autonomy the more that certain structural elements are included in them (the elements are ordered in terms of increasing local autonomy and power):

1. Intelligence gathering—stationing officials in localities to find out what is going on in the field.
2. Consultation and advisory planning—seeking out the opinion of local people on policy matters.
3. Program administration—making local people the administrative agents of central government programs and policies.
4. Administrative accountability—making district or neighborhood administrators responsible for government programs and accountable to local citizens.
5. Political accountability—establishing elected officials at the local level as representatives of local interests.
6. Authoritative decisionmaking—giving neighborhood representatives the power to make binding decisions on policy matters.
7. Political resources—giving localities control over resources such that local decision making involves real stakes and capacities.

If government involves elements 1 through 3, it constitutes a form of administrative decentralization or "command decentralization," as when a platoon leader in the field is given a measure of responsibility and decision-making autonomy. If government structure includes local decision making and control over resources (elements 4 through 7), it may constitute shared center-local control or full community control.[7] In sum, it seems that these seven elements constitute one dimension along which decentralization can be defined.

A second dimension that should be considered is the number of program functions involved, or "what is being decentralized." A neighborhood health clinic serves, for example, a single function, while neighborhood multiservice centers perform several functions. In light of both these two dimensions, it is clear that none of the current decentralization experiments come close to the ideal of a general-purpose, autonomous neighborhood government. What exists currently is a variety of single-function and multifunction experiments in which neighborhoods have limited power.

There are many examples of single-function experiments in administrative decentralization, such as municipal field offices of all kinds and district-based sys-

---

[7]Sherry Arnstein's article, "A ladder of citizen participation," *Journal of the American Institute of Planners,* 35:216–224 (July, 1969), presents another way of labelling the progression from weak to strong decentralization. [Arnstein's article appears on pp. 110–119.] The point of my analysis is to show the structural prerequisites to different kinds of participation.

tems of service delivery. Single-function experiments with substantial local power include neighborhood-run health clinics, community corporations dealing with poverty programs, and decentralized school boards (as in New York City). Multifunctional experiments include Little City Halls in twenty cities which provide information and receive citizen complaints. Of a multifunctional character, but with a somewhat greater amount of local power, are the Model Cities programs, multiservice centers in forty-two cities, and neighborhood corporations in New Haven. It is interesting to note that there seems to be a relationship between the number of functions decentralized and the degree of local power. In experiments existing at present, those performing single functions tend to possess relatively more local autonomy, and local autonomy seems to diminish with an increased number of functions.

The variety of existing decentralization experiments attests to, at the very least, the growing interest in neighborhood government strategies. Given this apparent enthusiasm, it is obviously important to know why government officials and community leaders wish to decentralize. That is, what answers are typically given to the nagging question: Why decentralize at all? Summarizing various written and spoken opinions on the subject, there are at least four different justifications for decentralization: (1) decentralization will increase administrative attentiveness and responsiveness to neighborhood needs; (2) decentralization will reduce the perceived distance between citizens and their government and therefore increase citizens' feelings of political efficacy; (3) decentralization will develop community cohesion and thereby focus local resources and concern on shared problems; and (4) decentralization will dramatically increase local democracy by developing local leaders and by providing wider opportunities for citizen involvement in decision making.

As against this positive view, critics of decentralization contend that it will increase racial segregation and strife, decrease due-process "fairness" and impartiality in administration, permit widespread corruption, create unchecked feudal baronies, and undermine the efficient allocation of resources (presumed to be enhanced by strong central management). To a lesser extent, critics also argue that decentralization will solve no problems; that without a massive commitment of resources to the cities, the structure of urban government makes little difference.

At present, the *a priori* and normative claims for and against decentralization have become so numerous and so passionate that one political scientist, Alan Altshuler, has devoted a book, *Community Control,*[8] to the task of sorting out and evaluating the conflicting arguments. The key point about this debate, however, is that it gives us almost no idea about the actual impact of decentralization on an urban neighborhood. In the first place, there has been little empirical research on the impacts of existing decentralization experiences. Secondly, as has been seen, decentralization, in the form of local autonomy or community control, has nowhere been achieved, and any evaluation of existing programs will necessarily deal with halfway measures and cannot indicate the effects of full decentralization. This being the case, it is foolish to expect a clear conclusion to the decentralization debate to arise from the present clash of rhetorical claims and speculative judgments. But it is possible to speculate more rigorously by considering the obstacles to and likely

---

[8]Alan Altshuler, *Community Control* (New York: Pegasus, 1970).

problems of decentralization. For if we consider these negative factors and still judge local control to be plausible, then advocacy of neighborhood government would rest on a careful assessment of possible dangers and deficiencies rather than on wishful thinking about structural change or blind despair about the present failures of urban government.

OBSTACLES TO NEIGHBORHOOD GOVERNMENT

If one considers the context of decentralization for only a minute, one should recognize certain obstacles to increasing neighborhood power. They are: (1) the costs of community organizing in time and effort, (2) community conflict, (3) city hall–neighborhood conflict, and (4) general political conflict.

First, it is a truism that political activism and citizen participation demand a considerable commitment of time, energy, and other personal resources. Doubtless, it is for this reason that the activist segment of any political community is very small indeed. Moreover, in order to persuade individuals to engage in collective action, it is necessary that the rewards of such action be greater than the personal costs. This means that serious participation is likely to occur only when neighborhood government offers visible rewards and works to solve concrete problems. As an added complication, there are many examples of desirable collective actions where it makes sense for the individual to participate only if he knows that everyone else in the community will join with him. This is true, for example, with garbage clean-ups and campaigns to curb dogs. If one or more people do not cooperate in the effort, the impact of everyone else's effort is necessarily vitiated.

As to community conflict, it has been noted by Bell and Held that a large number of community organizations already exist in poor neighborhoods.[9] One wonders whether these organizations, with their vested interests, will find any reason to promote and ultimately defer to a more generalized system of neighborhood government. Furthermore, many of the neighborhoods are characterized by racial and ethnic cleavages and, to a lesser extent, by religious differences and age differences (as between an old guard and "young turks"). If neighborhood government is to be a successful force for community cohesion and development, the various factions and vested interests will have to join together to pursue common purposes. Unfortunately, this has not always happened in recent experience. In some neighborhoods, Puerto Rican and black groups fight ceaselessly and bitterly; in other neighborhoods, entrenched community organizations have resisted any movement to neighborhoodwide structures.

City hall–neighborhood conflict has many manifestations. In some cases, community leaders claim that central government has consistently defaulted on the promise to give specific powers or resources to the neighborhoods. In other cases, local leaders complain about government interference with and surveillance of community programs. In still other instances, neighborhood leaders report that they cannot get the central government to act on requests or make decisions on issues of great importance to the neighborhood—the result being that neighborhood poli-

---

[9]Daniel Bell and Virginia Held, "The community revolution," *The Public Interest*, No. 16 (Summer, 1969), pp. 155–158.

cies are hamstrung by government inaction. Finally, some neighborhood governments find themselves caught between competing or warring government agencies, and their programs thereby become administrative footballs.

If the neighborhood-based organization is lucky enough to avoid these obstacles, there is still the possibility that neighborhood programs will ignite a political controversy that seriously damages the efforts at decentralization. The most dramatic political explosion over decentralization developed over the community control of schools in the Ocean Hill–Brownsville district of New York City. Before it was over, the teachers' union, City Hall, and the neighborhood had experienced a long and bloody political war, in which union rights were pitted against community authority, and charges of white racism met countercharges of black anti-Semitism. Other neighborhood programs, especially the Little City Hall Programs in Boston and New York, have also raised considerable controversy. The charge has been made in these cases that the neighborhood city halls were nothing more than political clubhouses for the incumbent mayor. The furor was such that no public money was allocated for the New York program, and the Boston program has been constantly under political attack.

FURTHER PROBLEMS AND QUESTIONS

If these obstacles are not enough, there are a number of further problems and questions that require consideration before neighborhood government is declared an unmitigated blessing.

For one thing, if neighborhood institutions are created for 150,000 or 300,000 people (as is commonly proposed in the large cities), will the citizen really feel that much closer to his government? Democratic theorists argue that a *city*, not to mention a neighborhood, should probably contain no more than 200,000 residents if anything remotely like direct democracy is to exist.[10] Or, if there is one neighborhood service center for every 150,000 to 300,000 people, will the citizen gain that much proximity and access to city services? Preliminary research indicates that, where only one such center exists in a neighborhood, only a tiny percentage of local residents will be aware of its existence.[11]

More importantly, if fresh resources are not committed to the cities, will decentralization make a concrete attack on any urban problem? And if so, on which problem? Surely new housing, parks, or subways will not be built with decentralization alone. Nor is it obvious how decentralization will make a dramatic effect on other service problems that also depend strongly on physical resources, such as garbage collection and fire protection. The problems that seem most readily treated by decentralization are those that involve social attitudes and human behavior. If

---

[10]Robert Dahl suggests that a population range of 50,000 to 200,000 is best suited for widespread citizen participation in a *city*. See his "The city the future of democracy," *American Political Science Review*, 61:967–970, (December, 1967).

[11]In a sidewalk survey on New York's Lower East Side, the author found that only three people out of 100 residents had heard of the neighborhood mayor's office, known as the Urban Action Task Force. Fifty of those interviews were conducted within a three-block radius of the government office. Several residents who were interviewed lived on the same block as the Task Force office and still were not aware of its existence.

a schoolchild feels alien in his own classroom, and if policemen and citizens hate each other, the community obviously suffers from a breakdown of political authority. But under decentralization, a new set of attitudes may arise that fosters citizen pride in the community and greater sensitivity on the part of public servants who are now accountable to local masters.

Following this logic, one wonders whether neighborhood government will affect those problems for which community people are both the source and the victims. Among those problems are widespread littering, turning in false alarms on fireboxes, vandalism against school property, drug pushing, and mugging. The question is: Will neighborhood governments be able to govern their own people—to establish and enforce community norms and sanctions—any better than the existing central government? Or is there a broad realm of uncontrollable, antisocial behavior that no government, whatever its location, can deal with under present social and economic conditions?

A further problem is that evidence to date suggests that citizens in poor neighborhoods do not turn out in large numbers to vote in community elections. A consequence of this in the decentralized school board elections in New York was that white Catholics were elected in wholly disproportionate numbers to govern schools in black neighborhoods. Decentralization in this case thus gave power to the wrong people, perhaps defeating the very purpose of the decentralization strategy. There is a larger point here as well. The poor have typically lost out in the one-man–one-vote and one-dollar–one-vote sweepstakes that determine who gets what in American political and economic life. Indeed, this is one meaning of powerlessness. The argument is therefore made that government should consciously protect and work for the poor and for poor neighborhoods, in a paternalistic way. Advocates of community control repudiate this principle of paternalism as colonialism, or worse, racism. But it is true that decentralization does represent a partial return to a free market system in political life. If in a racially mixed decentralized district, conservative whites win control of the neighborhood government, the poor and the blacks have no recourse. The effect of decentralization then is to establish the legitimate authority of those very forces that were viewed as the source of oppression. Clearly, too, if a central government does not redistribute resources in favor of poor districts, decentralization may produce an urban version of suburban feudalism, where the rich get richer and the poor get poorer.

The same dilemma also raises at least two contrasting alternatives regarding the encouragement of citizen participation. The first one calls for a disintegration of central government functions and powers, so that the localities can maximize their role. This view may be called the centrifugal concept of participation. The second one calls for the increased control of the central government apparatus by local groups (e.g., black minorities). This is, by contrast, the centripetal concept of participation. More concretely, the kind of local participation sought by a Rhody McCoy in Ocean Hill–Brownsville is bound to be radically different from the participation sought by Kenneth Gibson in Newark.

CONCLUSIONS

For the long-term future, neighborhood government may very well be a desirable goal. Aside from the commonly expressed justifications already mentioned, neighborhood government may constitute the "big push" that Gunnar Myrdal talks about, which will shake up a stagnant bureaucracy and also change the attitudes of citizens toward government and their own community. But it is also certainly true that the road to neighborhood government will be a difficult one, for there are several visible obstacles and a number of unresolved problems and questions. What is most important is that there is not enough knowledge about existing neighborhood government experiments to know if the road is worth taking in the first place.

As to the immediate prospects of neighborhood government, one can, I think, be more certain and more pessimistic. In New York City, where neighborhood government has proceeded further than anywhere else, there is a realization among city officials that strategies must be implemented very gradually if at all. There is a specific awareness that unions and many politicians will fight neighborhood government bitterly, and that they have the power to damage or destroy it. There is also the sense that, whereas there has been success in developing community structures, it has been very difficult to move government toward decentralization, toward more flexible administrative procedures. The new strategy in New York is to tackle the failures of government directly, before promising any new revolution in participatory democracy. More precisely, the strategy, manifest in programs like the police department's Operation Neighborhood, is to move toward command decentralization, to enhance administrative responsiveness by locating accountability and decision-making power at the neighborhood level. This is, of course, a long way from neighborhood government.

Furthermore, it is doubtful that the neighborhood government movement will take many cities by storm in the near future. In cities with black majorities or near majorities, the movement is likely to be toward centripetal participation—control of city hall. Conversely, in cities with a small black percentage of the population, the critical mass of political power may be missing that is needed to force government in the direction of local participation. It is also unclear whether neighborhood control is desired by citizens even where the power to produce it presumably exists. In Berkeley, California, for example, an electorate containing a strong black and white radical coalition was able to elect its candidates but came nowhere near winning a referendum to decentralize the police.

Finally, there is the question of whether neighborhood government is desirable for all urban neighborhoods in the same way at the same time. We must remember (and we tend to forget) that neighborhoods differ sharply in terms of their ethnic homogeneity, their level of community organization, and their assortment of needs. The New York experience has suggested that a uniform and grandiose plan will fail to distinguish among neighborhoods, and that it may be necessary to think of neighborhood government in different neighborhoods at different times.

D. PHYSICAL ENVIRONMENT

Any discussion of the physical environment seems particularly appropriate because of the current national concern with the human use and misuse of the earth's natural resources.[1] More people have become aware that our consumer-oriented society has grave effects on the air we breathe, the water we drink, and the land we live on. Typically, the problem is that both personal and industrial practices lead to the excessive pollution of the natural environment, to the point that life itself may be threatened. Examples of the seriousness of the matter are no longer hard to find, with birds threatened by oil spills, fish by industrial wastes dumped into rivers, and people by temperature inversions over polluted masses of air.

The recent concern with national and even world ecology has overshadowed the fact that cities have characteristically made great demands on the physical environment and have created their own special ecological strains. A city can be considered as a living organism that requires continued replenishment (e.g., building materials, electricity, and food) and that produces wastes and other by-products.[2] The organism depends heavily on economic markets to balance supply and demand and on transportation and communication networks to distribute the necessary commodities. From this point of view, one can marvel at the fact that a large city is so well organized that food and other essentials are distributed to millions of people every day. The routine of maintaining sustenance for so many people within a small area and of disposing of their wastes can thus be seen as a dominant feature of the urban environment.

From such a perspective, it should be apparent that the key environmental factors for a city are those that deal with either the provision of resources or the disposal of wastes. This is true even though the exact types

---

[1]See, for example, National Staff of Environmental Action, *Earth Day—The Beginning* (New York: Arno Press, Inc., 1970).

[2]Abel Wolman, "The metabolism of cities," *Scientific American,* 213:179–189 (September, 1965).

of resources and wastes may vary from city to city and from era to era. In Selection 21, Henry Still, for instance, points out how the nature of urban litter has changed. Fifty years ago, the removal of animal carcasses from the streets was of serious concern.[3] Today, carcasses may seldom be found, but their place has been taken by abandoned automobiles. Still's article also describes the large quantities of litter produced by the contemporary city, reflecting the somewhat excessive consumption of paper, bottles, and other mementos of our modern society. The subsequent articles by George Stewart (Selection 22) and Ron Linton (Selection 23) cover two environmental topics that have probably attracted the most consistent attention: waste disposal and air pollution. Stewart enumerates the alternative means of disposing of everyday household garbage, while Linton discusses the health hazards of air pollution and then describes the peculiar conditions leading to the Los Angeles smog.

Perhaps of equal importance is the consideration of the potential environmental concerns of the near future. Anthony Bailey (Selection 24) reports on the frequently high levels of urban noise that few cities have yet made large-scale attempts to reduce or eliminate. The increased noise is another manifestation of technological developments, but in many ways it should be easier to diagnose and treat than air or water pollution, since noise is more readily measurable and its sources are much more easily identifiable. A second concern for the near future may be associated with the burdens on a city's electrical and communications resources. J. Richard Udry (Selection 25) makes a brief analysis of childbirth incidence in relation to a famous electrical power failure in 1965. By so doing, he reminds us that there have indeed been large power failures, though they have been largely confined for the present to the northeastern United States. The urban dweller is beginning to learn how to live with these new hazards. He has even adapted to (though not necessarily accepted) the deteriorating telephone service that often exists in heavily populated areas.

The last article in this section, by Merril Eisenbud (Selection 26), examines the physical environment from the point of view of a city administrator. Eisenbud reviews New York City's environmental protection programs, describing some of their technical and managerial aspects. His account of the city's programs suggests the wide variety of environmental factors with which the contemporary city must cope.

---

[3]For a fuller discussion of the range of environmental concerns of a city of 100 years ago, see Council of Hygiene and Public Health, *Sanitary Condition of the City* (New York: Arno Press, Inc., 1970, orig. pub. in 1866).

21. Littered land

HENRY STILL

The time has arrived when manure heaps, slaughter houses, fat and bone boiling establishments, glue manufacturers, outdoor or unsewered privies and all kindred occupations and nuisances cannot be much longer tolerated within the built-up portions of New York or Brooklyn.

With the above edict, the Metropolitan Board of Health of New York City declared war on garbage, trash and other filth littering America's greatest city. It was issued on March 10, 1866, more than a century ago. The declaration forbade the "throwing of dead animals, garbage or ashes into the streets" and referred to "filthy and overcrowded tenements." The decree presaged the cry which now, a hundred years later, is being heard on the national scale, a plea for new awareness and methods for cleaning up our littered land.

In 1866 the New York Board of Health commented crisply that the "poor have the right of protection against avarice and inhumanity." Since then the life expectancy in that metropolis of steel and glass has gone up from forty-five to seventy years. In those days the killers were yellow fever, cholera, typhus, measles, scarlet fever, dysentery, tuberculosis and smallpox.

"The streets are extremely dirty and offensive," the Board's report said. "The gutters are obstructed with filth, composed of houseslops, refuse vegetables, decayed fruit, ashes, dead animals and even human excrement."

The writer commented that Manhattan visitors contracted disease in unclean hotels and eating places, that food markets were huddles of farm wagons and litter, and the only garbage collection was being done by private scavengers.

The Board of Health lost no time putting its words to work. Before the year 1866 was out, hundreds of cowbarn owners had been chased beyond the city limits. Two hundred and ninety-nine local piggeries were evicted from the city and 3949 refuse-heaped back yards were cleaned up. The Board introduced the first watertight garbage cans and persuaded garbage collectors to make regular rounds with sturdier vehicles. In its first eight months of operation, the New York Board of Health issued 23,000 orders and five thousand warnings to abate nuisances.

By 1869, all slaughterhouses had been shut down below 40th Street, but street-cleaning and rubbish removal was a dirtier problem because William Marcy ("Boss") Tweed had let out the work to private contractors on a ten-year basis. These contracts had to come to an end before efficiency could be instituted in the operation.

Carcass-strewn streets, in fact, remained a problem in New York City through 1914. That year, the Board of Health reported, it removed from streets the bodies

Abridged and edited from the book *The Dirty Animal* by Henry Still, pp. 35–47. Copyright © 1967 by Henry Still. Reprinted by permission of Hawthorn Books, Inc., 70 Fifth Avenue, New York 10011.

130

of 14,956 horses, 2105 steers, 56 mules, deer, monkeys and camels, and 56,903 dead dogs and cats.

Between 1869 and 1914, although not strictly limited by those years, the United States became the most industrialized nation on earth. At the beginning of the period, barely a fifth of all Americans lived in metropolitan areas; at the end, cities contained nearly one-half of the people. In 1906 hundreds of socialites climbed Russian Hill in San Francisco to view the great earthquake damage and watch their city burn. Other cities went up in flames and were rebuilt with new rules, new materials and new citizens. Immigrants flooded in from Europe. The railroads took trade and travel in all directions and concentrated commerce in the growing metropolitan areas. A concern for better sanitation led to such innovations as a three-story outdoor privy in St. Louis serving tenement dwellers. (An ingenious combination of multi-level piping offered some protection for people living on the ground floor.) In 1956, when nearly another half-century had passed, the city council of Trenton, New Jersey, passed an ordinance outlawing the last thirty outhouses within the city limits. Through a century, we learned not to leave the carcasses and natural wastes of man and animals lying around on the ground. To replace them came the world of paper, glass bottles, tin cans, plastic and the multimillion carcasses of dead automobiles.

The land is polluted with thousands of substances and things. These range from eroding mountainsides, where beautiful forests have been stripped away, to beer-can-littered miles of asphalt and concrete. Land pollution ranges also from salts and fertilizer deposited in the process of growing food, to residual pesticides and weed killers. While making our world ugly and increasingly unpleasant, all of these pollutants are the tracks we leave in trying to make our world a more pleasant place in which to live. Littering of the land, again, is the mark of a population which has outrun nature's waste conversion abilities.

.   .   .   .   .

... Although the land is great and the waters deep, we can no longer sweep our dirt under the rug in the blind faith that it will decay and go away. The major difficulty with solid wastes is that their disposal, by nature and quantity, generally results in polluting some other portion of our precious natural environment. If you burn trash, a common practice in thousands of town dumps, it pollutes the air. If you bury it improperly, it pollutes the land. If you dump it into a river, you help destroy the river.

"The well-known capacity of the modern city to drown in sewage is more than matched by its talent for smothering under a blanket of garbage and refuse," the Public Health Service commented. "The volume of solid waste has grown more rapidly than the population. At the same time, available economic space for waste disposal has declined. The consequence is that the garbage can, refuse pile and junk heap have moved out of the individual back yard, garage or attic into the major public charge."

Almost no part of the earth is free of man's rubbish, including many of the deepest parts of the ocean. As long ago as 1966, Andreas Rechnitzer, chief scientist of the North American Deep Submergence Systems Division, warned that we must stop using the ocean as a permanent rubbish dump. He says that almost any place you dive to the ocean floor, you can find junk (he called the objects "artifacts").

Rechnitzer, down there, has seen bedsprings, shell casings, unexploded projectiles, beer bottles, wash tubs and cans, as well as wrecked ships and automobile carcasses.

One time, seven thousand feet deep off the Marianas Islands in the western Pacific, he came within a foot of an unexploded five-inch projectile. "We decided it was an American shell because right next to it, in fact leaning on it, was a beer can," Rechnitzer commented with a smile. Another time he thought he had found a new spiral form of marine life capable of withstanding high pressure. It was a bedspring.

The millions of tons of military supplies and equipment which have been left to rot and rust after our wars is a story of its own, but the empty beer can and wrecked automobile have become symbols of our dirty age. During World War II at least one recreation island, a tiny piece of Eniwetok Atoll in the western Pacific, was protected against the rolling windward sea by a mile-long breakwater built entirely of discarded beer cans. This breakwater was the trace left behind by thousands of soldiers, sailors and marines who had been allowed ashore for a few hours to swim, play baseball and drink beer under the shade of a tropic palm.

Each time a modern housewife empties a vacuum-cleaner bag and her husband or son brings the family trash barrel to the street curb, they are contributing to the pollution of our land. In fact, every American (on the average) throws away 4.5 pounds of junk every day—paper, grass, brush cuttings, garbage, ashes, metal and glass. That is about 1,600 pounds, almost a ton, per person each year. The current national production of solid wastes amounts to 180 million tons per year. It costs $4.5 billion for collection and disposal of these solid wastes, a bill that will rise to $7 billion by 1980 if we do not change our ways.

The American Paper Institute recently published some facts and figures in support of the world's papermaking industry, which is much maligned for devouring the world's forests and polluting streams with its stinking chemical refuse. The Institute's ad man wrote:

Suppose, as you slept last night, some evil genie had withdrawn paper from the earth and blighted the forests which are the primary source of paper. . . .

The sunlight would glare through shadeless windows and bounce off empty picture frames on paperless walls. You could reach for the morning newspaper to discover there was no morning newspaper. And if you prayed, not even a Bible would have survived to help you.

Need a cigaret? There remains only a pile of loose tobacco on the floor. Breakfast? Orange juice and milk spill out of the refrigerator door. Loose cereal tumbles from the cupboard shelf. . . . No point in sending the kids to school, because what is school without books and paper and lunchbags?

What, for that matter, is civilization as we know it today without paper which separates us, as much as anything else, from the upper Pleistocene? Without paper there would be no commerce, no industry, no banks, not even a government, which does not really run on red tape, but on tons of paper.

That writer might also have pointed out that authors of books such as this one would be forced to ditch digging or farming as a livelihood. Without question, paper is more responsible for the forward movement of civilization than any other single product devised by man, but it also is a major component in our family trash barrel. According to the environmental pollution panel of the President's Science Advisory

Committee, paper and paper products account for *45 percent* of all municipal solid waste matter. Aside from obviously beneficial uses of paper (such as books and money), we have, as a by-product of our modern demand for sanitation, moved into a wrapper-happy age. The days when you could stand as a child amid the wonderful odors of a grocery and buy crackers and pickles from a barrel or candy from a glass display counter are virtually gone. Now every grocery store item, and half of those in a modern hardware store, are encased in paper (and plastic) so complex that in many instances the wrapping is more expensive than the product it contains! This is particularly true of the cereal box fetish which delivers to our youngsters a penny's worth of rolled, baked, sugared and odd-shaped cereal grain in a three-cent cardboard carton at a ridiculous retail price of thirty to forty cents. Likewise, potato chips, crackers and powdered soft drink mixes—considering the food substances alone—probably are worth less than their gaudy packages. That's only one example. The industry itself boasts that Americans are using more than 100,000 different paper and paperboard products, probably all of which are convenient but many unnecessary.

As might be expected, the United States uses more paper than any other nation in the world, 46 million tons per year, about 450 pounds for each man, woman and child. By comparison Sweden and Canada each consume 300 pounds per capita, Russia 42, and in China, where it all began with the discovery of the papermaking process in the first century A.D., the average person uses six pounds per year. As an indication of anticipated growth, the paper industry is spending more than one billion dollars a year on new research, experimentation and mills for production. Of all paper used, not more than one-third is reclaimed and remade into paper products at the present time. The other two-thirds goes to city dumps to be buried or burned.

Despite the vast quantities, paper at least is easily burnable, and if not burned, will decay and return to the soil in a reasonably short period of time. Grass clippings, brush and garbage will do the same, but not so with the hard junk.

Each year in America we discard 50 billion beverage and food cans; 30 billion bottles and jars; 65 billion metal, and glass and plastic caps. At the present time in America, glass and ceramics account for 6 percent of our municipal trash load; metallics 10 percent; ashes 10 percent; garbage 12 percent; grass, brush and cuttings, 15 percent, second only to paper which accounts for 45 percent. The remaining two percent contains miscellaneous material such as rubber, fabric and a growing quantity of plastics. As one newspaper reported: "Americans last year bought and presumably squeezed 1,244,126,428 metal squeeze tubes, half of which contained toothpaste" and all of which ended up in the junk pile.

The garbage can has been part of the American home for so many years that very few people think beyond the garbage truck to the mountain of rotting refuse which piles up across the nation. As a partial solution to this problem, the home garbage grinder has been one of the great inventions of our century. Because solids normally make up not more than one percent of the liquid flowing in city sewers, it is obvious this water flow also can disperse a great amount of garbage if it is properly pulverized so as not to clog the pipes with whole tomatoes and lettuce leaves. The garbage grinder, however, is far from universal in use, and millions of tons of food wastes still are heaped on slow burning fires which blacken the sky with foul-smelling smoke.

Although the horse has dwindled in both use and numbers since its displacement by the automobile, farm animal wastes still cause a considerable problem of land pollution. This is particularly true with modern feed lots, where thousands of cattle and hogs are fattened for slaughter, and poultry farms where millions of turkeys and chickens are raised by new force-feeding methods. Most of this waste, obviously, is usable fertilizer but the problem lies in the economics of processing and packaging these manures for sale. In southern California and a number of other areas feedlot steer manure is baked at high temperature to remove moisture and kill weed seeds and bacteria, then profitably sold for lawn and garden enrichment.

Although the average individual seldom thinks that broken concrete, rubble, and rock and mill tailings from mining operations are pollutants, millions of tons of these waste materials *are* added to the nation's junk pile each year.

In addition, the refining of ores, combustion of coal, and the production of metals and nonmetallic materials result in building vast mountains of slag, ash and other waste material. At the same time, enormous scars are slashed in the earth by strip mining, which leaves ugly gaping holes and raw gullies where land and woods once offered sweeps of calm, natural beauty.

American industry contributes vast quantities of scrap materials to the nation's solid waste totals, while at the same time helping to conserve useful raw materials. Industrial scrap is generated at a rate of twelve to fifteen million tons each year.

Another growing source of solid waste is the construction industry, particularly in the demolition of thousands of homes and other buildings to make way for urban renewal projects and new miles of superhighway. Much demolition material is burned on the site, but this complicates the air pollution problem. In Los Angeles County some five thousand *tons per day* of demolition material is going into sanitary landfills. Philadelphia reported disposal of fifty thousand tons of demolition waste in this manner in 1964.

The complexity and interrelation of pollution problems was shown in December 1965 when the New York City Council prohibited open burning of waste lumber. Wood began piling up at construction sites all over the city and Abraham Dollinger, attorney for the Wrecking Contractors Association of New York, cried: "This is the death knell of our industry." Before January 1, four city burning sites had accepted an average of 485 truckloads of demolition wastes per week. The ban on burning required the wrecking contractors to cut the waste lumber into three-foot sections and pack it solidly to eliminate holes where fires could start and rats could live in the sanitary landfill sites. In the first week following the ban, only 331 truckloads of debris were hauled to the landfill areas. On the site of the old Savoy Plaza Hotel on Fifth Avenue small mountains of splintered wood were growing. "Our problem is that we're choked up with lumber," commented an official of the wrecking company. "I have no idea what to do. It's tough to cut up everything here on the site because of nails." H. Earl Fullilove, chairman of the board of the Building Trade Employers Association, expressed the bitterness of wreckers who were hurt by the city's action. "It seems they singled out this industry," he said. "Everyone can see that the air pollution lumber creates is infinitesimal compared to other sources."

His comment is typical of every company and every individual who is against pollution of all kinds, but resents any control upon his particular contribution to the problem.

Whereas some land pollutants, such as radioactive wastes, are potentially harmful to man and other living organisms, most solid wastes are simply displeasing to the eye and are the residue from our increasingly complex technological civilization.

"I am concerned that just because we can build almost anything, we do build almost anything and usually with little or no thought to the side effects which these innovations produce," said Professor Hubert Heffner, Stanford University researcher. "Then when we find that new engineering advances have created social problems or political problems, or health problems, we seem to accept them as though they were completely inevitable."

One such engineering advance which today seems "completely inevitable" is the automobile, and the dead carcasses of this metal monster provide one of the ugliest blots on the American landscape today. More than seven million cars and trucks are consigned to the junk heap each year. Most of them, after they are stripped of usable parts, remain there. Every American city has one or a dozen auto graveyards, such as one outside Baltimore which covers many city blocks with hulks stacked four and five high. Now, in New York City, 1000 automobiles are abandoned on city streets each week; 52,000 a year. Their disposal is a greater problem than the removal of dead horses, cows and camels of another era.

The unsightly picture currently presented by junk cars has become of major national significance within the past decade [wrote the President's Science Advisory Committee in November 1965]. The negative reactions can be attributed to increased accumulations of hulks in scrap yards or scrap storage areas, and a "king size" litterbug tendency to abandon useless hulks on the streets or highways and in the farmyards. Essentially, the reason for the accumulation and casual discard of old automobiles is that although nominally a source of valuable metal, junk cars are not in surplus commodity.

A number of influences are acting to interrupt a normal recycling of scrap from old cars back into steel furnaces. The cost of collecting, processing, and transporting auto hulks is high and the price of the product is low compared to other more desired forms of ferrous metal scrap; changes in the steel-making process require less scrap than formerly; and closely paralleling the rapid increase in motor car production, the number of automobiles junked each year is steadily increasing.

The survival curve for passenger cars shows that about 50 percent of a given model will have disappeared from the roads in about ten years. Beginning at the age of five years, the rate of disappearance accelerates. This explains, in part, the tremendous increase in scrapped cars during recent years, because autos built in the high production years of the 1950s are now reaching the scrap pile in enormous numbers. These numbers in turn may be expected to increase because U.S. automobile production now is running between eight and nine million per year. Interior Secretary Stewart L. Udall estimates there are now 40 million junked cars rusting around the country and within another generation "a trash pile or piece of junk will be within a stone's throw of any person standing anywhere on the American land mass."

In the fall of 1965, Herman Streur, a resident of Ballflower, California, was moved to write the editor of the Los Angeles *Times* about the ugliness he observed on the road. "This spring and summer," he wrote, "I made a tour from Los Angeles to Florida, then to New York, Michigan, and then crossed into Canada. Of all the states and Canada, California has the worst littered highways. . . . Between litter on the highways, automobile graveyards, and signboards, we have the worst looking highways in the nation."

Californians have an eye for beauty and it is doubtful that that state has any monopoly on the hideous eyesore produced by the automobile, but it sometimes seems worse because the automobile population is so high in that western state. Los Angeles County, for example, because of its air pollution problems has been forced to prohibit burning of car seats, tires and other flammable waste from scrapped vehicles. As a result, the burning problem has moved to the high desert east of Los Angeles and has become so severe that it is jeopardizing flying safety around Edwards Air Force Base, one of the nation's most vital airfields.

There are few places left in America and the world where garbage and trash may be dumped in the open without offending nearby residents, and we must stop throwing our trash into the sky.

22. Garbage

GEORGE R. STEWART

From the point of view of the ordinary citizen, garbage may be defined as what goes into the can. The average city-dweller produces more than half a ton of it yearly. The emptying of the garbage cans of a city of a million inhabitants therefore amounts to a tonnage that anyone can more easily calculate with a pencil than really appreciate in terms of mass or odor.

Moreover, other urban solid wastes are closely allied to garbage in their composition and in their problem of disposal. Here, for instance, are grass cuttings and the prunings from street-plantings and from parks, in actual tonnage about equal to garbage.

First of all, and most essentially, garbage consists of food-remnants—the scrapings of plates, soured milk, grease from cooking, stale bread, peelings, spoiled fruit, wilted lettuce leaves, and much else equally given to quick decay and the emission of a sour smell. Along with food-leavings, as a second component, go food-containers, rarely clean, still harboring enough food or drink to attract flies and to create odor. Into the can thus go bottles, jars, wrapping paper (greasy with pork chops),

Abridged and edited from George R. Stewart, *Not So Rich as You Think* (Boston: Houghton Mifflin Co., 1967), Chapter 6. Copyright © 1967 by George R. Stewart. Reprinted by permission of the publisher, Houghton Mifflin Company.

paper bags, tin cans (with traces of baked beans and tomato soup), paper containers for frozen foods (no longer frozen). The third component consists of all the cleanings of the house or apartment, the disgorgement of the dustpan and the vacuum cleaner. From this one fraction, the British have, in fact, taken a name for the whole, and called it "dust."

The fourth and final component, if a mere heterogeneous collection can be called a component, consists of a whole miscellany of solid and semi-solid objects, having as their only common qualities that they are no longer wanted and are small enough to go into the can. Here we have, to catalog a few—old electric light bulbs (sometimes broken), pencil stubs and pencil sharpenings, cuttings and prunings of the potted geranium or African violet, wilted bunches of flowers and faded corsages, the cleanings of bird cages, paper (junk mail, crumpled letters, magazines, some newspapers), used paper handkerchiefs, the dumpings of ashtrays, worn-out shoes and clothes, squeezed tubes of toothpaste, "sanitary" napkins (scarcely any longer so to be distinguished), the puppy's "mess," used contraceptive devices, a dead kitten, the miscellaneous emptyings of wastebaskets, ashes.

By and large, the mixture is perhaps more disgusting and equally as dangerous as is sewage. Moreover, it suffers from the ordinary difficulty of mixtures, that is, the whole is "degraded" to the level of the "lowest" component. An old electric light bulb or a discarded magazine, in itself, is not disgusting. Yet, in the garbage cans they become no more attractive than the putrefying materials that are smeared over them.

The distinguishing qualities of garbage may therefore be said to be two. (1) It has a considerable "unpleasant" or "disgusting" fraction of once edible material that in a period of hours begins to rot and smell, and to attract flies and rats, and thus to become a public-health hazard. (2) Also, mingled with the putrescible material is the much larger bulking part of garbage, such components as metal, glass, plastic, paper, and ashes, which are highly resistant or even impervious to all processes of natural dissolution. Yet, by being thus mingled with the decaying part, they prevent the whole from being treated in the methods which have been developed for sewage.

A recent report to the President estimates that only one half of the American cities "currently have satisfactory refuse disposal systems." Even what is meant by "satisfactory" is probably to be very leniently interpreted, and what the unsatisfactory cities are doing or not doing had better be left unexpressed. Essentially, in the whole field, as the same report expresses the situation, things have "not moved very far from the invention of the garbage pail and the city dump."

As with sewage, the whole process splits into collection and disposal. Again as with sewage, the process of collection is working, in a somewhat archaic and shaky manner, but the process of disposal is raising difficulties. . . .

Though there has been, we may agree, little progress and certainly no technical breakthrough since the invention of the garbage pail, that implement in itself continues to work. The popularization of the garbage-disposal unit has produced an alternate, but even it demands time of the housewife. Moreover, this handy unit still leaves some material for the garbage can, and some housewives do not feel the device to be worth the extra complication. In any case, as long as our social structure rests upon the individual family unit and the private preparation of food, there seems to be no solution but that the one responsible for the housework must include the disposal of "urban solid waste" as part of the duties. Indeed, the can itself demands a certain amount of care and cleansing.

The next step involves the garbage-truck. On the whole, it seems to work well enough. In most cities the trucks are well painted, make a good appearance, and are associated with only a minimal smell. The old riddle, "What has four wheels and flies?" is hardly applicable any longer. . . .

The real difficulty arises with the question of where the truck is to dump its laboriously collected materials. What mechanism next takes charge? "This," as the epic poet sang in another connection, "This is the labor, this the burden."

There are almost as many ways of attempting to get rid of garbage as there are cities making the attempt. Not only are there several basic methods, with some sub-methods, but there are also an almost infinite number of variations, adaptations, and combinations of methods. The material itself is of such multiverse nature that a single method of disposal seldom suffices. Most of the procedures are traditional and crude, smack of the nineteenth century, and utterly fail to grapple with the Law of the Conservation of Matter.

1. Among the still-approved methods is that of burning. In a well-constructed municipal incinerator, burning has much to recommend it. But it is expensive; it makes use of the atmosphere as a dump; it leaves residues of ashes and noncombustibles that amount to about half of the original mass.

Open burning at dumps produces more smoke, and consumes only a small fraction of the whole. It means, essentially, mere dumping rather than burning.

Incineration at the source, that is, in the home, is not much practiced, and offers little possibility.

2. Traditional disposal usually meant feeding the garbage to animals. In the nineteenth century the method continued, chiefly with municipal hog farms. Some threat from trichinosis developed but this responsibility could be pushed off upon the consumer, who was advised to cook his pork thoroughly. Unfortunately, the feeding of garbage was found to spread vesicular exanthema, a deadly disease for hogs. An industry can take chances at killing a few consumers, but it cannot take chances with killing very many of its prime suppliers. Laws had to be passed requiring the sterilization of garbage, thus to kill the organisms of exanthema, and also, incidentally, those of trichinosis. But sterilization of garbage costs money, and the margin of profit of the industry decreased until, in many instances, it vanished.

Besides, there were positive objections to the hog farms. True, the system produced some meat, and thus represented a recycling of the organic material. But the farms circulated a pungent and wide-spreading odor. So they had to be pushed farther away from inhabited areas, still with increased costs of haulage.

In addition, the system took no account of the basic problem of matter. Ingenious agricultural statisticians estimated that a hog, at top efficiency, put on one pound a day by eating six pounds of garbage. What then must happen to the other five pounds? Some of it returned to the atmosphere as carbon dioxide, and as other gases, by unmentionable processes. But most of the five pounds, actually increased because of the water that the hog had drunk, piled up as manure.

Essentially, thus, the system disposed of only a small proportion of the material by recycling. It was merely a process of transforming garbage into manure, and such a procedure can be reckoned advantageous only if you prefer manure to garbage.

Most people would count this a hard choice, and modern agricultural economics seems to agree. When agriculture came to depend more upon commercial fertilizers, manure was a less needed commodity. Therefore, as the twentieth century advanced, the feeding of garbage to hogs declined, until it is now disappearing entirely from a highly urbanized civilization.

3. Mere dumping, crude as it is, has always been, and still remains, the simplest and commonest means of disposal of garbage. As long as land is cheap enough, the dump can be large and far enough isolated. "Collect-haul-dump" can then represent the whole process, and the minimal expense. Rats and flies raise problems, but they can be controlled, although they may sometimes not be.

The small towns and even the small cities may be able to continue with this cheapest of methods. Some of the great urban districts still rely on it essentially. Its time, however, seems definitely to be running out. Metropolitan centers begin to be surrounded by satellite cities, and then in turn by suburban districts. Land values soar. There is simply no room for garbage dumps, unless the trucks go many miles afield, and the expense of the long haul becomes prohibitive. Some large cities have already reached a point of crisis. Others can see into the future for ten years or a little more, but such a span of time is negligible in the life of a city. Unsightly, smelly, increasingly expensive with rising land-values, doubtfully sanitary, the open dump offers no hope.

4. Composting may be considered a step or two in advance of open dumping. It is, unfortunately, more expensive in many ways, although it consumes less land. It demands the separation of putrescible material from the rest of the mass. This material, that which we consider the garbage proper, is piled and allowed to decay into inoffensive compost. The compost then can be transferred to the fields. The method offers some possibilities for the future, but it cannot be a total solution.

5. Disposal at sea can only be available for coastal communities. But civilization itself has been described as a growth along the edge of salt water, and many millions of Americans live near the ocean or on navigable waters connecting with it. Moreover, the ocean is the natural sink of the world, so great in bulk that even civilized man cannot yet be concerned about polluting it with garbage. The chief trouble is that much garbage floats, and is likely to be drifted back to the shore while still in the process of decaying. To take it so far out that it will not drift back is expensive, and creates difficult problems in periods of stormy weather.

Various experiments have been conducted, and are being continued. In straightforward and typically American manner, the mere application of force has been tried, in an attempt to compress garbage to the point at which it will be heavier than sea-water and so sink docilely to the bottom. One such experiment has attained a measure of success, though the expense of the installation and operation of pressing machinery is far from negligible. The experimenters, however, were given pause by a horrible thought. Though compressed, the garbage still remained organic and subject to decay. In the course of months or years, gas might generate, and the compressed masses would then disintegrate, come floating gaily to the surface, and drift shoreward, where surf-bathers would find themselves swimming among last year's plate-scrapings.

Some other beginnings of disposal at sea may be considered tentatively successful. Some fruit-packing companies on San Francisco Bay load refuse into a good-sized barge, which is eventually towed fifty miles beyond the Golden Gate and pumped out. Most of the material is liquid or semiliquid and mingles quickly with the sea-water. The peach-pits and apple-peelings float off, and cannot be traced far, though no knows just what becomes of them. They may act as a fertilizer, and become food for plankton. Some of the pits may eventually wash up on the beaches of the Philippines.

With the land becoming more and more crowded, and with the ocean still as vast and uninhabited as ever, disposal of garbage at sea offers a tempting possibility. Obviously, it should be developed along with careful experiment.

6. By and large, as of the present time, the most advanced method of disposal for large cities is that known as sanitary fill, or "dump-and-cover." It is essentially a sophisticated version of the old open dumping, and superior in many ways. There is no burning, and therefore no problem of smoke or smog. Odors are so minimal as hardly to create a difficulty, and the erection of a high fence removes most of the "eye-blight."

In such an operation, bulldozers clear off the soil to permit the trucks to dump the garbage, and then the bulldozers push the soil back on top. At the end of every working day, all the dumped garbage is covered so that rats have no chance. In addition the earth is tamped down and made impermeable to fly-larvae. Such nuisances as blowing newspapers do not escape beyond the fence, and can be retrieved.

Offering little public offense, dump-and-cover creates much less protest from residents of an area than does open dumping, and so does not require such isolation. Therefore it does not so soon come up against the problem of crowding. Eventually, however, it must.

23. Breathing

RON M. LINTON

.   .   .   .   .

If air pollution is a contributing factor to increased respiratory disease, then it stands to reason that the adverse effects of air pollution on health are most serious in those urban communities which have the greatest concentration of air pollution sources and people. But the health hazards of air pollution are not limited to cities above a certain size; many small communities suffer to some extent from air pollu-

From *Terracide: America's Destruction of Her Living Environment* by Ron M. Linton by permission of Little, Brown and Co., pp. 57–63. Copyright © 1970 by Ron M. Linton. The author is Managing Associate, Linton, Mields, & Coston, Inc., urban environmental consultants, Washington, D.C.

tion problems. These problems may differ in degree from those experienced by larger cities and may be less complex, but they are still likely to produce adverse health effects on the people exposed to them.

A 1966 Public Health Service memorandum assessed the relationship of air pollution to several diseases as follows: Deaths from cancer of the lung, especially among males, have been increasing rapidly in recent years, with a striking urban-rural differential in mortality. As quoted in the memorandum Dr. Paul Kotin, Director of Environmental Science Services of the National Institutes of Health, stated: "The most satisfactory explanation for the consistent observation of an increased incidence of lung cancer in urban populations is exposure to polluted air." The Public Health Service memorandum notes that cancer of the lung is believed to reflect the interaction of a number of factors and that it is considered unlikely that a single factor can bring about lung cancer.

At present, available evidence of the role air pollution plays in lung cancer is based on findings of several research projects: Independent studies have indicated that individuals migrating from areas of low air pollution to areas of higher air pollution suffered a higher rate of lung cancer than did those who remained behind; and that the rate of deaths from lung cancer in the largest metropolitan areas in the United States is nearly twice that in the rural areas. A contrast continues even after full allowance is made for differences in smoking patterns. (But while air pollution can be considered partially responsible for an increase in lung cancer, or at least be called an aggravating factor, most scientific opinion considers cigarette smoking to be a much more significant factor.)

In Great Britain nearly 10 percent of all deaths and more than 10 percent of all industrial absences due to illness are caused by chronic bronchitis, and study and investigation now indicate that a similar condition exists in the United States. Cigarette smoking and air pollution are now accepted in Great Britain as distinct causes of chronic bronchitis, and the same is beginning to be accepted in the United States. Observation of individuals known to suffer from chronic bronchitis have shown a worsening of their symptoms on days of higher air pollution.

Illness and death from pulmonary emphysema are increasing rapidly in the United States. Between 1950 and 1959, deaths of males from this disease rose from fewer than 1.5 per hundred thousand population to nearly 8 per hundred thousand. A study of patients suffering from pulmonary emphysema showed they improved when protected from irritant air pollution. Patients in a room in which the outdoor air of a smoggy Los Angeles day had been purified by electrostatic precipitation and charcoal filtration showed relief and improvement after twenty-four hours.

It is harder to breathe when the air is polluted. Studies show that when the levels of irritant air pollution are beyond certain levels in the urban environment there is constriction in the air passages. While healthy persons may not notice the extra breathing efforts imposed by airway constriction, this added burden may become unbearable for persons whose lungs or hearts are already functioning marginally because of respiratory disease.

Indications are that bronchial asthma is another condition often made worse by air pollution. Because there is a long list of materials which are capable of triggering asthmatic attacks, it is difficult to ascertain the precise role of air pollutants. The Donora, Pennsylvania, castastrophe in 1948 provided a striking example of local aggravation of asthmatics. In New Orleans, epidemic outbreaks of asthmatic attacks have been shown to have been associated with air pollution.

The Public Health Service indicates that colds and other infections of the upper respiratory tract occur more frequently in areas with high air pollution levels. This was indicated in a study in a small Maryland city as long ago as 1950, and has since been confirmed by studies in Great Britain, Japan and the Soviet Union. A study of air pollution in the Detroit, Michigan–Windsor, Ontario, area indicated that people living in the two high-pollution areas of Detroit reported themselves afflicted with more symptoms of illness than people living in the two low-pollution areas. This was particularly true in regard to the prevalence of coughing and colds.

A twelve-year study on the causes of death completed in 1960 in Nashville, Tennessee, showed that the sections of the city subjected to the heaviest air pollution were areas of maximum deaths from all respiratory diseases. The mortality ratios were correlated with air pollution levels in the ambient air. Similar findings were made in a study conducted in the area of Buffalo, New York.

Moments of significant history often go unrecognized by those immediately affected. The participants and spectators are usually too busy coping with the immediate situation to reflect upon the broader implications of the event. Thus a newspaper on September 8, 1943, reported: "Thousands of eyes smarted; many wept, sneezed, and coughed. Throughout the downtown area and into the foothills, the fumes spread their irritations . . ." As the haze settled over the city, cut down the visibility, and invited a variety of citizen wheezes and tears, it is doubtful that Los Angeles realized that it was embarking upon a career as the smog capital of the world, a reputation that was to be subsequently investigated by experts, promulgated by comedians and castigated by its residents.

Smog had been experienced in Los Angeles previous to 1943. But September 8 is cited as the genesis of an air pollution condition that is known as "Los Angeles smog." The term smog is a combination of the words smoke and fog, and was historically used to describe the condition in London when coal smoke and soot combined with the famous London fogs to cause the thick impenetrable throat-wracking soup. Smog was also the name for pollution in Pittsburgh and St. Louis composed of smoke and soot from inefficient coal furnaces during the fall and winter months.

Los Angeles smog occurs on bright sunshiny days when there is no natural fog in the air, and is the result of invisible gases rather than smoke and soot from coal. The primary substances responsible for the smog are certain hydrocarbons and oxides of nitrogen. When these chemical ingredients are mixed together in the presence of ultraviolet light from the sun, a reaction takes place, and Los Angeles smog, or more exactly photochemical smog, is created. Adding to this mixture their own special flavor and flair are the sulfur compounds generated by the combustion of sulfur-containing fuels in power plants, from petroleum factories, and from industry. Together they have made Los Angeles unique in air pollution.

Three factors have been ascribed as the cause of Los Angeles smog: meteorology; the tremendous population growth since World War II; and the particular mode of housing, industry and transportation. The meteorology is unique to the Los Angeles Basin. The second two forces have corollaries in many other cities and regions in the country and the world.

The Los Angeles Basin geographically and meteorologically has a very limited air supply in which it can dump its effluents. Ringed by mountains on three sides and controlled by an inversion phenomenon centered over the Hawaiian Islands, the basin sometimes has an air supply less than 300 feet high in which to dilute all its contaminants (whereas in Chicago or New York the air supply mixing bowl is 3,000 feet high). In addition, Los Angeles has an average annual wind speed of only 6.2 miles per hour (compared with 10.1 for Chicago and 12.5 for Boston). Thus the inversion condition, a layer of warm air effectively putting a lid on the colder, denser air below, and the lack of a sufficient wind force to ventilate and disperse contaminated air, restrict Los Angeles to a limited air supply.

Into this fixed air supply Los Angeles has introduced the wastes produced by a population growing tremendously rapidly. In 1937 the population of the Los Angeles area was less than 3 million and there were about 1 million automobiles consuming less than 2 million gallons of gasoline daily, and there were also only 6,000 industrial units. In 1967 the population had more than doubled to 7.2 million, 3.84 million automobiles used 7.85 million gallons of gasoline daily, and there were approximately 18,500 manufacturing units. But the volume of air has remained the same. Projections to 1980 forecast 6 million cars on the Los Angeles freeways; the volume of air will remain the same.

Not only has the automobile molded the social character of Los Angeles, it has physically affected the area as well. The automobile has created a very decentralized city with industry dispersed uniformly throughout. Also dispersed throughout are the wastes from these autos, which are the largest source of hydrocarbon contamination and nitrogen oxides and the chief cause of photochemical smog which irritates the eyes and damages plant life. Today the automobile is the primary reason for the gray veil which hangs over the metropolitan area, contributing 90 percent of the effluents which pollute the air.

In 1947, the Los Angeles County Air Pollution Control District was formed to attack the smog and effluents in the Los Angeles Basin atmosphere. This pioneer effort has been praised as a model air pollution control system and copied and set up as an example for other governmental units. In 1967, the Los Angeles County Air Pollution Control District prevented 5,180 tons of pollution from entering the air by regulation of the 18,500 stationary sources in the area. It was estimated that this level of control represented the expenditure of almost three-quarters of a billion dollars, including the cost to industry for equipment, and the amounts spent by the Control District for research and operational expenses. Another 1,140 tons of air pollutants were controlled in 1967 by the installation of crankcase and exhaust control devices on motor vehicles, making the total amount controlled some 6,320 tons, after twenty years of work and the expenditure of millions of dollars.

Yet in 1967, 40,000 tons of material entered the Los Angeles atmosphere. Of this amount, 1,330 tons came from all stationary sources including industry, domestic heating, and cooking. The remaining 12,465 tons came from automobile exhaust pipes. As Louis J. Fuller, Air Pollution Control Officer for Los Angeles County summarized the twenty years of the nation's best air pollution control program,

Today, pollution from rubbish disposal has been eliminated, pollution from industry has been reduced almost to the practicable minimum, but pollution from motor vehicles has been controlled only slightly. In the meantime, the number of motor vehicles has more than doubled, and there is more than twice as much pollution from this source as there was when the control program began. . . . That is the balance sheet: 6,320 tons controlled; 14,000 tons uncontrolled. That which can be controlled from nonmoving sources has been almost completely controlled; that which can be controlled from automotive sources has been scarcely touched and makes up 90 percent of our problem.

The present level of control of the stationary sources of pollution is about 80 percent efficient. This has been achieved by rules and regulations of the Control District governing smoke, nuisance, particulate matter, sulfur compounds, combustion contaminants, storage of petroleum products, oil effluent–water separators, dusts and fumes, open fires, incinerator burning, gasoline loading, sulfur content of fuels, gasoline composition, solvents and animal reduction processes.

These rules and regulations have applied controls to incinerators, rendering cookers, coffee roasters, asphalt plants, open hearth furnaces, electric furnaces, restaurants, crematoriums, housing tract developers—from the smelting of metal to the production of dog food. Electric precipitators, baghouses, afterburners, separators, scrubbers, absorbers, and vapor collection equipment have been installed to prevent the air from becoming contaminated. The result of this diligent activity is that after twenty years, 10 percent of the air pollution can be controlled with an 80 percent efficiency.

Meanwhile, in Los Angeles, the population increases, the industries and manufacturing units multiply, the automobile sales rise, the consumption of gasoline grows, the ratio of air volume per person decreases, the exhausts spew forth, the sun shines, the cauldron bubbles, and Los Angeles coughs. And all cities are Los Angeles.

24. Noise is a slow agent of death

ANTHONY BAILEY

Isabel Halliburton says that she is going mad from noise. The comely director of casting at Young & Rubicam lives in a 12th-floor co-op apartment opposite an overpass entrance to the Queensboro Bridge, and the particular city noise which is driving her out of her mind is horns. When it gets bad enough, she calls the 17th Precinct, and sometimes the sergeant on duty says he will send over a patrolman, and sometimes he does. Then the policeman goes away and the honking (which has

Abridged and edited from Anthony Bailey, "Noise is a slow agent of death," *The New York Times Magazine,* November 23, 1969. Copyright © 1969 by The New York Times Company. Reprinted by permission.

died down during his presence) rises again. Sometimes Isabel Halliburton herself goes down. She approaches the driver of a honking car and suggests that he might serve himself and the public better by being patiently quiet. The other day a driver responded rudely, and Miss Halliburton took off her moderately high-heeled shoe and swung fiercely at his car hood, hammering in a big dent. The man screamed, "Do that again, and I'll call a cop!" "Nothing I'd like better," Miss Halliburton responded, and delivered a second blow, this time to the car door. She waited a moment or two, but the driver stayed where he was, imprisoned in his rage. He had, incidentally, stopped blowing his horn.

Horns aren't all. As indicated in a soon-to-be-issued report by Mayor Lindsay's Task Force on Noise, New Yorkers are subjected to a multiplicity of unwanted sounds. Some 80,000 street repair jobs and 10,000 construction and destruction projects take place every year, with attendant air compressors, jackhammers, pile drivers, wrecking balls and riveting equipment. In times past, city people complained about street cries—those of the rag-and-bone man, not the mugger's victim —and they were annoyed by church bells and the sound of ships hooting at dawn on the North River. Today, a group of people who live at 310 East 55th Street would be glad to have any or all of those romantic sounds in lieu of the low, whirring roar of the exhaust fans of the El Morocco night club. The fans are perched behind their house in a courtyard, a natural echo chamber; they run intermittently day and night, building in intensity around 11 P.M. and shutting off around 5 A.M. The tenants are furious, but they have no redress.

Of course, miniature El Morocco sound effects can easily be achieved in any well-to-do city family's kitchen by turning on the washing machine, blender and stove exhaust, letting the telephone and the back doorbell ring and getting a few children to start screaming at each other. But such noise is controllable. (Sock the children, put the blender in the dishwasher, stick the telephone outside the back door, blow the fuses, etc.) It is the noises you can't stop that are the worst—those in the Hudson Tube terminal, for instance, which has the sharpest railroad bend in the United States. When the PATH train comes in, the screech of wheels is such that strong men standing on the platforms stuff their fingers in their ears and women have been seen to cry.

"Noise," generally defined as unwanted sound, is a word of dubious origin, but two claimants to paternity are the Latin *nausea,* sickness, and *noxia,* harm; both fit neatly the shell-shocked condition of the New York citizen. It seems likely that people in New York start going deaf at 25, not like Nilotic tribesmen in "backward" Africa, at 70. Human hearing begins to be damaged by prolonged exposure to more than 85 decibels on the A scale (a scale devised to give greater weight to high-pitched sounds, which are more annoying to the human ear than the low-pitched variety). Heavy city traffic measures 90 db. A.

Medical research is beginning to show that loss of hearing is by no means the only ill effect of noise. Loud sounds cause blood vessels to constrict, the skin to pale, muscles to tense and adrenal hormone to be suddenly injected into the blood stream. Dr. Samuel Rosen, Clinical Professor of Otology (the science of the ear) at Mount Sinai School of Medicine in New York, says, "It would seem loud noise can increase body tensions, which can then affect the blood pressure, the functions of the heart and the nervous system." Dr. Rosen believes that the millions of city dwellers "with heart disease, high blood pressure and emotional illnesses need protection from the additional stress of noise." He adds that the ears cannot shut out noise the way eyelids shut out light: "The reflex effect which causes constriction of blood vessels occurs with equal intensity during sleep." Dr. Jerome Lukas of Stanford Research Institute says that many people show fatigue from the effort to remain asleep in spite of noise. One such man in the Bronx not long ago blamed his problem on some boys who were playing noisily outside; he shot and killed one of them.

A further effect of noise is to reduce communication: you can't hear other people; you can't hear yourself think; you put yourself in a room with Thermopane windows and a noisy air-conditioner to keep the other noises out. And because the city is getting noisier all the time, those who want to be heard shout louder, in the same way that the Fire Department has equipped its vehicles with a siren called the Grover T., whose oscillating note of great intensity cuts through the normal city din.

What can be done? Strangely, a great deal. Strangely, there are at hand numerous ways of preventing, suppressing and controlling noise. Strangely, all that is often needed to put those means into effect is—from a well-situated individual or from that morose, long-suffering giant, the public—a loud and prolonged *scream*. The technology which has produced the air compressor has also produced efficient plastic sound-damping materials. The jet engines for the new larger jet passenger planes will be more powerful and quieter than previous engines.

This sort of fact needs to be rubbed into the consciousness of people who are used—indeed, inured—to noise as a function of power. Frank Kirschner, who is director of engineering of the Soundcoat Company, a Brooklyn firm whose rapid growth exemplifies the rising technological interest in quiet, says: "Machines are not naturally noisy. And noise is not the inescapable price of progress. Machines can be designed to be quiet. It often means just being more careful in choosing the materials they are made of. . . ."

.   .   .   .

Take transportation first. As Rolls-Royce owners and advertisement readers know, the Rolls is so quiet you can hear the electric clock. Cadillac, rising to the challenge, has silenced its electric clock. Ford claims its cars are quieter than Rolls-Royces. Tires have recently been designed with treads that make less noise; according to Product Engineering magazine, a variation in tread pattern around the tire breaks up sound harmonics and frequencies. Car horns, as in Europe, can be two-tone, one for city use, one for the so-called open road. Truck noise, like car noise, can be minimized by larger mufflers and damping materials applied to body surfaces. City buses made by General Motors could be as quiet as G.M. cars, and with proper maintenance could be kept so. In fact, G.M. has produced the engine and chassis for a 60 percent quieter garbage truck; 1,100 of them are to be introduced in the city in the next two years. (Significantly, all that was needed to bring about this bonanza was the addition of a few strict lines to the specifications in the $4-million contract, which G.M. wanted and G.M. fulfilled; the "quiet" worked out at roughly $100 more per garbage truck.)

Down in the din-filled depths of the subways, quiet could be promoted *right now* by the application of a coating of vibration-damping material to subway car wheels. The Grand Central-Times Square shuttle has already benefited from resilient track fastenings which cut down car and track noise.

A new subway car can today be designed from the start to be quieter: sealed windows, complete air-conditioning, sound-absorbing and vibration-damping materials lining the cars and preferably (though expensive for maintenance) rubber-tired wheels; if it's possible in Montreal, Paris and Mexico City, it is conceivable in New York. No revolution is involved. The added cost would work out at about 1 per cent per car. The Pullmans of 30 years ago were built to such standards.

What has probably done more than anything else to prick the thickened skin of the public in regard to noise is the jet airplane. Here the city is immediately at a disadvantage, having no control over its own air space. The Federal Aviation Administration governs aircraft noise. The town of Hempstead, hard by John F. Kennedy airport, has attempted to enforce a tolerable-noise-level ordinance, aimed at the jets, but has so far been overruled in the courts.

One of the most bothersome noises for airport neighbors is not that of jets taking off and landing, which happens mostly in daytime, drowning the shouts of rival managers at Shea Stadium or the race announcer at Aqueduct, but that of ground-run-up noise from jets being overhauled and tested at night. Here technology can provide immediate help. Industrial Acoustics Company, a $15-million-a-year firm in the Bronx, makes run-up noise suppressors, which they have supplied for military air bases all over the world. The suppressors are basically big cylinders or boxes, placed behind the aircraft engine; they diffuse the exhaust gases, thereby reducing the generated noise level. Other airport devices which are being built include reflective walls and portable absorbent screens.

A further positive development is the new, more powerful, yet quieter jet engine. The National Aeronautics and Space Administration has helped on the research for producing engines with (to quote Product Engineering) "acoustically absorptive linings in nacelle ducts, fan tip speeds limited to those resulting in subsonic fluid flows, elimination of fan-inlet guide blades that produce annoying pure tones. . . ."

Moreover, this month the F.A.A. brought forth a regulation intended to halve the noise produced by jet aircraft landings and take-offs. The new rule, which sets maximum noise levels, will at first apply only to the big new jets scheduled to appear at airports within the next year. But it is expected that similar regulations will be ordered for current jet planes.

As for the helicopter, that irksome aerial lawnmower, a combination of Stradivarian concern with Sikorskian ingenuity *can* produce a quieter chopper: vibration-damping material applied on fuselage panels, better mufflers on the engine, improved rotor design. Yet the helicopter is not a particularly economic form of public transport now, and those improvements might make it less so. The simpler solution might be to ensure that it doesn't operate from central city locations.

To the noise of moving vehicles, New York adds the noise of standing machinery. The central air-conditioning plants, which proliferate with new office and apartment buildings, require cooling towers. These contain noisy fans and noisy water sprays. However, properly sited barriers together with discharge and intake silencers can greatly reduce the offending sounds. Lever House, exemplary in this as in many other features of its design, installed in 1951 a single louvered air intake silencer, which is still the largest ever built. In the air-cooled offices are more machines—computers and typewriters and tabulators—that can and are being shushed by sound-absorbing and vibration-damping materials. Meanwhile, employees look for silver linings. At Time-Life it has been found that a level of steady noise from, say, the airconditioning serves as "acoustical perfume." It camouflages other irritating noises caused by office machines and office conversation, and aggravated by partitions rather than walls between offices. However, workers cannot always adjust. One New York bank has suffered such employee turnover in its noisy check tabulating room that it has resorted to hiring deaf people—a good break for the deaf but hardly a cure for the noise; in fact, it suggests the notion that, if no remedial action is taken, the city might well be abandoned to those with severe handicaps, people without senses, lungs or feelings.

     ·   ·   ·   ·   ·

One noise that may soon be missing from the city streets is the clang of the garbage can. There have been trials of plastic cans and plastic bags. Now there is a quieter metal can—its ring deadened by such sound-damping materials as asphalt felt and rubber.

Meanwhile, in the home, the noise level is just about doubling every 10 years. It doesn't have to. The Soundcoat Company is currently testing a vacuum cleaner for dentists' offices which is 50 times more powerful than the average home vacuum and a good deal quieter. Plastic pipes for domestic plumbing are quieter and cheaper; it's a matter of getting plumbers to use them. The new city building code insists on no more sound transmission than 40 db. between apartments, to be 35 db. in two years' time. New York is the first American city with such a code, though it is still not as strict as most European standards. . . .

     ·   ·   ·   ·   ·

At this point, the reader may well ask why, if all these devices and materials exist, he is still being deafened? Why does he have a vision of a future city in which people scurry from one controlled-environment building to another, wearing gas masks, goggles and ear-muffs? It is at this point in surveys of pollution that he often reads, "Now it's up to the public." But he suspects that the public, which is 8 million strong, or weak, in this case, seems able to adjust quite gradually to whatever is killing it. It often doesn't even feel the pain.

     ·   ·   ·   ·   ·

Certainly the technological aspects of the problem are no longer the most urgent. Among the aspects which are, legislation and enforcement stand high, and both depend on our old friends, bold civic leadership and intelligent public awareness. New York has plenty of antihorn-blowing ordinances on the books, but in 1968 the police gave only 1,376 summons for unnecessary use of a car horn. One patrolman says that the last time he gave a summons for horn-blowing, the driver punched him in the nose.

There are presently no laws in the city demanding quieter compressors or muffled jackhammers, and the New York State regulations governing truck noise on the open highway clearly have little relation to narrow city streets flanked by high buildings. However, the Environmental Protection Administration is now pushing forward a city noise-control program. Guided by the Task Force report, which has recommended the creation of a complaint bureau, with investigative and enforcement powers, the E.P.A. intends to make a comprehensive survey in the city, as a result of which it will be able to establish noise standards and limits. . . .

Ultimately it is in that word "expect" that the *sine qua non* of noise control lies. Once people know that noise can be controlled, they will expect it to be controlled: by law, by enforcement, by inspectors, by business and by the public. The golden age! Bus drivers will perhaps realize it is *in their power,* while standing for 10 minutes in a waiting zone, to switch off the bloody engine. Truck drivers may start to brood about the fact that people might love them more if they replaced their stripped-out mufflers. Compressor operators might cease to question the patriotism of pedestrians who curse their machines. Companies might set their goals a trifle higher than "an acceptable rate of complaints." Traffic experts may think about traffic lights and traffic movement in terms of the noise of acceleration, gear-changing and braking, while highway designers will perhaps make maximum use of natural noise barriers such as woods and hills.

It isn't a pipe dream. Try blowing the open-road horn of your car in any French town, and see the angry looks you get, the furious remarks. What independent, intransigent Frenchmen have learned to take to be an assault upon liberty, fraternity and the common good, can also—with continuing education and enforcement—become the expectation of citizens in hard-edged, cacophonous New York. Hang on, Isabel Halliburton!

25. The effect of the great blackout of 1965 on births in New York City

J. RICHARD UDRY

Electric power went out in New York City and much of the Northeast in the late afternoon November 9, 1965, and stayed out for up to ten hours. On Wednesday, November 10, 1965, the New York Times carried a banner headline on page one, "POWER FAILURE SNARLS NORTHEAST; 800,000 ARE CAUGHT IN SUBWAYS HERE; AUTOS TIED UP, CITY GROPES IN DARK." Light and power first went out at 5:27 P.M. in New York City, and power in all areas was back on at 4:00 A.M.

On Wednesday, August 10, 1966, also in the Times, a page one mid-section headline announced, "BIRTHS UP 9 MONTHS AFTER THE BLACKOUT." Under the signature of Martin Tolchin, the following story appeared.

From J. Richard Udry, "The effect of the great blackout of 1965 on births in New York City," *Demography,* 7:325–327 (August, 1970). Copyright © 1970 by the Population Association of America. Reprinted by permission.

The author is Professor, School of Public Health, University of North Carolina, Chapel Hill, N.C.

A sharp increase in births has been reported by several large hospitals here, 9 months after the 1965 blackout.

Mount Sinai Hospital, which averages 11 births daily, had 28 births on Monday. This was a record for the hospital; its previous one-day high was 18. At Bellevue there were 29 new babies in the nursery yesterday, compared with 11 a week ago and an average of 20.

Columbia Presbyterian averages 11 births daily and had 15 Monday; St. Vincent's averages 7 and had 10; Brookdale averages 10 and had 13; and Coney Island averages 5 and had 8. However, New York and Brooklyn Jewish hospitals reported that their number of births was normal. . . .

There were 16 babies at Mount Sinai yesterday, 13 at Columbia Presbyterian, and 10 at St. Vincent's, all above average. The number of births was reported normal in Nassau and Suffolk counties, many of whose commuters were stranded in the city November 9, in Newark and Jersey City which were not affected, and in hospitals in Albany, Rochester, New Haven and Providence, where the lights went on in mid-evening.

Sociologists and obstetricians were requested to comment on the reported event. One sociologist was quoted as saying, "The lights went out and people were left to interact with one another." Others said that the disruption in routine caused by the blackout and the absence of television might have contributed to the phenomenon. Christopher Tietze was more cautious in his opinion: "I am skeptical until I see the data from the entire city. There can be daily fluctuations in individual hospitals that can be misleading. If it should be true, I would think it is because people may have had trouble finding their accustomed contraceptives, or just because it was dark." (Tolchin, 1966).

The effect of the blackout on birth rates is a relatively easy matter to determine. Through the cooperation of Carl Erhardt and the New York City Health Department, I obtained the number of births for each calendar day for the years 1961 through 1966. I took November 10, 1965, as the date of conception for the blackout babies, and assumed that the average gestational length was 280 days, counting from the last menstrual period, and therefore about 267 or 266 days from conception. Using a distribution of gestational ages at birth derived from vital statistics (Vital Statistics of the U.S., 1965), it was estimated that more than 90 percent of the births conceived on November 10th would have been born between June 27 and August 14. I reasoned that if there were an unusual number of conceptions on November 10th, then the period between June 27 and August 14, 1966, would contain a greater percentage of the year's births than that contained by the same period in other years.

Table 1 presents the percentages of the year's births occuring per week from June 27 through August 14 for the years 1961 through 1966. It can be seen that 1966 is not an unusual year in this comparison. For those who still imagine that all babies conceived on a given date are also born on an exact date 267 days later, Table 1 presents the number of births on the date corresponding to 267 days after the blackout, also for the years 1961 through 1966. This number of births is not at all remarkable for 1966 when compared to the previous five years. Figure 1 presents the critical data graphically. The unshaded area in Figure 1 is the limits of variation for the years 1961–1965 in percent of the year's births occurring in each of the critical weeks. The dotted line gives the average percent of the year's births occurring in each of these weeks for 1961–1965. The solid line is the percent of the year's births for each of these weeks for 1966.

Table 1
Births occurring in New York City from June 27 to August 16
(except 1964 when it was June 28 to August 15)
during the years 1961 through 1966

Year 19-	Mean births per		Percentage of year's total births	Number of births on 267th day
	Day	Week		
1961	478.7	3350.6	13.9	475
1962	467.2	3270.1	13.9	497
1963	476.2	3333.7	13.9	431
1964	470.2	3291.3	13.9	406
1965	457.7	3203.7	14.1	468
1966	434.5	3041.6	13.9	431

SOURCE: Unpublished tabulations furnished by the New York City Department of Health.

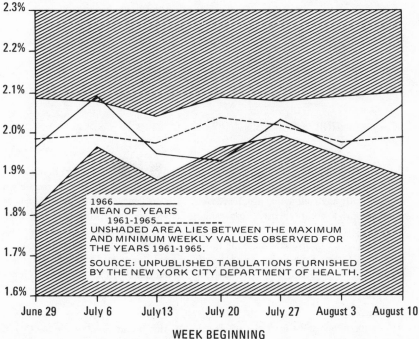

Figure 1
Percent of year's births occurring by week from June 29 to August 16 for the years
1961–1966

For no week is the 1966 value significantly above average for the previous five years. We therefore cannot conclude from the data presented here that the great blackout of 1965 produced any significant increase (or decrease) in the number of conceptions.

Let us not imagine that a simple statistical analysis such as this will lay to rest the myth of blackout babies. Nine months after the Great Snow of 1967 in Chicago, hospitals reported that they were preparing their facilities for an avalanche of "snow babies." It is evidently pleasing to many people to fantasy that when people are trapped by some immobilizing event which deprives them of their usual activities, most will turn to copulation.

REFERENCES

The New York Times, November 10, 1965.

Tolchin, Martin. "Births up nine months after blackout." *The New York Times,* August 10, 1966, p. 1.

U.S. Department of Health, Education, and Welfare, National Center for Health Statistics. *Vital Statistics of the United States, 1965.* Vol. I, *Natality.* Tables 1–42 and 1–46.

26. Environmental protection in the City of New York

MERRIL EISENBUD

The City of New York, by reason of its size, its geographic position in the midst of the world's most densely populated region, and decades of neglect, has been beset acutely with environmental problems. As has been generally true at all levels of government, a comprehensive approach to environmental protection had been handicapped in the past by traditional organizational separation of responsibilities, with inadequate coordination among the organizational units. To provide a unified approach, Mayor John V. Lindsay created the Environmental Protection Administration (EPA) in March 1968 to consolidate former administratively separate functions concerned with environmental hygiene. With its formation, EPA became

Abridged and edited from Merril Eisenbud, "Environmental protection in the City of New York," *Science,* 170:706–712 (November 13, 1970). Copyright © 1970 by the American Association for the Advancement of Science. Reprinted by permission.

The author is Professor of Environmental Medicine, New York University Medical Center, New York, N.Y.

responsible for street sanitation, water supply, water pollution control, air pollution, and noise abatement. It is an organization of more than 20,000 employees, with an annual operating budget of about $275 million, and a construction program of more than $2 billion during the next 5 years.

This article will deal with some of the pitfalls and successes of the program during its first 2 years of existence. Although no two communities are alike in all respects, the pollution problems of all cities do have many characteristics in common, and one generalization that can surely be made is that problems of urban pollution control present aspects of enormous legal, technical, sociological, and political complexities. No substantial progress can be made without huge expenditures of money and many years of sustained effort.

AIR POLLUTION CONTROL

The present active program of air pollution control began in the mid-1960's in response to widespread public interest. . . . A new air pollution control law (Local Law 14) was passed by the City Council early in 1966 and mandated certain basic requirements, among which were the following. (1) The sulfur content of all fuels burned in New York City would be limited to 1 percent by the 1969 to 1970 heating season. (2) No incinerators could be installed in newly constructed buildings. (3) All existing apartment house incinerators were to be shut down or upgraded according to a specified timetable. (4) Emission controls were to be installed as soon as possible on all municipal incinerators. (5) All open burning of leaves, refuse, and building demolition materials would be banned within city limits.

The overall emissions of sulfur dioxide to the city's atmosphere were reduced by 56 percent by the end of 1969. This has been reflected by progressive reductions in the hourly peak concentration of SO_2 (Figure 1). The annual maximum hourly concentration, which was 2.2 parts per million (ppm) in 1965, was reduced to 0.8 ppm by 1969, and further improvement has been observed in the early months of 1970.

Dust and soot are the most annoying form of air pollution in many cities. The sources of the particulate emissions in New York City are shown in Table 1, which indicates that space heating, municipal incineration, apartment house incineration, and power generation account for about 80 percent of the 69,100 tons (1 ton = 907 kilograms) emitted per year to the atmosphere as of November 1969.

During 1969, three of the city's eleven municipal incinerators were shut down, and another is scheduled to be closed as soon as alternate means of handling refuse can be arranged in the next year or two. The remaining seven incinerators are sufficiently modern so that air-cleaning equipment can be installed at a cost of about $12 million. However, because no equipment manufacturer would offer performance warranties, and in the absence of experience, an experimental program was designed to obtain the information needed to make the required engineering decisions. In addition to pilot plant tests of various air-cleaning techniques, full-scale installations have been made of two electrostatic precipitators and one Venturi scrubber. The early experience at these installations has been encouraging, but, because of the corrosive nature of the effluents and the generally arduous service to which equipment of this kind must be put, many months of testing will be necessary.

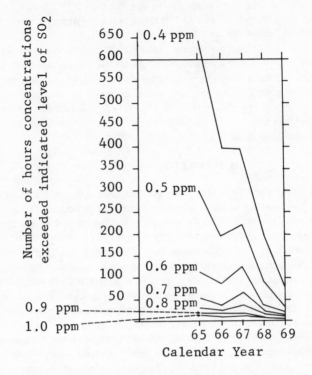

Figure 1
The number of hours the concentration of SO_2 exceeded the indicated level,
1965–69

Table 1
Sources of particulate emissions to the atmosphere
of New York City in November 1969

Source	Amount (ton/year)	Percent
Space heating	22,300	32.3
Municipal incineration	13,330	19.3
On-site incineration	12,690	18.4
Mobile sources	9,900	14.3
Power generation	6,400	9.2
Industrial sources	4,500	6.5
Total	69,120	100.0

These are the first installations of this type in the United States, and the information being obtained will be generally useful to communities throughout the country.

The largest single source of particulate emissions to the air of New York City is space heating from about 30,000 apartment houses that burn No. 6 residual fuel oil. The black smoke that one sees curling up from apartment house rooftops during the heating season is usually the result of improper operation of residual fuel oil boilers. Local Law 14 mandates installation of equipment modifications that will result in increased combustion efficiency and less particulate emission, and these are working well in about 1,500 furnaces where the change has been made.

The second largest source of particulates is apartment house incinerators, about 17,000 of which were constructed between about 1947 and 1967.

The improvements required for incinerators and residual oil burners proved practical, but the apartment owners nevertheless brought suit against the city, charging that the law was unconstitutional and imposed unreasonable hardships on the landlords. This suit has stalled compliance with the provisions of Local Law 14 that pertain to apartment house oil burners and incinerators.

The internal combustion engine is the main source of CO [carbon monoxide] in urban atmospheres at the present time. The concentration of CO exceeds the air quality target of 15 ppm near some heavily used streets, but it is not known to what extent people are exposed to these concentrations on a continuing basis. It is commonly believed that the automobile is the main source of urban pollution. This is certainly true in some localities where photochemical reactions involving components of automobile exhausts are known to contribute in a major way to the irritating smog characteristic of Los Angeles and certain other cities. However, this phenomenon has been less of a problem in New York City, where the subjective complaints due to air pollution can more properly be ascribed to sulfur oxides and particulates.

Another popular misconception is that the automobile is the main polluter because its emissions are greater in quantity than any other source of air pollution. Thus in New York City in 1967 it was estimated that automobiles discharged 1.7 million tons of CO per year. The next largest pollutant was SO_2, which was being emitted to the atmosphere at a rate of 828,000 tons per year. However, SO_2 is far more noxious than CO, for which the tentative air quality criterion is 15 ppm in New York State, as compared to about 0.1 ppm for SO_2. Thus the SO_2 emissions, though only about 48 percent of the CO emissions, are far more significant because its permissible concentration is less than 1 percent of that for CO.

The main source of CO exposure of city dwellers is apt to be cigarettes, the CO content of mainstream smoke being over 40,000 ppm.[1] Smoking one pack of cigarettes per day is said to be equivalent to continuous exposure to 50 ppm of CO in ambient air.

As the air of our cities gradually becomes cleaner, many communities will have to answer the questions, "How clean is clean?" or "How much is clean air worth?"

---

[1]Advisory Committee to the Surgeon General of the Public Health Service, *Smoking and Health* (Washington, D.C.: U.S. Government Printing Office, 1964).

Unfortunately, there is often insufficient basic knowledge with which to answer such questions intelligently. Air pollution imposes economic losses due to soiling and corrosion and also causes health effects. The economic losses due to air pollution include shorter shelf life of many types of goods, higher cleaning costs, and corrosion of certain materials. The economic loss in large urban areas is thought to average $65 per person per year, but there have been no studies as to how these costs can be apportioned among the various sources of air pollution.

One could argue that every city should have the cleanest air possible. The problem is that air pollution abatement measures cost a good deal of money, and the costs increase exponentially as the goals become more strict. The measures that must be adopted in New York City to implement the present provisions of the air pollution control law will cost about $500 million by about 1972. If the economic losses due to air pollution are as high as has been estimated, this is obviously a good investment, since the city's 8 million residents would receive a return on their investment of more than 100 percent per year, assuming the estimated economic loss to be $65 per capita.

There are many epidemiological studies in the literature, but there is as yet no satisfactory way of appraising the health effects of air pollutants at the concentrations experienced where reasonable abatement procedures are in effect. The results of these studies are highly equivocal at the levels of atmospheric pollution that will be reached when the present control program is fully implemented in 1972 to 1973. Should pressure develop for a higher degree of abatement than is now contemplated by Local Law 14, one would be justified in asking at what point any further investment would be less wisely spent on air pollution control than on housing, elimination of lead poisoning in the ghettos, better nutrition, better hospital service, or any other of the unlimited number of ways by which one can benefit the public health. We will see that this question arises again in connection with current policies on water pollution control.

For lack of a cost-benefit approach to the hygiene of urban atmospheres, we are doing surprisingly little about one class of particularly noxious pollutants, the aero-allergens. There are few data on the societal costs of disability from hay fever, but one source[2] estimates that 8 million people suffer from hay fever in the United States, that prescribed medicines for treatment of this affliction cost $65 million in this country in 1964, and that 25 million days are lost from work. The aero-allergens probably impose a greater cost in impairment of health than can be ascribed to any of the atmospheric pollutants for which control measures are now being developed. As noted earlier, about $500 million will be spent in New York City to implement the provisions of the air pollution law. This money will be spent over about a 5-year period and will be followed by increased annual operating costs of many millions of dollars per year. Nationwide, the Department of Health, Education, and Welfare estimates[3] that the annual cost of sulfur and particulate control in the United States, based on the use of 1 percent sulfur oil, will be about $500 million in 1971. In

---

[2]H. Finkelstein, *Air Pollution Aspects of Aero-allergens,* National Air Pollution Control Administration contract PH-22-68-25 (Washington, D.C., 1969).

[3]U.S. Department of Health, Education, and Welfare, *The Cost of Clean Air* (Washington, D.C.: U.S. Government Printing Office, 1969).

contrast, the total budget for ragweed control in New York City is about $5000 per year, which allows hardly enough to answer an occasional complaint.

If expenditures for ragweed control were of the same order of magnitude as for other pollutants, it might be feasible to control the pollen in a variety of ways. For example, specific herbicides might be developed, or the growth of ragweed might be controlled by some ecological process such as by adjusting the quality of soil in vacant fields and other areas where ragweed tends to grow. Or, as a last resort, the ragweed could be pulled out by hand, which would provide much needed summer employment for city youths. No doubt more meaningful control techniques would be suggested if there had been adequate research into the subject. Here clearly is an example of an environmental factor that deserves a higher priority.

Asbestos is an example of a relatively new contaminant of urban atmospheres, and there are ominous indications of the need for stringent controls.[4] When sprayed on structural steel, asbestos makes an excellent fire-retardant material, but it contaminates the urban atmosphere at the time of application and again when the building is demolished. It is known that inhaled asbestos can produce a rare form of cancer, mesothelioma, after long incubation periods, but there is as yet no information about the relation of the incidence of this disease to the concentration of asbestos in urban air. There is evidence that mesotheliomas are now being seen more frequently in the general population, and it has been suggested that this may be due to asbestos pollution. Cases being seen today may be due to exposure two or three decades ago, when exposure was presumably much less than it is today. However, today's exposure may not produce cases for 20 or 30 years. Thus, the people living in today's cities may be committed to a higher incidence of mesothelioma in the future. A thorough study of the use of asbestos in the building trades is needed, and recommendations must be developed to minimize urban exposure or to find a substitute for the asbestos. This is being done in New York City, and rules for the safe handling of asbestos are about to be issued.

When most people complain about air pollution they are referring to the dust that settles on furniture and other surfaces. Chemical and optical techniques must be developed that make it possible to apportion the settled dust among the various possible sources of pollution. Sometimes the sources are obvious, but sometimes not, and techniques are needed that would make it possible to ascertain if oil burners, incinerators, demolition dust, or natural dust is the offender in any given instance. Only with such information can one intelligently design a program of particulate emissions control.

The long-range prospects for clean air in New York, as in other large cities, are good and will be achieved in part as a by-product of the development of nuclear power. These plants are relatively pollution-free and will in time replace the fossil fuel plants unless the very existence of nuclear power as an alternative to fossil fuels causes the latter to undertake research and development that leads to a high degree of air pollution control. Recent developments in sulfur removal suggest that this may already be happening.

---

[4]J. G. Thomson and W. M. Graves, *Arch. Pathol.*, 81:458 (1966).

Whether the electrical generators operate on nuclear power or pollution-free fossil fuels, the central stations are destined to provide an increasing percentage of the energy needs of the community. Truly clean air will not be achieved until the thousands of inefficient individual space-heating boilers are eliminated in favor of steam or electric heat supplied from well-controlled central generating stations.

NOISE ABATEMENT

... A program of noise abatement in any large city is destined to be a long and arduous one. High on the list of priorities should be construction machinery, automotive equipment, aircraft, rooftop air conditioners, sirens, horns, and subways. A model noise abatement law, similar to the law dealing with air pollution control, must be developed, and rules and regulations must be adopted for enforcement purposes. Finally, new technological approaches must be developed.

Some progress has already been made in New York City in a small way. From the joint efforts of the Task Force, industry, and the Department of Sanitation, have come improvements now being incorporated into New York City's purchasing specifications which allow a marked reduction in the noise levels from sanitation trucks. Progress has also been made in the partial quieting of diesel compressors used in construction work.

Step by step it should be possible to provide a more quiet city. However, many of the sources of noise are beyond a city's powers to control. For example, all automotive equipment is subject to State control. The acoustic standards established by New York State call for a limit of 88 decibels, 50 feet (1 foot = 0.3 meter) from a truck. This may be satisfactory for a throughway in the open country, but is not acceptable for a truck passing through city streets where people are located closer than 50 feet and where the sound reverberates from buildings. Accordingly, state legislation is being prepared that will mandate acoustic specifications for motor vehicles that are more appropriate for urban needs.

Aircraft noise, so troublesome to many communities, is preempted by the federal government, and the city's role is therefore limited to persuasion or such influence as can be mounted by the collected efforts of legislators from urban areas.

WATER SUPPLY

The City of New York is blessed with a supply of excellent water carried in deep rock tunnels from reservoirs located on watersheds as far away as 125 miles. The city must provide water for its own needs, and is also required by state law to provide water to eight upstate counties.

The per capita demand for water has been rising steadily from about 25 gallons per day (gpd) (1 gallon = 3.8 liters) in the early 19th century to more than 150 gpd at present. Of the eleven largest cities in the United States, among which the per capita consumption of water ranges from 132 to 235 gpd, only three cities consume water at a rate lower than that of New York City. The reason for the wide range of per capita consumption among the various cities is not understood. The demand for water by the people living in the area served by the system is now 1400 million gallons per day (mgd) and is expected to increase to 2200 mgd by 2020, at which time the extrapolated per capita daily consumption would be about 185 gpd. Present projections indicate that the demand for water will exceed the dependable yield of the present system by sometime in the late 1980's unless steps are taken to conserve the use of water.

The extent to which water can be conserved is not fully understood. Intensive educational campaigns during past periods of drought have reduced water use by about 150 mgd, but public cooperation to this extent can reasonably be expected only during periods of near emergency—not under normal conditions. In the future, water conservation should be sought by adoption of a program of universal water metering and encouragement of plumbing manufacturers to develop fixtures that use less water.

A major objective of the water management program should be to stabilize, and possibly reduce, the per capita demand. In order to do this, one must first undertake studies designed to elucidate the reasons why the per capita demand is increasing. Second, there is a need to design plumbing fixtures that use less water. An excellent example is the toilet flush tank which in most cases uses about 6 gallons per flush. Assuming that the average person flushes the toilet four times per day (and there aren't even good data on this), this use would consume 24 gallons per day, or about 15 percent of the per capita consumption. Flush tanks are available that perform their function in a satisfactory manner with only 2 gallons per flush. The gradual changeover to more efficient tanks in the years ahead would thus reduce the per capita consumption of water by about 10 percent or more. This kind of innovation is also needed in kitchen faucets, shower baths, laundry machines, and other household or commercial plumbing fixtures.

Unless the use of water can be stabilized, additional sources of supply will be necessary in the decades ahead. Recent studies suggest that the Hudson River, which is now in the process of rehabilitation, could be used as a source of water in the latter part of this century. It will be necessary to assure that the freshwater flow is adequate to keep the saltwater tidal intrusion well below the proposed intakes presently planned for Hyde Park, and for this purpose water stored in Adirondack Mountains reservoirs would be released to the Hudson River during the dry summer months.

It is possible that, in time, reuse of water will become feasible on a scale suitable for large cities, or that large-scale desalination will be possible. Every effort should be made to further technology in these areas, but for potable water in the quantities required by large cities, no practical choice other than impoundment of surface water is available for the foreseeable future in many parts of the country.

WATER POLLUTION CONTROL

New York City currently provides some degree of secondary treatment for about 75 percent of the 1300 mgd of sewage generated. About 325 mgd of raw sewage continue to be discharged into the estuary, mainly from the west side of Manhattan. With the aid of the New York State Pure Waters Bond Issue, which provides for 60 percent reimbursement of expenditures for sewage plant construction, a $1.2-billion program has been started by New York City which, when completed in 1975, will provide high-degree secondary treatment for all its dry-weather waste water.

When the new plants are completed, there will remain the problem created by the fact that New York City, like many communities, uses combined sewers to collect both sanitary and storm drainage. The storm waters overwhelm the capacity of the sewage treatment plants, causing overflow of untreated sewage into the estuary. This problem is particularly acute in the 30-square-mile Jamaica Bay, which drains major portions of Brooklyn and Queens and which is intended to be included in the Gateway National Park, the first national park to be located within a city. Following completion of secondary sewage treatment facilities, a second program, not likely to be completed until the mid- or late 1980's, will provide for treatment of storm waters. In preparation, a $1-million ecological study of Jamaica Bay, financed by the Federal Water Pollution Control Administration, has been undertaken to provide a quantitative understanding of the hydrological, biological, and chemical characteristics of the bay. A demonstration storm water treatment plant is being built on the shore of Jamaica Bay and will serve as a prototype for a ring of several additional plants that will ultimately be built on its periphery. These plants will impound storm water which will be degritted, filtered, and chlorinated before being discharged into the estuary. Additional plants of this type will be constructed in the East Bronx. It is anticipated that by the late 1980's the estuary will have been sufficiently restored so that virtually the total shoreline of New York City may be available for recreational bathing.

The purpose of estuarine pollution control is to protect the water quality for recreational purposes, seafood harvesting, and wildlife preservation. Chemical indices of pollution such as biochemical oxygen demand (BOD), concentrations of nutrient ions and toxic substances, as well as biological indicators, such as the concentration of coliform organisms, are necessary adjuncts to a water pollution control program, but many of the standards currently in use have little basis, either theoretical or empirical, despite the fact that the standards have a fundamental influence on the design of sewage treatment plants and their cost. In most cases there is inadequate information about the hydrological and ecological characteristics of an estuary, and hence the design of water pollution control plants cannot be optimized in relation to the nature of the receiving waters. Sewage sent to plants located in one part of an estuary may require a higher degree of treatment than that treated in a plant located elsewhere. Moreover, the location and design of outfalls may influence the treatment requirements, and these designs should be based on the characteristics of the estuary. In the New York estuary, as in most places throughout the country, sufficient information does not exist. This is unfortunate because hundreds of millions of dollars are involved in decisions as to whether a plant should be designed, for example, for removal of either 67 or 90 percent of the BOD. There may, in fact, be no ecological or health gain in going to the higher value in one place, whereas in other cases a need for the highest possible secondary or even tertiary treatment might be indicated.

Each estuary should be studied thoroughly so that as complete as possible a mathematical model of the hydrological and biological characteristics can be developed. Such a program might take as much as 10 years to complete, and it should be financed out of the appropriations for capital construction.

Bathing water standards for saline waters are long overdue for reexamination; as in the case of certain of the air quality criteria, there is a need for extensive epidemiological research to provide a more quantitative understanding of the relation of various amounts of pollution to the public health. Recent literature[5] has suggested that the U.S. approach to the subject has been too conservative. The British, on the basis of studies of the health of bathers at a number of beaches in the United Kingdom, have concluded that marine beaches can be used for bathing if the water is esthetically acceptable! As earlier, we are faced with the question, "How clean is clean?"

SOLID WASTE MANAGEMENT

The City of New York is faced with enormous crises because of the burgeoning volume of solid waste. The streets are increasingly dirty, and the city will run out of disposal sites by the mid-1970's.

New York City's 8 million people live on 6000 miles of streets. They are joined each workday by an influx of more than 2 million people, approximately the population of the nation's second largest city, who come from outlying suburbs to earn their living. The rate of solid waste generation is increasing 2 to 4 percent per year and is currently about 5 pounds per capita per day. Depending on the part of town, the cost of collecting refuse varies from $15 to $30 per ton, and has increased steadily in recent years. The sanitation industry is one of the few in which wages have increased during the past decades without a commensurate increase in the productivity of labor, and it is frequently said that the only change in the technology of garbage collection is that the internal combustion engine has replaced the horse.

The garbage can is one of the principal impediments to higher efficiency and is long overdue for replacement. Numerous options are available as alternatives that will make the job easier for the sanitation man, thus increasing his productivity and making it possible to provide cleaner streets at less cost. Experiments conducted during 1969 demonstrated that plastic or paper bags are an efficient and sanitary alternative and that their use should be encouraged. The main advantage is that the sanitation man is no longer required to pick up a heavy can and laboriously shake the refuse from it. Bags have [been] found to be popular with both the householder and the men, and their use is increasing. The cost to the householder at the present time is approximately 8 cents per day per bag, and this will undoubtedly decrease as the bags are made available in mass distribution.

New high-rise apartment houses are still being built with no provision for refuse handling other than the garbage can. One large housing complex was planning to use 400 cans per day. While plastic or paper bags offer a suitable alternative for private homes or small multidwelling buildings, a whole spectrum of still more efficient alternatives are available for the larger buildings. These range from containers of 1-yard capacity that can be handled manually, to large 10-yard containers which are handled mechanically by special trucks. The building codes should be

[5]J. M. Henderson, "Enteric disease criteria for recreational waters," *Journal of the Sanitary Engineering Division, ASCE,* 94:1253–1275 (December, 1968).

changed to require all future buildings to incorporate efficient methods of handling solid waste.

. . . . .

The streets of a city become littered partly because of inefficient garbage collection activities and partly because of the high population density and the style of life in big cities. The origins of street litter are found deeply rooted in the complex technical and social system that comprises the metropolis. Economic trends, social mores, the complexities of the criminal courts system used to enforce the sanitary laws, and vehicular traffic congestion are all part of the problem.

The scrap automobile is a case in point. Until a few years ago the market for scrap steel was such that a scrap car could be disposed of by its owner at a price that offered incentive for him to arrange for its removal from the city streets. Changes in economics of the steel industry have altered this situation to the extent that in most parts of the city it costs more to remove a car than the car is worth. This has resulted in automobiles being abandoned on the streets of New York at an increasing rate—the total in 1969 was more than 57,000. The city has recently franchised scrap dealers to collect these cars from various parts of the city. In some cases, the scrap dealer is subsidized by the city and in others he pays the city a small price for the car. It is illegal to abandon a car in the city streets, but when the last owner removes the license plates and files off the engine number, it becomes prohibitively costly to trace him.

The nonreturnable bottle and its close relative the aluminum and steel can are another costly and offensive form of litter that owes some of its origins to the economics of our times. The beverage distributors insist that until recently a deposit bottle made as many as 30 round trips between the distributor and the customer, but that because of the indifference of the consumers to even a 5 cents deposit, the number of round trips in many communities gradually diminished to as few as four or five before the bottle was discarded. This is given as the reason for the shift from deposit bottles. There is little question that the consumer prefers the nonreturnable container, as does the supermarket, some of which will no longer handle deposit bottles. The result of this is an enormous net increase in the volume of solid waste imposed on the city and a very considerable amount of additional litter. The nonreturnable bottle and the abandoned vehicle are examples of problems that can only be solved by the local community with the greatest of difficulty. National policies are needed that apply uniform rules on a countrywide basis.

Vehicular congestion contributes as much to the littered appearance of streets as any other factor. Because it is prohibitively expensive to sweep streets by hand, most large cities have acquired mechanical brooms which are effective only when the curb is clear. In New York City, alternate side of the street parking rules have been promulgated that theoretically should make it possible to sweep the curbs mechanically, but these rules are honored as much in the breach as in their acceptance. The basic problem is that for lack of comfortable mass transportation there are too many cars in the city. Fewer cars would make the city a far more pleasant place, would avoid the enormous economic waste of traffic congestion, and would reduce air pollution. It would, incidentally, make the streets easier to clean.

The difficulties of enforcing alternate side of the street parking rules illustrate some of the frustrations of city government. For one reason or another the Police

Department was unable to enforce the parking rules with sufficient stringency, and the mayor attempted to obtain authority for the uniformed Sanitation Department officers, of whom there are about 1000, to issue summonses for parking violations. However, the state law specified that only a police officer could issue a summons. When city-sponsored legislation was introduced in Albany to make it possible for the Sanitation Department to issue summonses, its passage failed for two consecutive years. During the third year the law was passed, and late in 1969 the Sanitation Department began to issue summonses at a rate of about 5000 per week. However, within only a few months the new procedure, which was working very satisfactorily, was frustrated in the courts by a legal technicality. The ruling of the court in this case was so broad that it successfully blocked all the enforcement agents of the Environmental Protection Administration from issuing any summonses. No longer could the Sanitation Department officers issue summonses for littered sidewalks [nor] could the air pollution inspectors issue summonses for violation of local air pollution control laws. This matter has not as yet been resolved.

THE WASTE DISPOSAL CRISIS

This is a major problem to New York City because its refuse disposal sites will be exhausted by the mid-1970's. Ever since colonial days the city has followed the common practice of disposing of its solid wastes by filling its lowlands, and at the present time about 11 percent of the present land area of the city has been created in this way, including some of the most valuable commercial and recreational areas.

The largest land fill in the world is at Fresh Kills on Staten Island, but this will be completely filled by 1975. Smaller land fills exist in other parts of the city, and they too will be exhausted by that time.

The city at present produces about 21,000 tons of refuse per day, of which about 7,000 tons pass through municipal incinerators before going to the land fills. A basic strategy, therefore, must be to increase the municipal incineration capacity to reduce the volume of waste and to convert the refuse to a less offensive and more manageable form. A $200-million capital program has been begun, and construction of four giant incinerators is now contemplated; this will reduce the mass of refuse by about 75 percent, leaving a relatively innocuous ash that will occupy about 10 percent of the original volume. The present generation of municipal incinerators is one of the principal sources of atmospheric particulates. However, as noted earlier, these incinerators are being equipped with air cleaning equipment, and all new units will be provided with modern stack cleaning equipment. Since contemporary refuse has a heat value of about 5000 British thermal units per pound, every effort should be made to dispose of the heat either for power production or for generation of steam. It is estimated that the city can in this way recover about $2 per ton of refuse burned or as much as $12 million per year. The basic economics of such heat recovery is sound, assuming that the incinerators can be built near a market for the steam, and this practice is desirable from the conservation point of view.

In the long range, one must stabilize or, better yet, reverse the rising trend in the per capita production of refuse and use of water and other resources. To accomplish this will require development of new technology, changes in the habits of people, and new kinds of governmental regulation and participation. For example, New York City disposes of 350,000 tons of newsprint per year, at great cost in dollars, air pollution, and litter. From every point of view, including conservation of resources, it would be desirable to recycle this paper. By processing the paper in a modern, pollution-free plant for reuse by the newspaper industry, the streets and skies of New York would benefit, the tax dollar would go further, distant streams would be less polluted by effluents from paper mills, and extensive woodland areas would be conserved. Other examples could be given to illustrate the ways in which our economy must close on itself to reuse the products of its industry. This objective is one of the great technological challenges of the 1970's.

CONCLUSION

Before ending this account of the status of environmental protection in the nation's largest city, some additional thoughts may be desirable.

First, it should be stressed that in the long run environmental protection must go beyond pollution and must ultimately deal with other pressing problems including population control, poverty, raw materials conservation, vehicular traffic management, and land planning. A city that has clean air, clean streets, and clean water will not bring true quality to the way of life of its citizens until these and other monumental socioenvironmental problems are solved.

Second, it must be recognized that deficiencies in the political apparatus of communities have traditionally frustrated an orderly solution to complex problems, and it is hoped that this factor will not be an impediment to effective environmental rehabilitation. The elected officials, the bureaucracy of government, the unions, the community action groups, and the newspapers are important components of the social substrate from which all governmental programs must be developed and nourished. Professional environmental health specialists can define the objectives, develop the timetables, estimate the costs, and, as we have seen earlier, be given substantial sums of money with which to do the job. But factors that are related to the peculiar needs of the individual components of the political apparatus frequently cause issues to arise that seem extraneous to the job that must be done. The original objectives are sometimes overlooked, and priorities become misaligned. An important function of government is to permit the development of thoroughly considered plans of action that can be implemented by professional leaders who are given authority commensurate with the responsibilities assigned to them. A community that allows itself to fail in these respects will be unable to deal successfully with the ecological problems that face it.

PART TWO

The Study of the City

E. THE SYSTEMS VIEW

A major theme throughout Part One has been that there are complex and intricate relationships among the various components of the city. Population factors will have profound effects, for instance, on both the nature of neighborhood change and the structure of local government. As another example, changes like the increased unionization of municipal employees have to be understood in the light of other changes, like the trend towards community control and neighborhood government. Some of the relationships may be so obvious that even enumerating them seems a trivial matter. Other relationships may be much more subtle and may have completely unexpected consequences. As a result, it is important for some purposes to consider the city as a system and to attempt to understand how any single change is likely to have effects on the rest of the system; in turn, those effects may have their own impact or feedback on the original change.

Theorists have analyzed biological, physical, and social organizations as systems for some time,[1] but a new study of the city from the systems point of view is beginning to take root. The new type of study is based on recent progress in computer technology, which enables the researcher to deal with many variables and many complex relationships at the same time. It is also based on the development of policy research, in which the aim is to provide the best possible picture of policy alternatives to the top decision-maker of an organization.[2] Under these circumstances, the researcher must consider not only the structure of the whole organization but also the relationships between the organization and exogenous factors; he must therefore assume a systems view.

---

[1]For example, see L. von Bertalanffy, "The theory of open systems in physics and biology," *Science,* 111:23–29, (1950), and Talcott Parsons and Edward A. Shils (eds.), *Toward a General Theory of Action* (Cambridge, Mass.: Harvard University Press, 1951), pp. 190–233.

[2]For a recent view of policy research, see *Policy Sciences* Vol. 2 (March, 1971), whole issue.

The first two articles of this section provide glimpses of the methods that can be applied by the systems view. E. S. Savas (Selection 27) directs his attention to the organization of city government and suggests how its components can be studied as parts of a single system. Jay Forrester (Selection 28) describes his own computer model of the changes in a hypothetical city over a 250-year period. Similar quantitative models are being increasingly used in the computer laboratory for studying different kinds of social organizations.[3] The models allow the researcher to simulate or reproduce in the laboratory the organization's life span under different hypothetical situations. With Forrester's imagined city, for instance, predictions can be tested about the short and long-term consequences of many different government policies, including the construction of low-income housing units.

A somewhat parallel development, but one which complements very well the systems view, is the recent quest for more quantitative information about the city. This quest complements the systems view because the systems models demand much data in order to be more than mere heuristic devices. In other words, if a computer model or simulation is to produce accurate predictions, it must be based on the actual experiences in a given city; the more finely tuned the model, the more quantitative information is likely to be needed.

Besides the collection of numerous statistics (e.g., census data, crime reports, housing surveys, etc.), two types of information have been especially sought and will be increasingly important in the future: social indicators of the quality of life in the city, and measures assessing the performance of public programs. The original impetus behind social indicators was the development of economic indicators, which portray in rich and timely detail the state of the economy.[4] The aim of social indicators is to portray in a similar manner the state of society. For cities, social indicators have been difficult to develop. The Temperature-Humidity Index used by the U.S. Weather Bureau in many cities is perhaps the best example of an existing indicator: it purports to measure not the weather, but the amount of discomfort that the average person will experience due to the temperature and humidity of a given day. Daniel P. Moynihan (Selection 29) describes some of the pitfalls involved in the search for indicators and presents his own view of the major characteristics of good urban indicators.

---

[3]For some of the techniques and problems involved, see James M. Beshers (ed.), *Computer Methods in the Analysis of Large-Scale Social Systems* (Cambridge, Mass.: The M.I.T. Press, 1965), and Philip M. Morse (ed.), *Operations Research for Public Systems* (Cambridge, Mass.: The M.I.T. Press, 1967).

[4]For a broad review of social indicator work, see Bertram M. Gross (ed.), "Social goals and indicators for American society," *Annals of the American Academy of Political and Social Science,* Vol. 371 (May, 1967) and Vol. 373 (September, 1967).

Measures assessing the performance of public programs, like a city's health care program or its education program, are needed primarily for use in policy research. The decision maker often wants to know whether a taxpayer's dollar will be more effectively spent on one program than on another, and finding the answer depends partly on the ability to measure the success or performance of the program. As Harry Hatry (Selection 30) indicates, relevant performance measures are also not easy to formulate. In many cases, decision makers are forced to rely on quasi measures of performance, like the amount of work devoted to a given task, whereas what is needed is an assessment of the success in achieving the task. Hatry suggests several ways of developing the desired measures.

While the study and understanding of the city may be advanced by the intended comprehensiveness of the systems view, the same comprehensiveness may lead to undesirable situations in other ways. The collection of vast amounts of information may infringe, for instance, on the privacy of the individual. Edward Goldberg (Selection 31) reviews some of the crucial issues involved in the potential conflict between computer systems and individual privacy, a conflict likely to become more exacerbated in the future.

The implications of the new technology, however, can go much further. Suppose local citizens and their government want to guide the garbage department in doing one part of its job, collecting garbage. Various neighborhood representatives could call the garbage department every day, informing it of the location of garbage that has not been picked up. The procedure can be very inefficient, however, especially for a large city, and there is no guarantee that the information will be accurate. Nor is the situation drastically improved by having sanitation inspectors traveling around the city and making daily reports. A better way of obtaining the necessary guidance is for the city government to sponsor daily high-altitude airplane flights over the city, in which planes can take accurate and comprehensive photos of the street garbage. The photos are relatively cheap to obtain, and the accuracy of the information is unquestionable.[5] Furthermore, once obtained, the photos can also provide much other information, e.g., the general activity on the streets, and in some cases, such specific information as the identification of houses that do not have heat during the wintertime. This information may not infringe on individual privacy, for individuals will not necessarily be identifiable in the photos. But the question remains whether there has been a violation of collective privacies, like those belonging to groups of people in the form of neighborhoods, housing

---

[5]The example is far from hypothetical, for there has already been much research on the urban uses of high-aerial photography. For a bibliography, see G. Lenis and William W. Ray, "Application of aerial photographs and remote sensing imagery to urban research and studies," *Council of Planning Librarians Exchange Bibliography,* No. 119 (March 1970) (Monticello, Ill.).

owners, or even children. Second, it is not at all clear that government should be the collector of such information.

The final article by Paul Weaver (Selection 32) has been included not so much because it illustrates the systems view, but because it describes how some of the researcher's basic information sources can change. For many years, researchers have relied upon newspapers for documenting public events, and have often used news reports as a substitute for the "objective" recording of those events. Naturally, the shortcomings of such sources have also been long recognized. Among these are the reporter's inevitable bias, the inability of the newspaper to print all sides of a story, and the tendency for the news report to lack the proper perspective simply because the event was reported with as little delay as possible.[6] The shortcomings, however, have been viewed as being largely unavoidable; the newspapers are assumed to be doing their best job, given the nature of their business, and the researcher presumably compensates for the shortcomings when he uses news reports. Weaver's article points out how this situation can be changed by new editorial policy, and how a reputable newspaper like *The New York Times* can embark upon a new style of advocacy reporting without directly informing the public. The contemporary researcher cannot take any actions against the newspaper for following such a policy, but he must be even more careful in his use of these firsthand reports than in the past.

27. Cybernetics in city hall

E. S. SAVAS

The science which is parent to much of modern technology is cybernetics—the science of communication and control in organized systems. The word itself, introduced and popularized by Norbert Wiener,[1] is transliterated from the Greek word Κυβερνήτης. That same Greek word has also entered our language in a slightly different transliteration, and translation, as the word "governor." Etymologically, therefore, there is an equivalence between a governor and a cyberneticist, between government and cybernetics.

---

[6]Jacques Barzun and Henry F. Graff, *The Modern Researcher* (New York: Harcourt, Brace & World, Inc., 1970, rev. ed.).

Abridged and edited from E. S. Savas, "Cybernetics in city hall," *Science,* 168:1066–1701 (May 29, 1970). Copyright © 1970 by the American Association for the Advancement of Science. Reprinted by permission.

The author is First Deputy City Administrator, City of New York.

[1]Norbert Wiener, *Cybernetics* (Cambridge, Mass.: The M.I.T. Press, 1948).

This equivalence is worth exploring. What happens when a cyberneticist, perhaps naively, assumes that big-city government is "an organized system" and casts his practiced eye on it? What does he see, and what can he tell us about applying the principles of cybernetics to cities?

The cyberneticist brings to his task the view that an organized, adaptive system is a goal-seeking ensemble which can sense its relation to its objective and modify its behavior in order to approach the objective more closely The simple feedback-control diagram of Figure 1 is the basic tool of the cyberneticist, and it suffices to illustrate the elements of such a system. The desired condition of the system is selected by some goal-setting process, entered into a comparator, and then tested against the actual condition, which is observed and reported by some process of information feedback. Any discrepancy between the desired and the observed conditions causes the actuator to act upon the system to reduce the discrepancy. The continuing, dynamic nature of this entire process results from the disturbances— that is, causative factors outside the system which upset the system and make it necessary to apply control action to counteract their effects.

The discerning cyberneticist can identify corresponding elements of this feedback control system in city government, even though the latter is far from being a simple system with a single goal. The goal-setting mechanism, which establishes objectives and priorities, is the mayor's decision-making process. A comparison of the desired condition with the observed state of the city results in action to reduce the disparity; municipal administration (that is, the bureaucratic processes of city government) constitutes this action element of the system—a provocative thought indeed! The system being acted upon is the city and its people. It is subject to external upsets that may be classed as social, economic, political, and natural. The output, or observed condition of this living system, is the state of the city. Feedback

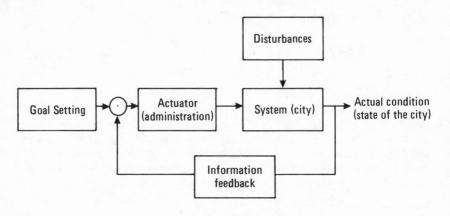

Figure 1
A basic feedback-control diagram

concerning the condition is transmitted to the mayoral decision center by way of an information system.

What happens when a cyberneticist, impelled by his students and his conscience to seek relevance, examines New York City's government? How would he interpret recent developments there in terms of the five basic attributes and elements of this cybernetic loop: (1) the overall dynamic characteristics of the process, (2) the information system, (3) administration, (4) goal-setting, and (5) disturbances?

DYNAMICS OF URBAN GOVERNMENT

The first disturbing realization is that the natural time constants of urban systems are unrelated to the term of elected office. Thus it is impossible for an official to show visible accomplishments in 4 years on a problem which may require at least a full generation—25 years—to solve. If Moynihan's thesis[2] is correct, for instance, then it will be necessary for a black male infant to grow to maturity, with his father as breadwinner and resident head of the house, before his family realizes its potential and acquires a life-style which puts it in harmony with the community.

Similarly, if it takes a year to determine the state of the system (that is, identify a major problem in a way which suggests approaches to its solution), another year to define objectives, to plan, and to allocate resources to attack the problem (in the annual budgeting ritual), and a third year to construct, staff, and test the appropriate administrative structure for implementing the plan, this leaves precious little time mostly the fourth (or election) year, to look for significant, tangible results. Awareness of these process dynamics may impel a political leader to settle for smaller goals, which are surer of attainment, or for highly visible acts which, initially, may be more symbolic than effective. Such acts can be further justified on the grounds that they will contribute to reelection, thereby making it possible to address the real problems systematically and fundamentally during the next term of office.

Forrester[3] has analyzed the feedback-control loops implicit in the everyday business activities of industrial firms, and has showed that their complex, time-varying interactions have profound consequences. Depending upon the amounts of time required to process orders, produce goods, bring the goods to market, and report sales, it is possible to generate wild instabilities and feast-or-famine conditions in the manufacturing plant, the warehouse, or the sales office. In other words, differing time constants for related processes can cause poor performance.

For a municipal analogy, take the embarrassing example of the housing administrator who approves an application to rehabilitate a decaying building, only to discover that the building has already been demolished by his agency. The time necessary to examine, evaluate, and approve a rehabilitation application exceeds the sum of the time required for the building to deteriorate past the point of no return, the time required to detect that deterioration (information feedback), and the administrative time required to make the decision and actually to effect demolition.

---

[2]U.S. Department of Labor, Office of Policy Planning and Research, *The Negro Family: The Case for National Action* (Washington, D.C., 1965).

[3]Jay W. Forrester, *Industrial Dynamics* (Cambridge, Mass.: The M.I.T. Press, 1961).

The large time constants and the incredibly involved multivariate nature of the city as a system require that we employ a very large, very sophisticated, very complicated governor—that is, a control device we call government. But, as any control engineer knows, it is difficult to keep a large, sophisticated controller tuned up and functioning well, for there are always component failures, gear slippages, time lags, loose connections, nonlinear effects, and other problems. In government, as in other large organizations, the analogous shortcomings are incompetent individuals in key posts, poor coordination, bureaucratic delays, bad communications, and conventional responses to unconventional situations.

The common cybernetic approach to this kind of problem is to apply minor-loop control—that is, to divide the control function among several smaller, simpler controllers. In doing this, one recognizes that *complete* decoupling of variables cannot be accomplished and that, by relegating such variables to different controllers, one is sacrificing the optimum that *theoretically* could be attained by a more integrated, comprehensive "total approach."

Decentralization is an example of minor-loop control. From the standpoint both of good government and of cybernetic theory, decentralized control of some government activities makes sense. Getting decision-making down into the community offers hope of getting more rapid response and more effective performance of the system. Thus, the concept of school decentralization, and of participatory democracy in general, is in accordance with cybernetic principles, although getting a new controller "on line" is always troublesome, as was demonstrated during the school turmoil in New York.

. . . . .

INFORMATION SYSTEM

Turning now to the second of the five areas, the information system, the cyberneticist begins by examining a mayor's sources of information and the characteristics of those sources.

One of these sources is direct personal observation: the mayor sees and hears things as he goes about the city. This is a good information channel, but obviously it is exposed only to signals within a restricted portion of the spectrum and has a limited capacity.

Information input to the mayor is also supplied by his subordinates, who constitute a well-structured feedback source, but whose signals are selectively amplified. Therefore, a mayor, like any chief executive anywhere, must maintain a subliminal defense and wonder, "Why is this particular individual giving me this information at this time?" Perhaps it is an effort to get a larger piece of a limited budget, or it could be an attempt to whitewash an incipient problem in the subordinate's area of responsibility.

The press and other public media represent yet another information source for a mayor—a good source, but only for carefully filtered signals, those that portray dramatic events.

A mayor also receives information from the "establishment"—the leaders of political, religious, business, labor, and academic groups, for instance. The cyberneticist recognizes, however, that these are high-impedance channels; that is, the signals transmitted by them may generate resistance and, therefore, careful matching throughout the entire communication circuit is necessary in order to conduct the signal with high fidelity from the individual members of the group to the mayor without excessive distortion.

Other channels of information connect the mayor to public officials at other levels and in other branches of government. These channels may also exhibit impedance problems.

The public constitutes a major source of information for the mayor. Four particular subgroups within this source are worth considering.

1. There are the highly vociferous individuals. The problem with their signals, of course, is that they have a rather low signal-to-noise ratio and, therefore, require long-term smoothing if meaningful information is to be extracted from them. In other words, one should look for persistent patterns in such complaints, and not overreact to isolated incidents.

2. On the other hand, special-interest groups emit signals which have very high signal-to-noise ratios, but these are biased signals. The bias must be detected and compensated for.

3. The cyberneticist also views civil disorders as information-bearing signals from the public. Unfortunately, these signals are rather powerful; they saturate the system, and this tends to set off the circuit protectors of the society, with the result that the only information received is the information that the system has failed— at least with respect to the groups immediately responsible for the disorders.

4. Finally, elections are the classical democratic institution for channeling feedback from the voters to the mayor. The problem with this channel, however, is that it is characterized by a very low sampling rate (one sampling per 4 years) and produces only one bit of information: yes or no! Polls are a means of increasing the sampling rate, and also of providing more bits of information. Elections, for example, fail to register the intensity of a voter's feelings. Why should the vote of a deeply committed individual have the same weight as that of a casual citizen whose vote is determined by a chance remark overheard at the supermarket, or by the most recent piece of campaign literature pressed upon him on election day? One might speculate about a hypothetical election where the voter has a choice of pulling one of four levers marked, respectively, "Have strong preference for candidate A," "Have mild preference for candidate A," "Have mild preference for candidate B," "Have strong preference for candidate B," where the "strong preference" votes have greater weight than the "mild preference" votes. This might be worth trying for referenda, at least, if this well-known concept from the market-research field is still considered too revolutionary to apply to a choice among political candidates.

Given the characteristics of the information feedback process discussed above, the cyberneticist can immediately identify ways to improve the quality, quantity, and flow of usable information to the mayor: increase the sampling rate, open more feedback channels, increase the bandwidth, enhance weak signals, match impedances, suppress noise, and correct biased signals. Recent innovations in New York City, although modest in scale, attempt to do just this.

One of these innovations was an effort to bring government from City Hall into the community by opening up several Neighborhood City Halls throughout the city and sending Mobile City Halls into various neighborhoods to find out what the local problems are and what the people are thinking—that is, to increase the sampling rate and open more channels. (One can speculate that, with computer consoles in Neighborhood City Halls, the computer may someday become the electronic equivalent of the old ward heeler, making possible convenient, decentralized data acquisition and delivery of services, but with centralized coordination and control.)

A second example of improved information feedback is the Mayor's Urban Action Task Force, now being emulated in other cities. In essence, the objective of the Task Force is to bridge the communication gap between the people and the executive branch of city government. High-ranking appointed officials are assigned liaison roles in specific neighborhoods, in addition to their normal duties. They tune in on the same wavelength as the community and keep in touch with local leaders, youth groups, neighborhood civic associations, and community corporations, and coordinate the delivery of municipal services in 44 areas, ranging in character from ghetto slum to upper-middle-class area.

The Action Center and the Night Mayor program, which together constitute a round-the-clock complaint bureau, serve the cybernetic role of enhancing weak signals and suppressing noise.

ADMINISTRATION

Administration is the weak link in the cybernetic loops of the cities. Goals may be set, but it is up to administrators to activate and guide the process by which broad goals are translated into specific objectives and by which resources are allocated and expended to convert objectives into achievements. This requires appropriate personnel, structure, and theory. All three are problem areas.

Salaries account for the largest part, by far, of local government costs. Yet, the decades of neglect since the Depression years—when cities had their pick of employees—have converted state and local government into a refuge for mediocrity. This shows up all over the country in the form of weak managers, uncivil servants, and employees going through preprogrammed motions while awaiting their pensions. The result is mindless bureaucracies which appear at times to function solely for the convenience of their staffs, rather than for the public whom they ostensibly serve. . . .

One step taken in New York to start changing this dismal picture was to increase executive salaries, a reform which preceded the Kappel Commission's recommendations[4] for analogous action at the federal level. In the past, a greater proportion of senior city officials came from political party circles, and city salaries (together with the fringe benefits of potential judicial appointment or other political rewards) were ample for purposes of recruiting from this limited labor pool, although not competitive in the free market for experienced executives. The increase in salary levels has enhanced the City's ability to compete for talented people from various relevant fields and to reward capable civil servants.

Another salutary change results from the "people power" marshaled by the Mayor's Volunteer Coordinating Council. Ten thousand volunteers, including cor-

---

[4]U.S. Civil Service Commission, *Report of the Commission on Executive, Legislative, and Judicial Salaries* (Washington, D.C., 1968).

porate executives, computer experts, lawyers, and housewives, work in 61 city agencies. More important than their contributed labor is the fact that, with their independence, they can challenge the status quo. They bring new ideas and fresh approaches to ventilate administrative bureaucracies which have sealed themselves off from the outside world with the bricks and mortar of inbreeding and complacency.

It is interesting to speculate on the effect on personnel of the 4- to 8-year turnover in government administrations. The new personnel usually enter office on a platform of promises to clean up the mess, make a clean sweep, reform the system, and otherwise tighten up and improve upon the flaccid performance of their predecessors. This would seem to lead to a permanently autocratic style of government management, a style which looks upon inherited employees as an alien force of sluggards who must be brought under control and made to toe the mark. This approach is the antithesis of the democratic, participatory style of management in which people are considered to be an organization's greatest asset. The latter style has been found consistently more effective than the former in achieving high productivity, in a variety of organizations throughout the world. Perhaps this explains why government bureaucracies tend to have low productivity: the political process produces a management style which brings this about.

It is also worth remarking on the observed American tradition that lawyers be represented in upper echelons of government in disproportionately large numbers. Young lawyers in private practice, to a much greater degree than other professionals, have control over their time, meet clients with means, and deal with the power structure. This gives them an advantage in political work, and leads to their election or appointment to government posts. However, their professional training is valuable only in the judiciary (and perhaps marginally in the legislative branch, where drafting bills is a minor aspect of the legislator's work). Legal experience is of no discernible value to a line commissioner or administrator in the executive branch of city government. The best experience for running large, complex government bureaus and departments is management experience in large, complex corporations, unions, universities, or other behemoths.

.   .   .   .   .

GOAL-SETTING

Goal-setting remains the most intuitive element in the city's cybernetic system, a wise choice of goals being dependent upon the acumen, sensitivity, and (apparently) extrasensory perception of the chief executive. However, he is aided in this task by information from the very same channels which report on the performance of his government, inputs which clearly affect his choice of goals and priorities.

It is important to recognize that citizens have multiple roles in the cybernetic process. Someone may be part of the system being acted upon by government, but he may also be a vocal element in the information feedback subsystem, he may be employed by the city in the administration subsystem, he may be a member of a politically powerful organization and add his strength to influence the setting of goals, and, if he takes advantage of federal mortgage subsidies and moves out of the city into the suburbs, his movement, although Brownian in scale, is a sociodemographic disturbance to the urban system.

The recent activation of community planning boards is a move to formalize participatory goal-setting. Neighborhoods which are historical and topographical entities have been recognized as community planning districts. They receive staff support, a modest budget to use for determining community sentiment and goals, and a mechanism for expression that goes beyond the traditional opportunity to write letters to their elected officials.

DISTURBANCES

Let us look now at the last element of the cybernetic loop, the disturbances which affect the system. Disturbances are the independent variables which act upon the system from the outside and over which local government has no direct control.

Primarily, the cyberneticist recognizes that municipal government is only one of the agents—and a minor one at that—acting upon the system of city and people. Corporations, banks, construction unions, and medical societies, for example, all have a more significant impact upon certain of the performance variables—certain conditions of the system—than local government has. In other words, with respect to many factors in city life, the "disturbances" are more important than the explicit actions of local government.

Disturbances can be classified as social, economic, political, or natural. As an example of a social disturbance, one can cite the revolution of rising expectations that is affecting not only our cities but the entire world. Recessions, wars, inflation, and high interest rates, which have a cataclysmic effect on the economy of the city, are economic disturbances which are beyond the control of a mayor. Political disturbances affect the city when changes in administration at the state or national level have a profound impact on urban programs. And, of course, there are natural disturbances, such as the droughts, floods, tornadoes, hurricanes, and earthquakes that afflict some cities.

For examples of government-induced disturbances originating at other levels of government, one has only to consider the highway construction and mortgage policies of the federal government, which "developed" the countryside surrounding the cities and peopled it with the cities' middle class. Also, it is evident that the nation's welfare policies, particularly as implemented in certain states, have influenced the rate of migration from southern rural shacks to northern urban slums.

For a more specific, local example, consider the change in federal law which led to a change in state law that forced New York City to drop 43 percent of the participants who had been enrolled in the Medicaid program. Over a million people were dropped—a disturbance indeed! This large and sudden fluctuation in load caused administrative havoc and made it appear that the City was incapable of handling routine administrative matters. The legislators failed to consider the response time of the administrative mechanism when they designated the effective date of the new law. To make matters worse, the load reappeared as an equivalent disturbance in the municipal hospitals, as patients who lost their eligibility for Medicaid no longer sought private medical care and crowded the municipal hospitals.

The cyberneticist deals with disturbances in one of two ways: through feedback control or through "feedforward" control (anticipatory control). Under feedback control, when a disturbance acts upon the system the performance deteriorates and information feedback causes control action to be taken to counteract the disturbance and thereby restore the system to the desired performance level. In contrast, feedforward control *anticipates* the effect of the disturbance on the system, and causes action to be taken to counteract the disturbance *before* the latter can affect the performance of the system. In other words, feedforward control involves planning to accommodate predictable, externally caused changes that would otherwise impact the system.

Clearly, feedforward control (planning) would appear to be the preferred mode of handling predictable disturbances, feedback control being used only to cope with unexpected upsets. Unfortunately, two characteristics of government conspire to limit the applicability of feedforward control.

1. Problems not perceived as problems by the mass public are problems not acted upon. In other words, if an intellectual or scientific elite points to a large problem (like the population explosion, for example), this is not sufficient to cause government to mobilize large resources to counteract the expected disturbance. Only when a sufficiently large body of opinion is aroused can government begin to plan and take anticipatory control action (such as fertility research or various birth control programs).

2. Feedforward control does not work too well, because the predictive models for social phenomena are poor. We have difficulty in forecasting the magnitude of the effect that a disturbance will have on system performance, and also difficulty in calculating the kind and quantity of anticipatory corrective action that should be taken in order to cancel out the disturbance. For example, it was predicted that the New York State Medicaid legislation (an external variable) would have a certain (budgetary) effect on the financial state of the City (and State). This prediction was wrong, and the cost to the taxpayer turned out to be much greater than had been expected. The reason: State planners assumed a low enrollment rate, due to ignorance and apathy, but welfare rights groups, neighborhood groups, and legal clinics in poverty areas were effective in making contact with, and educating, eligible patients and helping them enroll in the Medicaid program.

SUMMARY

The cyberneticist, practicing his profession in the environs of city hall, finds that city government can be viewed as a feedback control system. The basic elements of goal-setting, information feedback, actuation, and disturbances are present, although not in familiar form. An examination of those elements is useful for disclosing ways to improve urban government. This analogy suggests the possibility that the cybernetics sector of the intellectual community can be drawn to the problems of the cities in earnest, and that political scientists, public administrators, and urbanologists will avail themselves of the rich concepts and theories of cybernetics to help guide improvements in urban government.

28. Systems analysis as a tool for urban planning

JAY W. FORRESTER

New ways are becoming available for analyzing our social systems. These permit the design of revised policies to improve the behavior of the systems within which we live. Many of the ideas discussed here are treated more fully in *Urban Dynamics*,[1] which shows the city as an interacting system of industry, housing, and people. The book presents a theory, in the form of a computer model, that interrelates the components of a city. It shows how the interacting processes produce urban growth and cause growth to give way to stagnation. Various changes in policies are examined with the laboratory model to show their effect on an urban area. A number of presently popular proposals are tested: a job training program, job creation by bussing to suburban industries or by the government as employer of last resort, financial subsidies to the city, and low-cost housing programs. These are all shown to lie between neutral and detrimental in their effect on a depressed urban area. The evolution of an urban area from growth into stagnation creates a condition of excess housing. Housing is excess compared to the population and compared to the availability of income earning opportunities. To reestablish a healthy economic balance and a continuous process of internal renewal, it appears necessary to reduce the inherent excess housing of depressed areas and to encourage the conversion of part of the land to industrial use. By so doing, a large enough wage and salary stream can be brought from the outside economy to make the area self sustaining.

As you can see, these results are controversial. If they are right, it shows that most of the traditional steps taken to alleviate the conditions of our cities may actually be making matters worse. *Urban Dynamics* first appeared in May, 1969; it is already in the second printing. Although it has so far received little public notice in this country, it has become the center of a political tempest in Canada. North of the border, newspaper headlines, editorials, and radio and television panel discussions are debating its merits.

It is based on methods for studying complex systems that form a bridge between engineering and the social sciences. Although we will present here some of those results, my principal emphasis will be on the importance of the methods to all social systems.

Abridged and edited from Jay W. Forrester, "Systems analysis as a tool for urban planning," *IEEE Transactions on Systems Sciences and Cybernetics,* Vol. SSC-6 (October, 1970), pp. 258-265. Copyright © 1970 by the Institute of Electrical and Electronic Engineers. Reprinted by permission. The reader is referred to Professor Forrester's *Urban Dynamics* for full treatment of the subject.

The author is Professor, Alfred P. Sloan School of Management, Massachusetts Institute of Technology, Cambridge, Mass.

[1]J. W. Forrester, *Urban Dynamics* (Cambridge, Mass.: The M.I.T. Press, 1969).

Over a decade ago at M.I.T., we began to examine the dynamic characteristics of managerial systems. The field known as industrial dynamics resulted.[2] Industrial dynamics belongs to the same general subject area as feedback systems, servomechanisms theory, and cybernetics. Industrial dynamics is the study of how the feedback loop structure of a system produces the dynamic behavior of that system. In managerial terms industrial dynamics makes possible the structuring of the components and policies of a system to show how the resulting dynamic behavior is produced. In terms of social systems it deals with the forces that arise within a system to cause changes through time.

SYSTEMS PRINCIPLES

A design study of a social system seeks changes in structure and policies that will improve the behavior of the system. Some people recoil at the thought of designing social systems. They feel that designing a society is immoral. But we have no choice about living in a system that has been designed. The laws, tax policies, and traditions of a society constitute the design of a social system. Our available choice is only between different designs. If we lament the functioning of our cities, or the persistence of inflation, or the changes in our environment, we mean that we prefer a social system of a different design.

The design process is first to observe the behavior modes of a system to identify the symptoms of trouble. Second, the system is searched for the feedback structures that might produce the observed behavior. Third, the level and rate variables making up that structure are identified and explicitly described in the equations of a computer simulation model. Fourth, the computer model is then used to simulate in the laboratory the dynamic behavior implicit in the identified structure. Fifth, the structure is modified until components of the structure and the resulting behavior agree with the observed conditions in the actual system. Sixth, modified policies can then be introduced into the simulation model in search of usable and acceptable policies that give improved behavior.

This design process brings the essential substance of a social system into the laboratory where the system can be studied. Laboratory representation of a social system can be far more effective than most people would expect. Anything that can be stated or described about a social system can be represented in such a laboratory model. The major difficulty is the rarity of skilled professional talent. There are very few men with a knowledge of the proper guiding principles and with experience in perceiving the pertinent feedback structure of complex poorly defined systems. Whatever one may say about the shortcomings of the process, there is no comparably effective substitute.

A body of dynamic theory and principles of structure is emerging that allows us to organize and understand complex systems.[3] For example, the feedback loop

---

[2]J. W. Forrester, *Industrial Dynamics* (Cambridge, Mass.: The M.I.T. Press, 1961).
[3]J. W. Forrester, *Principles of Systems* (Cambridge, Mass.: Wright-Allen Press, 1968).

becomes the basic building block of systems. Within the feedback loop there are two and only two kinds of variables. One is the level variable produced by integration; the other is the policy statement or rate variable which governs the changes in a system. The level variables are changed only by the rates of flow. The rate variables depend only on the levels. Any path through a system network encounters alternating level and rate variables. These and many other principles of structure are universal in the entire sweep of systems that change through time. Furthermore, the structure of a system determines its possible modes of behavior. Identical structures recur as one moves between apparently dissimilar fields. These identical structures behave in identical ways wherever they are found.

Some diagrams showing urban behavior will illustrate these ideas. Figure 1 shows the central structure of an urban area. The nine rectangles represent the selected level variables. The 22 valve symbols represent the rates of flow that cause the nine system levels to change. Engineers often refer to these level variables as the state variables of a system. The distinction between level and rate variables is also familiar to anyone who examines financial statements. Balance sheet variables are always separated from variables on the profit and loss statement. They are separate because they are conceptually quite different. The balance sheet variables are system levels. They are created by accumulating financial flows. The profit and loss variables are system rates. This sharp distinction is found in all systems.

In this figure one can begin to detect the reasons for urban decline. The age of a building tends to determine the character of its occupants. New commercial buildings are constructed through the rate of flow NEC in the upper left corner of Figure 1. A new commercial building is occupied by a healthy successful commer-

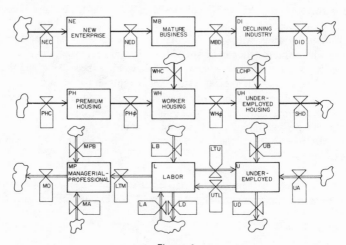

Figure 1
Urban structure
(See Appendix [page 186] for explanation of abbreviations.)

cial organization that uses relatively more managers and skilled workers than those who are unskilled. As the building ages first into the mature business category and then into the declining industry category, it tends to be occupied by a progressively less successful enterprise with lower employment skills. In addition to the changing employment mix as the industrial building ages, there is a tendency for total employment per unit of floor space to decline. This means that as industrial buildings age the total employment declines and also the average wage paid declines. On the other hand, as residential buildings age, there is a tendency for occupancy to increase as well as to shift to a lower economic category of population. As housing in Figure 1 moves from premium housing and worker housing into the older underemployed housing category, the housing is acceptable only to the lower income population. But the income of this group is not sufficient to use the buildings at the original population density. Lower incomes mean that the floor space must be used more intensively. As the building ages it attracts a lower income occupant and the building houses a higher population density. One perceives then a condition where the aging of buildings in an urban area simultaneously reduces the opportunities for employment and increases the population. The average income and standard of living decline.

· · · · ·

DEVELOPING A MODEL

In making a laboratory model of a social system one should not attempt straightaway to solve a problem. Instead one should generate a model which will create the trouble symptoms. Only if one fully understands the processes whereby difficulties are created can he hope to correct the causes. This means that we want a model of an urban area which can start with empty land, grow a city, and show the processes whereby economic health falters into stagnation and decay.

As another guide to modeling, one should start, not by building a model of a particular situation, but by modeling the general class of systems under study. This may seem surprising, but the general model is simpler and initially more informative than a model of a special case. Here we wish to model the general process of urban growth and stagnation. It should be a model which, with proper changes in parameters, is good for New York, Calcutta, a gold rush camp, or West Berlin. These all seem to have very different characteristics but they have certain elements in common which describe their urban processes. There are fewer concepts which are common to all than are to be found in any one. The general model can strip away the multitude of detail which confuses any one special situation. The general model identifies the central processes and is a statement of the theory for the entire class of systems.

Figure 2 shows the behavior of the laboratory model of an urban area. It presents the nine system level variables over 250 years. The first 100 years is a period of exponential growth; however, when the land area becomes filled, growth ceases, and the aging process begins. At year 100, near the end of the growth phase, the labor population is almost double the underemployed population. This is a healthy mix which is well matched to the job distribution in the area and which gives a high upward economic mobility to the underemployed population. But by year 150, the

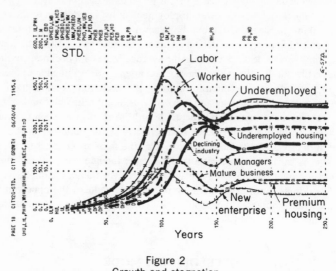

Figure 2
Growth and stagnation

labor population has fallen and the underemployed population has risen until these two groups are almost equal. Business activity has declined and the area has taken on the characteristics of a depressed city. This has occurred because of the way that the industry, housing, and populations in Figure 1 have interacted with each other.

EFFECTS OF DIFFERENT POLICIES

Figure 3 shows 50 years beginning with the conditions found at the end of Figure 2. At time 0, a low-cost housing program is [established with the intent to build housing for 5 percent of the underemployed each year]. Observe what happens. Underemployed housing, which is being actively constructed, rises 45 percent, but premium housing falls 35 percent, and worker housing falls 30 percent. New enterprise declines 50 percent and mature business declines 45 percent, all in the 50-year period. Economic conditions become sufficiently worse that even the underemployed population, although it rises initially, eventually falls to slightly less than its beginning value. These changes are a result of the low-cost housing program.

In this same manner, job training programs, job creation programs, and financial subsidies were examined. All lie between ineffective and harmful. The low-cost housing program was the most powerful in depressing the condition of a stagnant urban area.

The depressed areas of our cities seem to be characterized by excess housing compared to jobs and by excessive concentration of low-income population. These conditions, created by aging industrial and dwelling buildings, interact to drive out the upper-income population and business activity, and to reduce the tax base. Once

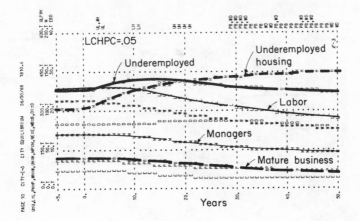

Figure 3
Decline of urban area caused by low-cost housing construction each year for 2.5
percent of underemployed

the decline starts, it tends to accelerate. Unless one can devise urban management policies that produce continuous renewal, difficulties are inherent.

Figure 4 shows an urban condition that begins with stagnation and then changes toward revival. Here, 5 percent of the slum housing is removed each year, and the incentives for new enterprise construction are increased somewhat. The result is a cascading of mutual interactions which raise the economic activity of the area, increase upward economic mobility for the underemployed population, and shift the population internally from the underemployed to the labor class. This is done without driving the existing low-income population out of the area. Underemployed housing is reduced. Initially this reduction comes largely from the empty housing. The resulting housing shortage restrains the population inflow which would otherwise defeat the revival of the area.

[In general when] a system misbehaves, we should ask ourselves what policies within that system cause the undesirable characteristics. If we examine the laws under which a city operates, we see a structure of regulations which could hardly be better designed to create stagnation and decline. The aging and decay of buildings is central to the urban decline process; yet we see throughout our tax laws and regulations numerous incentives to keep old buildings in place. As the value of a building decreases, so do the assessed taxes. The reduced expense makes it possible to retain the old building longer. For income tax purposes under some circumstances the value of a building can be depreciated several times. This produces incentives to keep an old building in place. Here is not the place for detail, but it seems clear that a different set of tax laws and city regulations could be devised to produce the individual incentives necessary for continuous renewal. As an example, I recently saw a suggestion that each building have a mandatory trust fund into which the owner must pay a levy each year. At any time, whoever owns the building can draw out the money in the trust fund if he demolishes the building and clears

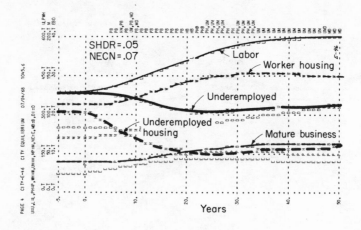

Figure 4
Revival caused by removing 5 percent of underemployed housing each year and
encouraging business construction to generate jobs

the land. This, you see, would create an earlier incentive for replacement. Property
tax levies and income tax accounting could both be changed to produce pressures
in the same direction.

CONCLUSIONS

Our studies of managerial, urban, and other social systems have uncovered
many general characteristics of complex systems to which we must be alert if we
are to avoid continuing to create detrimental modes of behavior.

First, complex systems are counterintuitive. They behave in ways that are
opposite to what most people expect. They are counterintuitive because our experience and intuition have been developed almost entirely from contact with simple
systems. But in many ways, simple systems behave exactly in the opposite way from
complex systems. Therefore, our experience misleads us into drawing the wrong
conclusions about complex social systems.

Second, complex systems are strongly resistant to most policy changes. A new
policy tends to warp the system so that slightly changed levels present new information to the policy points in the system. The new information, as processed through
the new policies, tends to give the old results. There are inherent reasons within
complex systems why so many of our attempts at correcting a city, a company, or
an economy are destined to fail.

But third, the converse is also true. There are points in systems from which
favorable influence will radiate. Often these points are difficult to perceive. Often the
action required is the opposite to that which might be expected. But when these
points are found, they tend to radiate new information streams in such a way that
the new circumstances, when processed through the old attitudes and policies,
produce a new result.

Fourth, complex systems tend to counteract most active programs aimed at alleviating symptoms. . . . When outside action tries to alter the condition of a system, the system relaxes its own internal processes aimed at the same result and throws the burden even more onto the outside force which is attempting to produce a correction. The internal need for action is reduced and the external supplier of action must work even harder.

Fifth, in complex systems the short-term response to a policy change is apt to be in the opposite direction from the long-term effect. This is especially treacherous. A policy change which improves matters in the short run lays a foundation for degradation in the long run. The short tenure of men in political office favors decisions which produce results quickly. These are often the very actions that eventually drive the system to ever-worsening performance. Short- versus long-run reversal processes are all around us. If an agricultural country is to industrialize, it must accumulate railroads, factories, and steel mills. This capital accumulation can only be done by forgoing consumption and reducing the standard of living first in order that the standard of living may rise at a later time. If a company faces declining earnings because its products are obsolete, it must invest more heavily in product research and incur even deeper short-term losses if it is to recover in the more distant future to a profitable product stream. A student forgoes short-term earning opportunities by attending college in order to increase his longer term earning capability. This reversal between the short run and the long run occurs repeatedly.

Sixth, a system contains internal dynamic mechanisms that produce the observed undesirable behavior. If we ignore the fundamental causes and simply try to overwhelm the symptoms, we pit two great sets of forces against one another. In general, our social systems have evolved to a very stable configuration. If the system is troublesome, we should expect that the causes of the trouble are deeply embedded. The causes will outlast our persistence in overwhelming the symptoms. Furthermore, the internal pressures usually rise to counteract a corrective force from the outside. We can expend all our energy to no avail in trying to compensate for the troubles unless we discover the basic causes and redesign the system so that it spontaneously moves to a new mode of behavior.

.   .   .   .   .

We are suggesting that the time is approaching when we can design social systems to obtain far better behavior. Different policies could change our urban areas from ones which are designed to deteriorate into ones which are designed for self renewal. One can foresee a time when we will understand far better the relationships between monetary policy, interest rates, unemployment, and foreign exchange. Already such studies have thrown new light on the processes of corporate growth, on the reasons for product stagnation and loss of market share, and on the growth and decline of cities.

But to design new policies for social systems requires a level of skill which is rare. The kind of system modeling and policy design which we have been describing requires a professional training at least as extensive as that in any of the established professions. The proper training requires theory, laboratory, case studies, apprenticeship, and practicing experience.

But in the area of designing the dynamic behavior of social systems, there are as yet no adequate professional schools. The educational materials are still in the development stage. The few who show skill in this area have learned by apprenticeship and by trial and error.

Those interested in the long-run improvement of society can make the greatest contribution by encouraging research and educational programs aimed at developing a high level of talent. Again the long run competes with the short run. Creating educational materials and teachers will at first absorb money and talent which in the short run might instead be devoted to solving particular present social problems. Unless a proper balance is maintained, with substantial energy devoted to establishing an educational capability for enlarging the future pools of skills in social system design, the time when we can master our own systems will be further delayed.

APPENDIX

Definitions for City Growth, Stagnation, and Revival Model

AMM	attractiveness-for-migration factor (dimensionless)
AMMP	attractiveness-for-migration multiplier perceived (dimensionless)
DID	declining-industry demolition (productive units per year)
LA	labor arrivals (men per year)
LB	labor births (men per year)
LD	labor deaths (men per year)
LTM	labor to manager (men per year)
LTU	labor to underemployed (men per year)
MA	manager arrivals (men per year)
MBD	mature-business decline (productive units per year)
MPB	managerial-professional births (men per year)
NEC	new-enterprise construction (productive units per year)
NED	new-enterprise decline (productive units per year)
PEM	public-expenditure multiplier (dimensionless)
PHC	premium-housing construction (housing units per year)
PHO	premium-housing obsolescence (housing units per year)
SHD	slum-housing demolition (housing units per year)
TC	tax collections (dollars per year)
TPCR	tax per capita ratio (dimensionless)
UA	underemployed arrivals (men per year)
UAMM	underemployed-arrivals-mobility multiplier (dimensionless)
UB	underemployed births (men per year)
UD	underemployed departures (men per year)
UHM	underemployed/housing multiplier (dimensionless)
UHPM	underemployed-housing-program multiplier (dimensionless)
UHPR	underemployed-housing-program rate (housing per year per man)
UHR	underemployed/housing ratio (dimensionless)
UJ	underemployed jobs (men)
UJM	underemployed/job multiplier (dimensionless)
UM	underemployed mobility (fraction per year)
UR	underemployed/job ratio (dimensionless)
UTL	underemployed to labor (men per year)
WHC	worker-housing construction (housing units per year)
WHO	worker-housing obsolescence (housing units per year).

29. Urban conditions: general

DANIEL P. MOYNIHAN

A characteristic theme of American politics at this time, and an emerging element of American sensibility, is that of "urban crisis." Shorn of a tendency to overdo, much of this comes down to a common-sense concern with the immediate social and physical environment on the part of a society that has been perhaps overmuch involved with questions of cosmic import—and cosmic inscrutability. This tendency is likely to become more, not less pronounced: the current military involvement in Asia is demonstrating to the nation clearly enough that there are limits to its desire to manage the world, just as there are limits to the world's desire to be managed. Peace is likely to bring a very considerable inward turning, and this is more than likely to be defined in terms of an "attack" (there is no avoiding an excess of aggressiveness in American life) on the problems of cities. Current expositions of the subject, for example, the hearings conducted by Senator Abraham Ribicoff's Subcommittee on Executive Reorganization of the United States Senate Committee on Government Operations, as well as President Johnson's plans for a model cities program, provide the rudiments of a postwar planning program. The proposals will be there when, as may be the case, the national government is, of a sudden, looking about for something else to do. Moreover, in a nation that increasingly senses the immense burdens imposed by the racial barriers and hostilities of the present, concern for "urban affairs" is certain to emerge as the most acceptable code word for "Negro" problems—and the white attitudes that give rise to so many of them.

In the familiar pattern, this poses both an opportunity and a problem for the social sciences. Irving Louis Horowitz has put it thus: "The problem of social policy becomes acute precisely to the degree to which social science becomes exact." The demonstrated feasibility of putting social science information and theory to work on social problems imposes a new and special set of strains both on policy-makers and on those who would advise them. To a degree that has not, perhaps, existed since the age of theological certitude, it becomes possible to be "right" or "wrong," and difficult—even impossible—to avoid scrutiny in just these terms. There is no turning back: we have bit this bullet, and had best get on with the slaughter of a good many of those cherished notions which are certain to perish in the first data runs. It will be easy enough to demonstrate what does not work: the job of social science must be to provide some plausible suggestions as to what will work.

Abridged and edited from Daniel P. Moynihan, "Urban conditions: General," *The Annals*, 371:159–177 (May, 1967). Copyright © 1967 by The American Academy of Political and Social Science. Reprinted by permission.

The author is Professor of Education and Urban Politics, Harvard University, Cambridge, Mass.

THREE GENERAL PROPOSITIONS

Three general propositions may be made. First of all, it is essential that all concerned with the development of a system of urban social indicators be prepared in advance to find themselves accused of having betrayed some of those very causes with which they have been most allied. Concern about urban affairs derives directly from concern about urban problems: it involves the statement by certain persons that certain things are not as they ought to be, and must be changed for the better. Such attitudes are almost always minority views, at least in the beginning. As a group, however, American social scientists are peculiarly prone to sharing and even to creating such concerns. They are problem-prone and reform-minded, and inevitably come to be seen as allies by those about whose problems they are most concerned. These latter, becoming accustomed to having social scientists on their side, easily come to assume that social science will be. This does not always happen, a fact not easily forgiven. Knowledge is power, and in contemporary society social scientists are often in the position of handing power about in an almost absent-minded way. Professional ethics, at least as ideally defined, can lead them to hand out the very best arguments to those whom they would consider the very worst contenders. This is a dilemma not yet well understood, and certainly not resolved. For the moment, the most than can be done is to be forewarned.[1]

The second proposition is that the way in which urban indicators are developed is likely to have considerable influence on the level of government—and of abstraction—at which the problems are dealt with. Specifically, if urban indicators remain for the most part "national" statistics, a powerful built-in tendency to seek "national" solutions will emerge.

This is no small matter. The economic policies of the federal government over the past two generations—beginning with the New Deal—have been brilliantly successful. But they have concentrated attention on data at the continental, even the global level—"aggregatics" in Bertram Gross's allusive term—to the exclusion, or at very least the neglect, of specific circumstances. Thus, the United States has, quite possibly, the best employment data in the world, but there is no city in the nation that knows what its unemployment rate is. And while the economy of the nation booms, sizzles, and soars, it has somehow become a practice for city workers to riot every summer; after which disturbances, enquiries determine that quite astonishing numbers of them were without work. An impressive number of contradictions have somehow slipped through the interstices of the macropolicy net. We are the richest nation on earth, with some of the worst slums; the most educated, with some of the most marginal school children; and the most mobile, with some of the most rigid caste confinements. One likely source of these contradictions is the reluctance, even the refusal, of many public organizations to report, much less to insist on, the relationship between their activities and concerns with other problems. This must be presumed to be part of the explanation behind Scott Greer's statement that "at a cost of more than three billion dollars, the Urban Renewal Agency has succeeded in materially reducing the supply of low cost housing in American cities." Insisting

---

[1]See Daniel P. Moynihan, "Education of the urban poor," address to the Harvard Club and the M.I.T. Alumni Center of New York City, March 1, 1967 (mimeographed).

that one thing has nothing to do with another is likely to have the effect of intensifying rather than moderating the unavoidable interactions.

A third general consideration may be termed a matter of temperament. It has to do with the fact that urban social indicators are almost certainly going to be developed by professors and government executives who will be far more concerned with what is bad about cities than with what is good about them. These men will judge good and bad in terms of their own rather special values acquired in the course of family, religious, educational, and occupational experiences that, by and large, are quite different from those of the urban masses whose conditions they will seek to measure. The idea of social indicators, and of an urban subset, is pre-eminently a product of the American intellectual world, although, of course, with a whole European tradition behind it. But the particular quality of the American intellectual —quite distinct from his European counterpart—has been the tendency to view cities with alarm, fear, and distaste, a history which Morton and Lucia White have summed up as "one of adverse metaphysical speculation and bad dreams about urban life, of aesthetic and moral recoil from the American city's ugliness, commercialism, and crime."[2] Surely some measure of the present concern with ugliness, commercialism, and crime is simply an inversion of the earlier views: precisely the same judgment about cities is handed down, with only a gloss of compassion and concern that things might somehow be made otherwise. The view that when one is tired of London one is tired of life is not one that has met much favor on American campuses—nor yet the proposition put to Hennessy by Dooley that while the country might be where the good things in life come from, it is the city that they go *to.* Neither the great Tory nor the Chicago saloonkeeper spoke with the accents of liberal academia: the one too confident, the other too clever for that special world.

The task, then, is to make the most of the special kinds of sensibility that will be brought to bear on cities by this group, including one of its most attractive qualities, the awareness that tastes differ and a willingness to allow, even to encourage them to do so. A further, almost a defining characteristic of American academics of the present age is the realization that everything has to do with everything else. American professors may be obscure, but they are hardly simple-minded. Their judgment as to what facts are relevant to the urban condition is likely to approach that condition itself in complexity and detail.

FOUR GUIDELINES

With these considerations in mind, it becomes possible to lay down four general guidelines for a system of urban social indicators, not so much as rules than as principles. It is contended merely that, to the extent information is organized along these principles, it is more likely than not to be useful and to be used.

First, urban social indicators should be the realm of disaggregation and correlation. To the greatest possible extent the data should be organized in terms of the Standard Metropolitan Statistical Areas (SMSA's) as defined by the Bureau of

---

[2]Morton and Lucia White, *The Intellectual versus the City* (Cambridge, Mass.: Harvard University Press and The M.I.T. Press, 1962), p. 75.

Census (there are now 227 SMSA's) and by census tract levels where this is highly significant, as in the case of poverty neighborhoods. Data should be organized in terms of political jurisdictions as well, so that they may be used by government organizations and by political candidates and parties. Moreover, if the relations between different phenomena are to be perceived and responded to in the workaday world of municipal affairs, it is necessary for the indicators to report such relations in the form of correlations and similar mathematical analyses, rather than to await the random initiatives of individual scholars. The relationships of functions such as unemployment to welfare dependency, to use but one example, are matters of fundamental interest to city government, but are rarely known, and even less often commented upon. Social indicators can bring these relations into the open, as it were, making them at once more visible and less threatening.

It will be obvious that some forms of urban indicators, such as air pollution or noise levels, are necessarily defined in terms of specific localities, and will automatically be reported in such terms. Similarly, there are apt to be many topics about which local data would be desirable, but for which survey costs would be greater than the likely return. The point in every instance is simply to collect as much specifically local data as resources permit.

Second, inasmuch as urban social indicators cannot be apolitical, they must be pan-political. The very existence of such indicators is a political fact, responding to the desire of a small body of opinion that there should be greater awareness of urban problems—in order that there should be more effective political action in dealing with them. Such information cannot be neutral. The choice of what is to be included, the manner of presenting it, and the interrelations that are sought out will reflect profound political attitudes and interests. They must, therefore, cater to as wide as possible a spectrum of political interests. Ideally, the volume of urban social indicators, should they become a reality, will be found on the desks of the head speech writers for *all* the mayoralty candidates in all the cities that are covered. What applies to the central cities should be equally the case for the surrounding suburbs: the distinction between city and suburb is merely a way of describing one aspect of the urban situation. The greatest danger of the enterprise is that the indicators will be shaped primarily in terms of the political attitudes and social programs of liberal Democrats, for the simple reason that most of the men conceiving the effort and carrying it forward will be of that persuasion. A deliberate effort should be made to include subjects of interest to other parties and more conservative points of view.

Crime is an important instance. It is, and for several generations has been, one of the most important political issues in the nation. There is probably no other issue that is so specifically identified by the public as an "urban" issue and an "urban" problem. It is also a racial problem. For that reason and for a combination of others, liberal academics have tended to ignore or skirt the issue, hoping, perhaps, that it would go away or in some way escape the attention of the public. Nothing of the sort has happened: crime in the streets has become, if anything, a more explosive issue as time has passed. Thus, in his special message proposing the Safe Streets and Crime Control Act of 1967, President Johnson reported that in a recent survey of two of our largest cities: "43 percent of those interviewed stayed off the streets at night." A survey conducted for the Commission on Law Enforcement and the Administration of Justice showed that crime, after race relations, is clearly thought to be the most important domestic problem.[3] This is the kind of information that can be collected in the present and which can be built into a time series from which important political arguments and deductions can be derived.

Similarly, the racial component of crime must be lived with. The President's Commission on Crime in the District of Columbia has reported that Negro males committed 76 percent of all serious offenses in the District in the years 1961–1965, and that Negro males and females together accounted for 86 per cent. This represents a rising proportion. In the decade 1950–1960, Negro males committed only 69 per cent of such offenses, while the male-female combination was only 77 per cent. These figures clearly correspond to the impressions of the white community, including the congressional community in the District, and these impressions will not recede simply because such information is not included in a series of urban indicators. If anything, the opposite might be the case: fears are often exaggerated, and will tend to persist for some time after the reality changes. Properly compiled urban crime statistics would probably show stable crime rates in terms of age groups, and will surely pick up declining crime rates well in advance of the popular perception. (Note the wide attention given to the recent announcement by the Bureau of Narcotics that the incidence of Negro drug addiction appears to be declining while that of whites is rising.) At a less heated level of concern is the Republican party's interest in increasing the opportunities of low-income Americans to own their own homes, as recently announced by Congressman Gerald R. Ford and Senator Charles H. Percy. This is a matter easily enough measured, and ought to be included in the housing data on American cities. As time passes, it may abet the Republican cause, or injure it, but in any event the indicators will be relevant to the political world which inspired them.

Third, urban social indicators should be concerned with the future as well as with the present. For some reason, government (and, to a lesser degree, business), although they collect and calculate a considerable range of "facts" about the future, are nonetheless curiously hesitant about making them public in any very assertive way. This is surely a mistake. Most public policy proceeds from assumptions as to what the future will be like, and these assumptions can often be significantly influenced by perfectly "knowable" information. In areas such as labor-force composition and school enrollment, this can be done with considerable accuracy, and can be used to much greater purpose than has been the case. As an example, current projections of the white and nonwhite population of the United States, when calculated in percentage terms, suggest that the school integration problem will be considerably greater than one might assume from the proposition that "Negroes make up about one-tenth of the population." The nonwhite proportion of the population between ages five and nine over the next twenty years is projected in Table 1. This would suggest, for example, that, in the very near future, upwards of one child in five entering public schools, nationally, will be nonwhite. Obviously, these proportions are much greater in certain central city areas, but, here again, it is possible to forecast with acceptable degrees of probable accuracy.

---

[3] *The Challenge of Crime in a Free Society,* report by President's Commission on Law Enforcement and Administration of Justice, February, 1967, p. 51.

Table 1
Projections of nonwhite proportion of
United States population aged five to nine, 1970-1985

Year	High fertility projection (%)	Low fertility projection (%)
1970	15.8	15.8
1975	16.3	15.9
1980	16.7	15.9
1985	17.2	16.1

Source: Derived from *Current Population Reports: Population Esti-mates,* Series P-25, No. 345, "Projections of the White and Non-White Population of the United States, by Age and Sex, to 1985," July 29, 1966.

Fourth, urban indicators should seek to provide comparisons between local data, average national data, and data corresponding to "best practice" in various fields. The Council of Economic Advisors' well-established practice of including in their Annual Report an analysis of the "gap" between the actual and the potential gross national product provides an excellent instance of the power of this type of analysis to create pressures for more effective social and economic policies.[4] A quite startling instance of wide disparities in performance will be found in the Selective Service rejection rates. Thus, in 1965, 48 per cent of the young men called up in South Carolina failed the mental examination, as contrasted with a failure rate of 5 per cent in Iowa. A wide difference in rejection rates exists between whites and nonwhites, and very probably between social class and neighborhood, if the data were available at this level of disaggregation. In 1965, for example, the disqualifica-tion rate for white draftees of 14.7 per cent contrasts sharply with a mental dis-qualification rate for Negroes of 59.6 per cent. With effort, it is likely that a considerable range of national test performance of this kind could be disaggregated to local areas, perhaps health and school districts, with possibly important conse-quences in terms of local judgments as to the adequacy of community services. In North Carolina, for example, the high rate of Selective Service mental-test rejections has become an issue of considerable concern.

Those things being said, it remains only to assert Bertram Gross's formulation: The object of social indicators should be to report "the condition of man in the metropolitan area" and to do so in three categories.[5] [The first category should include data on *people as individuals*—numbers, distribution, density, mobility, employment, income, antisocial behavior, health, and participation rates. The sec-

---

[4]See "The annual report of the Council of Economic Advisors," *Economic Report of the President, January 1967* (Washington, D.C., 1967), Chart 1, p. 43.

[5]Bertram M. Gross, "The city of man: A social systems reckoning," in William R. Ewald, Jr. (ed.), *Environment for Man: The Next Fifty Years* (Bloomington: University of Indiana Press, 1967), pp. 136–156.

ond should include data on *families*—unemployment and welfare statistics' correlations and poverty neighborhood studies. The third should include data on *institutions*—public service and voluntary organizations, business, mass media, education, and urban ecology.]

30. Measuring the effectiveness of nondefense public programs

HARRY P. HATRY

This paper discusses measuring the output, or effectiveness, of nondefense public programs, as related to its uses in making program and policy choices. We are not directly concerned with using such measurements for controlling ongoing operations, although, in many cases, the same measures may apply both to operational control and program choice. (Operational control also frequently involves workload and efficiency measures.)

In measuring the output, or effectiveness, of nondefense public programs, it is important to determine first what we should want to measure without being restricted by our current ability to measure things—we should avoid prejudging, based on current practice, what may be measurable and what may not be. Substantial improvements in data gathering and estimation clearly can be made, particularly as governments at all levels increasingly focus their attention on the end purposes of governmental activities, and not simply the immediate products.

For the purposes of this paper, such terms as "output measures," "evaluation criteria," "measures of effectiveness," and "program effects" are synonymous.

CRITERIA FOR PROGRAM SELECTION

My principal contention is that, of three approaches to criteria selection often used in government, all are inadequate for the purpose of program selection, and that a fourth, often neglected, approach should be used.

Abridged and edited from Harry P. Hatry, "Measuring the effectiveness of nondefense public programs," *Operations Research,* 18:772–784 (September–October, 1970). Copyright © 1970 by the Operations Research Society of America. Reprinted by permission.

The author is Director, State-Local Government Research Program, The Urban Institute, Washington, D.C.

1. The first inadequate approach can be disposed of rather quickly—at least conceptually, if not in practice. It assumes that effectiveness is either not measurable at all or is not needed. This assumption is implied by the use of program cost estimates to reflect the program's degree of effectiveness. Thus, if one program alternative calls for expending 10 per cent more than another, it does not necessarily follow that this program alternative will yield 10 per cent more benefits. Such an assumption begs the question. The key problem is to determine explicitly how much more effective, if at all, the one program is than the other. Program costs *are* necessary, of course, as one criterion in program selection, since they indicate the amount of scarce resources used by each program alternative. But program costs clearly should not be used to represent program effectiveness. While we can dismiss this approach quickly, it is still surprisingly prevalent throughout the country; for example, an "expenditure-per-pupil" factor is often used, implicitly if not explicitly, as a measure of effectiveness of public-school education.

2. The second inadequate approach to criteria is probably the most common: It uses "immediately" observable products, of which two types may be identified: (a) workload measures, and (b) physical standards.

a) The workload measure is the type of measure commonly found in current program and performance budgets. An example is one commonly used by Departments of Agriculture (state or federal) for cattle-inspection programs: "the number of livestock inspected" as a measure of output. Other examples are: "number of persons in employment-training programs," and "number of health-cases examined." As indicators of workload these are clearly useful. But these measures say little about the effectiveness of these programs, since they ignore such vital questions as: How effective will the livestock inspection, the employment training, the health examinations be? What would be the effects on citizens if the programs were reduced? increased? or revised? For the livestock case, measures are needed for the amount of potential human illness and livestock loss estimated for each program alternative. For employment-training-program proposals, estimates are needed of the employment that would occur (and for what durations) that otherwise would not have occurred—if little added employment is achieved, all the best training in the world is of little use. For health-examination program proposals, estimates are needed for the ultimate improvement in health (such as reduced mortality, morbidity, and disability) that is likely to result.

b) Physical standards are commonly used in state- and local-government physical-plan preparation and in certain federal programs, such as hospital construction. Examples of physical standards are: x acres of neighborhood parks per 1,000 population, y hospital beds per 1,000 population, and z teachers per so many students. But acreage, hospital beds, teachers, and the like, are not ends in themselves. Such numbers may be useful if related to more meaningful products, such as, respectively, the quantity and quality of recreation that will be delivered, health indicators, and learning measures.

3. The third unfortunate approach to criteria is quite different: It goes to the other extreme. This is the approach that insists upon translating each program effect into a common unit of measure, while at the same time suppressing (either consciously or unconsciously) more relevant, but noncommensurable, measures. This attempt to make measures commensurable (i.e., to express all measures in the same

units) is commendable, but is misguided—at least as generally practiced. Two forms of this approach commonly exist:

a) The first is often labeled a "cost-benefit" analysis, where the term "cost-benefit" is defined in the limited sense of translating program effects into monetary, dollar, terms.

b) The second form is the use of various "weighting" techniques to combine measures that are expressed in different units into a single overall index of worth for each alternative.

There is no doubt that the job of decision makers would be easier if a single effectiveness measure could appropriately be used. However, I contend that such procedures place the analyst in the position of making a considerable number of value judgments that rightfully should be made in the *political* decision-making process, and *not* by the analyst. Such value judgments are buried in the procedures used by the analysts and are seldom revealed to, or understood by, the decision makers.

Such hocus pocus in the long run tends to discredit analysis and distract significantly from what should be its principal role: to present to decision makers alternative ways of achieving objectives, and to estimate and display all the major trade-offs of cost and effectiveness that exist among these alternatives.

The number of very able professionals, in universities, consulting firms, and (though less frequently) in government who overdo this commensurability business is appalling. More will be presented on this point later.

4. What is needed for evaluation are criteria that come as close as possible to reflecting the basic, underlying objectives of the government—the effects upon people. These criteria should be expressed in any units that are appropriate.

. .   .   .   .

An example may be helpful. Let us assume that a government is considering assistance to communities for programs directed toward improving child health. The problem is to evaluate these proposals. What evaluation criteria are appropriate? As indicated earlier, such measures as the "number of children examined" and the "number of children treated" may be good workload measures, but they provide only limited information as to the more fundamental objective of helping to make these children healthier. The total magnitude of the health problem would be indicated best by estimating the total number of children with defects. The total actual effectiveness would much better be indicated by comparing the number of children with defects to the number whose defects would likely be corrected or at least alleviated. Thus, if (as an extreme case) no defects could be corrected or alleviated, all the examination in the world would be useless and would be a waste of resources.

THE SELECTION AND USE OF EVALUATION CRITERIA

I would now like to indicate briefly some of the major considerations in the selection and use of such criteria.

1. First, prior to selecting appropriate criteria, a governmental jurisdiction should identify, as specifically as possible, its basic objectives. One such classification of very general government objectives is shown in Table 1. Clearly, individual

programs often will be aimed at small portions of perhaps but one of the general objectives shown in the exhibit; for example, a disadvantaged-child health program would address just one part of the total health problem.

Table 1
An illustrative set of general governmental objectives

1. *Personal safety.* To reduce the amount and effects of external harm to individuals and, in general, to maintain an atmosphere of personal security from external events.
2. *Health.* To provide for the physical and mental health of the citizenry, including reduction of the number, length, and severity of illnesses and disabilities.
3. *Intellectual development.* To provide satisfactory opportunities for intellectual development to the citizenry.
4. *Satisfactory home and community environment.* To provide opportunity for satisfactory living conditions.
5. *Satisfactory economic status and work opportunity for the individual.* To permit each family and each person to meet basic economic–physical needs while maintaining dignity and self-respect; to permit any employable person desiring to work to obtain satisfactory employment without loss of dignity and self-respect.
6. *Satisfactory leisure-time opportunities.* To provide year-round leisure-time opportunities for the citizenry that are accessible, varied, safe, physically attractive, uncrowded, and, in general, enjoyable.
7. *Transportation, communication, location.* To transport needed amounts and types of human traffic quickly, safely, and pleasurably.

Governments need to identify what they are attempting to do (or, at least, *should* be attempting to do) for the citizens and then relate their program options to these objectives. (A number of local-government planning documents have done a reasonable job of identifying objectives, but they seem to ignore them when evaluating programs.) From these basic objectives, evaluation criteria should be developed.[1] It is also important to look for possible consequences, negative as well as beneficial, that government programs may have on objectives other than those at which the programs are explicitly aimed, a step that is often neglected. For example, early urban renewal efforts neglected the negative effects of destroying the homes of low-income families without providing for their relocation.

2. The real world being what it is, few problems are adequately considered in terms of a single criterion; most, if not all, problems involve more than one. . . . Transportation programs provide [a] good example of the need for multiple evaluation criteria. From the user's point of view, at least three major objectives need to be considered for transportation systems: the desires for shorter trip times, for safety, and for pleasure. Clearly, there are trade-offs among these objectives; for example, too much speed will likely diminish safety. In addition, transportation

---

[1]An illustrative set of evaluation criteria associated with such objectives is contained in my paper, "Criteria for evaluation in planning state and local programs," U.S. Senate Subcommittee on Intergovernmental Relations, July 21, 1967. Another recent report presenting some useful measures is U.S. Department of Health, Education, and Welfare, "Toward a Social Report," January 11, 1969.

systems have numerous effects on others than the immediate users: effects upon community physical environment (e.g., air and noise pollution), effects on job opportunities (through increased mobility), dislocation of families, disruption of neighborhoods, etc. Each of these factors should be considered and evaluated explicitly in transportation selection. Of course, for any given problem, the analysts may be able to eliminate some such effects as not being of significance for the situation under consideration; too often, however, analysts are often overly quick to make such eliminations.

As indicated earlier, it is my belief that attempts to combine the individual effects into a single unit of measure either by using some type of weighting procedure or by translating individual nonmonetary criteria into monetary terms, has been considerably overdone. For example, a considerable part of the cost-benefit work in the fields of water-resource programs, health, transportation, and education (at least until recently) has paid excessive attention to using monetary evaluations of program alternatives, with the result that many very important nonmonetary program effects were buried and ignored, or at least greatly underconsidered. The caveats contained in most such studies, slipped into the report somewhere to warn the reader that "intangibles" have not been included, have hardly been sufficient. Fortunately, the decision makers have probably been less misled by the final numbers presented in such studies than the analysts have.

Four of the deficiencies of this concentration on creating a single criterion of worth are worth discussing:

a) Key value judgments that are rightfully the task of the political decision-making process are instead made by analysts and buried in the report.

b) Key value concerns get ignored completely (even though this may not be intended by the analysts). An example, applying to (a) as well as here, is that of using future estimated earnings as a representation of the "value" of human life (in health studies, for example). The earning calculations (often based upon very sophisticated analysis) imply that the elderly have little, or possibly even negative, value; females (whether working or nonworking) fare badly compared to males; and the young (where a discount rate is used) are penalized compared to those just entering the age of work productivity. Similarly, in education studies, programs for those entering high-paying occupations would have the advantage over programs for those who might enter the lower-paying occupations (such as teaching and other more altruistic occupations). If economic growth were the sole or even primary objective of our society, such earning calculations might be a valid proxy for the value of human life. If this is not the case, however—and I do not believe it is—then such evaluations leave out vital considerations and, if not handled properly, tend to lead to governmental programs not as desirable from a social viewpoint as others.

c) The distributional effects, as will be discussed further below, are usually ignored in cost-benefit calculations. The program benefits, and the negative effects of proposed programs, seldom, if ever, will be spread evenly over population subgroups. In addition, the program costs and negative effects will generally be borne, at least in part, by groups different from those that receive the benefits (thus, even when both are expressed in dollars, costs and benefits are really not commensurable). Procedures are often proposed for weighting population subgroups, but, personally, I do not want to be the analyst with the task of selecting such weights.

Clearly, at least in my opinion, weighting the importance of population subgroups is the job of the political decision-making authority (though the analyst may be able to provide certain information on each subgroup to the study users).

d) Where dollar imputations are used, such as when a dollar figure is applied to represent the value of nonbusiness travel time saved or the value of a "recreation day," such figures are once again suspect. In a sense, they prejudge the determination that decision makers should make as to whether it is worth so many dollars of program cost to reduce travel time by so much or to provide a certain number of added recreational opportunities. In addition, when such figures are combined—as is usually done in such studies—with actual program-cost outlays, the results are a mixing of apples and oranges.

My position is not that decision makers should not in certain instances be shown such information as added earnings that might be obtained if illnesses are averted or if added years of education are provided, or information as to what alternative would be "optimum" if a certain weighting procedure is used. But this information should be provided only as additional information to the unweighted, undollared effects in whatever units are most meaningful and for each appropriate population subgroup. This will not make the job of political decision makers any easier, but will allow them to face the real, underlying issues that are relevant. The analyst should not be the one to make such choices.

3. As implied above, another important aspect of program analysis—one that until recently has been grossly neglected—complicates further the number of criteria that should be considered: the need to consider the various population subgroups affected by a given program. Government programs will, in general, affect different subgroups to different degrees; and different alternatives will generally differ in their distributions of effects. Too, different programs may be directed toward different beneficiary groups. In addition, groups other than those at whom the programs are directed may also be significantly affected—whether beneficially or negatively. For example, a program such as Medicaid directly affects all those in families with financial resources below specified eligibility levels; however, Medicaid probably also affects families not eligible under the program—for example, Medicaid has caused increased medical prices (and therefore causes lower real income to other families). In addition, Medicaid might cause medical services to be less available to other families by overloading private medical-care resources. Such characteristics as age, race, sex, special handicaps, and geographical location may distinguish important population subgroups. Most, if not all, program-selection problems should give explicit consideration to how each program alternative affects each of the various significant population subgroups. It is surprising how infrequently this is being done today.

4. Now we come to the real art of program analysis. Evaluation of program alternatives against their fundamental objectives may, in many instances, prove quite difficult. In some cases, lower-level, or proxy, criteria may need to be used. For example, response times may need to be used, at least temporarily, as a proxy for the reduction in unsolved crimes; or, the observed "going" price of narcotics may be useful as a proxy for the effectiveness of efforts to reduce narcotics flow.

However, there is a tendency for analysts to overdo this. Analysts seem to have a tendency to prefer to accept a proxy criterion that is readily quantifiable and that permits "optimization" than to attempt the difficult task of finding vital, but less quantifiable, relations. There are two related recent examples: The National Crime Commission, in its Crime Commission Report, presented an analysis of police communication and control systems and their effects on police response times in getting to the scene of a crime.[2] Similarly, New York City did an analytical study of its emergency ambulance-service system in which the number and location of ambulances were related to response times, e.g., both times until arrival at the scene and round-trip times until the patient was delivered to a hospital for care.[3] In both these cases the analysis was very good—with one qualification: A crucial problem in both analyses is the relation of response time to how response time affects other more important factors; in the ambulance problem, the health of the individuals, and in the crime study, the ability to solve past crimes and prevent future ones need to be related to the response times. In the ambulance-analysis report, one of the summary charts shows a reduction in average response times from roughly 14 minutes to 12 minutes. Now, I contend that the decision maker, who cannot be expected to be a medical expert, would have a very difficult time trying to determine for himself what it is worth to make this reduction from 14 to 12 minutes. It is not at all clear what this means in terms of improved health of the people who are emergency cases. My point is that, in both of these analyses, more time should have been spent on trying to relate response times to health in the one case and to crime solution and prevention in the other.[4] . . .

. . . .

5. Another important dimension to the criteria problem is the time dimension. That is, in evaluating competing program alternatives, each alternative needs to be evaluated, in general, against each relevant criterion for each year of the planning horizon. Few, if any, programs affect only the current and budget years; most will have implications for a number of years beyond. It is, therefore, inadequate to consider only the current and budget years; future implications need to be given explicit consideration—a point that is probably well appreciated by most analysts. This added dimension also adds to the multidimensionality of criteria since trade-offs are possible as to earlier versus later expenditures and benefits.

6. Finally, a major concern, of course, is the measurability of individual criteria. If a criterion cannot be reasonably measured in any manner, it will not be useful. However, this does not mean that a criterion has to be quantifiable in the absolute sense. Unfortunately, this point often seems to be misunderstood. Light can be shed on most criteria, even if done only in a qualitative sense—even if we can only say that alternative 1 is superior to alternative 2 on such-and-such a criterion, this

---

[2]See President's Commission on Law Enforcement and Administration of Justice, *Task Force Report: Science and Technology* (Washington, D.C., 1967), Chapter 2.

[3]See H. Spiegel and E. S. Savas, "Emergency ambulance service," Office of the Mayor, Office of Administration, New York City, May 8, 1968.

[4]It has occasionally been pointed out that an important consideration for a chief executive of a government is the public's perception as to the amount of response time before help arrives at the scene and that complaints do come in when this time is perceived as being too long. This suggests the need for a second criterion: the number (and perhaps severity) of complaints received of slow ambulance responses. However, even in this situation, we are left with the need to relate changes in response time to changes in the number of complaints.

statement is likely to be useful. Such procedures as rankings and ratings can be used effectively; e.g., alternative roads can be ranked, or rated, on attractiveness, say on a scale of one to ten. Thus the use of opinions and judgments by appropriate experts or clientele groups can certainly be used, if handled in a systematic manner. The scenario approach also has considerable potential for treating intangibles in a systematic and useful way.

Other examples where qualitative (i.e., subjective) information is needed and can be utilized are in measuring the "feeling of security" from crime, and in estimating the effects on mental health of proposed treatments.

SUMMARY AND RECOMMENDATIONS

In conclusion, here are some general recommendations for use in any government agency, federal, state, or local, that is concerned with measuring the effectiveness of public services.

1. All major program proposals should be required to identify explicitly the basic objectives toward which the programs are aimed.

2. Criteria should be selected that permit direct evaluation of programs against the identified objectives. If such criteria appear, after sufficient attention, to resist adequate measurement, carefully chosen proxy criteria may need to be substituted, but the real program objectives should not be forgotten. Where practical, information systems should be developed to obtain the needed information. The immediate physical outputs of programs such as workload measures and physical standards should not be used for these purposes without careful consideration as to their relevance. Workload measures and physical standards, though of considerable use for the purposes of evaluating the frugality of budgets and for aiding in the management control of current operations, will seldom be adequate for evaluation criteria for program-selection purposes.

3. Program proposals that contribute to the same basic objectives should be evaluated together, regardless of organizational lines.

4. The impacts of programs beyond the budget year, both as to costs and [as to] contributions to basic objectives, should be explicitly considered to see that future needs are not unduly penalized at the expense of current needs.

5. Multiple criteria are a complicating fact of life. Programs should be evaluated against all relevant criteria. Qualitative measurement is appropriate wherever purely quantitative measurement is insufficient.

Each program selection problem is likely to involve its own special considerations, which means that for each problem the question of appropriate evaluation criteria needs to be raised and criteria selected only after careful deliberation.

31. Urban information systems and invasions of privacy

EDWARD M. GOLDBERG

The development of modern, high speed, remote access computers has created a revolution in the accumulation, storage, processing, analysis, retrieval, and transmission of data. Urban governments, while not in the vanguard of the computer revolution, have in recent years joined the computer age. In common with other governmental and private agencies, state, regional, and local governments are participating in the information revolution with the development of large numbers of urban information systems. By 1968 there were 188 urban information systems of one kind or another in various stages of implementation in the United States, and it was projected that "hundreds" more such systems would be developed during the current decade (Dial, 1968: 1, 12).

As the capabilities of computers increase, thought must be given to the social problems created by the new technology. Although the technological problems of urban computers have been the subject of a mass of literature, little has been written on the social implications of urban information systems. Specifically, the literature is almost devoid of commentary on the problem of potential invasion of the right of personal privacy, defined by Justice Louis D. Brandeis as "the right to be let alone —the most valuable of the rights of man and the right most valued by civilized men" (*Olmstead* vs. *U.S.,* 1928). Thus, Hearle and Mason's seminal work (1963: 53–55) on urban information systems contains less than two full pages on the problem of confidentiality—and they do not consider it to be a problem. Even where the problem is recognized, little is said about it. Thus, Harold H. Haak (1967), discussing the evolution of a metropolitan data system for San Diego, California, raises the issue, but does nothing more than assert that it is a problem which "results from the fact that most of the laws regarding confidentiality were written long before anyone could have envisioned the capabilities of electronic data processing." Similarly, Dennis G. Price (1967: 23), reviewing the use of computers by state and local governments, devotes one short paragraph to the question of privacy, in which he observes that if and when the problem of compatibility of information is solved, the problem of invasion of privacy arises. But Price says nothing more about it, even in the section of his article concerned with "possible steps to solutions."

There are several reasons why the literature on urban information systems is so sparse when it comes to discussion of the problem of privacy. First, the technical experts who design, improve, maintain, use, and write about such systems honestly do not consider it to be a problem. Thus, Hearle and Mason (1963: 55) conclude

"Urban Information Systems and Invasions of Privacy" by Edward M. Goldberg is reprinted from *Urban Affairs Quarterly,* Vol. 5, No. 3 (March, 1970), pp. 249–264, by permission of the Publisher, Sage Publications, Inc. Abridged and edited.

The author is Professor of Political Science, California State College, Los Angeles, Cal.

that "the Unified Information System involves no new problems of confidentiality. On the contrary, any required restriction on data access can be enforced more effectively in such a system than in present separate systems" (cf. Baran, 1967: 119 ff.).

Second, they see so many benefits resulting from the development and maintenance of such systems, they cannot see the social problems. They are concerned with the elimination of technical problems in order to improve the efficiency and usefulness of the system. Third, they are enamored of the system for its own sake. And fourth, the problem is not unique to urban information systems. It is common to all data processing systems—private and governmental, national, state, regional, and local. Hence, one finds some concern expressed regarding the establishment of a national data bank, or with the general problem of privacy and the proliferation of information systems in general. However, it should be noted that this concern only emerged in the 1960s (Westin, 1967; Dial, 1968), and little of it is directed toward urban information systems per se.

· · · · ·

EXISTING URBAN INFORMATION SYSTEMS

A brief review of three existing urban information systems may illustrate the extent to which data are being gathered and stored today [for fuller discussions, see Black and Shaw, 1967; Milliman, 1967; and Garrison, 1967]. The city of Detroit maintains two data banks. The first is a "physical data bank," and it contains such information as the condition of the city's residential, commercial, and industrial buildings; property assessment figures; age characteristics of various structures; type of structure; the estimated costs of various kinds of physical treatment of residential structure (e.g., conservation, redevelopment, and code enforcement); population characteristics and occupancy patterns; and many other kinds of data. The second is a "social data bank." It contains data on crime rates, welfare, births and deaths, school truancy and dropout rates, the occurrence of venereal diseases and tuberculosis, and other information. The information in Detroit's data banks is available to any department of the city, and to any non-city agency that can make profitable use of the data.

Alameda County, California, maintains a "People Information System," which is used by many local agencies such as the assessor, auditor, tax collector, treasurer, retirement board, civil service, central service, public works, registrar of voters, surveyor, engineer, courts, sheriff, welfare, probation, health, hospitals, and so forth, as well as San Francisco Bay Area law enforcement agencies. The system maintains three basic types of files: an identification of I/D file to identify the person; an agency file describing the person's status with respect to each agency connected with the system; and cross reference files to link related I/D and agency records.

Similarly, Santa Clara County, California, maintains a system named LOGIC (Local Government Information Control). It contains information about residents such as: name, alias, birth record, driver's license data, vehicle license number, position (if a county employee), voter and jury status, property holdings; and 'other data' if the person has ever been involved with the county welfare or health departments, the district attorney, sheriff, adult or juvenile probation, court, and so on.

Now, the point of these illustrations is not that data ought not to be collected but that a wide variety of data *are* being collected today. And, as Westin (1967: 161) has pointed out:

> The most significant fact for the subject of privacy is that once an organization purchases a giant computer, it inevitably begins to collect more information about its employees, clients, members, taxpayers, or other persons in the interest of the organization. The result may be to provide better service, make more efficient use of personnel, know more facts on which to base decisions, pinpoint wrongdoers, and the like. But the inevitable result is that the investigator acquires two or three times as much personal information from respondents as was ever collected before because of the physical or cost limits of acquisition. The impact of computers on organizational life is to destroy practical boundaries of privacy in record giving which were once as meaningful in this area as walls and doors were to conversational privacy before the advent of new physical surveillance technology.

We must recognize the cognitive passion—the factual hunger—of all government bodies (Shils, 1967: 250–251). They wish and need to know more and more about those whom they rule in order to serve and protect them better. The need for information gathers a momentum, a dynamic of its own, which has become independent of the needs of policy. And computer technology, which opens new possibilities for otherwise impracticable manipulation of large bodies of data, extends and intensifies this passion for knowledge. This momentum, dynamic, and passion for knowledge is illustrated by Gordon Milliman, the man who runs Alameda County's "People Information System." Writing a mere two years after its inception, Milliman (1967: 30) looked forward to expansion of the system. It must be recognized that each such expansion of the system diminishes the sphere of the private (Shils, 1967: 233).

Moreover, the pressure immediately builds for the elimination of duplication of data and for sharing of data. Thus, Milliman asserts: "Because no unit of government is an island unto itself, we believe it is essential to communicate, cooperate and coordinate with the data processing efforts of other governmental units at the county, state and federal level." Another expert, Robert M. Hayes, sees the development of 'hundreds' of Urban Information Systems, many of which will form interrelationships with higher, lower and adjacent levels of government (see Dial, 1968: 12). Thus, we move inexorably toward the stage where interlocked data systems provide detailed, comprehensive information from a wide variety of sources almost at the touch of a button. The protection of privacy afforded by dispersion of records evaporates and the concentrated information becomes power.

Nevertheless, there are experts who do not view these developments as a problem. Edgar S. Dunn, Jr. (1967) has taken pains to point out that basically there are two different types of information systems: (1) statistical information systems, and (2) intelligence systems. The intelligence system generates data about individuals as individuals. They include things like medical records, educational records, tax records, and so forth. But, Dunn points out, they are restricted systems which have a specific administrative purpose and have not as their purpose the organization of intelligence about individuals into an integrated dossier of any kind.

The statistical information system, on the other hand, generates data that do not relate to individuals, but to groups or populations. Nevertheless, even a statistical information system can be made to contribute to an intelligence system or to double as an intelligence system. In order to process information, in order to avoid duplication, there has to be some sort of identification of individuals on each piece of datum. Such information is ultimately retrievable and, along with data in other systems—either intelligence or statistical—can be compiled into integrated, comprehensive dossiers.

Dunn's answer to this argument, like that of Hearle and Mason (1963: 54), is that the computer can be programmed to refuse to divulge such information about individuals (Dunn, 1967: 94; Bowman, 1967: 49 ff.). This is little comfort, for the computer obviously can also be programmed to divulge the data. Without appropriate *legal* safeguards there is no guarantee that information about individuals will be kept confidential, especially since some urban information systems—such as Alameda County's "People Information System"—are, whether intended or not, in effect, intelligence systems. Minimally, they can easily be made to function as intelligence systems.

.   .   .   .   .

THE CONCEPT OF PRIVACY

The legal right of privacy has its beginning with the decision of Lord Chancellor Hardwicke in *Pope* vs. *Curl,* 1741 (see Ernst and Schwartz, 1962: 6–9). Since that day, it has had a slow, progressive development in tort law (Ernst and Schwartz, 1962: 6–9 ff.; see also Gross, 1964; Prosser, 1960: 383; Westin, 1967: ch. 13; Beaney, 1966; Kalvin, 1966: 326). In the United States, the concept of privacy as a legal right was brought to the fore in 1890 in a very significant law review article, "The Right to Privacy," by Samuel D. Warren and Louis D. Brandeis (1890: 193). The first privacy statute in America was contained in the New York Civil Rights Act of 1903 (see Ernst and Schwartz, 1962: 127–129). The right of privacy in tort law is still undergoing change, both in statute and in court decision.

The framers of the United States Constitution expressed their concern with privacy in several provisions of the Bill of Rights (see Story, 1851: 560, 591, 597, 608–609; and Westin, 1967: 332–333). The First Amendment's guarantees of freedom of religion, speech, press, assembly, and petition were intended to secure the rights of private sentiment and private judgment. The "plain object" of the Third Amendment's prohibition against the quartering of troops in private homes without the owner's consent in peacetime was to secure the perfect enjoyment of that great right of the common law, that a man's house shall be his castle, privileged against all civil and military intrusion.

The Fourth Amendment, with its guarantee that "the right of the people to be secure in their persons, houses, papers and effects, against unreasonable searches and seizures, shall not be violated," was obviously a key element in American guarantees of privacy. The provision is indispensable to the full enjoyment of the rights of personal security, personal liberty, and private property. Similarly, Westin finds that the Fifth Amendment's privilege against self-incrimination was another major legal bulwark for personal privacy. The long-neglected Ninth Amendment's assertion that "the enumeration in the Constitution, of certain rights, shall not be construed to deny or disparage others retained by the people" did not deal with any specific right, such as privacy, but its presence in the Constitution, as will be shown below, may provide a vehicle for the development of a constitutional right of privacy.

Finally, one should take note of various provisions of the Sixth and Eighth Amendments. While not privacy measures when adopted, they bear on the problem of computer invasions of privacy today. The Sixth Amendment has provisions which guarantee the right of an accused in a criminal case to confront witnesses against him, to have compulsory process to compel witnesses to testify for him, and to have counsel. The Eighth Amendment guarantees against cruel and unusual punishments. When one deals with a computer, there is no trial, no lawyer, no opportunity to confront and discredit the supplier of information, no opportunity to supply countervailing information; yet the possible results in economic loss, damaged reputation, and so forth, may exceed the punishments inflicted in some criminal cases (Reich, 1967: 28-29).

Despite the constitutional provisions sketched above, there was no constitutional right of privacy until 1965. In that year, the Supreme Court took the first step —possibly a major step—towards the enunciation of a constitutional right of privacy. In *Griswold* vs. *Connecticut* (381 U.S. 479, 1965), the Supreme Court, by a vote of seven to two, invalidated a Connecticut law forbidding the dissemination of birth control information. Justice William O. Douglas, writing for the Court, spoke of zones of privacy created by various guarantees of the Bill of Rights. In particular, Douglas cited the First, Third, Fourth, Fifth, and Ninth Amendments, and concluded that the Connecticut statute unconstitutionally operated "directly on an intimate relation of husband and wife . . . a *right of privacy* older than the Bill of Rights" itself. Similarly, Justice Arthur J. Goldberg, in his concurring opinion, reasserted the oft-stated constitutional doctrine that the Fourteenth Amendment's due process clause protected those rights in the Bill of Rights which are so rooted in the traditions and conscience of our people as to be ranked as fundamental. The right of marital privacy, Goldberg asserted, could be protected even though it is not guaranteed in so many words by the first eight amendments, especially in view of the Ninth Amendment's statement that the fact that certain rights are guaranteed in the Constitution shall not be construed to deny or disparage others retained by the people. In Goldberg's view, the right of privacy in the marital relation was a fundamental personal liberty, one retained by the people—within the meaning of the Ninth Amendment.

LEGAL PROTECTION: FUTURE NEEDS

The implications of the evolving tort law of privacy and the emerging constitutional law of privacy for urban and other information systems are profound. As Reich (1967) has pointed out, "Any time bad information is supplied about an individual, his legal rights are being invaded at that moment. We have a great common law tradition that defamation of character is a wrong in the law. It seems to me absolutely clear as a starting proposition that anybody who supplies derogatory information about someone else invades his legal rights. A person has a right not to be defamed, whether by a machine or by a person. . . . He does not know what the computer says about him. He does not know what judgments people make on the basis of that. . . . In this day and age in which we have so much pressure to invade the individual's life, I think that we shouldn't stop with the Constitution, we should have affirmative laws to protect privacy more than the Constitution does."

What laws are needed? Reich has suggested three. First, a law prohibiting the eliciting, storing, or retrieving, by an officer or agency of the government, of certain types of information for any purpose; second, a law which would provide each person an effective right to inspect information collected about him and to compel corrections of inaccuracies and prejudicial omissions; third, a law limiting the access to stored information to the original recipient of that information. Other suggestions have been made by Garrison (1967): first, a law providing that certain files have a prescribed useful life and that they be destroyed at the end of a given period of time; second, when data are necessary for lawful research or statistical purposes, the law should require the removal of individual identification before the data are given to the researchers.

In more general terms, Westin (1967: 386, 398) has made the following suggestions:

> The effective use of computers calls for rational analysis and painstaking planning. If privacy is to survive, the growth of personal-data processing will necessitate the same high levels of analysis and planning by federal and state legislatures seeking to use computers for large-scale data processing. This means that fresh studies ought to be made of existing confidentiality and non-disclosure requirements for information acquired by government agencies in their regulatory and data-collecting roles. Provisions for confidentiality of information, restrictions on improper circulation, and sanctions against unauthorized use should be written into the basic legislation and administrative rules governing the new law enforcement computer systems.
>
> Similar legislative action is desirable for the government data centers that are rapidly coming into operation at both state and federal levels. The statute could provide that such information must be kept by the agency that collected it and can not be revealed to another government agency or to a private party unless certain conditions are met—national-security or defense needs; general permission in advance from those supplying information to circulate it freely; specific permission from the supplier for a particular use of the information to be made; and so forth. A process could be established for decision in the executive branch, subject to judicial review, of whether the auxiliary use is proper, has been authorized, and other limitations.

Finally, it ought to be made clear that the burden would be on those who wish to invade privacy to justify their activity, not on individuals to justify their right of privacy.

Michael (1967: 193) has observed that "in the face of the increasingly complex tasks of maintaining, to say nothing of improving, urban society, the special advantages the computer provides to increase information, command, and control . . . will generally be considered more important than protection or preservation of . . . freedom and privacy." Shils (1967: 270; italics added) does not appear to be more optimistic. Identifying the two problems raised by the development of information systems as: "(1) the protection of the privacy of the individual whose existence is the ultimate source of this information from divulgence beyond the circle of those who have legitimate access to the information system," and "(2) the protection of the individual whose privacy has been infringed from harassment by governmental and nongovernmental bodies on the basis of the information obtained by intrusion on privacy," he observes that "it all depends on whether satisfactory safeguards can be discovered and effectively established. The answer is a function of technological possibilities, legislative and administrative arrangements, and the moral character of the custodians of the information, programmers, supervisors, directors, etc. None of these alone will be adequate. *Perhaps all of them together might not be adequate.*"

It may, indeed, be true that this is a losing battle, but the effort must be made. Information is power, and it must be controlled, whether in urban information systems or elsewhere. For as Shils (1967: 275) has observed:

A civil society is not a society of complete transparency or visibility. Everyone needs to be allowed to live somewhat in the shade—both rulers and ruled —in order to "keep" what "belongs" to one.

Intrusions on privacy are baneful because they interfere with an individual in his control of what belongs to him. The "social space" around an individual, the recollection of his past, his conversation, his body and its image, all *belong* to him. He does not acquire them through purchase or inheritance. He possesses them and is entitled to possess them by virtue of the charisma which is inherent in his existence as an individual soul—as we say nowadays, in his individuality—and which is inherent in his membership in the civil community. They belong to him by virtue of his humanity and civility—his membership in the human species and his membership in his own society. A society which claims to be both humane and civil is committed to their respect. When its practice departs from that respect for what belongs to the private sphere, it also departs to that degree from humanity and civility. A civil society cannot exist without that respect.

REFERENCES

Baran, P. "Statement." In U.S. House of Representatives, Special Subcommittee on Invasion of Privacy, *The Computer and Invasion of Privacy.* New York: Arno Press, Inc., 1967. P. 119 ff.

Beaney, W. M. "The right to privacy and American law." *Law and Contemporary Problems* 31:253 (1966).

Black, H., and Shaw, E. "Detroit's data banks." *Datamation* 13:25–27 (March, 1967).

Bowman, R. T. "Statement." In U.S. House of Representatives, Special Subcommittee on Invasion of Privacy, *The Computer and Invasion of Privacy.* New York: Arno Press, Inc., 1967. P. 49 ff.

Dial, O. E. *Urban Information Systems: A Bibliographic Essay.* Urban Systems Laboratory, Massachusetts Institute of Technology. Cambridge, Mass., 1968.

Dunn, E. S., Jr. "Statement." In U.S. House of Representatives, Special Subcommittee on Invasion of Privacy, *The Computer and Invasion of Privacy.* New York: Arno Press, Inc., 1967. P. 92.

Ernst, M. L. and Schwartz, A. U. *Privacy: The Right to be Let Alone.* New York: The Macmillan Co., 1962.

Garrison, O. V. *Spy Government.* New York: Lyle Stuart, Inc., 1967.

Gross, H. *Privacy: Its Legal Protection.* Dobbs Ferry, N.Y.: Oceana Publications, Inc., 1964.

Haak, H. H. "The evolution of a metropolitan data system." *Urban Affairs Quarterly,* Vol. 3 (December, 1967).

Hearle, E. F., and Mason, R. J. *A Data Processing System for State and Local Governments.* Englewood Cliffs, N.J.: Prentice-Hall, Inc., 1963.

Kalvin, H., Jr. "Privacy in tort law—were Warren and Brandeis wrong?" *Law and Contemporary Problems* 31:326 (1966).

Michael, D. N. "Speculations on the relation of the computer to individual freedom and the right to privacy." In U.S. House of Representatives, Special Subcommittee on Invasion of Privacy, *The Computer and Invasion of Privacy.* New York: Arno Press, Inc., 1967.

Milliman, G. "Alameda County's 'People Information System.' " *Datamation* 13: 27–31 (March, 1967).

Olmstead vs. U.S., 277 U.S. 438, 478 (1928), dissenting opinion.

Price, D. G. "Automation in state and local governments." *Datamation* 13:22–25 (March, 1967).

Prosser, W. L. "Privacy." *California Law Review* 48 (1960).

Reich, C. A. "Statement." In U.S. House of Representatives, Special Subcommittee on Invasion of Privacy, *The Computer and Invasion of Privacy.* New York: Arno Press, Inc. 1967. Pp. 28–29.

Shils, E. "Privacy and power." In I. de Sola Pool (ed.), *Contemporary Political Science: Toward Empirical Theory.* New York: McGraw-Hill Book Co., 1967. Pp. 231–276.

Story, J. *Commentaries on the Constitution of the United States.* Boston: Little, Brown & Co., 1851.

Warren, S. D., and Brandeis, L. D. *Harvard Law Review* 4 (1890).

Westin, A. *Privacy and Freedom.* New York: Atheneum Publishers, 1967.

32. "Hard" reporting on *The New York Times*

PAUL H. WEAVER

Every newspaper arrives at a style (approach, method, and manner) of searching out and reporting the news. Its style is always to some degree, and often primarily, the product of a process of "muddling through," and once a newspaper settles into a style it rarely tries to change it very much. Newspapers avoid major change for good reasons: it can alienate readers; it almost always disrupts the news staff; and many editors, being traditionalists, see little need for it. In the case to be considered here, however, the executives of *The New York Times* made a deliberate and far-reaching effort to introduce a new style of metropolitan reporting. One outcome of this effort was, as planned, to improve the "readability" of local news coverage and to broaden its scope. But another outcome, unintended and largely unforeseen, was a seeming reduction in accuracy and neutrality and therefore in the influence the *Times* itself exerts. Was this, on balance, a good bargain, or did the costs of change exceed the benefits? Inescapably, this issue confronts each of the many newspapers which, like the *Times,* have joined the general trend of the fifties and sixties toward "interpretive" journalism.

The *Times* began this change in 1963, shortly after Arthur Ochs Sulzberger, as president and publisher, assumed responsibility for the management of the newspaper. His immediate predecessors, Orville E. Dryfoos (a brother-in-law) and Arthur Hays Sulzberger (his father), had overseen a decade's gradual alteration of the *Times's* style of foreign and Washington coverage. For several reasons, however, the metropolitan staff had been more or less exempt from these efforts to increase readability, breadth, and depth. But in 1963, A. M. Rosenthal, who had a distinguished record as a "new-style" foreign correspondent, was chosen as the man to liven up and otherwise improve the *Times's* metropolitan news.

As metropolitan editor, Rosenthal had some 200 employees under his jurisdiction; of these, about 110 were reporters and 40 were editors and copyreaders. Most of the editors and roughly a third of the reporters looked after specialized subject matter (society, religion, education, real estate, aerospace, and so on), and once hired or assigned, they required comparatively little attention from him. Almost 50 reporters were on general assignment, which meant that they reported news of any kind. (Some of them were kept available, as firemen are, just in case of emergencies; in between "fires" they did odd jobs like following out leads on possible stories and pulling together material for future obituaries, but their real function was to prevent the *Times* from ever being shorthanded.) The other major element of the metropolitan staff was its public-affairs section. Before 1963, there were fewer than ten public-affairs reporters: two or three of them usually reported state politics in Albany, and the rest covered city hall, the political parties and clubs, and (on a less

Reprinted with permission of The Macmillan Company from *Urban Government* by Edward C. Banfield, ed., (1969, rev. ed.) pp. 480–486. Copyright © 1969 by The Free Press, a Division of The Macmillan Company.

The author is Assistant Professor of Government, Harvard University, Cambridge, Mass.

routine basis) the major departments of city government. During his first two years, Rosenthal doubled the number of reporters assigned to New York City politics and government. The city, he thought, needed more and deeper coverage anyway; and the new administration of Mayor John V. Lindsay, which seemed to him to be of special importance not only to New York but also to urban America in general, deserved particularly close scrutiny from the *Times*.

It was with the work of the public-affairs and general-assignment reporters that Rosenthal was most concerned. He was determined to alter their reportorial style by introducing what he called "hard" reporting. Most newspapermen termed this kind of writing "interpretive," but Rosenthal preferred "hard." The word was perhaps more apt than he realized.

In the pre-Rosenthal days the metropolitan staff gathered and reported news in the same way that newspapers generally do. It scrutinized the flood of information that came to the newsroom from outside sources—wire services, press releases, books and articles, even anonymous tipsters—and when something of interest turned up it was usually given to a general-assignment reporter for rewriting or exploration. The primary reliance, however, was on reporters who "covered beats." As an editor of those days once explained, "News breaks through definite channels; it cannot do otherwise. Cover these channels and you catch the news—much like casting a net across a salmon stream."[1] Naturally the structure of the search process to a large extent determined what was found and considered news. And naturally, too, what was considered news to a large extent determined the way facts were selected, organized, and presented to the reader. Tacitly the *Times* defined news as what happened on a reporter's beat during a twenty-four-hour period. A well-written story was regarded as one which set forth the facts about a happening in order of their descriptive importance and in the most sober, neutral way possible. What good reporting mainly required, therefore, was respect for facts and an instinct for the newsworthy happening. The best reporter was the one who missed the fewest happenings, gathered the most facts, made the fewest errors, and showed the least bias. Usually a reporter served a long apprenticeship before being allowed to report political news on his own. This was not because the *Times* wanted to give him the time to develop a deep understanding of some subject matter: on the contrary, it was held that a capable reporter did not need any special study or substantive knowledge to write an adequate story about almost anything. The long apprenticeship was necessary because the *Times* felt that a record of reliable performance in getting and presenting facts was the best indicator of a reporter's ability. It also gave a reporter time to learn the "territory"—who was who, and what was really new. As one might expect the best stories were generally given to the senior reporters. These men might not have been the liveliest writers—in fact, they tended to be the dullest—but they had proven their ability to get the facts and to treat them with respect, and that, in those days, was what really mattered.

For this traditional conception of news and news-gathering, Rosenthal substituted "hard" reporting. This, he said,

---

[1]Edwin L. James, "The organization of a newspaper," *The New York Times; The Newspaper: Its Making and Its Meaning* (New York: Charles Scribner's Sons, 1945), p. 103.

is not taking things at their surface value. You try to find the genesis of the thing, the why. What motivates the people involved? Basically, hard reporting is a style of inquiry, an approach to reporting. It has nothing to do with subject matter.

The terminology was somewhat confusing. Newspapermen had generally used the term "hard news" to refer to a story which was about a bona fide happening and accordingly had a news value that did not depend upon mere opinion, certainly not the caprice of an editor or the cunning of a public relations counselor. (At the opposite extreme was the "puff," something passed off as news when it was not, or something manufactured to look like news.) Rosenthal used the word *hard* in an entirely new sense: for him, "hardness" had to do not with an event's claim to being news but rather with the manner in which an event was reported.

For the *Times* metropolitan reporter, the changes "hard" reporting entailed were clear enough. He could no longer confine his attention simply to digging out facts and setting them down. He had to do more than just describe an event: now he had to discuss its significance as well—tell what its causes were, what its effects might be, and how it could bear on the private citizen's concerns—and do so in terms the reader could understand. In order to do this the reporter would have to think and analyze, weigh evidence, and make judgments. In what he wrote he would have to set forth a reasoned argument in support of his conclusions, and he would have to do this in a way that would engage the attention and interest of the reader. Needless to say, a competent "hard" reporter would have to have a very unusual set of qualities. He would have to have a deep understanding of every subject matter on which he reported, the ability to analyze and synthesize, and extraordinary skill as a writer.

More obscure, perhaps, but no less important were the changes "hard" reporting demanded in the structure of the news-gathering process. Because the "hard" reporter had to look beyond the mere happening to the "broad issues and trends" it symbolized, the *Times'* conception of news itself became more inclusive. News could therefore be found in places where it had not been found before, and the beat system accordingly changed. A reporter was still assigned to cover the police department, for example, but he no longer reported "crime"; instead, he concentrated on "the big issues" in law enforcement and the administration of justice—the relationship between mayor and police department, brutality, discrimination, defendants' rights, civilian review, and so on (The *Times* kept staffers at the various police headquarters to inform the metropolitan desk of criminal happenings, but these were rarely reported in the paper.) Moreover, Rosenthal created several new beats: for the first time, a reporter was assigned to the city departments having responsibility for maintaining the quality of the urban environment—sanitation, parks, air pollution, city planning, and water. Another reporter was assigned to health and hospitals. "Hard" reporting was one reason why the size of the public-affairs staff was doubled. It also accounted for the rehabilitation of the general-assignment reporter, who now began to write stories about topics in urban sociology and anthropology and other aspects of the city which, because they rarely crystallized into a happening, had formerly received little notice in the *Times.*

If "hard" reporting required more reporters, it also required a different kind of reporter. Since news was not only "what happened" on a beat but also anything of "significance," whether expressed by a happening or not, the *Times* reporter needed a broader "news sense" than before. Since more things were potential news, he had to make more judgments about what to report and what to ignore, but his criteria for deciding were less clear-cut and unambiguous. This was true as well of the reporter's judgments concerning what to say in a story and how to say it. Moreover, there was more pressure on reporters in making these decisions, for under Rosenthal what counted was how imaginatively a story was developed and how interestingly it was written. Many of the senior reporters found it difficult and uncongenial to adapt to the demands of "hard" reporting, and Rosenthal relied on them less and less. He also broke tradition by reassigning the aerospace editor as chief political reporter. As older reporters left the paper—which they did in greater numbers than normal—Rosenthal hired many young men with more and better college degrees. These relatively inexperienced reporters began to get many of the best assignments because they were better able to produce "hard" stories and they were more responsive to Rosenthal's purpose.

The role of the metropolitan editor underwent an equivalent change. Previously, his principal job had been to see that beats were properly covered. Rosenthal's conception of news required that he do more than this, for if a "hard" reporter had to make judgments about the meaning of the news, then a "hard" editor had to make judgments about those judgments, and to do this he had to be personally in touch with the scene that was being reported. Rosenthal therefore established a network of personal contacts in the city, just as he had as a foreign correspondent. As metropolitan editor, he told an interviewer,

> I would want to know all the important people involved in making the news. So when I got to New York, I set out to know the mayors, judges, lawyers, theatrical people, and all other important figures in the news. I did this because it's interesting, and I did it because you get stories by knowing these people. I don't see how an editor can judge what is a good story, what isn't, without knowing the people involved. My assistant and I try all the time to think of stories—and the only reason we can do it is that we know the people.

Nor was Rosenthal reluctant to make use of this knowledge. If his predecessors had adopted a laissez-faire attitude toward reporters, he actively involved himself in the process of searching for, making judgments about, and writing the news.

These changes were not without their disadvantages. The *Times,* for example, had always been scrupulously careful not to "boost" political candidates in its news columns. "Hard" reporting put this longstanding practice under strain. Since the news included "big issues" and what was typical (as opposed to the atypical and discrete happening), reporters and editors had to make choices that they had not had to make when news was only what happened on a beat. This meant that there was a better chance that political figures would receive more publicity than their political importance warranted. Thus when Rosenthal decided to do a story on how a neophyte politician campaigns for the Democratic nomination for assemblyman, a by-product was the unexpected nomination of the candidate whom the reporter on the story chose to write about. (The reporter and candidate, incidentally, were old college friends.) To Timesmen brought up in the old tradition, it looked as if the man had been "boosted," as it did to political professionals around town. Rosenthal's view, of course, was that the *Times* had merely taken a look at a typical but neglected aspect of the political process.

In general, "hard" reporting found it difficult to be neutral. Like most serious newspapers, the *Times* had always been reluctant to make explicit assessments of the meaning of the news itself. But making such assessments was one of the defining characteristics of "hard" reporting, and under Rosenthal interpretive statements began to appear "high up" in stories, sometimes even in the lead paragraph or headline. Since there was often room for differences of opinion about what interpretation was the proper one, the *Times* occasionally was in the position of taking sides in its news columns. Sometimes it was suspected of doing so for partisan reasons. Many Democrats, for example, concluded that it "slanted" the news to support Mayor Lindsay. To Rosenthal, who rejected the notion of biased reporting as emphatically as the most traditionalistic Timesman, there was a big difference between "slanting" the news and interpreting it. That he was in personal contact with figures like Lindsay was bound, some thought, to affect his judgment and make him less neutral. But it was, of course, precisely in order to have his judgment affected—that is, to gain a perspective on the big issues as well as on the little facts —that he had established these contacts in the first place.

Perhaps the most important effect of "hard" reporting was its impact on the attitudes and values of reporters. As the ability to write interestingly and to interpret gained in importance, the old values of accuracy, completeness, and neutrality were of necessity cherished somewhat less. This change could be seen in the contrast between the older and younger reporters on the metropolitan staff. The younger ones, most of whom Rosenthal had hired, were better educated than their seniors and seemingly more intelligent. Certainly, as a group, they had proven themselves better writers. But one senses—it is, of course, impossible to provide any objective measure of this—that they are not as deeply attached to the *Times* and do not feel the same fervor for facts.

There can be little doubt that the *Times's* metropolitan stories are written in a livelier style and are better organized than they used to be. Whether they explain things any better, however, is open to question. Even the "hard" reporter gets almost all his information from the people involved in the events and institutions he covers. His interpretation, far from being an original conclusion that he himself draws, is almost invariably an amalgam of *their* views. Thus the "hard" reporter's interpretation rarely goes beyond the conventional wisdom on the subject under consideration. There are several reasons why a reporter's interpretation cannot be really serious (perhaps one should say really "hard" as opposed to merely brittle). First, no newspaper, not even the lavishly staffed *Times,* can afford a reporter the large amount of time and assistance required for a really serious report. Second, even if the reporter were given the necessary time and assistance, he would not in most cases have the special knowledge and talents needed to produce something really serious. Indeed, even the most highly educated academic experts rarely have the information, understanding, judgment, and expository skill that the ideal of "hard" reporting presupposes. And in any event, the reporter—even the "good" reporter—demonstrates little inclination for serious reading or thinking. Third, even if he had the time and ability, the reporter would not for long be permitted to offer really "hard" reportage: no newspaper, not even the *Times,* could suffer the consequences of trying its readers' patience with stories that go very far beneath the surface.

If "hard" reporting has not done more than increase somewhat the "readability" of the *Times,* it may have done even this at a price higher than anyone would have wanted to pay. Most longtime observers of New York politics agree that there has been some loss of accuracy and neutrality in *Times* metropolitan affairs coverage. Some might well say that even if the loss is small it is too high a price to pay for any gain in readability. But this loss may not be the full price. A further, indirect consequence may be a decline in the influence of the *Times.* An editor spoke frankly of this to an interviewer:

> What has kept the *Times* what it is, what has made it able to survive all the mergers, is that it was always authoritative and correct, even at the expense, sometimes, of readability. You were forming the opinions of the people in the power structure. . . . By losing authoritativeness, you lose influence in the power structure but gain popular influence. So the changes going on in the *Times* today mean that we're losing the one thing that separates the *Times* from all other newspapers. I'll be interested to find out what you learn from the politicians. If they don't like the *Times* as it is today, we've done a very, very bad thing. Our attempt is most certainly not to oversimplify and distort but only to add readability. It is not impossible to be readable and accurate at the same time, but it is very hard.

In fact, many politicians in New York do think that the *Times* is not as accurate as it used to be. No one can say, of course, whether there has been a gain in "popular influence" sufficient to compensate for whatever loss there may have been in "influence in the power structure." On the whole, however, it seems unlikely that the *Times's* bargain will prove to be a particularly good one, either for it or for New York. Ultimately the influence of a newspaper arises from the respect people feel for it, and readability, one would think, cannot inspire as much respect as reliability.

F. THE SIDEWALK VIEW

In contrast to the systems view and its attempt to characterize the city primarily for policymaking purposes, the sidewalk view is used here to refer to research aimed at uncovering the significant aspects of urban social life. Although some major differences might be cited between systems and sidewalk research, the contrasts should not be overdrawn. A basic knowledge of the city will ultimately be based on a diverse array of research styles and methods, in which any systems-sidewalk dichotomy will surely disappear.

However, for the present purposes it is instructive to consider various types of sidewalk research as a group because of some common problems and issues. These stem from the fact that sidewalk research usually involves the direct confrontation between an investigator and an urban dweller in his normal environment. The confrontation occurs whether the research employs participant observation, surveys, or actual field experimentation as its prime method. The researcher–urban dweller interface creates both practical problems, such as maintaining effective communication, and ethical problems, such as whether the research should be carried out in the first place. On this latter point, many urban citizens, whether members of a local neighborhood or part of the municipal bureaucracy, have now become highly cynical about the motivations of the researcher. In their minds, previous research has brought few of the desired changes in their lives and has generally resulted only in professional accolades for the researcher. As one outcome, cooperating on any new research project may be deemed a waste of time. The contemporary urban researcher must therefore satisfy such citizens and himself as to the main justifications for his investigation. He must then deal in a sincere, compassionate, and honest manner with all the people who will be involved in his research.

Of all the research methods available, participant observation raises most clearly the problems just mentioned. The method was first developed by anthropologists studying small communities[1] and involves the investigator acting simultaneously as a participant in and an observer of local events, usually over a period of at least one year. By being a participant, the researcher becomes privy to much information and has many experiences that are unavailable through any other means. This type of involvement can lead to a much better understanding of how people live, especially where the people may have a value system and language different from the ones to which the researcher is accustomed. William Foote Whyte used participant observation to study the street-corner life of Italian young adults in Boston thirty years ago,[2] and thereby demonstrated how the method could be used to advantage in studying urban subcultures. Whyte's comments on participant observation are still an excellent guide for the field worker today, and it was Whyte who described so well the difficult course that a successful field worker must follow: He must avoid the trap of becoming either a nonparticipating observer or a nonobserving participant.[3] During the past ten years, there have been a number of participant-observer studies in the Whyte style.[4] Given the continued diversity of life styles in American cities, it is clear that participant observation will remain one of the more useful parts of the future researcher's repertoire. In the article selected for this reader, Elliot Liebow (Selection 33) reports his experiences in studying a neighborhood in Washington, D.C., during the early 1960's.

Survey research generally involves the administering of formal questionnaires or interviews to gain information about a specific sample or group of people. Because the questions are usually structured, the answers are more easily tabulated and quantified, and many detailed analyses and comparisons are possible. As survey techniques have become more refined, the use of the survey has become more popular. For instance, social science groups in at least two large cities (Boston and Detroit) now carry out surveys annually; in a smaller city like Dayton, Ohio, surveys can be made even more frequently.[5] This type of regular reporting is one of the few ways

---

[1]For example, see Florence Rockwood Kluckhohn, "The participant observer technique in small communities," *American Journal of Sociology,* 46:331–343 (November, 1940).

[2]William Foote Whyte, *Street Corner Society: The Social Structure of an Italian Slum* (Chicago: University of Chicago Press, 1955, 2nd ed.). See especially the Appendix.

[3]*Ibid.,* p. 321.

[4]For example, see Herbert J. Gans, *The Urban Villagers: Group and Class in the Life of Italian-Americans* (New York: The Free Press, 1962); Elliot Liebow, *Tally's Corner* (Boston: Little, Brown & Co., 1967); Gerald D. Suttles, *The Social Order of the Slum: Ethnicity and Territory in the Inner City* (Chicago: University of Chicago Press, 1968); and Ulf Hannerz, *Soulside: Inquiries into Ghetto Culture and Community* (New York: Columbia University Press, 1969).

[5]The Detroit Area Survey is carried out by the University of Michigan, the Boston Area Survey by the Harvard–M.I.T. Joint Center for Urban Studies, and the Dayton surveys by the Public Opinion Center, Dayton, Ohio.

of assessing residents' perceptions and attitudes on a citywide basis and can be expected to become of more popular use. In this respect, the growth in the use of public opinion polls in recent years should be seen as following the same general trend. Two articles in the present reader deal with some of the issues that the contemporary survey researcher must face. Carol Weiss (Selection 34) examines the problem of assessing the validity of the answers to a questionnaire, with particular attention given to the interviewer's role. Eric Josephson (Selection 35) reports his own experiences in carrying out a survey in a community setting and shows how the broader concerns of the community inevitably interact with the conduct of any specific research project.

A third type of sidewalk research is based on the design of simple but usually ingenious experiments that can actually be carried out on the sidewalks (or other natural settings) of a city. The issues studied tend to be concerned with the psychological inquiry into the nature of the urban dweller. Georg Simmel, for instance, long ago pointed out how the blasé attitude attributed to urban dwellers could be interpreted as an adaptive response; without such an attitude, the urban dwellers' mental life would be severely strained by the numerous human and nonhuman incidents that occur every moment in the city.[6] It is this type of curiosity about ordinary behavior in the city and the images of the city that is reflected in Stanley Milgram's article (Selection 36) and his review of some of the experiments that have been conducted. Milgram's review should give the social science student of the city an excellent idea of the ways in which routine urban situations can be used as the basis for well-planned and controlled experiments.

---

[6]Georg Simmel, "The metropolis and mental life," in Kurt H. Wolff (ed.), *The Sociology of Georg Simmel* (Glencoe, Ill.: The Free Press, 1956), pp. 401–422. The article was originally written in 1902.

33. A field experience in retrospect

ELLIOT LIEBOW

BACKGROUND

When I came to the Child Rearing Study Project on January 1, 1962, this NIMH [National Institute of Mental Health]-supported study of "Child Rearing Practices Among Low Income Families in the District of Columbia" was well into its third year. My job was to collect field material on low-income adult males to complement the data already secured through family interviews.

From the very beginning I felt comfortable with the prospect of working with lower-class Negroes. I was born and raised in Washington, D.C. My father and mother were both Jewish immigrants from Eastern Europe—my mother from Latvia, my father from Russia. My father was a grocer and we lived in rooms above or behind the various stores which he operated. All were in predominantly Negro neighborhoods.

School and playground were white, but all of our customers and most of the neighbors were Negroes. Among them and their children I had many acquaintances, several playmates and a few friends. The color line, retraced daily at school and playground and home, was always there; but so were my day-by-day contacts with Negro men, women, and children in the store, on the street, and occasionally in their houses; watching a crap game in Sam's place; witnessing the Devil being exorcised from a woman writhing on the floor of a storefront church from my seat in the back row; shooting crap for pennies in a dark hallway; sitting with Benton on the curb, poking aimlessly at debris, waiting for something interesting to happen. It was not until I was seventeen and enlisted in the Marine Corps that I began to move in an almost exclusively white world.

PREPARING FOR THE FIELD

I spent the first week in familiarizing myself with the project and with the work that had already been done. I had several informal discussions with Dr. Hylan Lewis, the director of the project, and gradually gained a feeling for the kind of material that was wanted. Importantly, he laid down no hard-and-fast ground rules on the assumption that the job could best be done if I were free to feel my way around for a few weeks and discover for myself the techniques that were most congenial to me. His one prescription was that the work be securely anchored in the purposes of the project, remembering, too, that "Everything is grist for our mill." As I think back on this now, I see a clear connection between his instructions and his fondness for the quotation, "The scientific method is doing one's darndest with his brains, no holds barred."

Abridged and edited from *Tally's Corner* by Elliot Liebow, by permission of Little, Brown and Co., Inc., pp. 232–256. Copyright © 1967 by Little, Brown and Company, Inc.

The author is Chief, Center for Studies of Metropolitan Problems, National Institute of Mental Health, Rockville, Md.

Having partially digested the project literature, I told the director that I was ready to get started. He suggested a neighborhood that might be "a good place to get your feet wet." His instructions were: "Go out there and make like an anthropologist."

"Out there" was not at all like the Indian village of Winisk on Hudson Bay in which I had done field work. I was not at all sure how one "makes like an anthropologist" in this kind of "out there." Somewhat wistfully, perhaps, I thought how much neater things would be if anthropologists, as they had done in the early thirties, limited themselves to the study of "wholes," a tribe, a village, or some other social unit with distinct boundaries and small enough to be encompassed in its entirety by direct observation.

.   .   .   .   .

IN THE FIELD

In taking up the director's suggestion that this would be "a good place to get your feet wet," I went in so deep that I was completely submerged and my plan to do three or four separate studies, each with its own neat, clean boundaries, dropped forever out of sight. My initial excursions into the street—to poke around, get the feel of things, and to lay out the lines of my field work—seldom carried me more than a block or two from the corner where I started. From the very first weeks or even days, I found myself in the middle of things; the principal lines of my field work were laid out, almost without my being aware of it. For the next year or so, and intermittently thereafter, my base of operations was the corner Carry-out across the street from my starting point.

The first time out, I had gone less than one short block when I noticed a commotion up the street. A man—Detective Wesley, I learned later—was dragging a kicking, screaming woman to a police call box. A small crowd had gathered on each of the four corners to watch. I approached two men and asked what the woman had done. Both were uncertain. The younger of the two said that he had heard two stories and proceeded to tell me both of them, concluding with the observation that he had known Detective Wesley for six or seven years and that he was "nobody to fool with."

I said that sometimes being a cop seems to do something to a man. This led to a discussion of policemen and each of us contributed personal experiences or anecdotes on the subject. After ten or fifteen minutes of this, the older man said goodbye and walked off. The younger man stayed on. Across the street from where we were standing was the Downtown Cafe. I suggested that we go in and have some coffee and he agreed. As we walked across the street he asked if I was a policeman. I told him no and explained that I was working on a study of family life in the city. There was no more discussion about who I was or why I was there. We sat at the bar for several hours talking over coffee.

I had not accomplished what I set out to do, but this was only the first day. And, anyway, when I wrote up this experience that evening, I felt that it presented a fairly good picture of this young man and that most of the material was to the point. Tomorrow, I decided, I would go back to my original plan—nothing had been lost.

But tomorrow never came. At nine the next morning, I headed down the same street. Four men were standing in a group in front of the Carry-out.

Three were winos, in their forties—all marked with old scars on face and neck, dressed shabbily, but sober. The fourth was a man of thirty-two or thirty-three, who looked as if he had just stepped out of a slick magazine advertisement. . . . One of the winos had a month-old puppy stuck in the front of his overcoat. Only the dog's head was exposed.

The group approached me and one of the older men said, "Isn't he a nice puppy?" I said yes, and began patting the dog. "He just bought him," one man said. "I wanted the female, too, to breed them," said the man holding the dog, "but that woman, she sold the female to her friend."

The puppy was whining. "Maybe it's hungry," said the older man, "let's get him some hamburger." "No man, he'll get worms from that stuff," said one of the others. I suggested milk and we all went into the Carry-out. I asked the waitress for a half pint of milk. The man asked for a saucer. "You can't feed him here," the waitress said, "the Health Department would close us up." She gave us a paper plate and the milk (paid for by me). We took the dog into a hallway next door. Everyone was pleased at how eagerly the puppy drank.

A man who had been in the Carry-out joined us in the hallway. "That's a shepherd, isn't he? Just what I want for my little boy." I said, "I wish I could get one for my little girl, but she's allergic to all animals, dust, and lots of things." "It's better that way," said one of the winos. "She'll outgrow it. But man, if you don't have that until you're full grown—man, look out." "Yes, that's right," the newcomer agreed. "I know a woman who got allergies after she was grown and she got bronica asthma with it."

The dog finished the milk. The owner put him back in his overcoat and I shook hands all around with the winos. We split up three ways. The winos went up the street, the well-dressed man down the street, and the newcomer —who turned out to be Tally Jackson—and I went into the Carry-out.

For more than four hours Tally and I lounged around in the Carry-out, talking, drinking coffee, watching people come in and go out, watching other hangers-on as they bantered with the waitresses, horsed around among themselves, or danced to the jukebox. Everyone knew Tally and some frequently sought out his attention. Tally sometimes participated in the banter but we were generally left undisturbed when we were talking. When I left at two o'clock, Tally and I were addressing each other by first names ("Elliot" was strange to him and we settled for "Ellix") and I was able to address the two waitresses by their first names without feeling uncomfortable. I had also learned to identify several other men by their first names or nicknames, had gotten hints on personal relationships, and had a biographical sketch (part of it untrue I learned later) of Tally.

Back on the street, I ended up at the Downtown Cafe, this time by way of the morning's now very drunk owner of the puppy, who was standing near the entrance. The puppy was our bond and we talked about him with an enthusiasm that perhaps neither of us felt. Later, the well-dressed man who had also been part of the puppy episode came in and joined me at the bar. Then, still drinking beer at the bar stool, I met two other men in quick succession. The first man had to leave shortly for his night-shift busboy job at the restaurant. The other was a surly man in his middle thirties who initiated the contact by taking the stool next to me and asking what kind of work I did, adding that he had seen me around the day before, watching Detective Wesley drag that woman across the street.

I told him briefly what my job was.

"Well, if you hang around here you'll see it all. Anything can happen and it does happen here. It can get rough and you can get your head knocked in. You'll be okay though, if you know one or two of the right people."

"That's good to know," I told him, guessing (and hoping) that he was one of the "right people." He left me with the impression that he was being friendly and, in a left-handed sort of way, was offering me his protection.

By the end of the second day I had met nine men, learned the names of several more, and spent many hours in close public association with several men, at least two of whom were well known. And perhaps most important of all, in my own mind I had partly sloughed off that feeling of being a stranger and achieved that minimum sense of "belonging" which alone permits an ease of manner and mind so essential in building personal relationships.

Over the next three or four weeks, I made several excursions into other neighborhoods and followed up at the Downtown Cafe and the Carry-out shop on an irregular basis, getting to know some of the people better and many others for the first time. Frequently I ate breakfast and lunch at the Carry-out and began putting occasional dimes in the jukebox and in the pinball machine. Ted Moore, who worked at a liquor store nearby and whom I had first met in the Carry-out while he was waiting for the store to open, regularly alternated with me in buying coffee and doughnuts in the morning. At the Downtown Cafe the man who told me that I'd be okay if I knew "one or two of the right people" publicly identified me as his friend. ("Sure I know him," he told another man in my presence. "We had a long talk the other day. He's my friend and he's okay, man, he's okay. At first I thought he was a cop, but he's no cop. He's okay.")

All in all, I felt I was making steady progress. There was still plenty of suspicion and mistrust, however. At least two men who hung around the Carry-out—one of them the local numbers man—had seen me dozens of times in close quarters, but they kept their distance and I kept mine. Once, accidentally, I caught the numbers man's eye as I walked in. We held the stare for three or four seconds and I nodded slightly but he wouldn't let go. I went on about my business, determined that I wasn't going to be stared down next time and that he'd get no more nods from me unless he nodded first. As it turned out, I didn't have long to wait.

One mid-February day, I walked into the Carry-out.

. . . Tally was having a cup of coffee. "Look here," he said. "Where is this place?" Tally took out a sheet of paper from an envelope and handed it to me. It was a summons to appear as a witness for the defense in the case of the United States versus Lonny Reginald Small. A faint stamp indicated that Tally was to report to the United States District Court for the District of Columbia at 3rd and Pennsylvania Avenue, Northwest, at ten o'clock this morning. I read off the address. It was then 9:40. I suggested that Tally take a cab, but when Tally said he didn't have the money I offered to drive him down. He quickly accepted. On the way, Tally explained that Lonny was a friend of his. Lonny was being tried for murdering his wife last summer. "Lonny is a nice guy," he said. "He's one hundred percent."

Thus began a three-week odyssey into the world of Lonny Small, a young man of twenty-six who, according to the jury's subsequent verdict of "not guilty," had choked his wife to death accidentally. Upon his acquittal, Lonny was rearrested in the courthouse for a violation of probation (on a previous grand larceny conviction) in another jurisdiction. He waived extradition, was given a hearing, was released on an appearance bond, and after another hearing he was again placed on probation.

Almost imperceptibly, my association with Tally, and through him with Lonny, was projecting me into the role of a principal actor in Lonny's life. By being with Tally through the trial, I found that first Tally, then Lonny, were looking to me for leadership and, as in the question of waiving extradition, for decision making. Court officials, apparently taking their cues from Lonny, began looking to me as his spokesman.

The follow-up of Lonny, which took most of my time for at least the next two weeks, carried me into dozens of places and into contact with scores of people. Throughout this period I stayed in close touch with the project director, getting clearance for and weighing the possible consequences of my growing involvement with the authorities. I went to three different jails during this time, sat through one murder trial and two hearings in judges' chambers, testifying at one of them. I went to bondsmen's offices, to the United States Employment Service, to the Blessed Martin de Porres Hostel (for homeless men) and into several private homes. I met policemen, judges, lawyers, bondsmen, probation officers, and one of Lonny's former employers. I talked with his friends and at least one enemy, his mother-in-law, whose daughter he had killed. I met in council several times with various members of his extended family (who accepted me, through Tally, as Lonny's friend, no' questions asked) in their houses, and drove around with them to the houses of other members of the family trying to raise money for Lonny's bond.

Meanwhile, back at the Carry-out, where Tally and I were meeting regularly at night and where I tried to stop in during the day whenever possible, people I had never seen, or others I had seen but never spoken to, began coming up to me and asking, "Is Lonny out yet?" or "Did you raise his bail yet?" or simply, "How's it going?" Bumdoodle, the numbers man, one of those who had not known Lonny, was especially solicitous of Lonny's welfare. He, too, began calling me by my first name and, although I kept no record of it, I think it was at this time that he dropped all subterfuge in taking numbers in my presence and soon began taking bets from me.

By the middle of March, Tally and I were close friends ("up tight") and I was to let him know if I wanted or needed "anything, anytime." By April, the number of men whom I had come to know fairly well and their acceptance of me had reached the point at which I was free to go to the rooms or apartments where they lived or hung out, at almost any time, needing neither an excuse nor an explanation for doing so. Like other friends, I was there to pass the time, to hang around, to find out "what's happening."

I switched my day around to coincide with the day worker's leisure hours: from four in the afternoon until late at night, according to what was going on. Alone, or with one, two or half a dozen others, I went to poolrooms, to bars, or to somebody's room or apartment. Much of the time we just hung around the Carry-out, playing the pinball machine or standing on the corner watching the world go by. Regularly at five, I met my five "drinking buddies" when they came off from work and we went into a hallway for an hour or so of good drinking and easy talk.

Friday afternoon to Sunday night was especially exciting and productive. I'd go to Nancy's "place" (apartment) where, at almost any hour, one could get liquor, listen to music, or engage in conversation. Or perhaps seven or eight of us would buy some beer and whiskey and go up to Tonk's apartment near the Carry-out where he lived with his wife. Occasionally, I'd pair up with one or two men and go to a party, a movie, or a crap game, which might be in almost any part of town. Sunday afternoon was an especially good time to pick up news or happenings of the preceding forty-eight hours. People were generally rested up from the night before, relaxed, and ready to fill one another in on events which involved the police, breakups of husband-wife relations and bed-and-board arrangements, drink-stimulated brawls, sex adventures, and parties they had witnessed, heard about, or participated in over Friday and Saturday.

By April most people seemed to be taking it for granted that I belonged in the area. At least two men did not trust me or like me, but by then I was too strongly entrenched for them to challenge successfully my right to be there, even had they chosen to do so. New people moved into the area and I found myself being regarded as an old-timer, sometimes being asked to corroborate events which predated my arrival.

Throughout this period, my field observations were focused on individuals: what they said, what they did, and the contexts in which they said them or did them. I sought them out and was sought out by them.

My field notes contain a record of what I saw when I looked at Tally, Richard, Sea Cat and the others. I have only a small notion—and one that I myself consider suspect—of what they saw when they looked at me.

Some things, however, are very clear. They saw, first of all, a white man. In my opinion, this brute fact of color, as they understood it in their experience and as I understood it in mine, irrevocably and absolutely relegated me to the status of outsider. I am not certain, but I have a hunch that they were more continuously aware of the color difference than I was. When four of us sat around a kitchen table, for example, I saw three Negroes; each of them saw two Negroes and a white man.

Sometimes, when the word "nigger" was being used easily and conversationally or when, standing on the corner with several men, one would have a few words with a white passerby and call him a "white mother-fucker," I used to play with the idea that maybe I wasn't as much of an outsider as I thought. Other events, and later readings of the field materials, have disabused me of this particular touch of vanity. Whenever the fact of my being white was openly introduced, it pointed up the distance between me and the other person, even when the intent of introducing it was, I believe, to narrow that distance.

. . . All of us left Tally's room together. Tally grabbed my arm and pulled me aside near the store-front church and said, "I want to talk to you." With no further introduction, he looked me straight in the eye and started talking.

"I'm a liar. I been lying to you all along now and I want to set it straight, even if it means we can't be friends no more. I only lied to you about one thing.

Everything else I told you is gospel truth but I did lie about one thing and that makes me a liar. I know that some white people think that if you catch a man in a lie one time you can't never trust him after that. And even if you feel that way about it I still got to tell you. You remember when you first come around here, I told you. . . . Well, that was a lie. . . . I didn't think nothing of it at first, but then you and me started going around together and when we started getting real tight, my conscience started whomping me. I kept looking for a place to tell you but it never seemed right. Then tonight . . . I knew this was the right time. I knew you were going to find out and I didn't want you to find out from somebody else. . . ."

Once I was with Richard in his hometown. It was his first visit in five years. We arrived in the middle of the night and had to leave before daybreak because Richard was wanted by the local police. We were in his grandmother's house. Besides Richard, there were his grandmother, his aunt, and two unrelated men, both long-time friends of Richard.

The group was discussing the possibility of Richard's coming home to stay and weighing the probable consequences. In the middle of the discussion, Richard interrupted and nodded at me. "Now Ellix here is white, as you can see, but he's one of my best friends. Him and me are real tight. You can say anything you want, right to his face. He's real nice." "Well," said his Aunt Pearl, "I always did say there are some nice white people."

Whether or not there is more to these citations than "Some of my best friends are . . ." or "Yes, but you're different," the wall between us remained, or better, the chain-link fence, since despite the barriers we were able to look at each other, walk alongside each other, talk and occasionally touch fingers. When two people stand up close to the fence on either side, without touching it, they can look through the interstices and forget that they are looking through a fence.

The disadvantage of being white was offset in part by the fact that, as an outsider, I was not a competitor. Thus, in the matter of skin color, I saw myself nowhere in the spectrum of black- to light-skinned (or "bright"); I was completely out of it, with no vested interest. It could be that this made it possible for some people to speak freely to me about skin color.

"You know, I'm the darkest one in my family. All my aunts, uncles, everybody is light-skinned and they were all down on me, except my grandmother. . . . She'd do anything for me, maybe because she saw everyone else against me. . . . All the time I was coming up, I kept hoping somebody would have a baby darker than me."

Looking at me, however, the people I came to know in the area probably saw more than a "white male adult." They saw or knew many other things as well, any one of which relegated me to outside status. Those with whom I was in regular contact knew, for example, that I was with them because it was my job to be with them, and they knew, according to their individual comprehension and my ability to communicate, just what my job was. They knew that I lived outside the area. They knew that I was a college graduate, or at least they associated an advanced education with the work I was doing. Moreover, it was apparent, certainly to me, that I was not fluent in their language. Thus, I was an outsider not only because of race, but also because of occupation, education, residence, and speech. The fact that I was Jewish came up only twice. Once, a man who worked but did not live in the area threw some Yiddish expressions at me because "I thought you looked Jewish." The other time was when I met a soldier in a local bootleg joint. We had been talking for some ten minutes or so when he asked me whether I was "Eyetalian." I told him I was Jewish. "That's just as good," he said. "I'm glad you're not white."

The fact that I was married and a father, and that I was bigger than average size—6'1", 185 pounds—probably didn't matter much, except as they entered incidentally into my personal relationship with one or another individual. Since the people I spent most of my time with ranged in age from twenty to the middle forties, I would guess that my age (thirty-seven) was not significant in itself.

On several different counts I was an outsider[1] but I also was a participant in a full sense of the word. The people I was observing knew that I was observing them, yet they allowed me to participate in their activities and take part in their lives to a degree that continues to surprise me. Some "exploited" me, not as an outsider but rather as one who as a rule had more resources then they did. When one of them came up with the resouces—money or a car, for example—he too was "exploited" in the same way. I usually tried to limit money or other favors to what I thought each would have gotten from another friend had he the same resources as I. I tried to meet requests as best I could without becoming conspicuous. I was not always on the giving end and learned somewhat too slowly to accept food or let myself be treated to drinks even though I knew this would work a hardship on the giver.

When in the field, I participated as fully and as whole-mindedly as I could, limited only by my own sense of personal and professional propriety and by what I assumed to be the boundaries of acceptable behavior as seen by those I was with.

Occasionally, when I wanted to record a physical description of say, a neighborhood, an apartment, or a social event, I tried to be an observer only. In practice, I found it impossible to keep all traces of participation out of a straight observer role.

One Saturday night, with my observer role clearly in mind, I went to a dance at the Capitol Arena where more than a thousand people were jammed together. I was the only white male, this was my first time at such an event, the music was so foreign to me that I picked out the wrong beat, and I was unable to identify several of the band instruments. I was, willy-nilly, an observer. But here are a few lines excerpted from the field observation:

> It was very hot, it was very noisy, it was very smelly, and it was all very exciting. It was impossible to remain simply an observer in a place like this, even for someone as phlegmatic as I. It was only a few minutes after Jackie Wilson started singing that I discovered that the noise wasn't nearly loud

---

[1]From the outset, I had decided that I would never shoot crap, pool, or play cards for money, or bet money in any way (numbers excepted, since playing numbers is safely impersonal), and would meticulously avoid the slightest suspicion of a personal involvement with any woman. These self-imposed restrictions to some extent did underline my marginality. My explanation that I couldn't afford to chance a fight or bad feelings because of my job was usually accepted and I was generally excused from participating in these activities rather than excluded from them.

enough, the heat wasn't nearly hot enough, and the odor from more than a thousand closely packed people was not really strong enough at all. Like everyone else, I wanted more of everything.

Almost from the beginning, I adopted the dress and something of the speech of the people with whom I was in most frequent contact, as best I could without looking silly or feeling uncomfortable. I came close in dress (in warm weather, tee or sport shirt and khakis or other slacks) with almost no effort at all. My vocabulary and diction changed, but not radically. Cursing and using ungrammatical constructions at times—though they came easily—did not make any of my adaptations confusable with the speech of the street. Thus, while remaining conspicuous in speech and perhaps in dress, I had dulled some of the characteristics of my background. I probably made myself more accessible to others, and certainly more acceptable to myself. This last point was forcefully brought home to me one evening when, on my way to a professional meeting, I stopped off at the Carry-out in a suit and tie. My loss of ease made me clearly aware that the change in dress, speech, and general carriage was as important for its effect on me as it was for its effect on others.

In retrospect, it seems as if the degree to which one becomes a participant is as much a matter of perceiving oneself as a participant as it is of being accepted as a participant by others.

34. Validity of welfare mothers' interview responses

CAROL H. WEISS

Because survey research is open to the criticism that respondents do not always tell the truth to interviewers, validation studies have long been an honored pursuit.[1] They have led to progressive clarification of the extent and direction of response error, and to its increasing control. In recent years, as more research has focused on poor people in our society, special concerns about response error have come to the fore. Some critics claim that the poor present interviewing problems different in kind and degree from other respondent groups. Poor people, they say, misunderstand the interviewer, or defer to him, or try to con him; the interviewer stereotypes the respondent and biases his answers; or else poor people have such difficulty in knowing or remembering or verbalizing that the interview becomes a very leaky vessel indeed for taking out questions and bringing back answers.[2]

In an effort to test these assertions, this study validated responses of a sample of Negro welfare mothers. They were New York City residents receiving public assistance in 1966 who had been interviewed by the National Opinion Research Center for a study on the use of health services.

Their responses to five questions in the original interview were compared with official records—registration status in 1964, voting in the 1964 presidential election, receipt of money from welfare, child's failure of a subject on his last report card, child's ever being left back to repeat a grade in school. Of the 1,002 Negro respondents to the interview, validation data on registration and voting were available for 549. The other cases were lost because:

389 respondents reported moving from their neighborhood between the election and the interview; since back addresses were unavailable, records could not be checked;

54 were too young to have voted in 1964;

10 did not answer the survey questions on registration and voting.

From Carol H. Weiss, "Validity of welfare mothers' interview responses," *Public Opinion Quarterly*, 32:622–633 (Winter, 1968–1969). Copyright © 1969 by Columbia University Press. Reprinted by permission.

The author is Research Associate, Bureau of Applied Social Research, Columbia University, New York.

[1] Among the validation studies of this decade are John B. Lansing, Gerald P. Ginsburg, and Kaisa Braaten, *An Investigation of Response Error* (Urbana, University of Illinois Press, 1961); David J. Weiss *et al., Validity of Work Histories Obtained by Interview,* Minnesota Studies in Vocational Rehabilitation, Vol. 12, Bulletin 34, (Minneapolis, 1961); Michael E. Borus, "Response error in survey reports of earnings information," *Journal of the American Statistical Association,* 61:729–738 (1966).

[2] For a review of earlier research on this topic, see Carol H. Weiss, "Interviewing low-income respondents: A preliminary view," *Welfare in Review,* October, 1966, pp. 1–9.

Similarly, the number of cases for which school data could be checked was reduced because families had no child in New York City public schools at the fourth grade level or above, because records were lost or unavailable in the schools, because children could not be located in the schools reported, and not every school could be visited before the end of the school year. In all, some validation data were available for 680 respondents.

Rates of error to the different questions varied from a low of 2 percent on the welfare question[3] to a high of 37 percent on child's failure of a subject on his last report card. (See Table 1.) Most error lay in reporting more socially desirable behavior than facts warranted, and this type of error is here called bias. On the school questions there was also a considerable amount of reverse error, or confusion. That is, mothers reported more subject failure, and especially more left-back, than their children merited. Evidently many mothers were unaware of the facts on children's school performance.

TABLE 1
Response error on five questions

Question	N	% Reporting	% Actual	Precentage of Error In Socially Desirable Direction (Bias)	In Undesirable Direction (Confusion)	Total %
Registration	549	47.9	34.4	16	2	18
Voting	549	43.7	29.1	16	2	18
Child ever left back in school	400	42.2	39.7	10	12	22
Child failed subject on last report card	416	37.5	54.6	27	10	37
Received money from welfare	680	94.3	96.2*	2	—	2

* A small number of respondents had gone off the welfare rolls between the selection of the sample and the date of the interview.

NO GENERAL TRAIT OF RESPONSE ERROR

Error on the different questions was uncorrelated. Except for the questions on registration and voting, where registration was a filter question for the question on voting, respondents inaccurate on one question were not more likely to be inaccurate

---

[3]Two special factors contributed to the low rate of error about receiving welfare. Half of the interviews—for experimental purposes—were introduced with a statement that this was a survey of welfare mothers. Also, the question on welfare followed a series of questions that assumed participation in the welfare system, such as "Do you ever talk with a welfare investigator about the children's future?"

on others.[4] Even when questions were closely related in content, error was specific to the item. There was apparently no general trait or condition of response error, all phi coefficients being less than .10.[5]

ACCURACY ON VOTING

On the voting and registration questions, 82 percent of the welfare mothers answered accurately. Sixteen percent overreported their registration and voting and 2 per cent underreported. The amount and direction of response error are similar to those of the largely middle-class populations whose voting self-reports have been validated in previous studies (see Table 2).

The Negro welfare mothers in the study actually voted much less often than other groups studied. Only 29 per cent voted in the 1964 election.[6] Nevertheless, they acknowledge their nonvoting with as much candor as other groups. When they erred, they—like everybody else—overclaimed voting.

Insofar as response bias reflects allegiance to social values, it appears that the low-income Negro respondent group adheres to much the same values in the area of voting as do middle-class groups. They wish to be considered participants in the political process.

CHARACTERISTICS OF THE BIASED RESPONDENT

Two sets of characteristics distinguish the accurate from the biased respondent on the voting questions. The biased respondent is high on community integration. That is, she has lived in the neighborhood longer, is older, better educated, has had longer work experience, and spent her childhood in an urban place. Secondly, she is oriented to middle-class values. She expressed views consonant with societal norms on questions regarding teaching children to live for today and letting tomorrow take care of itself, the likelihood of her children's being on welfare when they have their own homes, her educational expectations for her children, her attitude toward receiving welfare, satisfaction with the extent of her own education, and having a clock in the apartment. The biased respondent is likely to reject welfare status for herself and her children, to value education, and to indicate a future time orientation. The low-income mother with fewer linkages to society, in experience and values, is less likely to idealize her voting behavior.

Much the same characteristics that are associated with bias are also associated with actual voting. On four out of the five community integration items, respondents with high integration are more likely to vote. (The exception is the length of time

---

[4]This agrees with the finding that "the use of a given item to identify a class of inaccurate respondents apparently has little utility in estimating the general influence of misinformation," in Charles R. Tittle and Richard I. Hill, "The accuracy of self-reported data and prediction of political activity," *Public Opinion Quarterly,* 31:106 (1967).

[5]The highest correlation, .081, was between error on the school failure question and error on the question about the child's having been left back.

[6]Note that they are not only low-income and Negro but also women with children, a group that tends to vote appreciably less often than equivalent males. *Cf.* Angus Campbell *et al., The American Voter* (New York: John Wiley & Sons, Inc., 1960), pp. 487–488.

TABLE 2
Accuracy of self-reported voting behavior in five studies

	Parry and Crossley Denver 1948	Miller Waukegan 1950	Freeman Washington State 1950	Bell and Buchanan Los Angeles 1961 Registration		Weiss N.Y.C. Welfare Mothers 1964
				General Population	Low Education (0–11 yrs.)	
Accurate	86%	89%	83%	70%	69%	82%
Voted	60	54	56	53+	44	27
Did not vote	26	35	27	16+	25	55
Inaccurate	14	11	17	30	31	18
Said they voted, didn't	13	11	15	27	28	16
Said they didn't vote, did	1	—	2	3	3	2
% of Nonvoters admitting not voting	67	77	63	38	47	77
N	920	204	374	712	242	549

Source: Hugh J. Parry and Helen M. Crossley, "Validity of responses to survey questions," *Public Opinion Quarterly*, 14:61–80(1950); Mungo Miller, "The Waukegan study of voter turnout prediction," *Public Opinion Quarterly*, 16:381–398(1952); Howard E. Freeman, "A note on the prediction of who votes," *Public Opinion Quarterly*, 17:288–292 (1953); Charles G. Bell and William Buchanan, "Reliable and unreliable respondents: Party registration and prestige pressure," *Western Political Quarterly*, 29:37–43 (1966). The Bell and Buchanan data, which concern registration, not voting were supplemented by personal communication.

worked for pay.) On all six of the value orientation items, respondents giving the middle-class response are more likely to vote. It turns out that it is not the biased respondent who is highest in community integration and middle-class orientation. Highest of all is the true voter—the person who actually registered and voted and said so. On those characteristics that differentiate actual voters from actual nonvoters, the biased respondent is part-way between the two groups. As shown in Table 3, she approximates the true voter in attitudes and attributes. She appears to be similar enough to the actual voter to have accepted the norm of political participation, if not to the extent of getting to the polling booth, at least to the extent of claiming to have voted. She is, in effect, the almost voter.[7]

TABLE 3
Percentage of true voters, of biased nonvoters, and of true nonvoters with given characteristics and attitudes*

Characteristics and Attitudes	True Voters (N = 148)ᵃ	Biased Nonvoters (N = 100)ᵃ	True Nonvoters (N = 274)ᵃ
Community Integration Characteristics			
Age:	63.5%	60.0%	42.1%
35 years and older	(94)	(60)	(115)
Time in the neighborhood:	39.5	39.0	18.4
Over 10 years	(58)	(39)	(50)
Place of childhood:	79.7	72.0	65.8
City or town	(118)	(72)	(179)
Education: 12th grade	30.4	27.0	19.0
or higher	(45)	(27)	(52)
Time worked:	37.4	46.0	32.5
Over 10 years	(55)	(46)	(88)
Value Orientations			
Strongly disagrees that you should teach child to live	65.3	57.0	53.0
for today	(96)	(57)	(142)
Says her child(ren) will	57.0	52.8	45.4
surely not be on welfare	(73)	(47)	(104)
Did not get as much	72.1	71.7	71.4
education as she wanted	(106)	(71)	(195)
Expects child(ren) to continue education past	51.8	47.8	33.1
high school	(59)	(32)	(50)
Feels bothered a lot about	41.8	33.0	29.2
being on welfare	(59)	(32)	(79)

* "True voters" and "true nonvoters" are those accurate on both registration and voting questions.
ᵃ On some questions, "no answers" reduce the N.

[7] On the school questions, fewer characteristics differentiate mothers of achieving children from mothers of nonachievers. The community integration characteristics are irrelevant to actual school performance. They are also irrelevant to response bias. The middle-class orientation items, on the other hand, *are* related to differences in children's school performance. Middle-class responses are also related to bias. The biased respondent is not as clearly in the middle between achievers and nonachievers as on the voting questions, although traces of the pattern appear. The clearest association with bias is mother's placing a high value on education.

EFFECTS OF ERROR

The fact that the same characteristics that are associated with voting are associated with response bias distorts not only the absolute figures but also the analysis of relationships among variables. When nonvoters who are most like actual voters tend to overreport voting, the effect is to inflate the correlations between background characteristics and voting. For example, length of residence in the neighborhood is associated with voting and also with the biased error that claims voting. The percentages of those actually voting and those reporting voting are as follows:

Length of Time in Neighborhood	% Actually Voting	% Reporting Voting
Less than 3 yrs.	22	30
3-10 yrs.	26	40
Over 10 yrs.	39	59

Reported voting thus appears to be more closely associated with length of neighborhood residence than in fact it is.

In some cases, the effect of response error is to deflate the true correlations. For example, residents of public housing were a maverick group. They were more likely to vote but less likely to give biased responses. They were less likely to have children who failed in school but more likely to admit it. In the latter case, the reported data show the reverse relationship of the actual data.

Residence in Public Housing	% With Child Actually Failing a Subject	% Reporting Child Failing a Subject
Public housing residents	48	46
Nonresidents	56	36

EFFECTS OF SOCIAL DISTANCE BETWEEN INTERVIEWER AND RESPONDENT

It is usually assumed that social distance between respondent and interviewer will adversely affect response accuracy. Evidence for the biasing effects of social distance comes from two major sources: studies reporting Negro response bias to white interviewers[8] and studies where social class was directly related to the topics under inquiry, as in Katz's study of opinions on labor and economic issues.[9] In the present case, it was possible to investigate the effects of social distance between interviewer and respondents on response accuracy when neither of these conditions obtained. Both respondents and interviewers were Negro, so that no racial difference intruded; and the questions validated were relatively remote from class concerns.

Disparities in social status were limited to socioeconomic status, education, and age. It was expected that welfare mothers would give the interviewers most unlike themselves a more biased, idealized story. To "like" interviewers, they need not defer and could comfortably acknowledge less desirable behaviors.

The data do not support this contention. Table 4 shows that when each pair of respondents and interviewers was matched on education, age, and socioeconomic status, the "unlike" interviewer on each item, as well as on the three-item "disparity index," does not generally receive more biased responses. The differences were small, but, if there was any pattern, it was status similarity, not status disparity, that was associated with bias. [See table 4, pg. 234.]

EFFECTS OF RAPPORT

Even more of an effect on response bias was made by the degree of rapport between respondent and interviewer. Interviewers rated rapport at the end of the interview on a five-point scale: confiding, frank, equivocal, guarded, and hostile. The respondents who were rated highest in rapport were the most biased.

This finding underscores the differentiation made by investigators like Hyman[10] between "task involvement" and "social involvement" of the respondent in the interview. Survey organizations tend to stress the building of rapport, "for by and large, the greater the involvement of the respondent in the situation, the greater his motivation and interest in the task at hand."[11] But, Hyman continues, "While rapport may be a function of degree of *total* involvement, validity may be conceived

---

[8]For example, evidence of bias in Negroes' responses to white interviewers is presented by James Allen Williams, Jr., "Interviewer-respondent interaction: A study of bias in the information interview," *Sociometry,* 27:338–352 (1964); Daniel O. Price and Ruth Searles, "Some effects of interviewer-respondent interaction on responses in a survey situation," *Proceedings of the Social Statistics Section* (American Statistical Association, 1961), pp. 211–221; Gerhard E. Lenski and John C. Leggett, "Caste, class, and deference in the research interview," *American Journal of Sociology,* 65:463–467 (1960); Barbara S. Dohrenwend, John Colombotos, and Bruce P. Dohrenwend, "Social Distance and Interviewer Effects," *Public Opinion Quarterly,* 32:410–422 (1968); Thomas F. Pettigrew, *A Profile of the Negro American* (Princeton, N.J.:D. Van Nostrand Co., Inc., 1964).

[9]Daniel Katz, "Do interviewers bias polls?" *Public Opinion Quarterly,* 6:248–268 (1942).

[10]Herbert H. Hyman *et al., Interviewing in Social Research* (Chicago: University of Chicago Press, 1954), pp. 138–150.

[11]*Ibid.,* p. 138.

TABLE 4
Net bias* in responses to registration, voting, left back, and subject failure questions, by characteristics of interviewer

Interviewer Characteristics	Registration	Voting	Left Back	Subject Failure
Interviewer-Respondent Disparity Index				
High	17	16	0	22
Low	20	22	8	29
Present socioeconomic status of interviewer:				
30–59	19	22	2	30
60–79	15	15	8	25
80 or more	21	19	0	27
Education match between interviewer and respondent:				
Same education	24	23	7	39
Interviewer 1 level higher	17	17	0	24
Interviewer 2 levels higher	15	17	4	24
Age match between interviewer and respondent:				
Same age	19	21	8	26
Interviewer 10 or more years younger	17	15	4	24
Interviewer 10 or more years older	18	14	−17	36

* "Net bias" is a measure designed to eliminate responses based on lack of knowledge or faulty memory rather than purposeful distortion. It is derived by computing the percentage error among persons whose actual behavior was desirable (e.g. actual voters who said that they didn't vote), and subtracting that percentage from the percentage error of persons overclaiming the desirable behavior (e.g. nonvoters who said that they voted.) The assumption is that an equal proportion of both groups is confused or uninformed; by chance, one set made the socially desirable, i.e. biased, error, and they are eliminated in the measure of "net bias."

as increasing with *task* involvement rather than with *total* involvement. To the extent that a respondent's reaction derives from social or interpersonal involvement, we may expect it to result in bias . . ."[12]

That appears to be the situation here. On almost every question, the better the rapport, the greater the proportion of biased responses. Net bias on each question, by degree of rapport, is shown in Table 5.

Interviewers who rated rapport highest tended to be of higher social status. They had some college education, high current socioeconomic status, and were not dark-skinned. Thus, the possibility arises that it is the combination of interviewer-respondent disparity and high rapport that leads to response bias.

However, the data show that whatever the status disparity or similarity, however like or unlike the interviewer and respondent are, high rapport is associated with greater bias. Thus, for like interviewers, net bias on the registration question was 28 per cent when rapport was high, 16 per cent when rapport was low. For unlike interviewers, net bias was 24 per cent when rapport was high, 11 per cent

[12] *Ibid.*

when rapport was low. High rapport plus high status similarity led to the highest rate of bias.[13]

EFFECT OF SOCIAL DISTANCE AND RAPPORT
ON ATTITUDINAL RESPONSES

Besides the factual questions, the study contained a number of attitude questions. Although there is no way to validate answers of opinion, it is possible to look at the social desirability of the responses and make inferences about bias.

TABLE 5
**Net bias* in responses to registration, voting, left back, and subject
failure questions, by rapport between interviewer and respondent**

Rapport	Registration	Voting	Left Back	Subject Failure
Confiding	25	26	6	26
Frank	16	14	4	33
Poor	3	2	1	2

*See note to Table 4.

Interviewer-respondent similarity and rapport each had an effect. As with the voting data, each increased the social desirability of attitude responses. However, the order of importance changed; status similarity showed a stronger relation to social desirability than did rapport.

Respondents told interviewers most like themselves (in socioeconomic status, education, and age) that they were bothered about receiving welfare significantly more often than they gave this response to unlike interviewers. They more often told like interviewers that their children will surely not be on welfare, that they strongly disagree with teaching children to live for today, that at least one of their children will continue his education past high school, and that they have a political party affiliation.

Rapport operated in the same direction. In situations of high rapport, respondents gave more socially desirable answers. This was true on all of the attitude questions listed, but the differences tended to be small.

When interviewer-respondent disparity was held constant, high rapport had a tendency to increase the social desirability of responses. Table 6 shows that out of the 15 possible cases (three disparity categories, five questions), high rapport was associated with the more desirable response in eleven.

The combination of similarity and high rapport led to the highest percentage of socially desirable answers on three questions—bothered about welfare, teaching

---

[13]Response bias on the school questions was also associated with status similarity and rapport, but the relationships were cloudier.

TABLE 6
Attitude responses, by interviewer-respondent disparity and rapport

| Attitude Responses | *Interviewer-Respondent Disparity* | | | | | |
| | *Unlike* | | *Medium* | | *Like* | |
	High Rapport	*Lower Rapport*	*High Rapport*	*Lower Rapport*	*High Rapport*	*Lower Rapport*
Bothered about receiving welfare: Yes	61.1 (66)	53.7 (51)	72.4 (71)	64.1 (98)	83.5 (66)	77.2 (88)
Teach children to live for today: Strongly disagree	54.6 (59)	58.5 (55)	58.0 (58)	59.1 (94)	65.8 (52)	57.0 (54)
Will children be on welfare Surely not	63.3 (57)	54.8 (46)	43.7 (38)	33.8 (45)	53.3 (40)	67.7 (63)
Educational expectations for children: Post-high school for any child	46.3 (38)	35.3 (24)	40.8 (29)	38.1 (43)	40.0 (24)	54.1 (40)
Political party affiliation: None (low percentage is desirable)	14.5 (16)	17.9 (17)	13.1 (13)	21.4 (34)	10.0 (88)	14.9 (17)

children to live for today, and having a party affiliation. On the other two questions, highest bias occurred under conditions of high similarity and lower rapport. Although both similarity and rapport were associated with bias, on the attitude questions similarity had the stronger effect.

DISCUSSION

The validity of welfare mothers' voting responses appears reassuring, both substantively and technically. With similar norms operating, the respondents do not appear to be drastically alienated from society and its political institutions. Technically, no special definitions of social desirability or special response distortions appear to bedevil the survey enterprise among the poor—at least on this type of question.

The data on interviewer-respondent interaction, on the other hand, raise some unexpected issues. If these data are supported by further research, should the trend toward use of "indigenous interviewers" in studies of the poor be halted?

There have been previous indications that status-similar interviewers who interact with respondents on a personal basis tend to get biased answers.[14] Not only poor people, but all respondents, may bias answers in the kaffeeklatsch atmosphere set by the overly friendly interviewer. If the association between rapport and bias hasn't shown up as clearly before, it may be that the interviewers in this study, and of the poor generally, are more likely to establish rapport on a personal basis, rather than on a task-oriented basis.

The implications may be not to stop recruiting lower-status interviewers. It is likely to be advisable—for reasons of community acceptance, increase in contact and interview completion, creation of interviewing jobs for local people, and other considerations—to use "like" interviewers in studies of the poor. But the training for them may need to be reconsidered. Ways may have to be found to help them develop task involvement, rather than personal involvement, as the basis for rapport and to concentrate on the business aspect of completing the interview.

---

[14]Cf. Dohrenwend, Colombotos, and Dohrenwend, *op. cit.;* and Richard J. Hill and Nason E. Hall, "A note on rapport and the quality of interview data," *Southwestern Social Science Quarterly,* 44:247–255 (1963).

If we consider our "high rapport" measure similar to Dohrenwend's "intrusive-non-rejecting" category, our data agree with the Dohrenwend model of strong bias for respondents and interviewers of closest similarity. However, unlike their model, high rapport in our study is also associated with greater bias among respondents similar to the interviewer in ethnicity but dissimilar in social status. Differences of definition abound, however, and as "rapport" becomes better specified in terms of interviewer behaviors and attitudes, the different biasing effects reported in recent papers by Williams (*Public Opinion Quarterly,* 32:287–294 [1968]), Dohrenwend, and others may seem less inconsistent.

35. Resistance to community surveys

ERIC JOSEPHSON

THE PROBLEM

The cooperation—passive or active—of respondents and the communities in which they live is the *sine qua non* of survey research. Carlson (1967) commented to the American Association of Public Opinion Research recently, "We are able to collect our research data only because the general public continues to be willing to submit to our interviews. This acceptance of us by the public is the basic natural resource on which our industry is built. Without it, we would be out of business tomorrow." So far, those engaged in surveys which are relatively innocuous as regards purpose, content, and population being studied have been able to take that cooperation—or inertia—for granted.

However, judging by the experience which my colleagues and I at the Columbia University School of Public Health have had with protests against a study of adolescents in a well-known ghetto, research projects dealing with the "pathologies" of slums or with deviant behavior should be prepared for trouble. The situation is by no means desperate, but it is serious and worthy of serious consideration. Ironically, at a time when there are greater demands on survey research than ever before to deal with problems of demonstrable public concern, such as poverty, ill health, or youthful drug use, resistance to surveys threatens to make such research increasingly difficult and sometimes impossible. Based chiefly on a single episode, my paper addresses itself to the sources of this resistance, some of the forms which it takes, and its implications for our field.

Before describing the opposition which confronted me and my colleagues, I want to distinguish between studies or projects which are national in their scope or in the interest they arouse, and those which are essentially local in their focus and significance.

At the national level there have been controversies over Project Camelot and the Moynihan Report, debates inside and outside Congress about psychological testing and data banks, and most recently, the apparently successful campaign to get the Census Bureau to eliminate questions about flush toilets and other embarrassing matters. In the controversies which these and other such *causes celebres* have aroused at home and abroad, attacks have been made against the sponsorship of research projects (especially when it is concealed or Establishmentarian), their alleged uselessness, the failure of investigators to consult with the communities or populations being studied, the threat to individual privacy (as in reporting deviant

From Eric Josephson, "Resistance to community surveys," *Social Problems,* 18:117–129 (Summer, 1970). Copyright © 1970 by The Society for the Study of Social Problems. Reprinted by permission.

The author is Associate Professor, Sociomedical Sciences, School of Public Health, Columbia University, New York.

behavior), and the invidiousness of research findings. These are charges which have been made against social research by intellectuals, politicians of left and right, and spokesmen for the black community.

In view of what appears to be a rising chorus of protest against research, it is worth noting that nationwide survey organizations have, so far as I know, continued to conduct studies on a variety of controversial topics—e.g., the urban riot studies. What explains this success, in my opinion, is that the investigators and interviewers are rarely in evidence long enough to become conspicuous targets for attack. In other words, such studies have relatively limited and brief impact on the communities being sampled.

But studies, such as ours, which focus on a single community for a fairly extended period of time lack this advantage of low visibility. The investigators become part of the local landscape, so to speak, thereby increasing the chance that they will become embroiled in local controversy. I have made no attempt to catalogue such episodes, although I think it should be done. Among the relatively few published reports of such cases are those by Rainwater and Pittman (1967) regarding their problems in studying deviant behavior in a St. Louis housing project and Moore's (1967) description of the difficulties which she and her colleagues encountered in a study of Mexican Americans in the Southwest. What these and other such reports add up to is a picture of lower-class sensitivity about being studied, suspicion of outside investigators and their motives, skepticism about the benefits of research —in short, disenchantment with the nature and conduct of social research—especially among local community leaders. This is not new. What is new, as some of these reports suggest, is that community leaders, demanding a voice in the research enterprise, are in a position to exact a price for their cooperation. As a consequence, research may at times be diverted from its original, "purer" purpose. These issues became central in the controversy that developed over our project.

AIMS OF THE PROJECT

Our original objective was to produce data on the relationship between poverty and adolescent health. At the beginning we found that, despite the almost inordinate attention which has been paid by social scientists to adolescents, rich and poor, relatively little was known about their health. We know a great deal about the health status and medical care needs of the very young and the very old; but very little about those between childhood and adulthood. This neglect has been due partly to the assumption that at least the physical, if not the emotional, health of adolescents can be taken for granted. And to be sure, in terms of morbidity, adolescents are in an advantageous position as compared with their juniors and seniors. But evidence from studies of draft rejects, the National Health Survey, job training programs, accident, suicide, and homicide statistics, suggested to us that this neglect was unjustified and that adolescents living in slums were in a particularly disadvantageous position.

As social scientists, we approached the problem by taking a broad view of "health," i.e., not only concerning ourselves with traditional measures of health status and medical care needs, but also with self-perceptions regarding health, health practices, moods, aspirations and expectations, sexual behavior, the use of drugs, violence, thoughts about death, etc. Our aim from the beginning was to collect two kinds of data about adolescent health: one based on what youngsters themselves might report in interviews and the other based on examinations of them by medical teams. The result, we hoped, would be a comprehensive picture of the health status and medical care needs of adolescents which would contribute to planning for improved delivery of medical care in disadvantaged communities. I must add that since we were planning to deal with minors in the eyes of the law, we recognized from the start that we would have to obtain some form of parental consent both for interviews with and medical examinations of adolescents (Smith, 1967).

In 1967, we obtained funds from the Children's Bureau to undertake a pilot study of adolescent health in the Washington Heights health district of New York City. The opportunity to do so was presented to us by the work done earlier on a comprehensive family health survey of the community conducted by Elinson (1969), referred to as the Master Sample Survey. Our technique was to go back to adolescents, here defined as between 12 and 17 years of age, in households which had previously been approached in the most recent Master Sample Survey. This we did in the summer of 1967, completing 122 interviews with youngsters and arranging for medical examinations of half of them at the nearby Washington Heights Health Center. From a methodological point of view, it was successful; that is, it gave us an opportunity to produce and test instruments for a larger study. Although the average length of the interview was two and a half hours, adolescents and their families were extremely cooperative. There was no controversy about the project.

But Washington Heights, although diverse in its ethnic and income characteristics, is not exactly a slum; and, as noted earlier, our intention was to study the poor. Once again, an unusual opportunity presented itself given the new role which Columbia University began to play in Harlem's medical affairs. As part of the affiliation contract between the University and the City of New York with regard to Harlem Hospital (a municipal institution), plans had been laid for a comprehensive evaluation of the health status and medical care utilization patterns of the community being served by Harlem Hospital, including a sample survey of households in the community. Directing the overall evaluation was Elinson.

As previously in Washington Heights, our plan was to go back to households which had been approached in the larger survey and, with parental consent, interview adolescents about their health and offer them free medical examinations at Harlem Hospital. Starting at the end of 1967, we intended to interview as many as 1000 adolescents 12 to 17 years of age. Since the larger community survey had been under way for six months and had been proceeding without any unusual difficulties, we anticipated none with regard to our project. Once again, funds for the study were made available by the Children's Bureau.

While ours was to be the first large-scale study of adolescent health in Harlem, it was not the first study of adolescents in that community. Several years earlier, Haryou-Act, the major local anti-poverty agency, had conducted a survey of adolescents in Harlem which focused particularly on their educational and occupational aspirations and expectations but also included many questions about "antisocial" behavior. So far as I know, the Haryou-Act investigation produced no controversy. But in 1967, we at Columbia represented a university with which Harlem was beginning to have increasingly strained relations. This would later culminate in the controversy over plans for a gymnasium in Morningside Park; but there were other issues at stake as well—for example, the charge had already been made that Columbia was exploiting Harlem Hospital for its own purposes and ignoring the wishes of the community with regard to health matters. Such, in brief, is the background of the episode I shall now describe.

THE PROTEST

Late in 1967, we made the necessary arrangements with our colleagues in charge of the larger community health survey and with the staff at Harlem Hospital. Our own team of interviewers would go to households already visited in the other survey; with parental consent, adolescents would be interviewed and offered a medical examination at the Hospital. Before starting field work, however, it seemed necessary and desirable to determine whether the questionnaire we had used successfully in ethnically mixed Washington Heights would be appropriate for a survey in which most of the respondents would be black residents of Central Harlem.

Therefore, we decided to conduct a small number of (approximately 30) unstructured interviews with adolescents in households previously contacted by the larger community health survey. The chief purpose of these interviews was to provide information about the salience of "health" and medical care for adolescents in these households and about ways of questioning them about such matters—in short, to help us revise the questionnaire which we had used previously in Washington Heights.

Since the new questionnaire became controversial, a brief description of it is in order. It contained such innocuous items as "When, roughly, was the last time you saw a doctor—for any reason at all?" or "Some people feel that, when you come right down to it, there's not much a person can do about his health. Do you feel this way or not?" But the questionnaire also sought to elicit from youngsters suggestions as to how we might best interview their contemporaries about health matters. Thus, we asked: "The word 'health'—what does it mean to you? (Probe: How would you describe a healthy person?)" We also asked: "What do you think we should ask young people about sex? (Probe: What should we ask about their sexual relations and sexual experiences?)" Regarding drugs, we did not ask adolescents whether they themselves were taking drugs but rather what they knew about drug use among others their age. Regarding "trouble with the police," we asked them whether they had ever had such trouble and also what kind of trouble their neighbors had had. Regarding riots, we did not ask whether they themselves had participated but merely what they thought about riots. Perhaps the most sensitive questions were, "Have you ever thought about killing yourself?", "When was the last time you beat somebody?" and "Do you ever carry a knife?" In somewhat different form, all of these questions had been tested successfully in our Washington Heights pilot study and in other surveys. Also, the Central Harlem Adolescent Study, conducted earlier by Haryou-Act and to which I referred above, included such questions as "When was the last time you carried a knife, gun or some other weapon?", "When was the last time you tried reefers or another drug?", "When was the last time you had been in any kind of a fist fight?" and "When was the last time you had been in gang fights?" Our plan was to conduct these unstructured interviews early in December 1967.

Precisely because of the nature of these exploratory interviews—requiring a considerable amount of probing—we hoped to recruit field workers with some experience in social surveys as well as the ability to improvise variations in the wording and sequence of questions. Friends at the Bureau of Applied Social Research and at the National Opinion Research Center referred a number of interviewers to us who worked out well; others (about whom we knew little) were recommended to us by members of our own staff. Of a total of seven interviewers who were finally recruited for the exploratory study and asked to come to a training session, three (all graduate students in the social sciences) at the very outset began to raise serious questions about Columbia's "image" in Harlem and about the propriety of the study. Although our staff began to have misgivings about letting them undertake interviews, we did nothing at first, permitting them to leave with their assignments. However, the day after the training session, we decided that the three interviewers who had expressed such strong doubts about the project should not be permitted to proceed with their assignments. Our fear was that they might antagonize respondents and thereby jeopardize further contacts by other investigators with these households; this was a risk we did not want to take. They were, therefore, called back before doing any interviews, asked to return all study materials, and offered another, more consultative role on the project. This offer they declined. Meanwhile, the other four interviewers completed their assignments, reporting no difficulties in obtaining parental consent for the interviews or in conducting the interviews with adolescents. Altogether, eight interviews were completed.

So far, this had been a fairly ordinary situation in which a few interviewers felt uncomfortable about a project and then withdrew from it. However, although we did not know it at the time and for reasons which remain speculative, the three discharged interviewers had managed to make copies of our questionnaire before returning their assignments kits and began to circulate copies of the questionnaire in Harlem, thereby setting in motion a protest against the project and against the university under whose auspices it was being conducted.

Within two weeks of our initial training session and the departure of the three hostile interviewers, a story appeared in *The Amsterdam News* announcing the formation of an "Ad Hoc Citizens Committee Against Columbia University . . . to protest a health survey being conducted among Harlem adolescents." Spokesmen for the committee were reported as having taken this action "after seeing samples of the survey questionnaire which, they claim, contains 'derogatory and prejudicial' questions." More specifically, we were attacked for asking questions about narcotics, beatings, knives, and street fights and riots. At approximately the same time, under the aegis of a "Harlem Committee for Self-Defense" (another name for the Ad Hoc Committee) leaflets regarding the project began to circulate in Harlem. One of them charged that Columbia "was doing a study under the guise of health" and attacked us for asking 12-year-olds about their sex lives, their use of drugs and alcohol, their friends, the last time they beat someone or were beaten, their militancy, the weapons they carried, whether they had ever thought of killing themselves, and their participation in riots. "If the Man was interested in your health," this leaflet continued, "he would send a doctor not an interviewer. They are using black interviewers to fool you. They know white cops can't do it. So now they are sending black ones. There will be other studies and other disguises. Don't tell anyone anything about your business!!! Protect yourself and your black brothers and sisters. Join with the Harlem Committee for Self-Defense to stop this study before this study stops you!!!" Still another leaflet referred to our project as a "Trick Health Survey."

What followed was a meeting devoted to our project held at the Abyssinian Baptist Church; approximately 75 people attended. Chaired by one of the interviewers we had discharged, the meeting heard him say (according to a published report) that our survey was intended "to determine just how far (Columbia) can go before people rebel and resist." Also aired at the meeting were charges that the results of the survey would "wind up in police precincts, not in the halls of the University" and that the survey was a "fraud." After the chairman asked, "What can we do to stop Columbia?" one suggestion from the floor was to "give the interviewer a good head whipping." To which another participant added: "You will have to spill your own blood to fight Columbia." In addition, a woman described as an "indignant mother" took the floor to say that "I would not allow anyone to come into my house and ask my children anything." A young man on our staff who attempted to defend and justify the project was shouted down, accused of "selling his people down the river for a few pieces of silver," and ordered out of the church.

How much interest the protest was beginning to generate is hard to determine. A few radio broadcasts mentioned it, as did local and student newspapers. In a story about Columbia's relations with Harlem, *The New York Times* quoted one of the leaflets but did not mention the project. The radical organ, *Challenge,* devoted a full page to our survey under the headline, "Harlem Hits Columbia Snoopers." According to the story in *Challenge,* "the project and the interview form have just enough questions dealing with health to make it look good, but in reality it has nothing to do with improving anyone's health. It's just one more method used by the ruling class to determine how best to suppress the Black people with the least amount of trouble. But some of the people who were supposed to be interviewers, after reading the letter, the 'interviewer's guide' and the questions they were supposed to ask, saw how Columbia and its masters, the U.S. Government, had something besides 'health' in mind." *Challenge* went on to describe how the three interviewers had "called a meeting of people from Harlem to discuss this situation and map out a plan of action to combat this and every other attempt to use Harlem as a laboratory to experiment on our people like the Nazis did in Germany." I must add that the *Challenge* story also suggested that " 'Surveys' and interviews have been flooding Harlem since the 1964 rebellion. Hundreds of 'foundations' and 'agencies' are sticking their noses into the people's lives. The antipoverty agencies have been the major front for these 'studies.' "

As the protest continued, our project was linked by militant blacks with a number of other activities in which Columbia was engaged. Under the general charge that the University was threatening to "take over" Harlem, Columbia was denounced for its plans to build a gymnasium in Morningside Park, for evicting its black neighbors, for taking over Harlem Hospital—as well as for our study of adolescents.

So far as I and my colleagues were concerned, however, the climax of the protest against our survey was reached late in January, 1968 when a demonstration by black militants and their supporters took place at Columbia University's main campus; this, I should add, happened nearly three months before what the Cox Commission described as the "disturbances" at the University took place. Perhaps as many as 50 demonstrators marched along Broadway for half an hour, some of them carrying placards which said "Don't let Columbia interview Blacks" and others with signs saying "We need hospitals, not surveys." Our project was not the only target at this time; as noted, Columbia was also being attacked for its plans to build a gymnasium and for evicting some of the tenants in University-owned apartment buildings. The spirit of the occasion was summed up by the placard with the phrase, "Columbia get the hell out and stay out."

Although the Harlem Committee for Self-Defense and its supporters continued their agitation, repeating the charges made earlier urging a "boycott of this 'sinister' research," and demanding "hands off Harlem," it is probable that other issues began to take priority over our project. When the Columbia campus finally exploded over the gymnasium issue in April 1968 and black students seized Hamilton Hall, the crowds of black sympathizers who came up the hill from Harlem to show their solidarity were far larger than the ones who had attacked our project. More recently, there has been further agitation in Harlem regarding the Hospital; but so far as we know the controversy over our project either died a natural death or was displaced by other, more pressing concerns.

AFTERMATH

Such, in brief, is the history of the protest against our project in Harlem. Before discussing some of the more general implications of the attack, let me describe what we tried to do about it.

First of all, it was important that we evaluate the extent to which the attack against the project reflected community sentiment. Our judgment was that a small group of people in Harlem were exploiting our survey for their own political purposes and that they had little community support; most people in Harlem, we assumed, knew little about our survey, or if they did, were indifferent. Indirect support for this assumption has been provided by the telephone survey which Nash and Epstein (1968) of the Bureau of Applied Social Research conducted in Central Harlem soon after the disturbances at the lower campus; they found that relatively few people had strong feelings about Columbia and that most were either favorably disposed toward the planned gymnasium or neutral on the subject. To the best of my knowledge, nobody mentioned our study.

But even if most residents of Harlem were neutral toward our survey, the fact that agitation against it had become linked with a much broader attack against Columbia University and its role in the surrounding community meant that more was at stake than the survival of the adolescent health survey. As noted earlier, Columbia had assumed major responsibility for staffing the municipal hospital in Harlem; part of this responsibility included an evaluation by our colleagues at the School of Public Health of the quality of care provided at Harlem Hospital and of the health status of the population being served by it.

In view of all that was involved, we faced the following alternatives: to abandon the project, to continue as if nothing had happened, or to modify our plans. The first of these alternatives was not entirely unthinkable: one of the deans on the main campus (no longer at Columbia) strongly urged us to delay the start of the project and even to consider abandoning it. To their great credit, this suggestion was rejected by our colleagues at the School of Public Health. The second alternative was obviously unthinkable. Therefore, if we were to continue, certain changes in objectives and procedure would have to be made.

These changes consisted chiefly of taking out of the questionnaire almost all items dealing with deviant behavior, meeting with spokesmen for some of the protesting groups in an attempt to have some dialogue with them about the project and their feelings about it, and discussing the project at meetings of the Harlem Health Council—a voluntary body of individuals and agency representatives with an interest in the health of the community. In March, 1968 the Health Council agreed to form an ad hoc advisory committee in order to facilitate community participation in the project.

As conceived by the Harlem Health Council, the advisory committee was not expected to have veto power over the project or its staff. Rather, in establishing the committee, the aim was to alert project staff members to health problems of particular interest to the community and to provide a means of getting reactions to our objectives and methods, particularly our interviewing procedures. Committee members, in turn, could help explain our project in the community. Since its formation, the advisory committee has held about half a dozen meetings and has been supportive in many ways, as in strongly backing our requests to the federal government for continued funding. Suggestions by committee members have been incorporated in revisions of our interviewing procedures; indeed, it was at the instigation of the committee that we restored the controversial question on adolescent drinking behavior to the household interview schedule. It is fair to say that the committee is less interested in the research than in the service aspects of the project—i.e., the direct benefit to the adolescents who would be provided with free, comprehensive medical examinations at Harlem Hospital—and in the more indirect benefits to the community in having available information which may be useful in planning for improvements in the delivery of health care to youth in Harlem. But this would be expected, since the committee may be involved in the implementation of findings from our survey.

Another consequence of the protest was that we were forced to delay the start of field work approximately six months. This period of time was used in revising our questionnaire and in seeking some measure of community support. But it was a costly delay, for the Children's Bureau, dissatisfied with the progress we were making, sharply reduced the size of our grant. This in turn compelled us to limit the scope of the project and the size of the sample to be studied.

However, by mid-1968 we were back in the field and have since completed approximately 700 interviews with adolescents 12 to 17 years of age—achieving a respectable completion rate of approximately 80 percent of those assigned to interviewers; cooperation in the medical examination phase of the project has been equally high. So far as we know, none of the relatively few refusals to cooperate with either interviewer or medical examination team can be attributed to the controversy. Most non-interviews have been due to our dependence on a list which is at least six months old. Furthermore, the much larger community health survey (never a source of controversy) has been continuing without prolonged interruption and is now approaching a total of 9,000 completed interviews in Harlem.

But if the protest failed to prevent us from resuming our work, it succeeded in forcing us to narrow the scope of the project. To be sure, we are collecting data on the physical health status of adolescents in Harlem; but we have been unable to pursue certain related areas of interest to us such as drug use. What makes this particularly ironic is that if there is any single health problem about which there is widespread concern in Harlem, it is adolescent drug use. Indeed, one of the leading political figures in the community, consulted about the project, told us that he regarded the youthful drug problem as *the* most important of all social questions facing Harlem. And yet we have been unable to interview youngsters about drugs. This has been part of the cost of continuing the project.

IMPLICATIONS

Two kinds of lessons can be drawn from the protest against this project. One has to do with the practical problems of doing research under such circumstances; the other has to do with the more basic questions which such attacks raise about social research.

At the practical level, one obvious lesson is to screen prospective interviewers more carefully than we did, since in this case (as in several other surveys about which reports are circulating) they started the controversy. But under the circumstances of rising tensions between Harlem and Columbia, we could hardly have given them a test of loyalty to Columbia. Besides, who is going to screen the investigators themselves?

Another lesson is that there are times when and places where it is difficult, if not impossible, to collect data on deviant behavior; in our case I suppose we should have been more cautious about the content of the questionnaire which got us in trouble. But again, experience elsewhere has demonstrated that even the most innocuous questions can be upsetting to some respondents or to the communities in which they live. In other words, while the content of questionnaires may have something to do with the fate of a survey, many other factors are involved. How else explain why some surveys of ghetto life have been attacked, while others have been spared?

Perhaps our greatest error was that we failed to obtain some degree of community participation in planning the project. Once again, however, the problem was how and at what points to make contact with the community. Actually, we had considered forming an advisory committee earlier but were uncertain about how to proceed. Who represented "the community" in such matters? And obviously, there was far less community interest in our project at the beginning than after the controversy had started. Nevertheless, if there is anything practical to be learned from our experience, I think it is here: investigators of ghetto life should make a serious effort to obtain some degree of community support and involvement before starting their research. This may create problems for researchers, as I shall suggest later; but the alternatives are even less attractive.

But even the most loyal interviewers, the most innocuous questionnaire, and a sympathetic advisory committee are no guarantee that a project will remain uncontroversial. While the community as a whole and most prospective respondents may be neutral or even indifferent to such research, the fact remains that a handful of people can disrupt it. We can speculate about their motives or draw up elaborate plans for coping with such controversies after they begin; more important, however, are the implications of such attacks for social research in times like these.

In turning to the broader significance of the protest against our project, I want to make it clear that I do not regard such resistance as necessarily unhealthy. On the contrary, I feel that such episodes have something positive to teach us—if we are prepared to listen.

One issue has to do with the perception of studies, such as ours, as threatening; this was illustrated in the charge that we were planning to turn information over to the police, or that what we were doing was part of a genocidal plot against Harlem. I am not suggesting that fear of research is widespread; indeed, our subsequent experience and that of most research teams suggest that it is not. What is significant, however, is that research can be perceived as a mechanism of control. Nor is this completely farfetched; much of social science research *is* manipulative in its intent or purpose. It is awareness of this purpose which underlies fear of the invasion of privacy and skepticism regarding our ability to protect that privacy.

This is particularly the case when researchers deal with "deviant" behavior. Here the implication is that such research is invidious in its purpose—i.e., that its intent is to show how much more "deviant" or "pathological" the ghetto is than other communities, or that findings regarding pathology will be misinterpreted by the investigators and misused by the institutions they serve. Sensitivity about these issues is one of the more serious obstacles to such research.

Fear of research is also related to awareness on the part of some ghetto residents that most studies of their communities are initiated on the outside. People in communities such as Harlem may wish for information about certain problems, such as drug use, but usually lack the resources and the expertise with which to study them. But those resources and expertise may be found on the outside. Hence the feeling that social surveys are a form of exploitation (by the investigators for their gain) of helpless or powerless communities which gain little or nothing from the research.

One reaction to this is the demand for participation in the research process, both in terms of planning surveys and in terms of jobs. Another response is the notion that communities like Harlem have been over-studied by outsiders. There is no evidence that this has in fact been the case; indeed, our impression is that there have been relatively few systematic surveys of Harlem (and until now none dealing with health) apart from national or citywide studies which merely include its population as part of a larger universe. Nevertheless, the idea of over-exposure to surveys prevails.

These are just some of the issues which such protests raise. Whether representative of community sentiment or merely the product of a few who seek political gain, negative or hostile feelings about the work we do confront us with the problem of demonstrating more effectively than heretofore, first, precisely what safeguards we can offer our respondents in regard to the information they give us, and second, the utility—immediate or long-range—of our findings.

With regard to safeguards for informants, I feel that we need much more than elegantly phrased codes of ethical conduct which we are scarcely able to enforce among ourselves. Of course, investigators may deny that they will turn information over to the police; but if pressed, they have no legal grounds for not doing so. Or, if they have special "understandings" with the police and other agencies of law enforcement so that self-informants of "deviant" behavior will not be prosecuted, investigators risk compromising themselves. Here is a dilemma. "In situations of this type," says the President's Panel on Privacy and Behavioral Research (1967), "investigators are well advised to seek expressions of confidence from the entire community about the importance of their studies and of the absolute necessity of maintaining the confidentiality of their data." But what is meant by "the entire community" and how can researchers get expressions of confidence from it, particularly in a period of conflict? This needs much more attention; for as Wolfle (1968) recently pointed out, if we as investigators fail to codify the relationship of researcher to subject, the courts will do it for us—and in ways that we may not like.

With regard to the utility of research—which I personally consider the most important of all the issues raised by protests against surveys—a number of questions present themselves. First, utility for whom? For us as social scientists, for the elite policy makers we usually serve, or for the community we are studying? The distinctions are important. Irving Louis Horowitz (1967) has asserted, "There is a direct relationship between the ability to pay and belief in the utility of the social sciences. Who are the high users? The federal government, some state governments, basic industries, marketing industries. Who are the low users? Farmer-labor groups, the poor in general, minority groups (with the exception of highly sophisticated groups such as affluent religious organizations that spill over into the high-users category). In the main, racial and ethnic groups do not place much value on the use of social science. Perhaps the use of social science research is itself a suave reflection of wealth. Those who wish to use social science agencies extensively are wealthy enough to afford them; those who disparage social science groups are often rationalizing their own lack of affluence."

Finally, there is the basic question as to the real importance of the research we do. If we as researchers cannot easily persuade ourselves of the utility of what we do, how can we hope to convince the communities and populations which we are studying? To be sure, there may be payoff from social surveys over the long run; but as Keynes said, in the long run we are all dead, and communities such as Harlem are impatient.

To recapitulate, while overt resistance to surveys is not as yet widespread and there is no reason to believe it will become so, I think it is necessary to recognize its significance when it occurs. In some communities and in some populations, there is apparently the feeling that survey research is useless, representing merely a form of exploitation by the investigators for their gain or for the gain of the institutions and powers they serve. What, if any, are the rights of communities and study populations to know about the aims and sponsorship of the research? How can communities participate more actively and constructively in the research enterprise? And if they are to become involved, how can social scientists preserve their autonomy with regard to the nature of the problems being studied, the findings produced, and the implications drawn? Then too, in an age of data banks there is some fear—not altogether unjustified—that information collected in surveys will be used for purposes of controlling the populations being studied. How can this fear be overcome? How can we demonstrate the utility of such research?

Moore (1967, 242) has written of her experiences in studying the poor, "The license we are given by our subjects to collect a great deal of information—much of it confidential—entails in our case an almost explicit bargain with them that this information will be used discreetly and presented expertly in such a way that they will collectively benefit. This bargain also implies that we may not be able to afford —either ethically or financially—the kind of theoretically oriented research that runs the risk of accomplishing little more than the verification of null hypotheses."

In short, we face the problem of justifying ourselves and the work we do. Not only is our usefulness to communities and study populations uncertain, but we have yet systematically to codify our relationships with informants, as in medicine or law. Resistance to social research will be overcome when we have done far more than heretofore to win the confidence of the communities and populations we are studying by protecting their rights to privacy and by demonstrating that what we are doing can be of some value to them—in other words, by committing ourselves as social scientists to major social change. Whether we can achieve these objectives remains to be seen.

REFERENCES

Carlson, R. O. "The issue of privacy in public opinion research." *Public Opinion Quarterly* 31:1 (Spring, 1967).

Executive Office of the President. *Privacy and Behavioral Research.* Office of Science and Technology. Washington, D.C.: U.S. Government Printing Office, 1967. P. 21.

Gell, C., and Elinson, Jack (eds.). "The Washington Heights Master Sample Survey." *The Milbank Memorial Fund Quarterly* 47:1 (January, 1969). Part 2.

Horowitz, I. L. *The Rise and Fall of Project Camelot.* Cambridge, Mass.: the M.I.T. Press, 1967. P. 353.

Moore, Joan W. "Political and ethical problems in a large-scale study of a minority population." In Gideon Sjoberg (ed.), *Ethics, Politics, and Social Research.* Cambridge, Mass.: Schenkman Publishing Co., Inc., 1967.

Nash, G., and Epstein, Cynthia. "Harlem views Columbia University." *New York,* July, 1968.

Rainwater, L., and Pittman, David J. "Ethical problems in studying a politically sensitive and deviant community." *Social Problems* 14:4 (Spring, 1967).

Smith, B. M. "Conflicting values affecting behavioral research with children." *Children* 14:2 (March–April, 1967).

Wolfle, D. "Editorial." *Science* 159:3817 (February, 1968).

36. The experience of living in cities

STANLEY MILGRAM

When I first came to New York it seemed like a nightmare. As soon as I got off the train at Grand Central I was caught up in pushing, shoving crowds on 42nd Street. Sometimes people bumped into me without apology; what really frightened me was to see two people literally engaged in combat for possession of a cab. Why were they so rushed? Even drunks on the street were bypassed without a glance. People didn't seem to care about each other at all.

This statement represents a common reaction to a great city, but it does not tell the whole story. Obviously cities have great appeal because of their variety, eventfulness, possibility of choice, and the stimulation of an intense atmosphere that many individuals find a desirable background to their lives. Where face-to-face contacts are important, the city offers unparalleled possibilities. It has been calculated by the Regional Plan Association[1] that in Nassau County, a suburb of New York City, an individual can meet 11,000 others within a 10-minute radius of his office by foot or car. In Newark, a moderate-sized city, he can meet more than 20,000 persons within this radius. But in midtown Manhattan he can meet fully 220,000. So there is an order-of-magnitude increment in the communication possibilities offered by a great city. That is one of the bases of its appeal and, indeed, of its functional necessity. The city provides options that no other social arrangement permits. But there is a negative side also, as we shall see.

Granted that cities are indispensable in complex society, we may still ask what contribution psychology can make to understanding the experience of living in them. What theories are relevant? How can we extend our knowledge of the psychological aspects of life in cities through empirical inquiry? If empirical inquiry is possible, along what lines should it proceed? In short, where do we start in constructing urban theory and in laying out lines of research?

Observation is the indispensable starting point. Any observer in the streets of midtown Manhattan will see (i) large numbers of people, (ii) a high population density, and (iii) heterogeneity of population. These three factors need to be at the root of any sociopsychological theory of city life, for they condition all aspects of our experience in the metropolis. Louis Wirth,[2] if not the first to point to these

---

Abridged and edited from Stanley Milgram, "The experience of living in cities," *Science,* 167:1461–1468 (March 13, 1970). Copyright © 1970 by the American Association for the Advancement of Science. Reprinted by permission.

The author is Professor of Psychology, The City University of New York Graduate Center, New York, N.Y.

[1] *The New York Times,* June 15, 1969.

[2] L. Wirth, "Urbanism as a way of life," *American Journal of Sociology,* 44:1–24 (July, 1938). Wirth's ideas have come under heavy criticism by contemporary city planners, who point out that the city is broken down into neighborhoods, which fulfill many of the functions of small towns. See, for example, H. J. Gans, *People and Plans: Essays on Urban Problems and Solutions* (New York: Basic Books, Inc., 1968); J. Jacobs, *The Death and Life of Great American Cities* (New York: Random House, Inc., 1961); G. D. Suttles, *The Social Order of the Slum* (Chicago: University of Chicago Press, 1968).

250

factors, is nonetheless the sociologist who relied most heavily on them in his analysis of the city. Yet, for a psychologist, there is something unsatisfactory about Wirth's theoretical variables. Numbers, density, and heterogeneity are demographic facts but they are not yet psychological facts. They are external to the individual. Psychology needs an idea that links the individual's *experience* to the demographic circumstances of urban life.

One link is provided by the concept of overload. This term, drawn from systems analysis, refers to a system's inability to process inputs from the environment because there are too many inputs for the system to cope with, or because successive inputs come so fast that input A cannot be processed when input B is presented. When overload is present, adaptations occur. The system must set priorities and make choices. A may be processed first while B is kept in abeyance, or one input may be sacrificed altogether. City life, as we experience it, constitutes a continuous set of encounters with overload, and of resultant adaptations. Overload characteristically deforms daily life on several levels, impinging on role performance, the evolution of social norms, cognitive functioning, and the use of facilities.

The concept has been implicit in several theories of urban experience. In 1903 George Simmel[3] pointed out that, since urban dwellers come into contact with vast numbers of people each day, they conserve psychic energy by becoming acquainted with a far smaller proportion of people than their rural counterparts do, and by maintaining more superficial relationships even with these acquaintances. Wirth points specifically to "the superficiality, the anonymity, and the transitory character of urban social relations."

One adaptive response to overload, therefore, is the allocation of less time to each input. A second adaptive mechanism is disregard of low-priority inputs. Principles of selectivity are formulated such that investments of time and energy are reserved for carefully defined inputs (the urbanite disregards the drunk sick on the street as he purposefully navigates through the crowd). Third, boundaries are redrawn in certain social transactions so that the overloaded system can shift the burden to the other party in the exchange; thus, harried New York bus drivers once made change for customers, but now this responsibility has been shifted to the client, who must have the exact fare ready. Fourth, reception is blocked off prior to entrance into a system; city dwellers increasingly use unlisted telephone numbers to prevent individuals from calling them, and a small but growing number resort to keeping the telephone off the hook to prevent incoming calls. More subtly, a city dweller blocks inputs by assuming an unfriendly countenance, which discourages others from initiating contact. Additionally, social screening devices are interposed between the individual and environmental inputs (in a town of 5000 anyone can drop in to chat with the mayor, but in the metropolis organizational screening devices deflect inputs to other destinations). Fifth, the intensity of inputs is diminished by filtering devices, so that only weak and relatively superficial forms of involvement with others are allowed. Sixth, specialized institutions are created to absorb inputs that would otherwise swamp the individual (welfare departments handle the financial needs of a million individuals in New York City, who would otherwise create

---

[3]G. Simmel, *The Sociology of Georg Simmel,* ed. by K. H. Wolff. (New York: The Macmillan Co., 1950). English translation of G. Simmel, *Die Grossstadte und das Geistesleben die Grossstadt* (Dresden: Jansch, 1903).

an army of mendicants continuously importuning the pedestrian). The interposition of institutions between the individual and the social world, a characteristic of all modern society, and most notably of the large metropolis, has its negative side. It deprives the individual of a sense of direct contact and spontaneous integration in the life around him. It simultaneously protects and estranges the individual from his social environment.

Many of these adaptive mechanisms apply not only to individuals but to institutional systems as well, as Meier[4] has so brilliantly shown in connection with the library and the stock exchange.

In sum, the observed behavior of the urbanite in a wide range of situations appears to be determined largely by a variety of adaptations to overload. I now deal with several specific consequences of responses to overload, which make for differences in the tone of city and town.

SOCIAL RESPONSIBILITY

The principal point of interest for a social psychology of the city is that moral and social involvement with individuals is necessarily restricted. This is a direct and necessary function of excess of input over capacity to process. Such restriction of involvement runs a broad spectrum from refusal to become involved in the needs of another person, even when the person desperately needs assistance, through refusal to do favors, to the simple withdrawal of courtesies (such as offering a lady a seat, or saying "sorry" when a pedestrian collision occurs). In any transaction more and more details need to be dropped as the total number of units to be processed increases and assaults an instrument of limited processing capacity.

The ultimate adaptation to an overloaded social environment is to totally disregard the needs, interests, and demands of those whom one does not define as relevant to the satisfaction of personal needs, and to develop highly efficient perceptual means of determining whether an individual falls into the category of friend or stranger. The disparity in the treatment of friends and strangers ought to be greater in cities than in towns; the time allotment and willingness to become involved with those who have no personal claim on one's time is likely to be less in cities than in towns.

The most striking deficiencies in social responsibility in cities occur in crisis situations, such as the Genovese murder in Queens. In 1964, Catherine Genovese, coming home from a night job in the early hours of an April morning, was stabbed repeatedly, over an extended period of time. Thirty-eight residents of a respectable New York City neighborhood admit to having witnessed at least a part of the attack, but none went to her aid or called the police until after she was dead. Milgram and Hollander, writing in *The Nation,*[5] analyzed the event in these terms:

> Urban friendships and associations are not primarily formed on the basis of physical proximity. A person with numerous close friends in different parts of

---

[4]R. L. Meier, *A Communications Theory of Urban Growth* (Cambridge, Mass.: The M.I.T. Press, 1962).

[5]S. Milgram and P. Hollander, "The murder they heard," *Nation,* 198:602–604 (June 15, 1964).

the city may not know the occupant of an adjacent apartment. This does not mean that a city dweller has fewer friends than does a villager, or knows fewer persons who will come to his aid; however, it does mean that his allies are not constantly at hand. Miss Genovese required immediate aid from those physically present. There is no evidence that the city had deprived Miss Genovese of human associations, but the friends who might have rushed to her side were miles from the scene of her tragedy.

Further, it is known that her cries for help were not directed to a specific person; they were general. But only individuals can act, and as the cries were not specifically directed, no particular person felt a special responsibility. The crime and the failure of community response seem absurd to us. At the time, it may well have seemed equally absurd to the Kew Gardens residents that not one of the neighbors would have called the police. A collective paralysis may have developed from the belief of each of the witnesses that someone else must surely have taken that obvious step.

Latané and Darley[6] have reported laboratory approaches to the study of bystander intervention and have established experimentally the following principle: the larger the number of bystanders, the less the likelihood that any one of them will intervene in an emergency. . . .

In any quantitative characterization of the social texture of city life, a necessary first step is the application of such experimental methods as these to field situations in large cities and small towns. Theorists argue that the indifference shown in the Genovese case would not be found in a small town, but in the absence of solid experimental evidence the question remains an open one.

More than just callousness prevents bystanders from participating in altercations between people. A rule of urban life is respect for other people's emotional and social privacy, perhaps because physical privacy is so hard to achieve. And in situations for which the standards are heterogeneous, it is much harder to know whether taking an active role is unwarranted meddling or an appropriate response to a critical situation. If a husband and wife are quarreling in public, at what point should a bystander step in? On the one hand, the heterogeneity of the city produces substantially greater tolerance about behavior, dress, and codes of ethics than is generally found in the small town, but this diversity also encourages people to withhold aid for fear of antagonizing the participants or crossing an inappropriate and difficult-to-define line.

Moreover, the frequency of demands present in the city gives rise to norms of noninvolvement. There are practical limitations to the Samaritan impulse in a major city. If a citizen attended to every needy person, if he were sensitive to and acted on every altruistic impulse that was evoked in the city, he could scarcely keep his own affairs in order.

.   .   .   .   .

FURTHER ASPECTS OF URBAN EXPERIENCE

Some features of urban experience . . . are difficult to treat in quantitative fashion. Yet I prefer discussing them in a loose way to excluding them because

---

[6]B. Latané and J. Darley, "Bystander apathy," *American Scientist,* 57:244 (Summer, 1969).

appropriate language and data have not yet been developed. My aim is to suggest how phenomena such as "urban atmosphere" can be pinned down through techniques of measurement.

The contrast in the behavior of city and town dwellers has been a natural starting point for urban social scientists. But even among great cities there are marked differences in "atmosphere." The tone, pacing, and texture of social encounters are different in London and New York, and many persons willingly make financial sacrifices for the privilege of living within a specific urban atmosphere which they find pleasing or stimulating. A second perspective in the study of cities, therefore, is to define exactly what is meant by the atmosphere of a city and to pinpoint the factors that give rise to it. It may seem that urban atmosphere is too evanescent a quality to be reduced to a set of measurable variables, but I do not believe the matter can be judged before substantial effort has been made in this direction. It is obvious that any such approach must be comparative. It makes no sense at all to say that New York is "vibrant" and "frenetic" unless one has some specific city in mind as a basis of comparison.

In an undergraduate tutorial that I conducted at Harvard University some years ago, New York, London, and Paris were selected as reference points for attempts to measure urban atmosphere. We began with a simple question: Does any consensus exist about the qualities that typify given cities? To answer this question one could undertake a content analysis of travelbook, literary, and journalistic accounts of cities. A second approach, which we adopted, is to ask people to characterize (with descriptive terms and accounts of typical experiences) cities they have lived in or visited. In advertisements placed in the *New York Times* and the *Harvard Crimson* we asked people to give us accounts of specific incidents in London, Paris, or New York that best illuminated the character of that particular city. Questionnaires were then developed, and administered to persons who were familiar with at least two of the three cities.

Some distinctive patterns emerged.[7] The distinguishing themes concerning New York, for example, dealt with its diversity, its great size, its pace and level of activity, its cultural and entertainment opportunities, and the heterogeneity and segmentation ("ghettoization") of its population. New York elicited more descriptions in terms of physical qualities, pace, and emotional impact than Paris or London did, a fact which suggests that these are particularly important aspects of New York's ambiance.

A contrasting profile emerges for London; in this case respondents placed far greater emphasis on their interactions with the inhabitants than on physical surroundings. There was near unanimity on certain themes: those dealing with the tolerance and courtesy of London's inhabitants. One respondent said:

When I was 12, my grandfather took me to the British Museum . . . one day by tube and recited the *Aeneid* in Latin for my benefit. . . . He is rather deaf, speaks very loudly and it embarrassed the hell out of me, until I realized that nobody was paying any attention. Londoners are extremely worldly and tolerant.

---

[7]N. Abuza, "The Paris-London-New York questionnaires" (unpublished manuscript, Harvard University).

In contrast, respondents who described New Yorkers as aloof, cold, and rude referred to such incidents as the following:

I saw a boy of 19 passing out anti-war leaflets to passersby. When he stopped at a corner, a man dressed in a business suit walked by him at a brisk pace, hit the boy's arm and scattered the leaflets all over the street. The man kept walking at the same pace down the block.

We need to obtain many more such descriptions of incidents, using careful methods of sampling. By the application of factor-analytic techniques, relevant dimensions for each city can be discerned.

The responses for Paris were about equally divided between responses concerning its inhabitants and those regarding its physical and sensory attributes. Cafés and parks were often mentioned as contributing to the sense that Paris is a city of amenities, but many respondents complained that Parisians were inhospitable, nasty, and cold.

We cannot be certain, of course, to what degree these statements reflect actual characteristics of the cities in question and to what degree they simply tap the respondents' knowledge of widely held preconceptions. Indeed, one may point to three factors, apart from the actual atmospheres of the cities, that determine the subjects' responses.

1. A person's impression of a given city depends on his implicit standard of comparison. A New Yorker who visits Paris may well describe that city as "leisurely," whereas a compatriot from Richmond, Virginia, may consider Paris too "hectic." Obtaining reciprocal judgment, in which New Yorkers judge Londoners, and Londoners judge New Yorkers, seems a useful way to take into account not only the city being judged but also the home city that serves as the visitor's base line.

2. Perceptions of a city are also affected by whether the observer is a tourist, a newcomer, or a longer-term resident. First, a tourist will be exposed to features of the city different from those familiar to a long-time resident. Second, a prerequisite for adapting to continuing life in a given city seems to be the filtering out of many observations about the city that the newcomer or tourist finds particularly arresting; this selective process seems to be part of the long-term resident's mechanism for coping with overload. In the interest of psychic economy, the resident simply learns to tune out many aspects of daily life. One method for studying the specific impact of adaptation on perception of the city is to ask several pairs of newcomers and old-timers (one newcomer and one old-timer to a pair) to walk down certain city blocks and then report separately what each has observed.

Additionally, many persons have noted that when travelers return to New York from an extended sojourn abroad they often feel themselves confronted with "brutal ugliness"[8] and a distinctive, frenetic atmosphere whose contributing details are, for a few hours or days, remarkably sharp and clear. This period of fresh perception should receive special attention in the study of city atmosphere. For, in a few days, details which are initially arresting become less easy to specify. They are assimilated into an increasingly familiar background atmosphere which, though important in setting the tone of things, is difficult to analyze. There is no better point at which

---

[8]P. Abelson, "Microcosms in a world apart," *Science,* 165:853 (August 29, 1969).

to begin the study of city atmosphere than at the moment when a traveler returns from abroad.

3. The popular myths and expectations each visitor brings to the city will also affect the way in which he perceives it.[9] Sometimes a person's preconceptions about a city are relatively accurate distillations of its character, but preconceptions may also reinforce myths by filtering the visitor's perceptions to conform with his expectations. Preconceptions affect not only a person's perceptions of a city but what he reports about it.

The influence of a person's urban base line on his perceptions of a given city, the differences between the observations of the long-time inhabitant and those of the newcomer, and the filtering effect of personal expectations and stereotypes raise serious questions about the validity of travelers' reports. Moreover, no social psychologist wants to rely exclusively on verbal accounts if he is attempting to obtain an accurate and objective description of the cities' social texture, pace, and general atmosphere. What he needs to do is to devise means of embedding objective experimental measures in the daily flux of city life, measures that can accurately index the qualities of a given urban atmosphere.

EXPERIMENTAL COMPARISONS OF BEHAVIOR

Roy Feldman[10] incorporated these principles in a comparative study of behavior toward compatriots and foreigners in Paris, Athens, and Boston. Feldman wanted to see (1) whether absolute levels and patterns of helpfulness varied significantly from city to city, and (2) whether inhabitants in each city tended to treat compatriots differently from foreigners. He examined five concrete behavioral episodes, each carried out by a team of native experimenters and a team of American experimenters in the three cities. The episodes involved (1) asking natives of the city for street directions; (2) asking natives to mail a letter for the experimenter; (3) asking natives if they had just dropped a dollar bill (or the Greek or French equivalent) when the money actually belonged to the experimenter himself; (4) deliberately overpaying for goods in a store to see if the cashier would correct the mistake and return the excess money; and (5) determining whether taxicab drivers overcharged strangers and whether they took the most direct route available.

Feldman's results suggest some interesting contrasts in the profiles of the three cities. In Paris, for instance, certain stereotypes were borne out. Parisian cab drivers overcharged foreigners significantly more often than they overcharged compatriots. But other aspects of the Parisians' behavior were not in accord with American preconceptions: in mailing a letter for a stranger, Parisians treated foreigners significantly better than Athenians or Bostonians did, and, when asked to mail letters that were already stamped, Parisians actually treated foreigners better than they treated compatriots. Similarly, Parisians were significantly more honest than Athenians or Bostonians in resisting the temptation to claim money that was not theirs, and

---

[9]A. L. Strauss (ed.), *The American City: A Sourcebook of Urban Imagery* (Chicago: Aldine Publishing Co., 1968).

[10]R. E. Feldman, "Response to compatriot and foreigner who seek assistance," *Journal of Personality and Social Psychology,* 10:202–214 (1968).

Parisians were the only citizens who were more honest with foreigners than with compatriots in this experiment.

Feldman's studies not only begin to quantify some of the variables that give a city its distinctive texture but they also provide a methodological model for other comparative research. His most important contribution is his successful application of objective, experimental measures to everyday situations, a mode of study which provides conclusions about urban life that are more pertinent than those achieved through laboratory experiments.

TEMPO AND PACE

Another important component of a city's atmosphere is its tempo or pace, an attribute frequently remarked on but less often studied. Does a city have a frenetic, hectic quality, or is it easygoing and leisurely? In any empirical treatment of this question, it is best to start in a very simple way. Walking speeds of pedestrians in different cities and in cities and towns should be measured and compared. William Berkowitz[11] of Lafayette College has undertaken an extensive series of studies of walking speeds in Philadelphia, New York, and Boston, as well as in small and moderate-sized towns. Berkowitz writes that "there does appear to be a significant linear relation between walking speed and size of municipality, but the absolute size of the difference varies by less than ten percent."

Perhaps the feeling of rapid tempo is due not so much to absolute pedestrian speeds as to the constant need to dodge others in a large city to avoid collisions with other pedestrians. (One basis for computing the adjustments needed to avoid collisions is to hypothesize a set of mechanical manikins sent walking along a city street and to calculate the number of collisions when no adjustments are made. Clearly, the higher the density of manikins the greater the number of collisions per unit of time, or, conversely, the greater the frequency of adjustments needed in higher population densities to avoid collisions.)

Patterns of automobile traffic contribute to a city's tempo. Driving an automobile provides a direct means of translating feelings about tempo into measurable acceleration, and a city's pace should be particularly evident in vehicular velocities, patterns of acceleration, and latency of response to traffic signals. The inexorable tempo of New York is expressed, further, in the manner in which pedestrians stand at busy intersections, impatiently awaiting a change in traffic light, making tentative excursions into the intersection, and frequently surging into the street even before the green light appears.

·   ·   ·   ·

COGNITIVE MAPS OF CITIES

When we speak of "behavioral comparisons" among cities, we must specify which parts of the city are most relevant for sampling purposes. In a sampling of "New Yorkers," should we include residents of Bay Ridge or Flatbush as well as

---

[11]W. Berkowitz, personal communication.

inhabitants of Manhattan? And, if so, how should we weight our sample distribution? One approach to defining relevant boundaries in sampling is to determine which areas form the psychological or cognitive core of the city. We weight our samples most heavily in the areas considered by most people to represent the "essence" of the city.

The psychologist is less interested in the geographic layout of a city or in its political boundaries than in the cognitive representation of the city. . . .In *The Image of the City*,[12] Kevin Lynch created a cognitive map of Boston by interviewing Bostonians. Perhaps his most significant finding was that, while certain landmarks, such as Paul Revere's house and the Boston Common, as well as the paths linking them, are known to almost all Bostonians, vast areas of the city are simply unknown to its inhabitants.

Using Lynch's technique, Donald Hooper[13] created a psychological map of New York from the answers to the study questionnaire on Paris, London, and New York. Hooper's results were similar to those of Lynch: New York appears to have a dense core of well-known landmarks in midtown Manhattan, surrounded by the vast unknown reaches of Queens, Brooklyn, and the Bronx. Times Square, Rockefeller Center, and the Fifth Avenue department stores alone comprise half the places specifically cited by respondents as the haunts in which they spent most of their time. However, outside the midtown area, only scattered landmarks were recognized. Another interesting pattern is evident: even the best-known symbols of New York are relatively self-contained, and the pathways joining them appear to be insignificant on the map.

The psychological map can be used for more than just sampling techniques. Lynch argues, for instance, that a good city is highly "imageable," having many known symbols joined by widely known pathways, whereas dull cities are gray and nondescript. We might test the relative "imagibility" of several cities by determining the proportion of residents who recognize sampled geographic points and their accompanying pathways.

If we wanted to be even more precise we could construct a cognitive map that would not only show the symbols of the city but would measure the precise degree of cognitive significance of any given point in the city relative to any other. By applying a pattern of points to a map of New York City, for example, and taking photographs from each point, we could determine what proportion of a sample of the city's inhabitants could identify the locale specified by each point. We might even take the subjects blindfolded to a point represented on the map, then remove the blindfold and ask them to identify their location from the view around them.

One might also use psychological maps to gain insight into the differing perceptions of a given city that are held by members of its cultural subgroups, and into the manner in which their perceptions may change. In the earlier stages of life, whites and Negroes alike probably have only a limited view of the city, centering on the immediate neighborhood in which they are raised. In adolescence, however, the field of knowledge of the white teen-ager probably undergoes rapid enlargement;

---

[12]K. Lynch, *The Image of the City* (Cambridge: Mass.: Harvard University Press and The M.I.T. Press, 1960).

[13]D. Hooper (unpublished manuscript, Harvard University).

he learns of opportunities in midtown and outlying sections and comes to see himself as functioning in a larger urban field. But the process of ghettoization, to which the black teen-ager is subjected, may well hamper the expansion of his sense of the city. These are speculative notions, but they are readily subject to precise test.

CONCLUSION

I have tried to indicate some organizing theory that starts with the basic facts of city life: large numbers, density, and heterogeneity. These are external to the individual. He experiences these factors as overloads at the level of roles, norms, cognitive functions, and facilities. These overloads lead to adaptive mechanisms which create the distinctive tone and behaviors of city life. These notions, of course, need to be examined by objective comparative studies of cities and towns.

A second perspective concerns the differing atmospheres of great cities, such as Paris, London, and New York. Each has a distinctive flavor, offering a differentiable quality of experience. More precise knowledge of urban atmosphere seems attainable through application of the tools of experimental inquiry.

PART THREE

A Glimpse of the Future

INTRODUCTION

The final selection of *The City in the Seventies* is an interview with a prominent urbanologist, George Sternlieb (Selection 37). In the interview, Sternlieb speculates about the possible future of the central city. His observations reflect his own recent experiences in studying urban development, and his comments provide a reasonably comprehensive and realistic appraisal of the city's future (though one need not agree with his conclusions).

Some of Sternlieb's themes (e.g., the role of modern transportation in making urban labor markets less competitive and the role of modern communications technology in making the advantages of urban propinquity a less important factor in everyday business affairs) suggest that the city may perhaps be thought of as a major victim of technological change. If this is so, cities are likely to suffer even more in the future, since technology will continue to advance. For instance, a possible future factor in communications is the development of high-capacity cable television systems, where one goal will be to reduce the need for people to travel by enabling them to communicate via television. Up until now, the impact of cable television has been mainly on small rural communities; however with technological and federal regulatory changes, large cities will increasingly be the markets for new cable television systems. Thus cable television will present yet another challenge to cities—to see whether they can take advantage of new technology rather than vice versa.

Some of Sternlieb's other themes—e.g., that American people have relatively high housing standards or that the availability of suburban land makes the development of new communities cheaper (though, as Sternlieb makes clear, also more wasteful) than the renewal of existing urban structures—suggest that the experience of the central city in the United States may be quite different from that of cities in other countries. To this extent, parallels drawn between U.S. cities and the older European cities, for instance, may be inappropriate. But more important, the potentially distinctive American flavor also implies that the future of the cities may not be a strictly urban dilemma, but rather a dilemma involving the basic values of all of American society.

37. Are big cities worth saving?

GEORGE S. STERNLIEB

Q. Dr. Sternlieb, is there any way to stop the flight of people and business out of the cities and into the suburbs?

A. I don't think so.

Q. Why do you say that?

A. First, I want to suggest that the crisis of the city is not a crisis of race. The existence of race as an issue obscures much more important facts of life.

The problem of the city is a crisis of function. What is left to the city that it does better than someplace else? In our free market we have considerable fluidity of mortgaging and debt structure. We have people who can vote with their feet or with their automobile—and they are voting for the suburbs.

What actually does the city have to offer to keep people? The answer today is: very little.

There was a time when the city offered a variety of important things.

The city as a manufacturing place was very significant. The city was a place where you could put together a lot of cheap labor, strong backs. So the city and the immigration that went into the city made sense because there was a market for those people—for their skills or lack of skills, for their exploitability.

Today there isn't that kind of market for their work. Many of the jobs that used to be found in the tenement-house industries of New York and Philadelphia, for example, were jobs that we have since exported. We exported them first to Puerto Rico. Now the Puerto Ricans are discovering that Formosa and Hong Kong and a number of other places can do those jobs even more cheaply.

Q. What kinds of jobs?

A. Such jobs as needlework, for example. Take the cut-and-sew establishments that existed in my youth. I was a member of the Fur and Leather Workers Union

"Are big cities worth saving?" is reprinted from *U.S. News & World Report,* July 26, 1971 issue. Copyright © 1971 by U.S. News & World Report, Inc.

The author is Director, Center for Urban Policy Research, Rutgers University, Newark, N.J.

at one time, so I know whereof I speak here. Then, the cutting was all done in New York—in Manhattan—and the sewing used to be done in the tenements—first in the Bowery, then it migrated to Coney Island, then to Queens. It followed the Italians because at that time they were the cheapest labor available. It followed the Jews for a while.

Then we got trucks and we got better highways, and we discovered that there were a lot of coal miners' wives in Pennsylvania and jobless thread-mill workers in Fall River, Mass., who could do the work even more cheaply, and trucks could haul it into the city in a few hours. Eventually—in my own time—these trucks became able to make overnight hauls from as far away as South Carolina.

Then air freight began to come in and for a dollar a dozen you could bring stuff up from shops as far away as Mississippi and Texas.

Take something that is very labor-intensive: Let's take brassieres, which require a lot of needlework. There was a time when something more than 50 percent of all the brassieres sold in the U.S. were made in Puerto Rico. The bulk of that business has now even moved out of Puerto Rico. So now what the newest immigrants find in the central city is a society which has priced them out of the labor market.

Q. Are you saying that the flight of business from the cities is largely a search for cheaper labor?

A. No. I think the first thing that initiated this flight was the search for space. The second thing that began to move it very strongly was fashion. It became highly fashionable to be outside the city. I remember a little company that I worked with in Boston. We had excellent space for $1.25 a square foot. We moved out to Bedford at $4.75 a foot. It was inconvenient, but in Bedford we were in high fashion, and in Boston we weren't.

Q. Do you mean business firms pay such prices just to be in fashion?

A. For many companies the decision to seek more space outside a city does not represent an important outlay of funds. Typically, it does not involve capital funds; it involves flow of funds, and therefore it does not appear to hurt much.

Once this move began, it was augmented by a number of innovations that made it more feasible.

First of all, the bosses, too, moved out. The time was when society lived in the central city and to be in society you had to be in the central city—but not any more. So the bosses have moved out.

And it also turns out that there is a very substantial virtue in having your facilities in a place that is relatively easy to reach.

Now, let me touch on another factor here. One of the things that the central city had working for it—and still has working for it—is propinquity: nearness to others with whom you do business.

I recall some years ago a firm in the theater business decided to move to the West Coast because of the production facilities there: They could make films there. But within a year and a half after leaving, everybody came back to New York.

Production in America is easy. What you need is somebody who can sell the stuff, and in this case, at least, the guys who buy it were in New York. So let me be the last to belittle that factor. It is still a very significant thing.

Q. Can you see the time coming when New York will no longer be the financial center of the nation?

A. Yes, very easily. You see, in terms of paperwork processing, we are just at the beginnings of a technology.

Now you have telephone communication lines and computers that can talk to each other and videophones over which you can actually see as well as hear the man you are talking to.

The next stage of the game here is the three-dimensional image, so you will be able to communicate directly without bringing everybody together in New York.

I think the appeals of New York are beginning to show their age.

Q. Do you think the deterioration of cities has grown out of these changes in the functions of the city, or is it the deterioration of the cities that is chasing people away?

A. You get into a dynamic here. All it takes is a 2 or 3 or 4 or 5 percent drop in business volume—it doesn't have to be a 50 percent drop—and you begin to feel it. Your stock-turnover rate turns soggy. You mark down stock, and you cut down on inventory. Then the customer begins to say your store isn't what it used to be. The decline begins to feed on itself.

Now, I have said before in print and I'll repeat again: New York City is—with the possible exception of Washington, D.C.—the only city in the United States which I feel does have the market capacity to reshape itself. It still has that vital critical mass. But I am afraid that its capacity is rapidly being dissipated.

Q. What about other large cities, such as Philadelphia, Boston and Chicago?

A. I see very limited futures for them.

Q. What do you see ahead for Washington, D.C.?

A. Government employment—pure and simple.

Q. But a lot of the Government workers don't actually live in Washington. They live in suburbs in Virginia or Maryland, and shopping centers are growing up out there, too—

A. That's right. Washington is an artificial city. It is an administrative hub.

Q. You say cities don't have the jobs any more. Yet every city has a traffic jam morning and evening, with suburban commuters coming in to work at city jobs. So how can it be just the lack of jobs that has killed the city?

A. Remember, the city isn't dead yet—though it is pretty far gone—and I would say in terms of putting money in it the city is no longer a good bet. But now let's look at jobs a number of different ways.

Manufacturing: Let's face it—manufacturing has moved out of the city. Retailing: The saga of the central-city department stores is not ended. On the other hand, I noticed that one big firm in its recent annual report said with pride that 58 percent of all its department-store business is now outside the central city.

What we've done is to move from the convenience centers to shopping centers. When you have a shopping center with 2 million square feet of space and an air-conditioned mall, you don't need downtown any more. The retailing employment in many major cities is marginal at best.

Now, what are cities left with? They are left with offices. These offices have been very significant, and we have had a wonderful bloom in office buildings. But will the central-city office business continue to grow? I am highly dubious. One of the least recorded but most significant developments of the last several years is the growth of suburban office space.

WHY CITY WORKERS LIVE IN SUBURBS

Q. Still, there are enormous numbers of people who work at city jobs but live in the suburbs. Why don't they live in the city where their jobs are?

A. Because the housing that is available to them in the city no longer fits the American dream of appropriate housing.

Who are the people that live in central-city housing? And what we are talking about here is not the "ghettos" but the high-rise, fairly high-cost rental facilities and the co-operative or condominium apartments.

Ninety percent of the heads of the households living in these places are more than 35 years old; 95 percent have no children of school age; 90 percent of them are employed in the central city or are lawyers or professional people who have some very strong reasons for being in the central city.

Ninety percent of the people can't afford to live well in the city, especially if they have kids of school age.

Q. Do you mean city living has priced itself out of the market?

A. Well, that's part of it, but in part it's also that the level of amenities that the city once could offer just isn't there any more. The good medical services and the good schools have moved out to the suburbs.

Q. Didn't those good services move out to the suburbs because the people moved out? The question is why the people moved out—

A. Well, this outward movement, this suburbanization, is not really new. It began as far back as 1910 with the coming of the automobile. The movement was halted temporarily by the Depression and the war, but after World War II it began again.

Then what should have taken place slowly and gracefully, giving us time to adjust over a generation or two, suddenly uncoiled like a broken spring, and the outward movement has kept growing.

Q. The heavy migration of Negroes into central cities came at about the same time as the migration of whites to the suburbs. Did the Negro migration speed up the departure of white people?

A. It speeded up what would have taken place anyway.

Q. Why did so many Negroes move to the cities?

A. They came for the very same reason that all the other migrants have come. They are part of what is really one worldwide phenomenon of our time: the movement off the land.

The amount of labor required to turn out a bale of cotton in 1940 was approximately 24 times the amount required to turn out a bale of cotton in 1968. You can say almost the same about corn or chickens—everything that is grown on a farm. So, with their jobs disappearing, farm workers had to go somewhere, and they came to the cities.

Q. Now that this has happened, what can be done about it?

A. That, it seems to me, is the real question.

Q. Would you give up on the central city?

A. Yes.

Q. Isn't that a pretty drastic judgment about the places where so many millions of Americans live?

A. O.K., let me suggest to you that the bulk of our inputs into the central city are a form of what I would refer to as "high-class ritual"—a form of symbolic reaction, of going through the motions.

Much of our effort in housing and in job development is really trivial in terms of realistic throughput. In psychological terms—to show that somebody cares—it is very important. But in terms of putting real dollars into central cities, let me suggest that people put in real bucks where they get the most bang for their buck —and the place where you get the most bang for your buck is not in the central city.

The reasons for this are many, but one of the most significant elements is the fact that the central city typically is a very high-cost area. Whether it is the repair of sewage lines or new transportation facilities or a rehabilitation project, you are fitting to pre-existing structures, and that requires a maximum degree of human intervention and decision-making, and it minimizes the role of capital intensification.

The only way we can get that big bang for the buck is to maximize the capital intensification. And that is what takes place outside of the central city—in a place where you are starting from scratch.

CREATION OF A HOUSING MONSTER

Q. Do you advocate that the Federal Government try to guide the flow of people? If so, how?

A. I don't think we have much choice any more.

A colleague of mine was asked why construction costs have gone up far in excess of other major inputs into our economy. His response was that, essentially, this was a by-product of Government funding; that the Government has artificially subsidized the market by meeting the demands of labor, etc., without a real test of the market, until we have finally come to the point where we now have 1 percent interest money for home construction.

The Government has created a housing Frankenstein, and it's going to have to live with it, because we don't know how to get down off that tiger.

Q. What are we going to do then: build more suburbs, or build new cities?

A. All the acorns for tomorrow's oak trees are already around. Take a look at them. It would be my guess that while the Government is messing around with the "new city" concept, the American genius for seizing the vitals of a program and adapting it to American conditions is being shown by the growth of the PUD.

Q. What is a "PUD"?

A. Planned unit development. The PUD is to the new town what an $8.95 knockoff is to a $400 Paris original. It's built for America.

The capital flows—the cash flows, I should say—involved in new-town construction are ridiculously inadequate. They take too long. Why, you're dealing with a project that takes 20 or 30 years to finish, whereas you can put a PUD into the ground from start to finish in a relatively short time.

Q. What is the difference between a PUD and a new city?

A. A PUD is smaller. It packages the following: retailing facilities, some manufacturing, and residential facilities of three or four different configurations.

Under enabling legislation that has been adopted by a number of States, local zoning or master plans can be abrogated for a PUD which meets certain standards.

Q. Where have PUD's been built?

A. There is one in Twin Rivers—which is East Windsor, N.J.—that is nearly finished. It has 3,000 residential units. They broke ground for the first residential structure two and a half years ago, and today they have 1,600 units sold.

Q. Is a PUD a form of suburban subdivision?

A. Right—with the inclusion, typically, of nonresidential buildings.

Q. Is this PUD concept spreading?

A. In New Jersey alone there are 13 PUD's for which ground has been broken with 50,000 units that will house close to 200,000 people. Pennsylvania has PUD's in depth. And the idea is growing elsewhere.

In New Jersey there are three pieces of land, each of which is more than 10,000 acres, which have been put together by a variety of different syndicates with real money. The Governor estimates that New Jersey needs a minimum of 60,000 units a year—and preferably, in order to make up for lost time, 100,000 units a year.

Q. As these new suburban areas are developed, will we find the same problems of congestion and deterioration in schools creeping out into the older suburbs?

A. Really there are two questions here: First of all, what happens to the older suburbs? And secondly, are the new suburbs going to end up being old suburbs?

Now, the older suburbs—the zone of emergence for the middle-class-oriented emigré from the central city—nobody cares much about them. There are no programs that make any sense for them. They are going down the drain. Their fiscal problems are enormous. They are not equipped for their changing role, they do not have a capital plan, and they cannot manage to keep operating expeditures to cope with the new population which they're getting.

Q. Are old suburbs getting more people with low incomes? Is that their problem?

A. In part it is a population with a little lower income, but it is also the problems that the population brings with it, even when it has solid income.

The children that these newcomers bring with them often bear the stigmata of the central city. They're already behind a year or two years in reading ability, and they're behind a generation in behavior patterns. It costs money to cope with them —and there just isn't enough money, and there are no programs.

You know, when you talk about people who are desperate to get out of the central city, you're not talking about whites any more; you are talking about the black middle-class-oriented individual. He is desperate to get out. He is not going to move into a new town for a long time, if ever. What can he buy? He can buy into an older suburb.

The prime question which is not being approached in our day is this: Will this older suburb serve as a satisfactory valve for this guy, or will it over a period of time convince him that all this business of trying to make it in America really doesn't work? I am afraid that the odds right now are on the latter.

Q. In time, will the newer suburbs develop the same kinds of problems?

A. You remember the jokes about Levittown in Long Island. Well, it has worked very well, and it's still holding up. How long do you want it to hold up?

One thing that we have in the suburbs—and this is a very important thing to keep in mind—is a relatively low level of density, so if or when we decide that we're tired of what the suburb is like, we can take it down. Now, contrast that with our central cities—with the public-housing areas in central cities, for example. It has been said that the worst thing about public housing is how much it is going to cost to take those things down. They're built to last for an eternity.

What I like about the suburbs is that they permit you to retain some options.

Q. If this deterioration you talk about continues, what do we do with the central cities?

A. You can plan a number of alternate scenarios:

One of the scenarios I call "sandbox." This is a reference to what you provide for children to play in to keep them out of your hair. If you take a hard look at much that has been done under the name of "local community participation" or "model cities" involvement of one kind or another, what you see is basically "sandboxism" in disguise. In effect, we are telling people: "Here is a nice new program. Go play with it and don't bother us too much."

Q. Do you mean we're just putting people out of the way to keep them quiet?

A. That's right. Let me cite an example: Newark, after the 1967 riots.

One of the things that set the riots going was that a medical school had been projected to take 185 acres of land. Obviously, that was too much. The medical school was reduced to 50 acres, and 64 acres of land already cleared was up for grabs. The Governor and other officials told the black people who had fought the school: "This land is now yours. Develop housing."

Well, the years have come and gone, and there is no housing. Studies, yes. Committees, yes. Patronage, yes. But housing, no.

Q. Who is it that is fighting over who is going to develop this housing? Is it black vs. white?

A. No. This is no longer black vs. white; it is all black now. It's just an ordinary fight for patronage. Black men are human, just like the rest of us.

In the meantime, who pays the price? It's paid by people who have no houses to live in.

Today it is no longer the question of 15 or 20 years ago of "How do we keep the middle-class white in the central city?" Now it's "How do we keep the middle-class black in the central city?" The only thing that is keeping him in the city right now is the fact that there's no place for him to move to.

As soon as we get substantial suburban housing built you're going to see a second hegira from the central city—and this one is going to be much more speckled.

BATTLE FOR OPEN HOUSING IS WON

Q. Does this depend on the acceptance of the principle of open housing for all races?

A. I think the battle for open housing—not economic integration but for open housing—is substantially won. Every man's dollar is becoming as good as every other man's dollar.

Q. If middle-class blacks follow middle-class whites in moving out of the central city, then all the cities will have left will be not just blacks but poor blacks—

A. Poor blacks, and some rich people—people who are rich enough to insulate themselves from the reality.

Q. Isn't this kind of central city naturally explosive?

A. There will be explosions, but they are going to be contained explosions.

Humanity in general—and Americans particularly—have a capacity for being outraged and alarmed the first few times something happens, but after that the TV cameras won't even bother with it.

Q. If central cities follow the pattern you predict, won't it mean more abandoned buildings, more crime and more incentive for everybody who can to get out of the city?

A. This is absolutely the case—and we don't have to imagine the future because the future is already right with us. The level of abandoned buildings is increasing in all the older cities, and we simply do not know how to cope with this.

Q. Is there a point at which it is possible to clear out large areas in central cities and develop them as we do new suburbs?

A. We haven't reached that point, yet, and my guess is that here you run into the sandbox idea again.

You see, part of the sandbox deal is that the adults don't go into it. So you have people, very frequently, sitting on what potentially could be enormously useful, valuable, reusable space. But it's now their thing.

Q. If so much city housing is being abandoned, why do we need to keep building new housing in the same areas?

A. That's a good question. The central city at this moment in history is really different from its predecessors.

How did the early immigrant groups accumulate capital? One way was through the purchase of property and the exploitation of that property—and the classic way was for a man to buy a tenement. You find generation after generation has risen as tenement landlords—"slumlords" we call them now. In the course of time they moved up to better buildings. The older buildings were taken over by a newer group of immigrants.

But now there is nobody coming into the central cities to take advantage of because this is the last group of immigrants.

Q. Why is so much housing being abandoned?

A. Housing is abandoned because it is unlivable—at least by today's American standards. There was a time when this housing, even though unlivable, would have been lived in because there would have been a new immigrant group so poor, so desperate that they would have moved in. And later this new group—whether it were Puerto Rican or black—would have had its turn at becoming slumlords.

Now there are a number of minority-group buyers of this stuff, but there is no money left in the slums, and there is no new group coming in.

CHANGING PATTERNS OF MIGRATION

Q. Are you saying that the migration of the blacks off the farms of the South and of the poor whites out of Appalachia is about over?

A. The big sources of supply for such migration have largely been exhausted. And a great deal of the migration that is taking place is bypassing the older places that they used to go to. They don't want to go where there is trouble.

Q. Where are the immigrants going now?

A. To cities such as Seattle, for example, or to places like Buffalo or Rochester or Milwaukee or the Minneapolis-St. Paul area. These were not the places where blacks used to go, but they do now. The rate of black immigration to such places is startling.

Q. Does this indicate a likelihood that the smaller industrial cities will soon be facing the same pattern of deterioration and suburban spread as the big cities?

A. They are now, I would say, even more functionless and more evidently marked for the scrap heap.

Q. How far out is our urban decay going to spread? Is industry going to keep chasing people madly through the suburbs as they go farther and farther away? Or is there going to be a time when the trend is reversed and people start coming back to the cities?

A. Implicit in much of the questioning here today has been the concept that going out of cities is essentially a perverse act and that we've got to get back to normalcy and that normalcy means people living in cities. That simply isn't so.

Q. But in the cities we already have paved streets and subways, mains and sewers. Why keep going farther out and building new subways, streets and sewers?

A. Because it's cheaper in a high-labor-cost area to build from scratch than it is to rebuild. Wasteful? Yes—but it's cheaper.

Q. Can the Government turn this trend around some way?

A. It's been trying very hard, but what you end up with is phony bookkeeping. What you do is take some old place which costs a fortune to rehabilitate, and the only way you can make the flow of funds look appropriate is by saying that this old place is going to last 50 years.

Q. How about the cost of what we've got on our hands now in central cities? Whatever it costs to revive these areas would seem worthwhile, wouldn't it?

A. To a European, yes—but what a European might regard as acceptable housing is not acceptable to Americans. In Belfast [Northern Ireland], for example, 70 percent of all the housing units have no indoor toilets. Glasgow [in Scotland] is about as bad. Here in America we have much higher standards of what is appropriate housing.

If you interview a slum kid in America on what is the good life, you'll find he already has a toilet and a heated apartment. Unlike his parent—who says, "Public housing is the greatest thing that ever happened to me"—this kid says, "The good life is a house in the suburbs with a two-car garage." And anything less than that is simply not regarded as a good life.

Q. Do you see any likelihood of small towns becoming starting points for cities of the future?

A. We now have the technical capacity to turn them into growth centers, but I can't see the money flowing into it. The cash-flow requirements would be very onerous. The cost level of something as massive as what we're talking about would be enormous.

When we talk about developing isolated areas we should look at the experience of the new towns in Great Britain which started out with a concept of a closed-cell type of existence. But neither in the English new towns nor, for that matter, in their Scandinavian equivalents have they ever been able to achieve more than about 35 percent local employment.

Suppose we start with a city of 100,000 households. There would have to be 60,000 additional jobs outside the context of this place. How do we get them? Jobs don't grow in the fields.

Q. Should the Government discontinue its urban-renewal and model-cities programs?

A. No. We've got to have a sandbox.

Q. Are you saying that facetiously, or for real?

A. I am saying that for real because I don't want those people climbing up over the walls, and that's a tax that I am willing to pay.

Q. Suppose we are willing to spend the money it would take to salvage the old central cities? How much money would it take?

A. We simply don't have a state of the art right now to do this, no matter how hard we try. We have run through all the platitudes of the social sciences.

Fifteen years ago, you couldn't find an academic—or many nonacademics—who didn't have a solution. They all had answers. Well, we tried their answers, and they didn't work. Now they say, "It wasn't enough," or "It wasn't administered right," or they blame "those incompetents" in city hall or in Washington.

That's just a lot of noise. Sure, we could have used a lot more dough, but what we really needed was more expertise. The fact is we really don't know what to do.

Q. Would welfare reform have a measurable impact on our migration problem?

A. I think the Administration has a migration policy, but I am afraid it is too little and too late.

A migration policy, very simply, involves the question of: How do you shape the market so that people either move or don't move in line with a plan?

This concept is shown by this example: There is much more housing being built with Government aid in the South than there is in the North. And this makes sense. You can build about 2-1/2 units in the South for what one unit will cost in New York, and in certain parts of the South people can live on the $1,600 or $2,400 or whatever you provide in welfare funds.

But it's too late to draw the people back to the South. The vast bulk of welfare recipients in New York, excluding the Puerto Ricans for the moment, were either born in New York or have lived there 15 years or more. And the younger generation that is coming on welfare—we lack adequate data here, but my impression is that it substantially is born into welfare.

So the migration policy that would have been eminently sensible in the late 1940s or might have made some sense in the 1950s—it's too late for that now. The people won't go back south. They are not living on $1,600 or $2,400 in New York; they are living on $3,500 or $4,000 or $4,500. And the newcomers to welfare in New York are not from the South; while some are from Puerto Rico, the bulk are "made in New York."

There are some very interesting data which indicate that Southern blacks who migrate to the North have a higher employment rate than blacks born in the North. I say this very sadly because for many years the Northern "liberals"—myself included—could view most of our human problems as being the product of Southern injustice exported to the North.

Psychologically, this was very rewarding. But, unfortunately, it is simply not the case.

NAME INDEX

SUBJECT INDEX

BOOK MANUFACTURE

The City in the Seventies was composed by computerized typography at Datagraphics in Phoenix. The printing and binding were performed at Kingsport Press, Inc. The paper is Perkins & Squier Company's Glatfelter Special Book, XL. The cover was designed by Evelyn Hansen. The type is Video Times Roman.